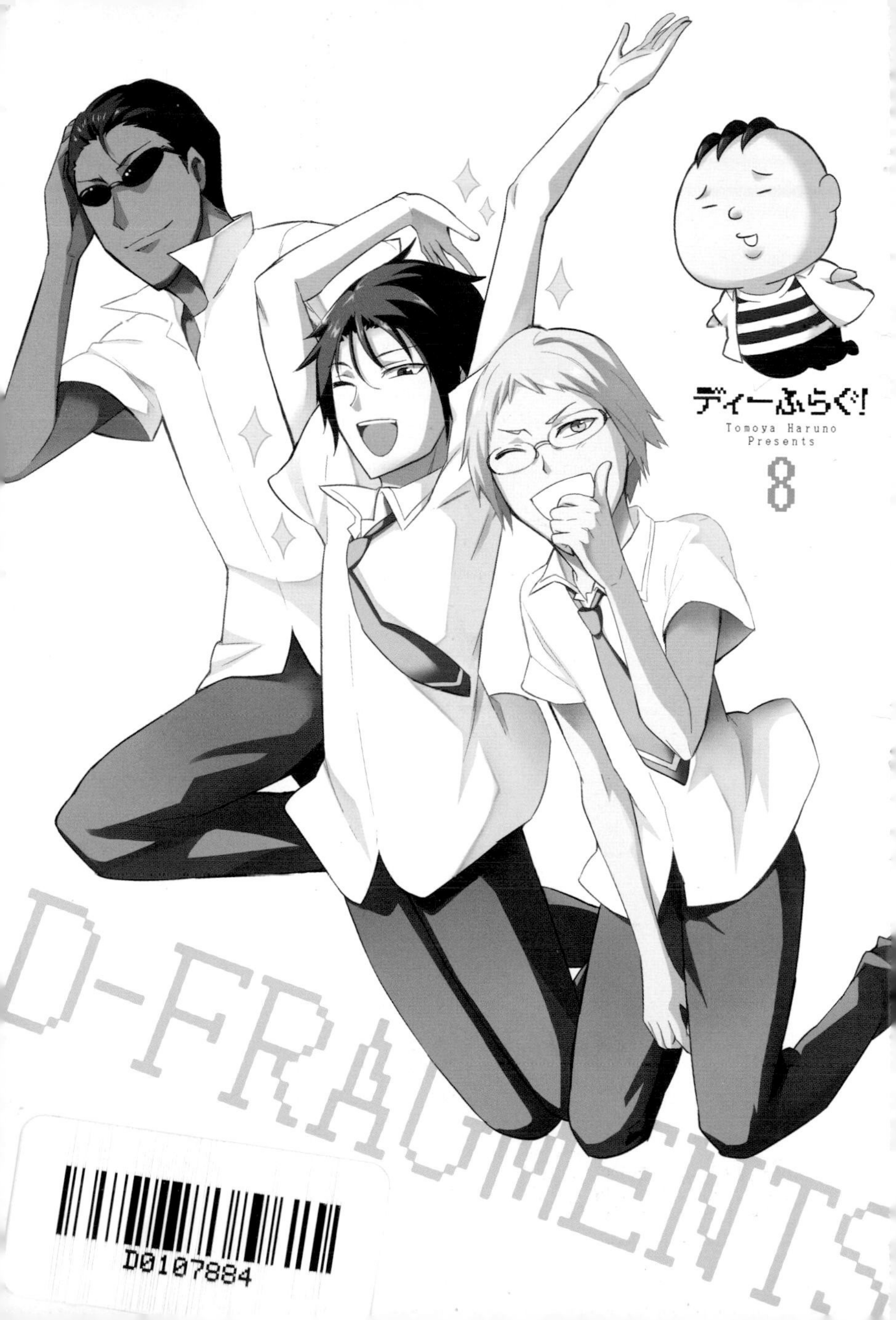
ディーふらぐ!
Tomoya Haruno
Presents
8
D-FRAGMENTS

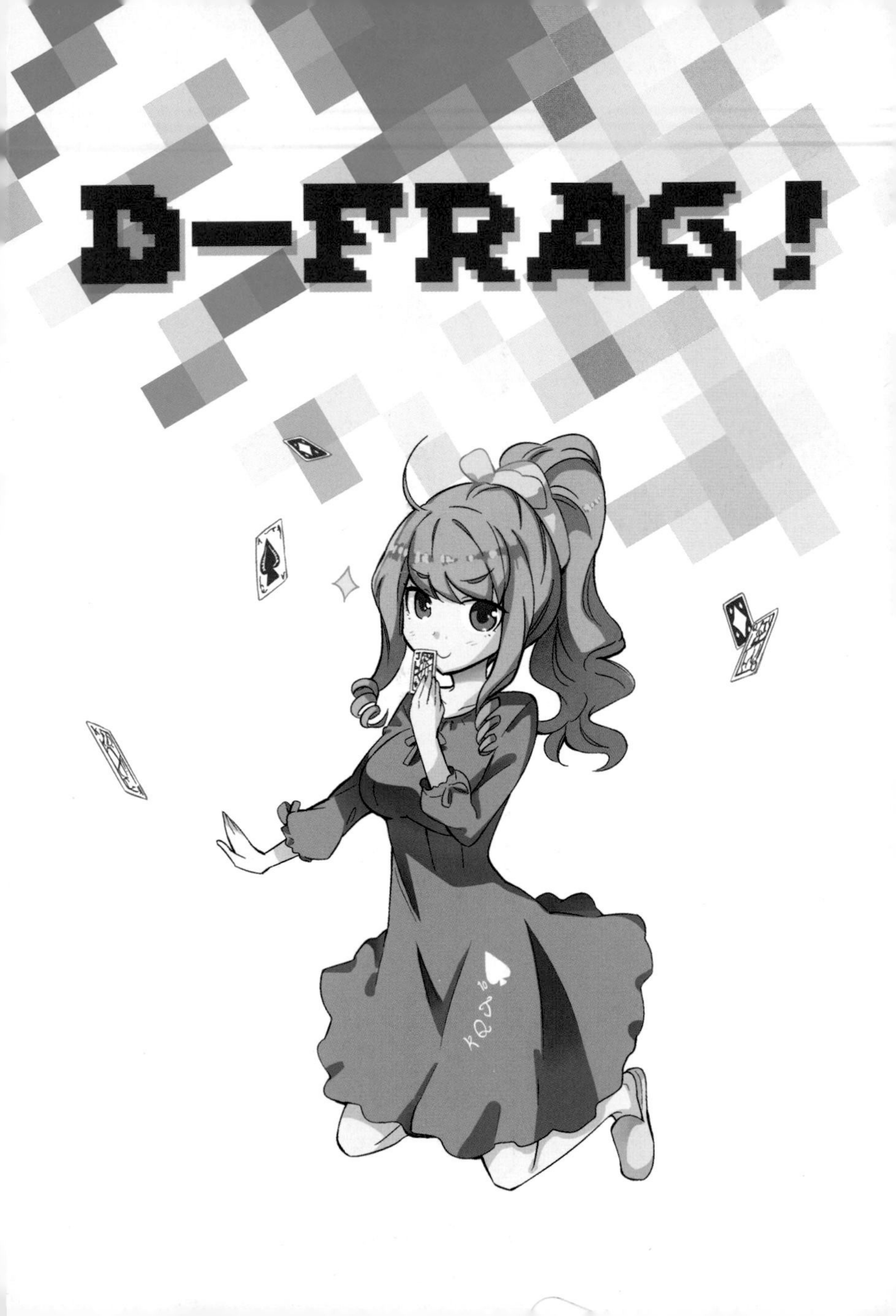
D-FRAG!

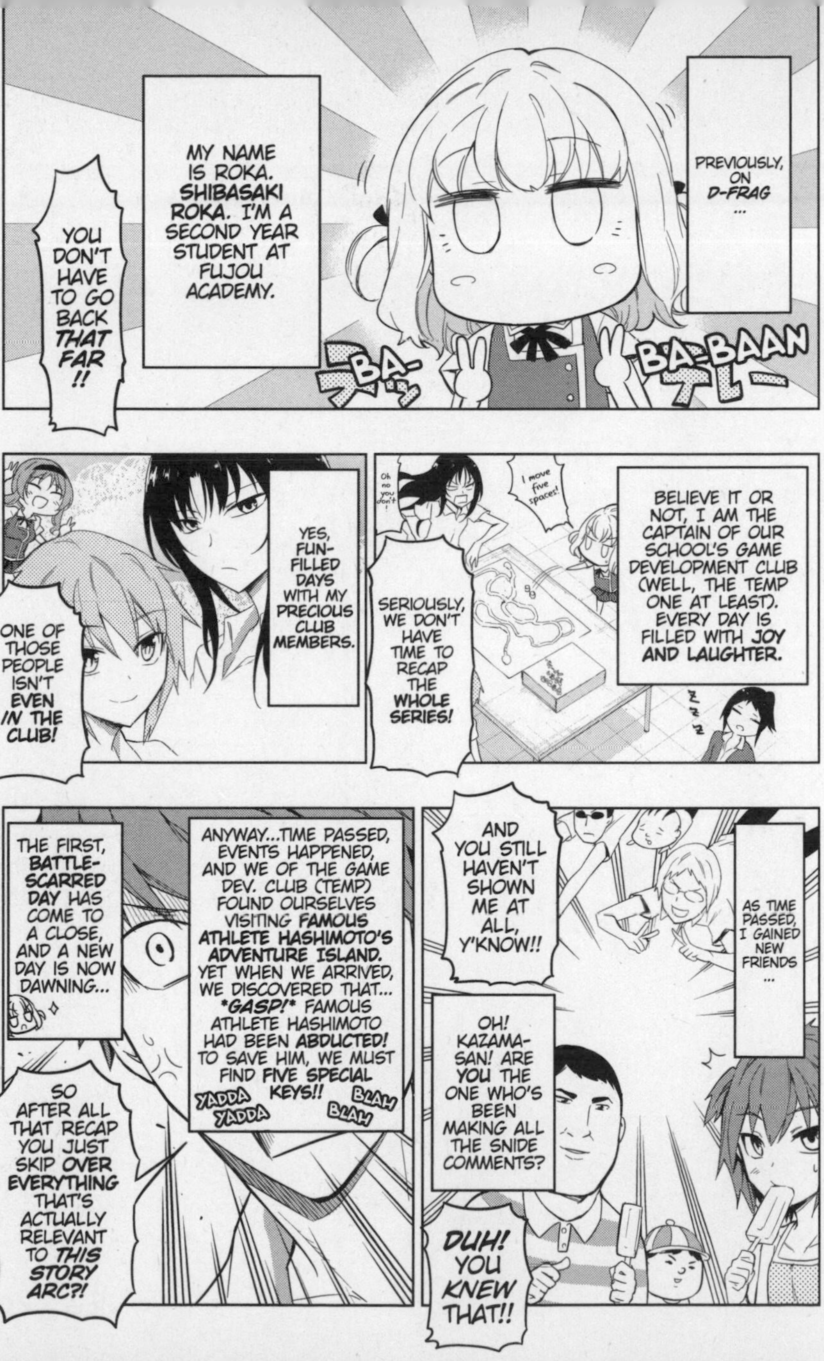
PREVIOUSLY, ON D-FRAG ...
MY NAME IS ROKA. SHIBASAKI ROKA. I'M A SECOND YEAR STUDENT AT FUJOU ACADEMY.
BA-
BA-BAAN
YOU DON'T HAVE TO GO BACK THAT FAR!!
BELIEVE IT OR NOT, I AM THE CAPTAIN OF OUR SCHOOL'S GAME DEVELOPMENT CLUB (WELL, THE TEMP ONE AT LEAST). EVERY DAY IS FILLED WITH JOY AND LAUGHTER.
I move five spaces!
Oh no you don't!
SERIOUSLY, WE DON'T HAVE TIME TO RECAP THE WHOLE SERIES!
YES, FUN-FILLED DAYS WITH MY PRECIOUS CLUB MEMBERS.
ONE OF THOSE PEOPLE ISN'T EVEN IN THE CLUB!
AS TIME PASSED, I GAINED NEW FRIENDS ...
AND YOU STILL HAVEN'T SHOWN ME AT ALL, Y'KNOW!!
OH! KAZAMA-SAN! ARE YOU THE ONE WHO'S BEEN MAKING ALL THE SNIDE COMMENTS?
DUH! YOU KNEW THAT!!
ANYWAY...TIME PASSED, EVENTS HAPPENED, AND WE OF THE GAME DEV. CLUB (TEMP) FOUND OURSELVES VISITING FAMOUS ATHLETE HASHIMOTO'S ADVENTURE ISLAND. YET WHEN WE ARRIVED, WE DISCOVERED THAT... *GASP!* FAMOUS ATHLETE HASHIMOTO HAD BEEN ABDUCTED! TO SAVE HIM, WE MUST FIND FIVE SPECIAL KEYS!!
BLAH BLAH
YADDA YADDA
THE FIRST, BATTLE-SCARRED DAY HAS COME TO A CLOSE, AND A NEW DAY IS NOW DAWNING...
SO AFTER ALL THAT RECAP YOU JUST SKIP OVER EVERYTHING THAT'S ACTUALLY RELEVANT TO THIS STORY ARC?!

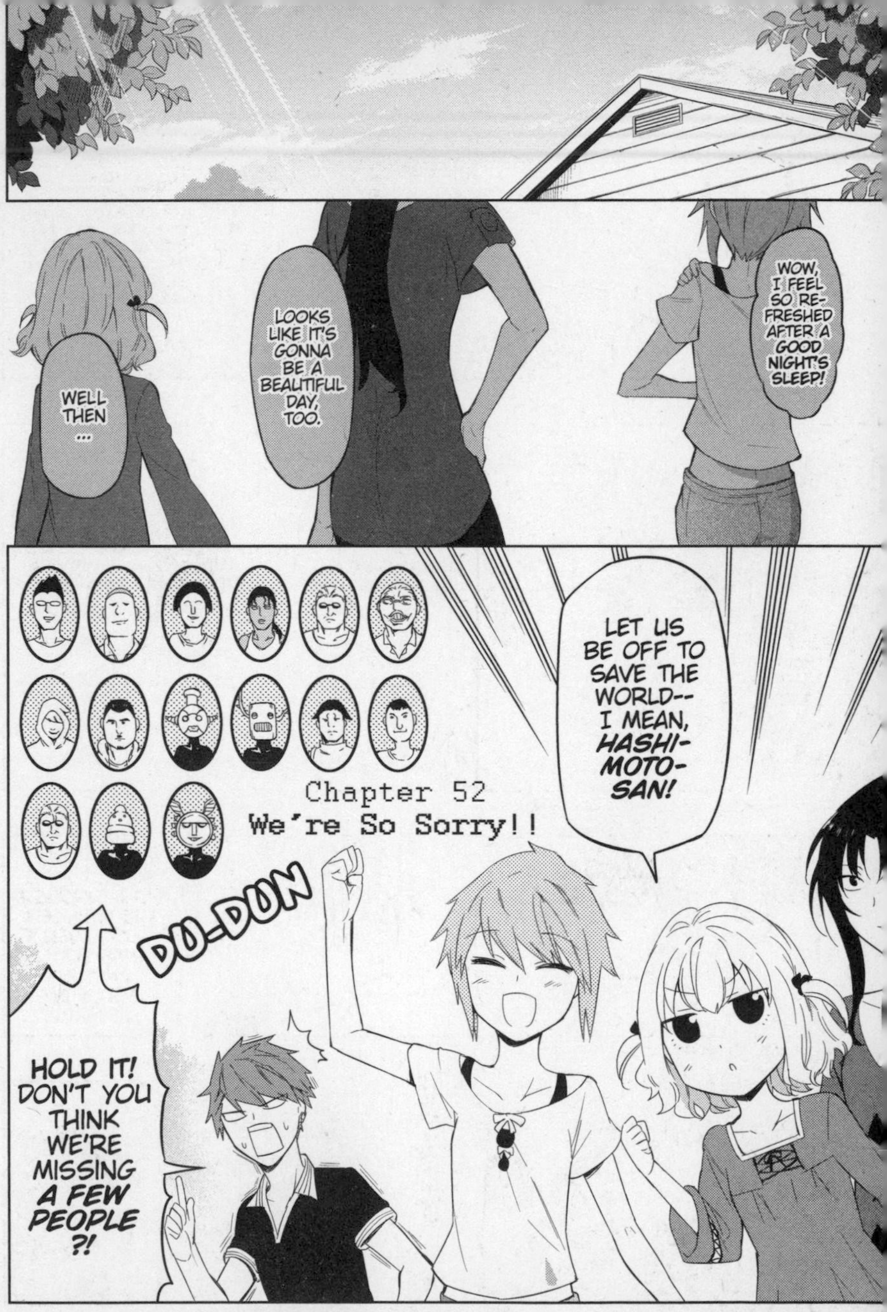
WOW, I FEEL SO RE-FRESHED AFTER A GOOD NIGHT'S SLEEP!
LOOKS LIKE IT'S GONNA BE A BEAUTIFUL DAY, TOO.
WELL THEN ...
LET US BE OFF TO SAVE THE WORLD-- I MEAN, HASHIMOTO-SAN!
Chapter 52
We're So Sorry!!
DU-DON
HOLD IT! DON'T YOU THINK WE'RE MISSING A FEW PEOPLE ?!

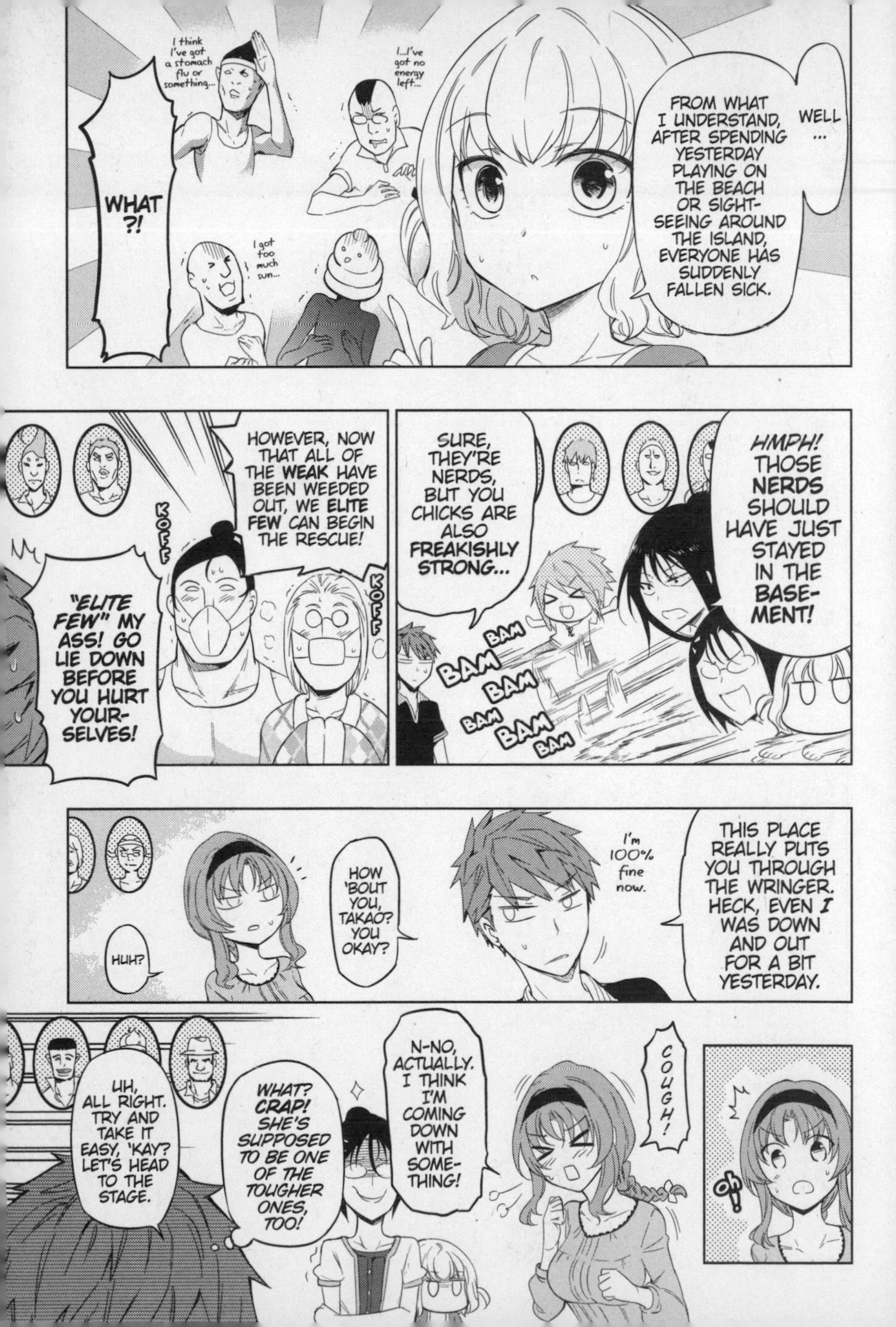
WELL ...
FROM WHAT I UNDERSTAND, AFTER SPENDING YESTERDAY PLAYING ON THE BEACH OR SIGHT-SEEING AROUND THE ISLAND, EVERYONE HAS SUDDENLY FALLEN SICK.
I...I've got no energy left...
I think I've got a stomach flu or something...
I got too much sun...
WHAT?!
HMPH! THOSE NERDS SHOULD HAVE JUST STAYED IN THE BASEMENT!
BAM BAM BAM BAM BAM BAM BAM BAM
SURE, THEY'RE NERDS, BUT YOU CHICKS ARE ALSO FREAKISHLY STRONG...
KOFF
HOWEVER, NOW THAT ALL OF THE WEAK HAVE BEEN WEEDED OUT, WE ELITE FEW CAN BEGIN THE RESCUE!
KOFF
"ELITE FEW" MY ASS! GO LIE DOWN BEFORE YOU HURT YOUR-SELVES!
THIS PLACE REALLY PUTS YOU THROUGH THE WRINGER. HECK, EVEN I WAS DOWN AND OUT FOR A BIT YESTERDAY.
I'm 100% fine now.
HOW 'BOUT YOU, TAKAO? YOU OKAY?
HUH?
Oh!
COUGH!
N-NO, ACTUALLY. I THINK I'M COMING DOWN WITH SOME-THING!
WHAT? CRAP! SHE'S SUPPOSED TO BE ONE OF THE TOUGHER ONES, TOO!
UH, ALL RIGHT. TRY AND TAKE IT EASY, 'KAY? LET'S HEAD TO THE STAGE.

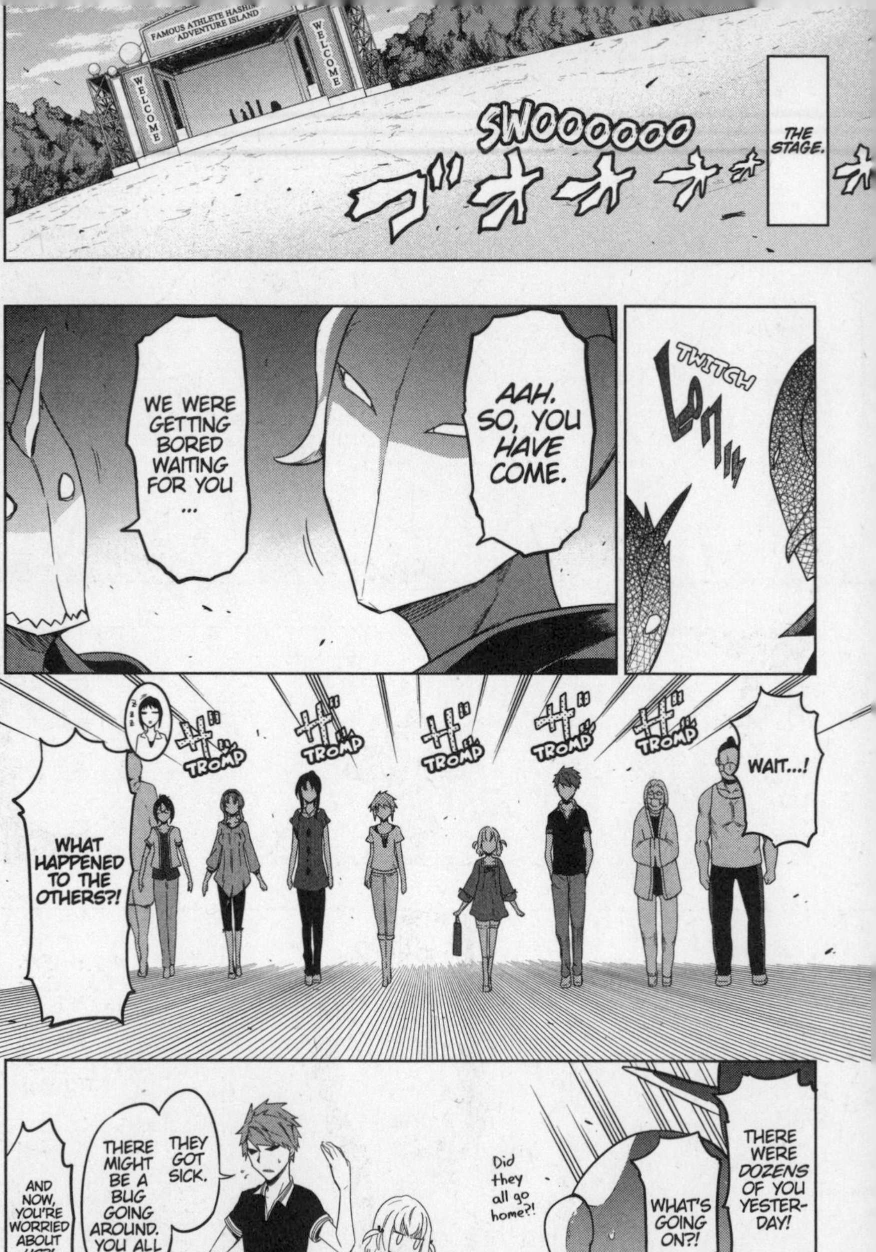
THE STAGE.
SWOOOOOOO
FAMOUS ATHLETE HASHI
ADVENTURE ISLAND
WELCOME
WELCOME
TWITCH
AAH. SO, YOU HAVE COME.
WE WERE GETTING BORED WAITING FOR YOU ...
WAIT...!
TROMP
TROMP
TROMP
TROMP
TROMP
WHAT HAPPENED TO THE OTHERS?!
THERE WERE DOZENS OF YOU YESTER-DAY!
WHAT'S GOING ON?!
Did they all go home?!
THEY GOT SICK.
THERE MIGHT BE A BUG GOING AROUND. YOU ALL OKAY?
AND NOW, YOU'RE WORRIED ABOUT US?!

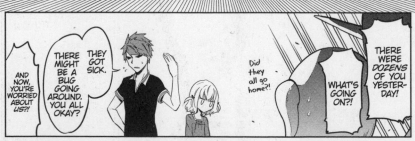

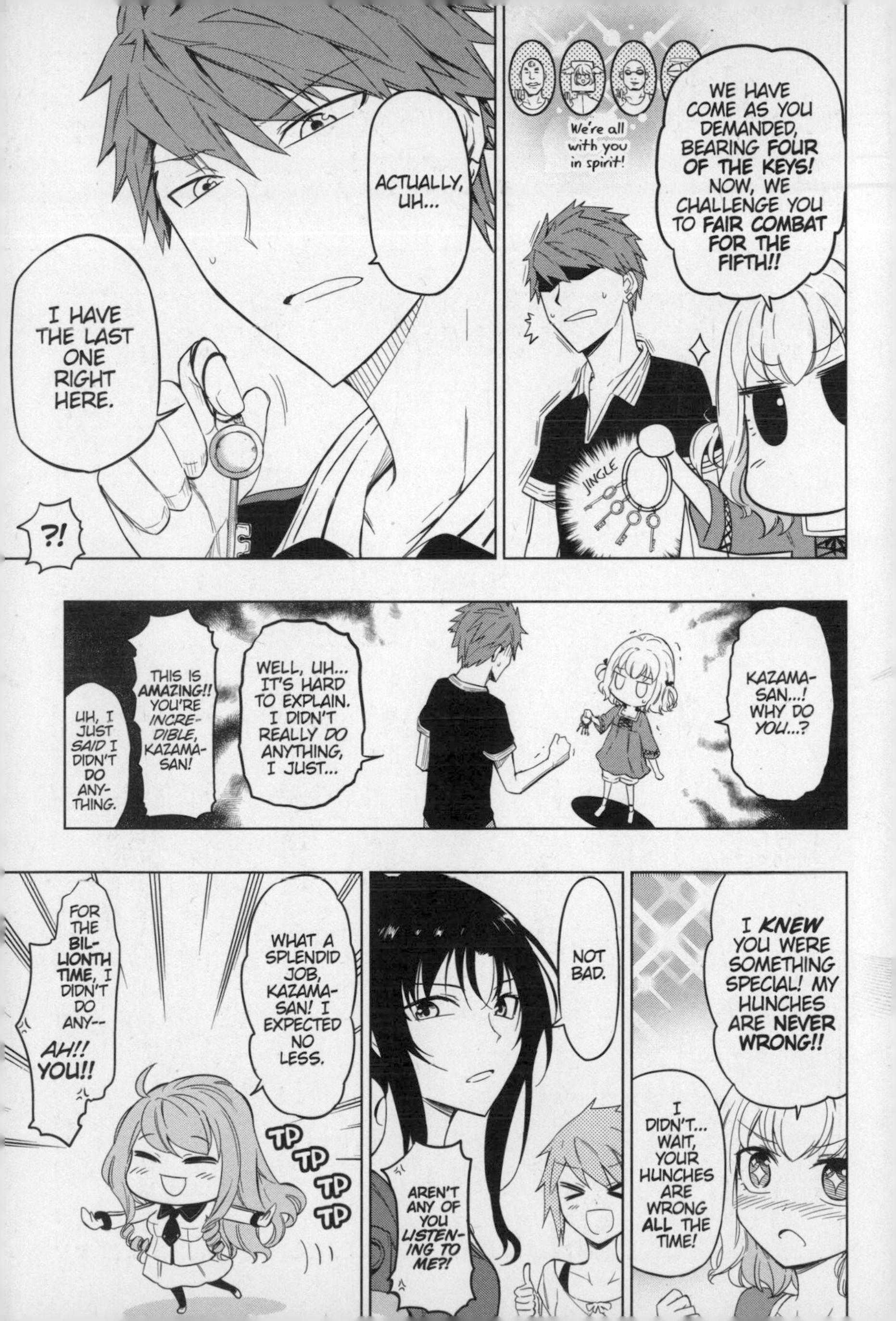
WE HAVE COME AS YOU DEMANDED, BEARING FOUR OF THE KEYS! NOW, WE CHALLENGE YOU TO FAIR COMBAT FOR THE FIFTH!!
We're all with you in spirit!
JINGLE
ACTUALLY, UH...
I HAVE THE LAST ONE RIGHT HERE.
?!
KAZAMA-SAN...! WHY DO YOU...?
WELL, UH... IT'S HARD TO EXPLAIN. I DIDN'T REALLY DO ANYTHING, I JUST...
THIS IS AMAZING!! YOU'RE INCREDIBLE, KAZAMA-SAN!
UH, I JUST SAID I DIDN'T DO ANYTHING.
I KNEW YOU WERE SOMETHING SPECIAL! MY HUNCHES ARE NEVER WRONG!!
I DIDN'T... WAIT, YOUR HUNCHES ARE WRONG ALL THE TIME!
NOT BAD.
AREN'T ANY OF YOU LISTENING TO ME?!
WHAT A SPLENDID JOB, KAZAMA-SAN! I EXPECTED NO LESS.
FOR THE BILLIONTH TIME, I DIDN'T DO ANY-- AH!! YOU!!
TP TP TP TP

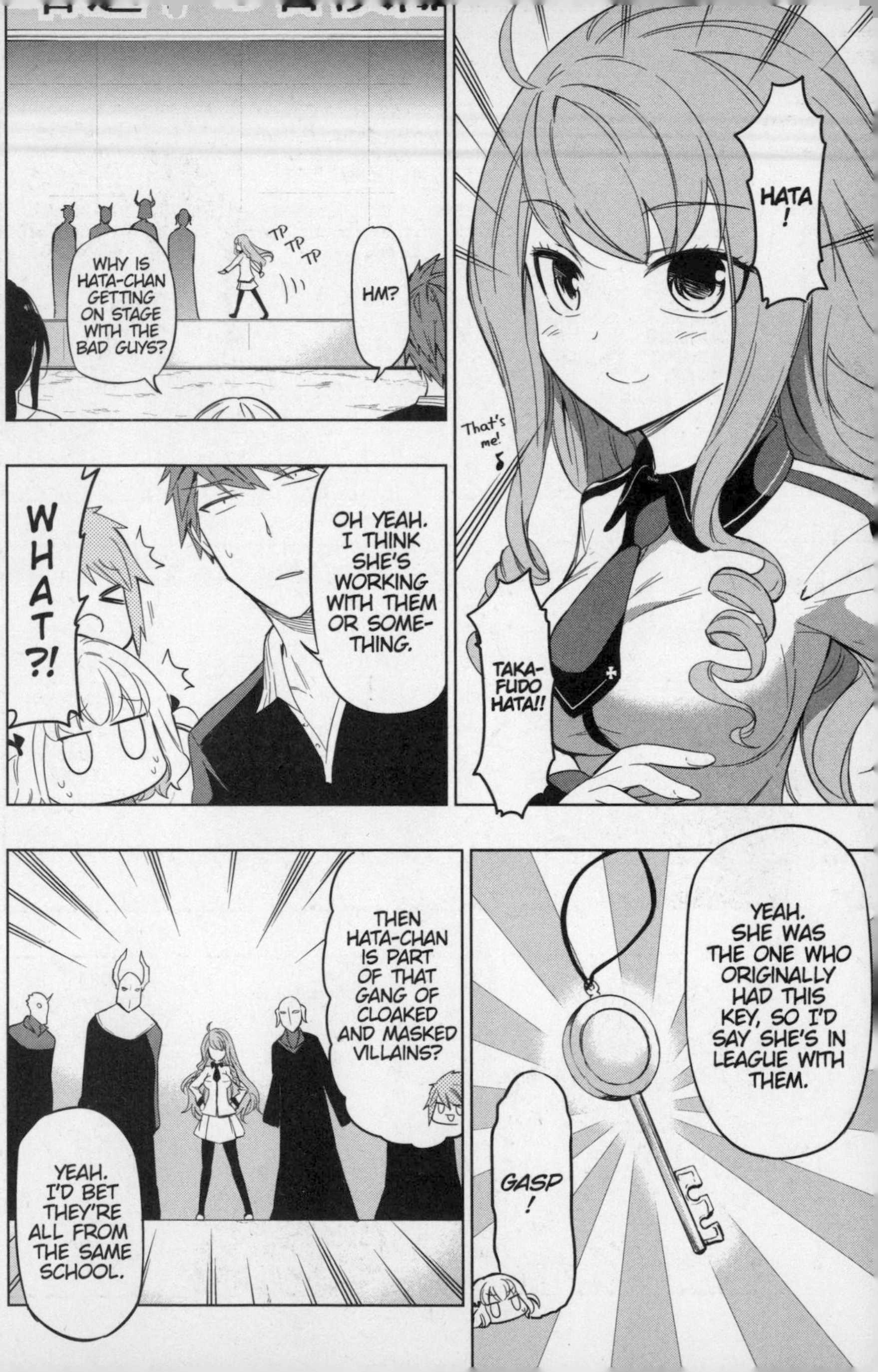
HATA!
That's me! ♪
TAKA-FUDO HATA!!
TP TP TP
HM?
WHY IS HATA-CHAN GETTING ON STAGE WITH THE BAD GUYS?
OH YEAH. I THINK SHE'S WORKING WITH THEM OR SOME-THING.
WHAT?!
YEAH. SHE WAS THE ONE WHO ORIGINALLY HAD THIS KEY, SO I'D SAY SHE'S IN LEAGUE WITH THEM.
GASP!
THEN HATA-CHAN IS PART OF THAT GANG OF CLOAKED AND MASKED VILLAINS?
YEAH. I'D BET THEY'RE ALL FROM THE SAME SCHOOL.

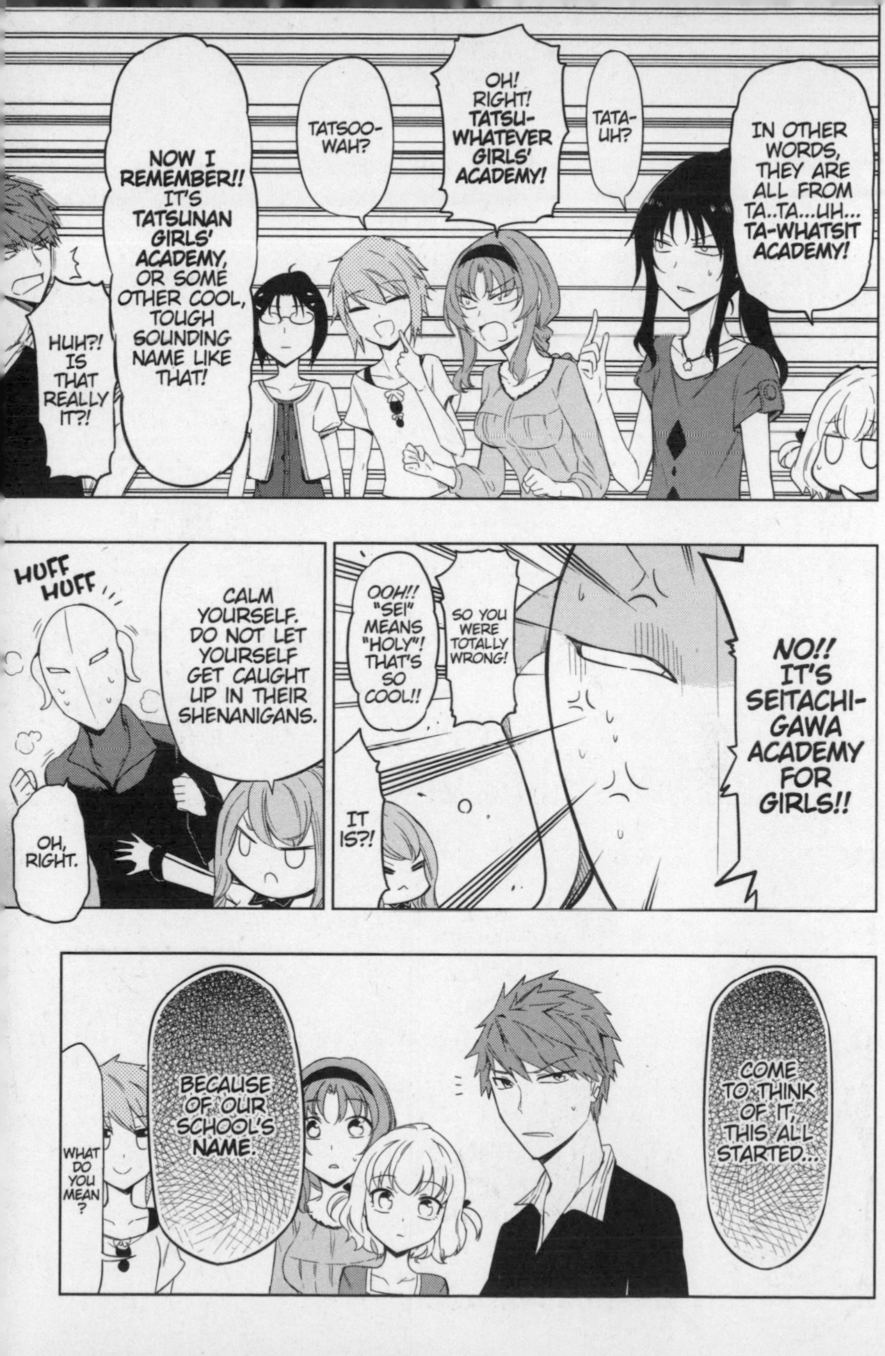
IN OTHER WORDS, THEY ARE ALL FROM TA..TA...UH... TA-WHATSIT ACADEMY!
TATA-UH?
OH! RIGHT! TATSU-WHATEVER GIRLS' ACADEMY!
TATSOO-WAH?
NOW I REMEMBER!! IT'S TATSUNAN GIRLS' ACADEMY, OR SOME OTHER COOL, TOUGH SOUNDING NAME LIKE THAT!
HUH?! IS THAT REALLY IT?!
NO!! IT'S SEITACHI-GAWA ACADEMY FOR GIRLS!!
SO YOU WERE TOTALLY WRONG!
OOH!! "SEI" MEANS "HOLY"! THAT'S SO COOL!!
IT IS?!
HUFF HUFF
CALM YOURSELF. DO NOT LET YOURSELF GET CAUGHT UP IN THEIR SHENANIGANS.
OH, RIGHT.
COME TO THINK OF IT, THIS ALL STARTED...
BECAUSE OF OUR SCHOOL'S NAME.
WHAT DO YOU MEAN?

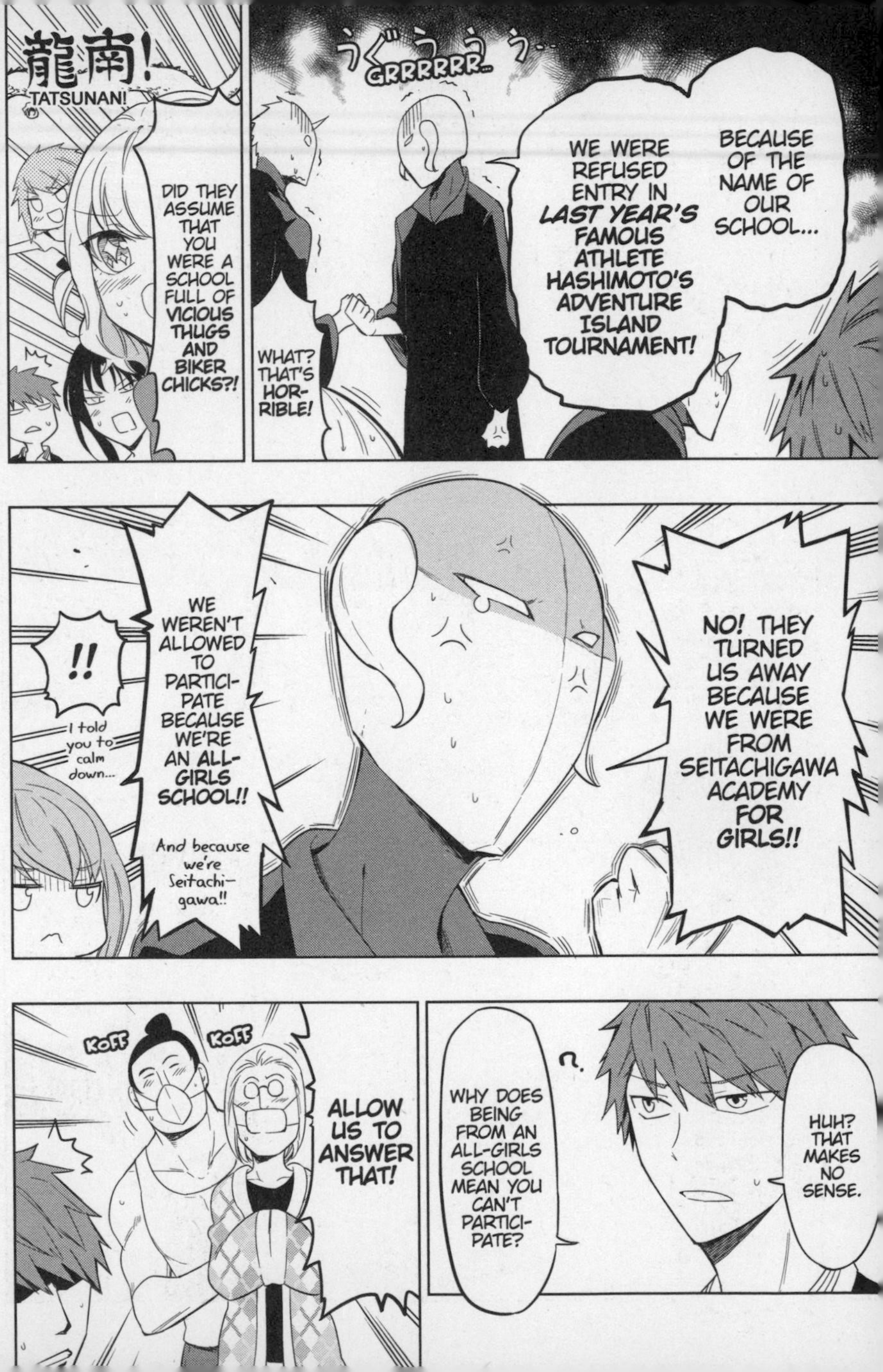
うぐぅぅぅ…
GRRRRRR...
BECAUSE OF THE NAME OF OUR SCHOOL...
WE WERE REFUSED ENTRY IN LAST YEAR'S FAMOUS ATHLETE HASHIMOTO'S ADVENTURE ISLAND TOURNAMENT!
WHAT? THAT'S HOR-RIBLE!
龍南!
TATSUNAN!
DID THEY ASSUME THAT YOU WERE A SCHOOL FULL OF VICIOUS THUGS AND BIKER CHICKS?!
NO! THEY TURNED US AWAY BECAUSE WE WERE FROM SEITACHIGAWA ACADEMY FOR GIRLS!!
WE WEREN'T ALLOWED TO PARTICI-PATE BECAUSE WE'RE AN ALL-GIRLS SCHOOL!!
And because we're Seitachi-gawa!!
!!
I told you to calm down...
HUH? THAT MAKES NO SENSE.
WHY DOES BEING FROM AN ALL-GIRLS SCHOOL MEAN YOU CAN'T PARTICI-PATE?
?
ALLOW US TO ANSWER THAT!
KOFF
KOFF

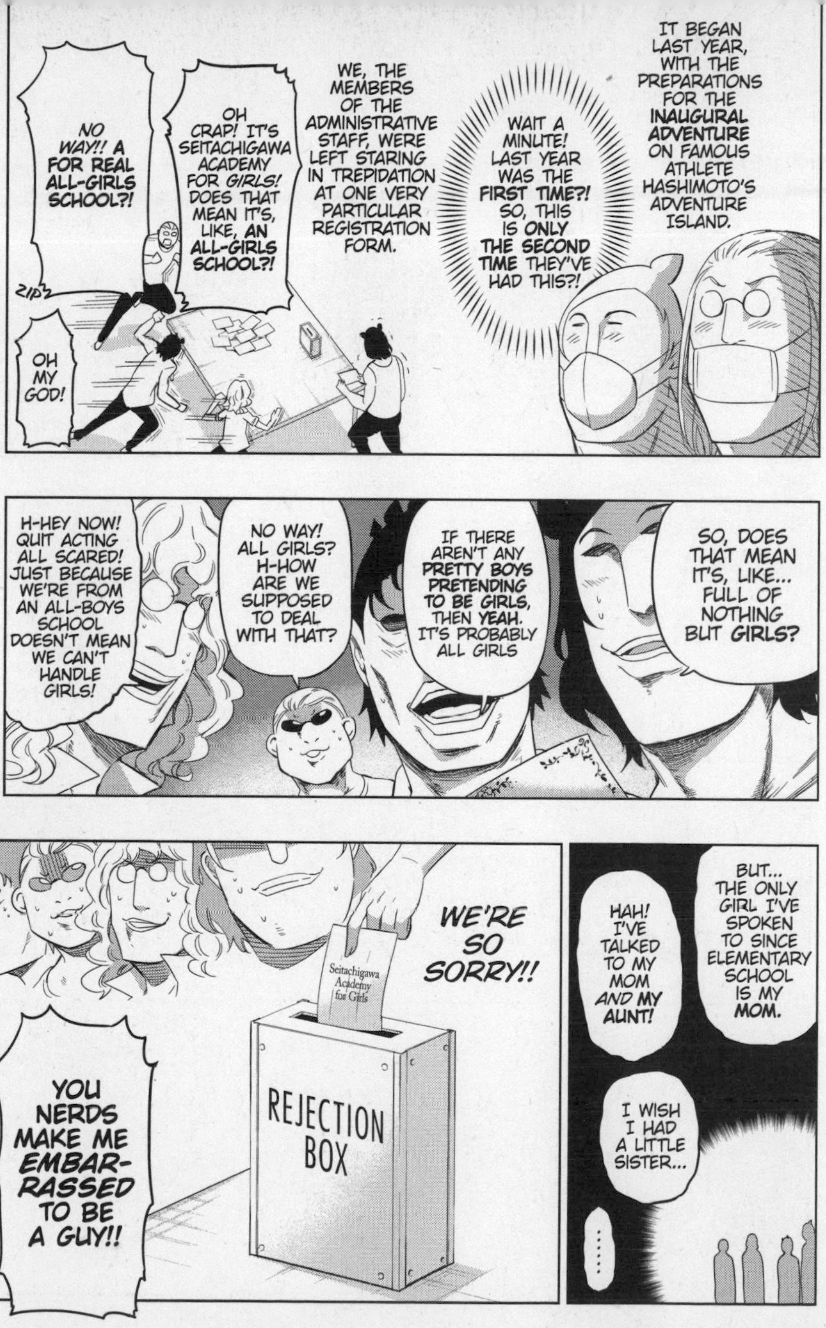
IT BEGAN LAST YEAR, WITH THE PREPARATIONS FOR THE INAUGURAL ADVENTURE ON FAMOUS ATHLETE HASHIMOTO'S ADVENTURE ISLAND.
WAIT A MINUTE! LAST YEAR WAS THE FIRST TIME?! SO, THIS IS ONLY THE SECOND TIME THEY'VE HAD THIS?!
WE, THE MEMBERS OF THE ADMINISTRATIVE STAFF, WERE LEFT STARING IN TREPIDATION AT ONE VERY PARTICULAR REGISTRATION FORM.
OH CRAP! IT'S SEITACHIGAWA ACADEMY FOR GIRLS! DOES THAT MEAN IT'S, LIKE, AN ALL-GIRLS SCHOOL?!
NO WAY!! A FOR REAL ALL-GIRLS SCHOOL?!
ZIP
OH MY GOD!
SO, DOES THAT MEAN IT'S, LIKE... FULL OF NOTHING BUT GIRLS?
IF THERE AREN'T ANY PRETTY BOYS PRETENDING TO BE GIRLS, THEN YEAH. IT'S PROBABLY ALL GIRLS
NO WAY! ALL GIRLS? H-HOW ARE WE SUPPOSED TO DEAL WITH THAT?
H-HEY NOW! QUIT ACTING ALL SCARED! JUST BECAUSE WE'RE FROM AN ALL-BOYS SCHOOL DOESN'T MEAN WE CAN'T HANDLE GIRLS!
BUT... THE ONLY GIRL I'VE SPOKEN TO SINCE ELEMENTARY SCHOOL IS MY MOM.
HAH! I'VE TALKED TO MY MOM AND MY AUNT!
I WISH I HAD A LITTLE SISTER...
......
WE'RE SO SORRY!!
Seitachigawa Academy for Girls
REJECTION BOX
YOU NERDS MAKE ME EMBARRASSED TO BE A GUY!!

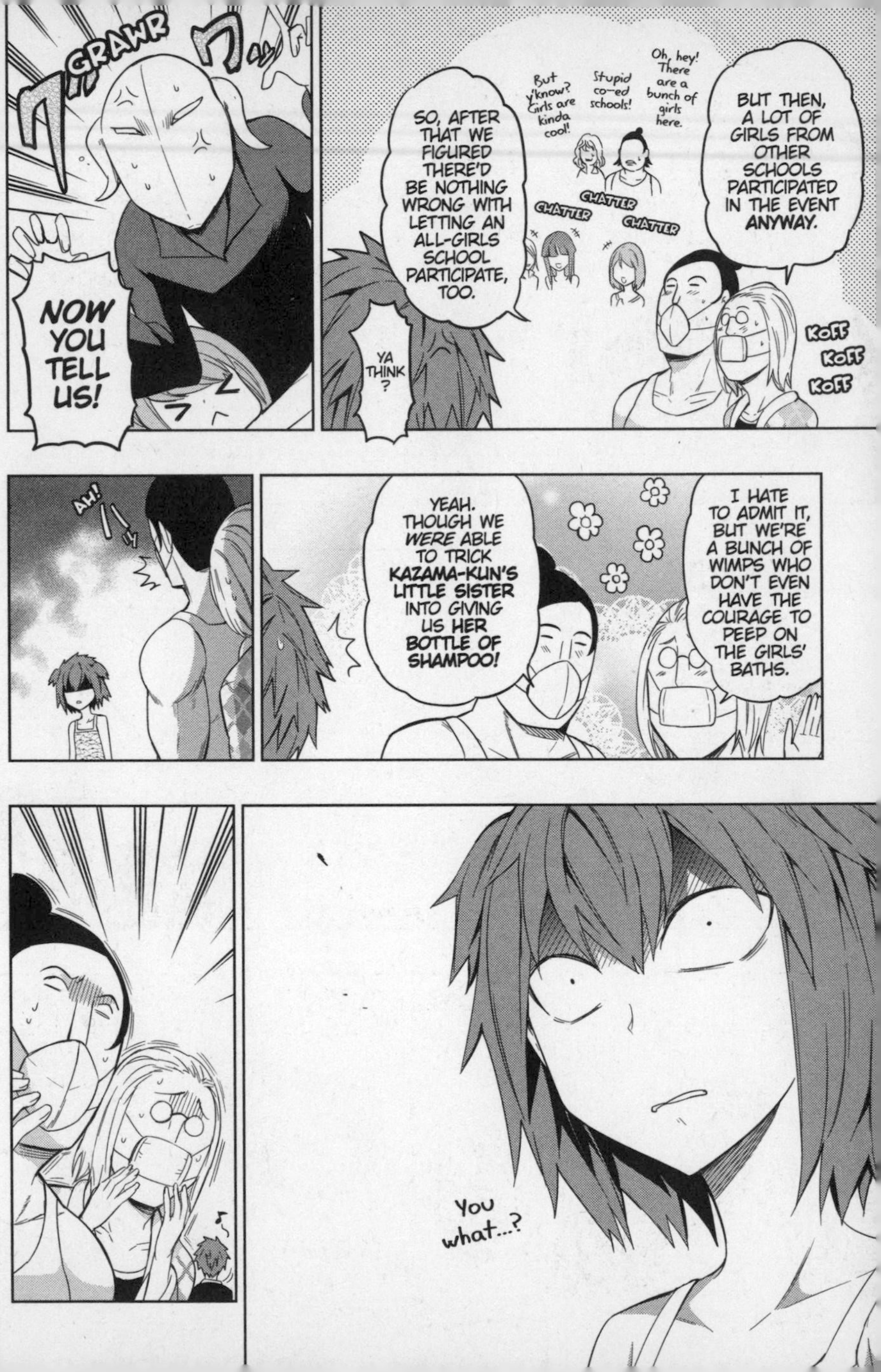
BUT THEN, A LOT OF GIRLS FROM OTHER SCHOOLS PARTICIPATED IN THE EVENT ANYWAY.
Oh, hey! There are a bunch of girls here.
Stupid co-ed schools!
But y'know? Girls are kinda cool!
CHATTER
CHATTER
CHATTER
KOFF
KOFF
KOFF
SO, AFTER THAT WE FIGURED THERE'D BE NOTHING WRONG WITH LETTING AN ALL-GIRLS SCHOOL PARTICIPATE, TOO.
YA THINK?
GRAWR
NOW YOU TELL US!
I HATE TO ADMIT IT, BUT WE'RE A BUNCH OF WIMPS WHO DON'T EVEN HAVE THE COURAGE TO PEEP ON THE GIRLS' BATHS.
YEAH. THOUGH WE *WERE* ABLE TO TRICK KAZAMA-KUN'S LITTLE SISTER INTO GIVING US HER BOTTLE OF SHAMPOO!
AH!
You what...?

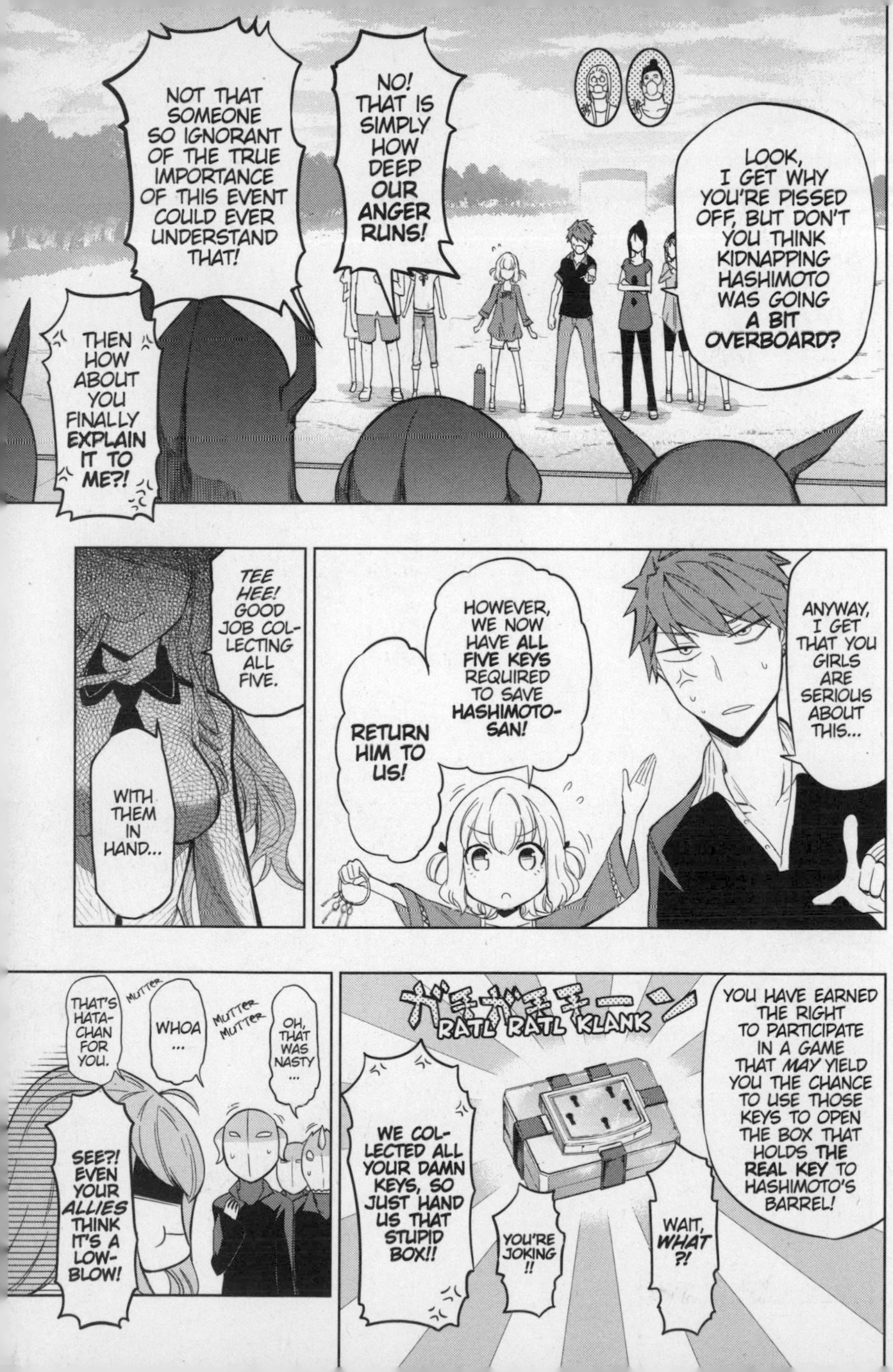
LOOK, I GET WHY YOU'RE PISSED OFF, BUT DON'T YOU THINK KIDNAPPING HASHIMOTO WAS GOING A BIT OVERBOARD?
NO! THAT IS SIMPLY HOW DEEP OUR ANGER RUNS!
NOT THAT SOMEONE SO IGNORANT OF THE TRUE IMPORTANCE OF THIS EVENT COULD EVER UNDERSTAND THAT!
THEN HOW ABOUT YOU FINALLY EXPLAIN IT TO ME?!
ANYWAY, I GET THAT YOU GIRLS ARE SERIOUS ABOUT THIS...
HOWEVER, WE NOW HAVE ALL FIVE KEYS REQUIRED TO SAVE HASHIMOTO-SAN!
RETURN HIM TO US!
TEE HEE! GOOD JOB COL-LECTING ALL FIVE.
WITH THEM IN HAND...
RATL RATL KLANK
YOU HAVE EARNED THE RIGHT TO PARTICIPATE IN A GAME THAT MAY YIELD YOU THE CHANCE TO USE THOSE KEYS TO OPEN THE BOX THAT HOLDS THE REAL KEY TO HASHIMOTO'S BARREL!
WAIT, WHAT?!
YOU'RE JOKING!!
WE COL-LECTED ALL YOUR DAMN KEYS, SO JUST HAND US THAT STUPID BOX!!
OH, THAT WAS NASTY...
MUTTER MUTTER
WHOA...
MUTTER
THAT'S HATA-CHAN FOR YOU.
SEE?! EVEN YOUR ALLIES THINK IT'S A LOW-BLOW!

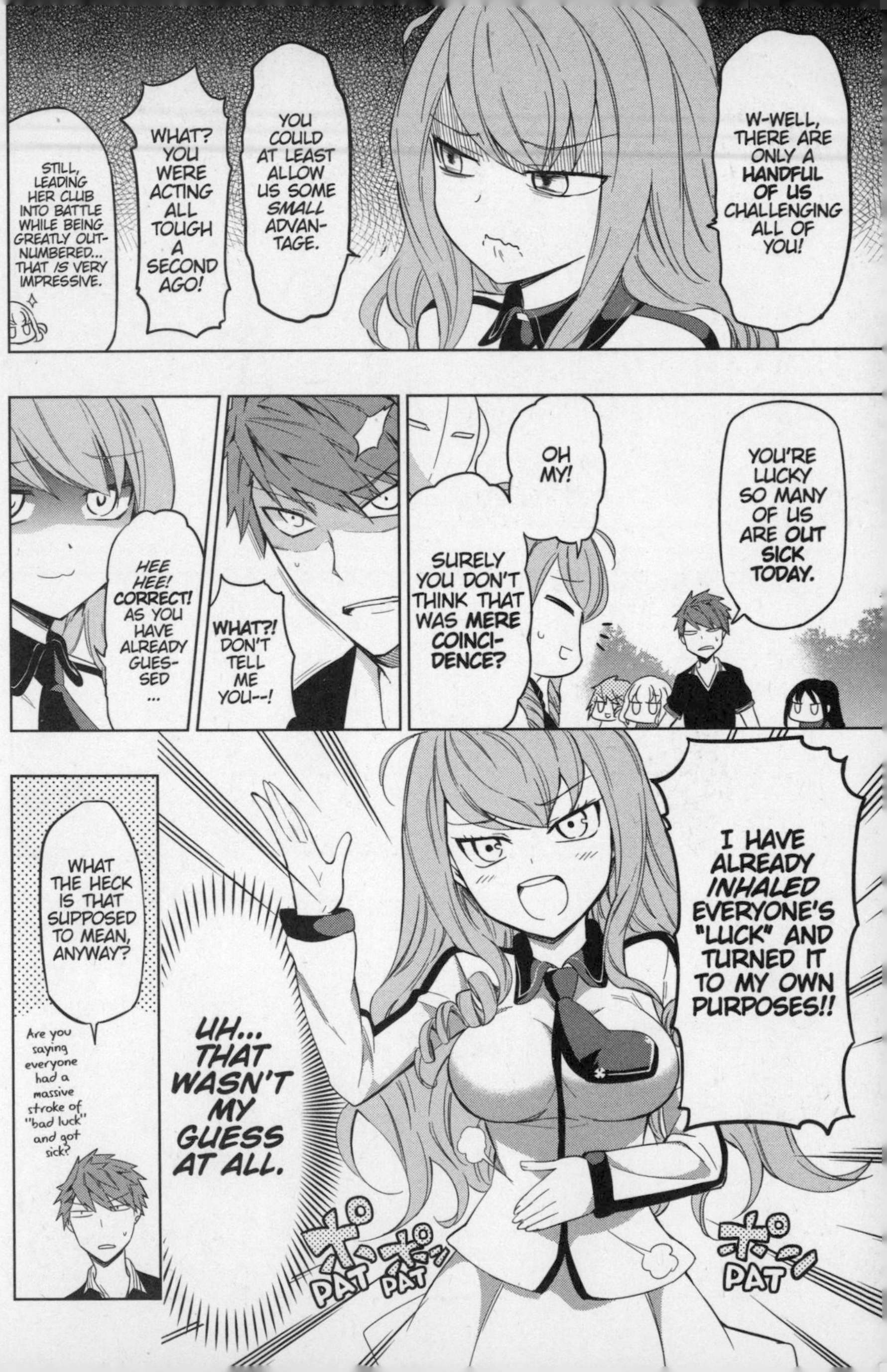
W-WELL, THERE ARE ONLY A HANDFUL OF US CHALLENGING ALL OF YOU!
YOU COULD AT LEAST ALLOW US SOME SMALL ADVANTAGE.
WHAT? YOU WERE ACTING ALL TOUGH A SECOND AGO!
STILL, LEADING HER CLUB INTO BATTLE WHILE BEING GREATLY OUT-NUMBERED... THAT IS VERY IMPRESSIVE.
YOU'RE LUCKY SO MANY OF US ARE OUT SICK TODAY.
OH MY!
SURELY YOU DON'T THINK THAT WAS MERE COINCIDENCE?
WHAT?! DON'T TELL ME YOU--!
HEE HEE! CORRECT! AS YOU HAVE ALREADY GUES-SED...
I HAVE ALREADY INHALED EVERYONE'S "LUCK" AND TURNED IT TO MY OWN PURPOSES!!
PAT
UH... THAT WASN'T MY GUESS AT ALL.
PAT PAT
WHAT THE HECK IS THAT SUPPOSED TO MEAN, ANYWAY?
Are you saying everyone had a massive stroke of "bad luck" and got sick?

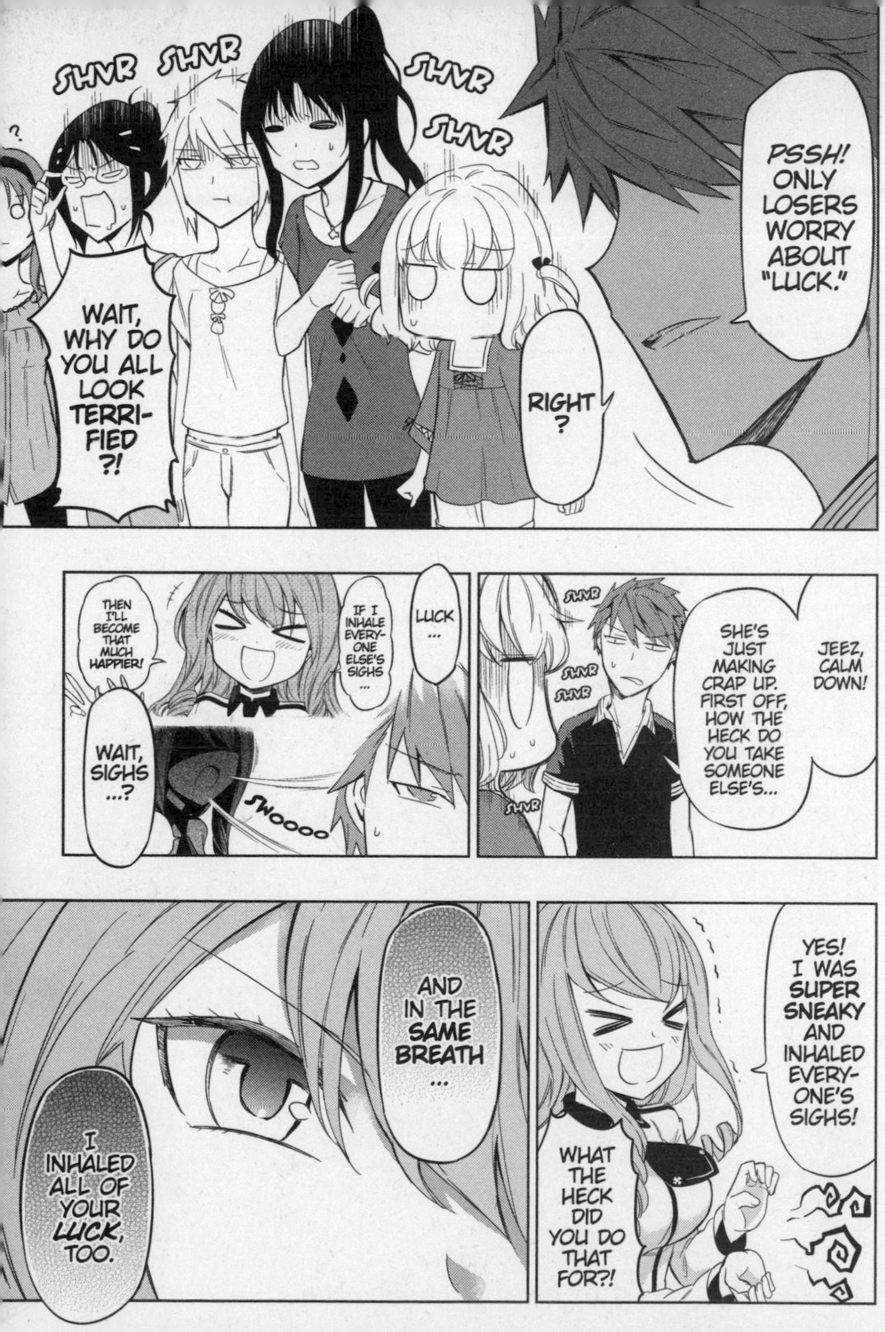
PSSH! ONLY LOSERS WORRY ABOUT "LUCK."
SHVR
SHVR
RIGHT ?
SHVR
SHVR
WAIT, WHY DO YOU ALL LOOK TERRI-FIED ?!
?
JEEZ, CALM DOWN!
SHE'S JUST MAKING CRAP UP. FIRST OFF, HOW THE HECK DO YOU TAKE SOMEONE ELSE'S...
SHVR
SHVR
SHVR
SHVR
LUCK ...
IF I INHALE EVERY-ONE ELSE'S SIGHS ...
THEN I'LL BECOME THAT MUCH HAPPIER!
WAIT, SIGHS ...?
SWOOOO
YES! I WAS SUPER SNEAKY AND INHALED EVERY-ONE'S SIGHS!
WHAT THE HECK DID YOU DO THAT FOR?!
AND IN THE SAME BREATH ...
I INHALED ALL OF YOUR LUCK, TOO.

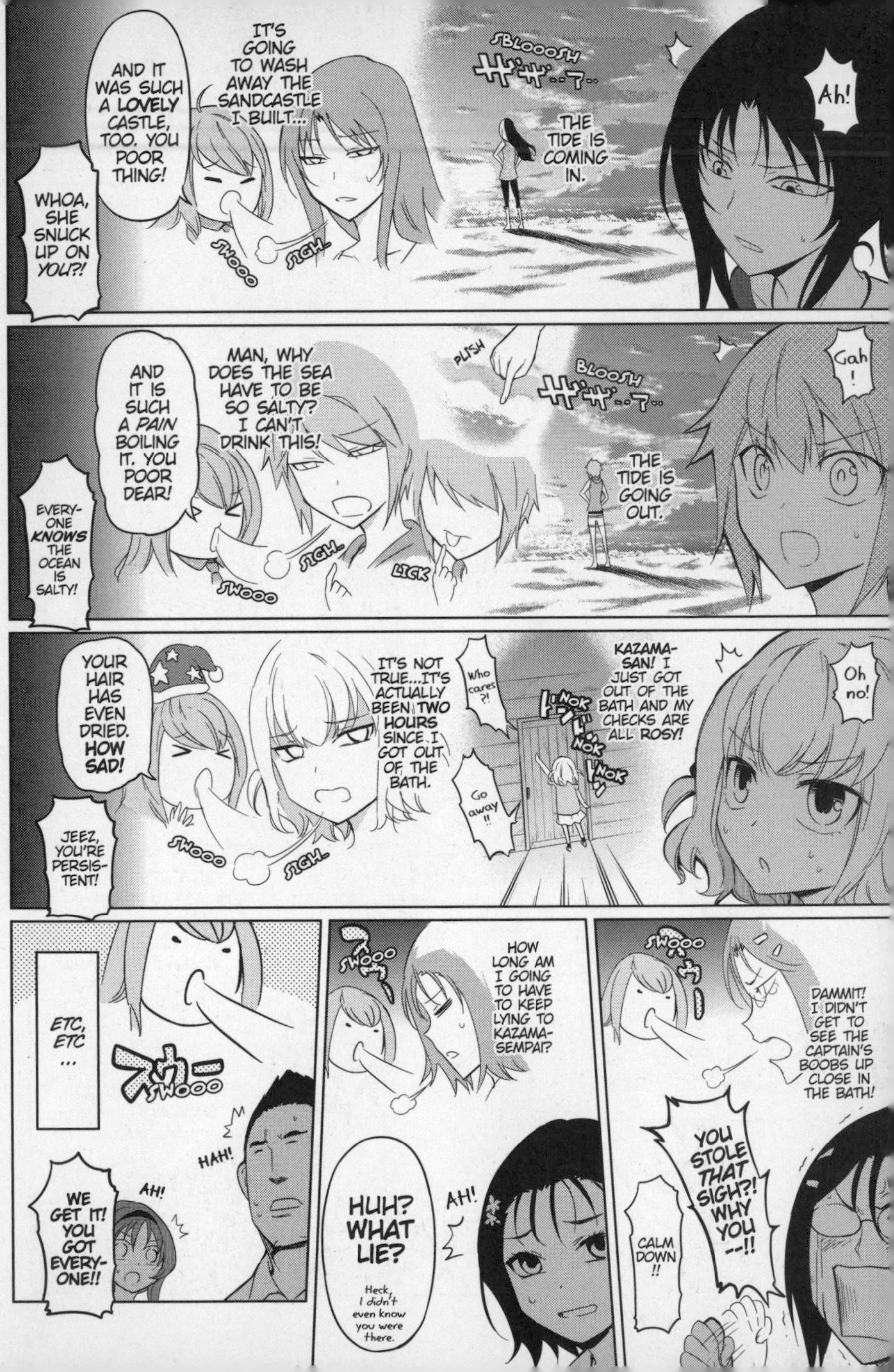
Ah!
SBLOOOSH
THE TIDE IS COMING IN.
IT'S GOING TO WASH AWAY THE SANDCASTLE I BUILT...
SIGH..
AND IT WAS SUCH A LOVELY CASTLE, TOO. YOU POOR THING!
SWOOO
WHOA, SHE SNUCK UP ON YOU?!
Gah!
BLOOSH
THE TIDE IS GOING OUT.
PLISH
MAN, WHY DOES THE SEA HAVE TO BE SO SALTY? I CAN'T DRINK THIS!
LICK
SIGH..
AND IT IS SUCH A PAIN BOILING IT. YOU POOR DEAR!
SWOOO
EVERY-ONE KNOWS THE OCEAN IS SALTY!
Oh no!
KAZAMA-SAN! I JUST GOT OUT OF THE BATH AND MY CHECKS ARE ALL ROSY!
NOK
NOK
NOK
Who cares?!
Go away!!
IT'S NOT TRUE...IT'S ACTUALLY BEEN TWO HOURS SINCE I GOT OUT OF THE BATH.
SIGH..
YOUR HAIR HAS EVEN DRIED. HOW SAD!
SWOOO
JEEZ, YOU'RE PERSIS-TENT!
SWOOO
DAMMIT! I DIDN'T GET TO SEE THE CAPTAIN'S BOOBS UP CLOSE IN THE BATH!
YOU STOLE THAT SIGH?! WHY YOU--!!
CALM DOWN!!
SWOOO
HOW LONG AM I GOING TO HAVE TO KEEP LYING TO KAZAMA-SEMPAI?
AH!
HUH? WHAT LIE?
Heck, I didn't even know you were there.
ETC, ETC ...
SWOOO
HAH!
AH!
WE GET IT! YOU GOT EVERY-ONE!!

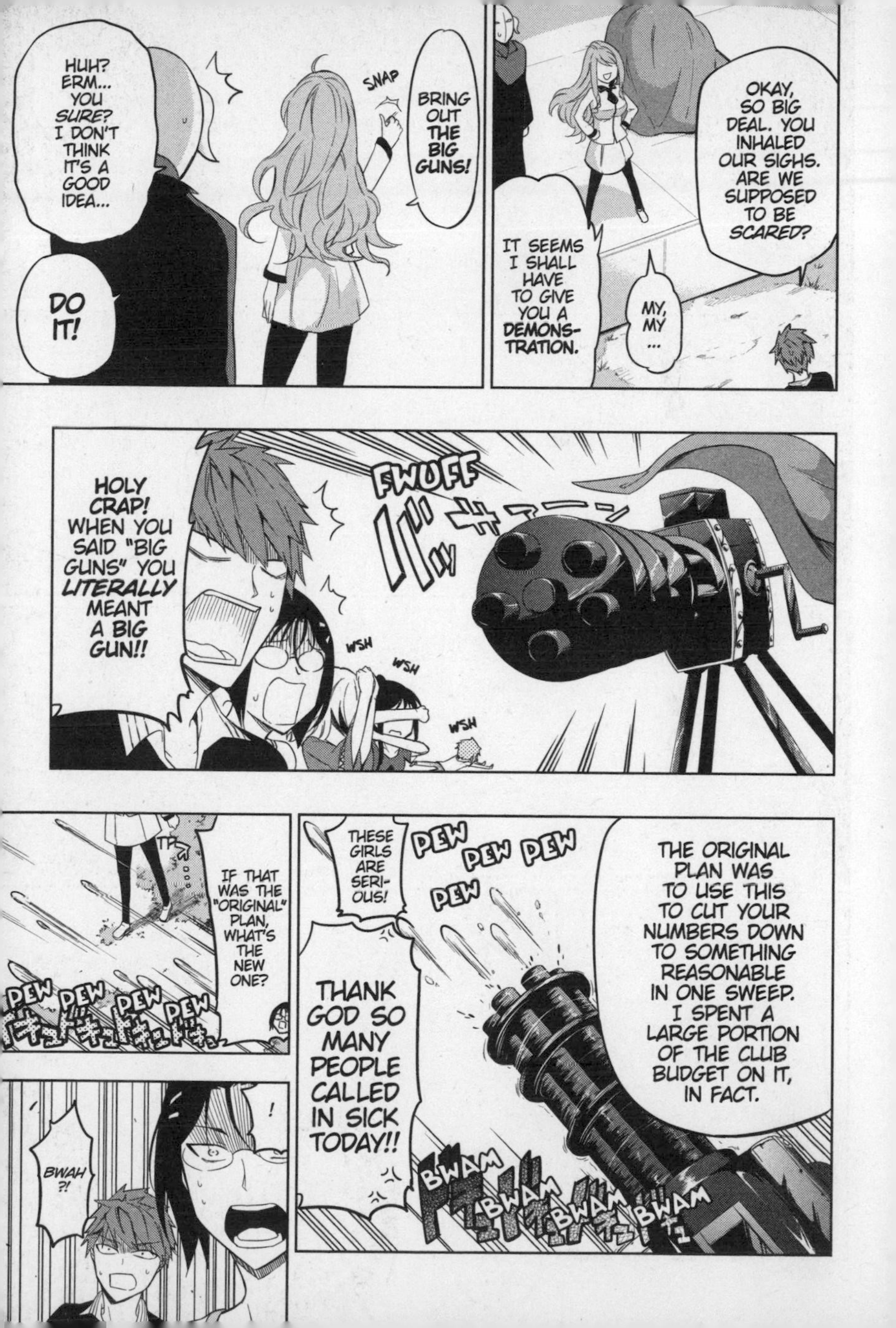
OKAY, SO BIG DEAL. YOU INHALED OUR SIGHS. ARE WE SUPPOSED TO BE SCARED?
MY, MY ...
IT SEEMS I SHALL HAVE TO GIVE YOU A DEMONSTRATION.
BRING OUT THE BIG GUNS!
SNAP
HUH? ERM... YOU SURE? I DON'T THINK IT'S A GOOD IDEA...
DO IT!
FWUFF
HOLY CRAP! WHEN YOU SAID "BIG GUNS" YOU LITERALLY MEANT A BIG GUN!!
WSH
WSH
WSH
THE ORIGINAL PLAN WAS TO USE THIS TO CUT YOUR NUMBERS DOWN TO SOMETHING REASONABLE IN ONE SWEEP. I SPENT A LARGE PORTION OF THE CLUB BUDGET ON IT, IN FACT.
PEW PEW PEW PEW
THESE GIRLS ARE SERIOUS!
THANK GOD SO MANY PEOPLE CALLED IN SICK TODAY!!
BWAM BWAM BWAM BWAM
IF THAT WAS THE "ORIGINAL" PLAN, WHAT'S THE NEW ONE?
PEW PEW PEW PEW
BWAH ?!

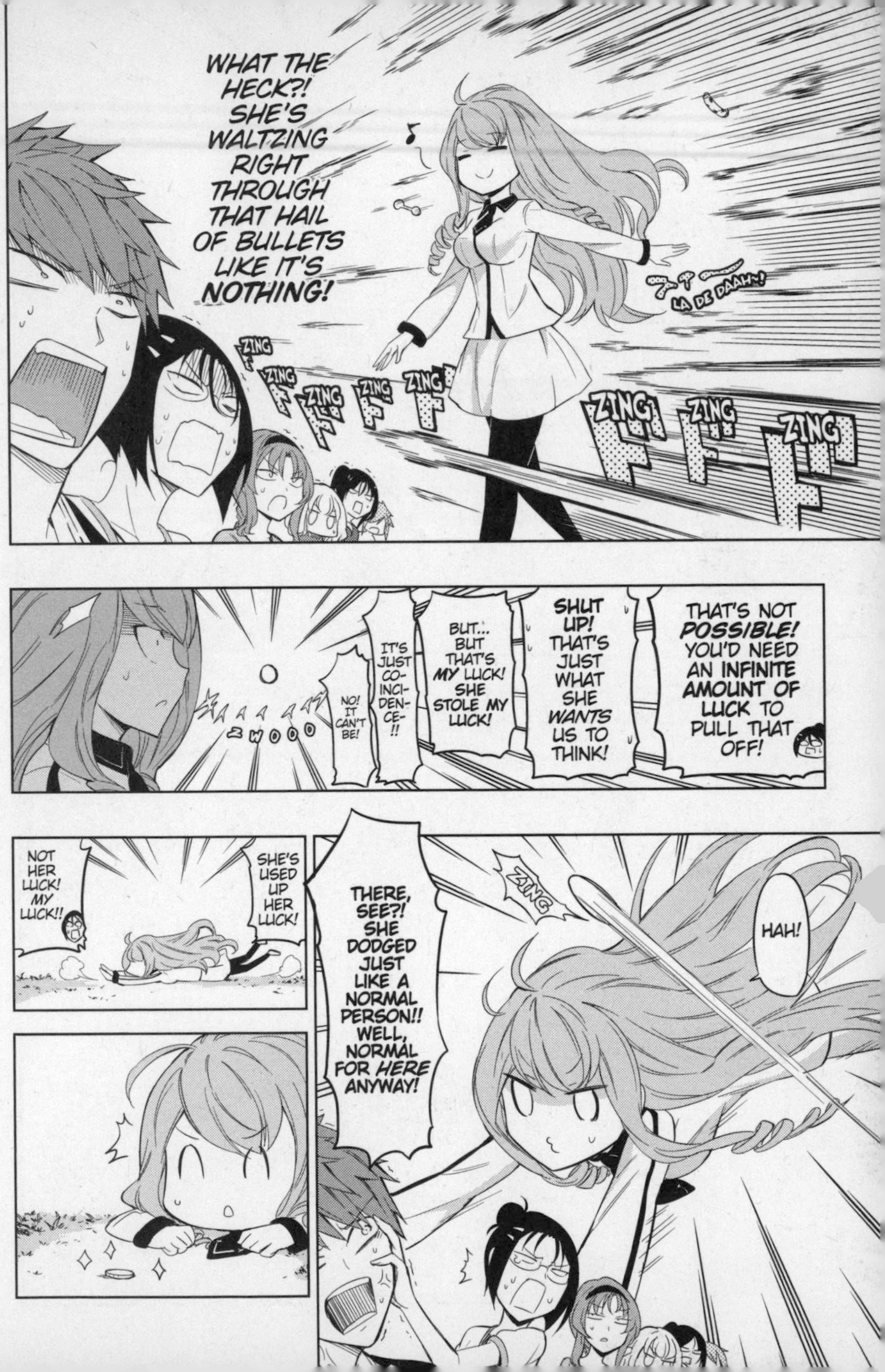
WHAT THE HECK?! SHE'S WALTZING RIGHT THROUGH THAT HAIL OF BULLETS LIKE IT'S NOTHING!
LA DE DAAH~!
ZING
ZING
ZING
ZING
ZING
ZING
ZING
ZING
THAT'S NOT POSSIBLE! YOU'D NEED AN INFINITE AMOUNT OF LUCK TO PULL THAT OFF!
SHUT UP! THAT'S JUST WHAT SHE WANTS US TO THINK!
BUT... BUT THAT'S MY LUCK! SHE STOLE MY LUCK!
IT'S JUST COINCIDENCE!!
NO! IT CAN'T BE!
ZWOOO
HAH!
ZING
THERE, SEE?! SHE DODGED JUST LIKE A NORMAL PERSON!! WELL, NORMAL FOR HERE ANYWAY!
SHE'S USED UP HER LUCK!
NOT HER LUCK! MY LUCK!!

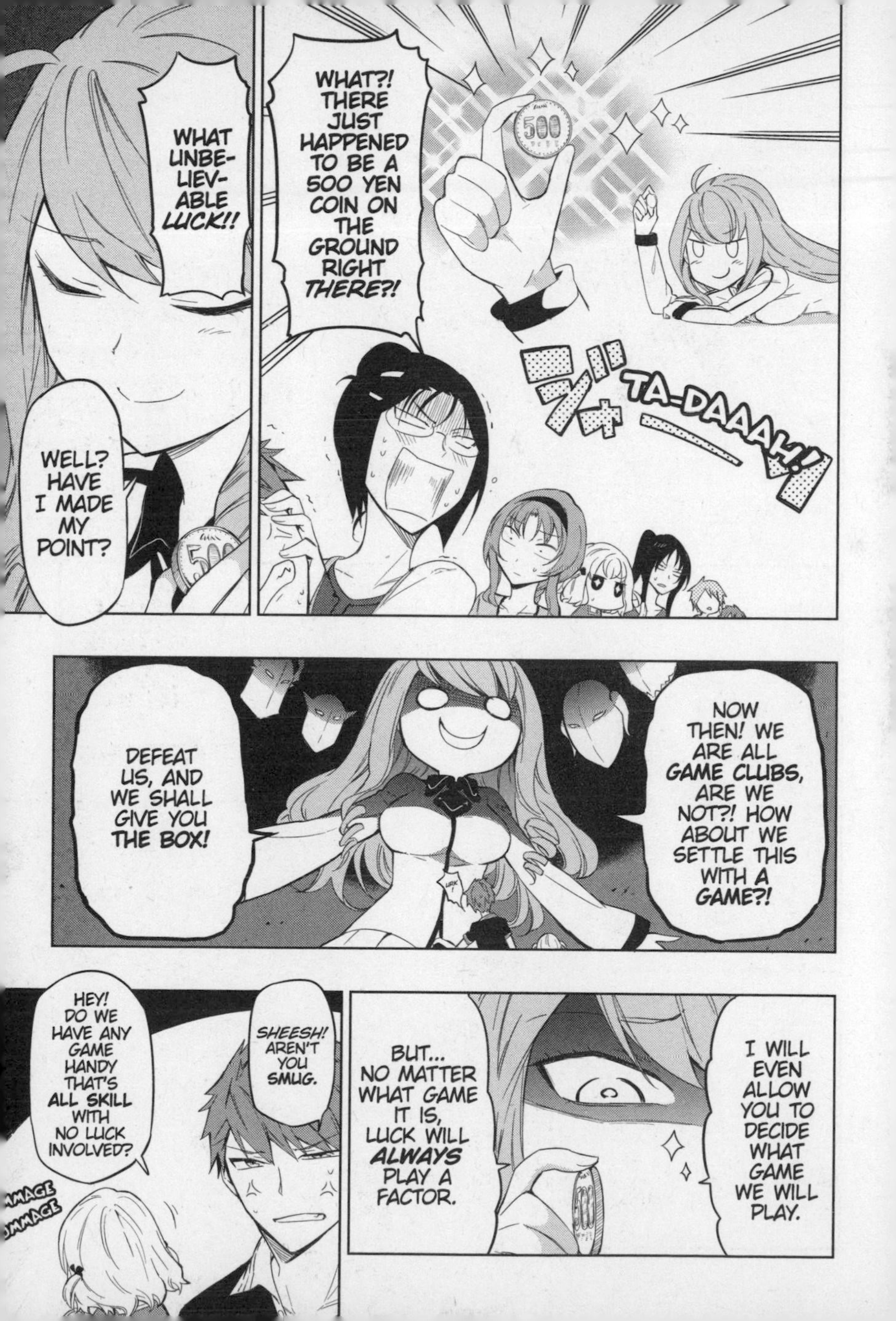
TA-DAAAH!
WHAT?! THERE JUST HAPPENED TO BE A 500 YEN COIN ON THE GROUND RIGHT *THERE?!*
WHAT UNBELIEVABLE *LUCK!!*
WELL? HAVE I MADE MY POINT?
NOW THEN! WE ARE ALL **GAME CLUBS**, ARE WE NOT?! HOW ABOUT WE SETTLE THIS WITH A **GAME?!**
DEFEAT US, AND WE SHALL GIVE YOU **THE BOX!**
I WILL EVEN ALLOW YOU TO DECIDE WHAT GAME WE WILL PLAY.
BUT... NO MATTER WHAT GAME IT IS, LUCK WILL ***ALWAYS*** PLAY A FACTOR.
SHEESH! AREN'T YOU SMUG.
HEY! DO WE HAVE ANY GAME HANDY THAT'S **ALL SKILL** WITH NO LUCK INVOLVED?

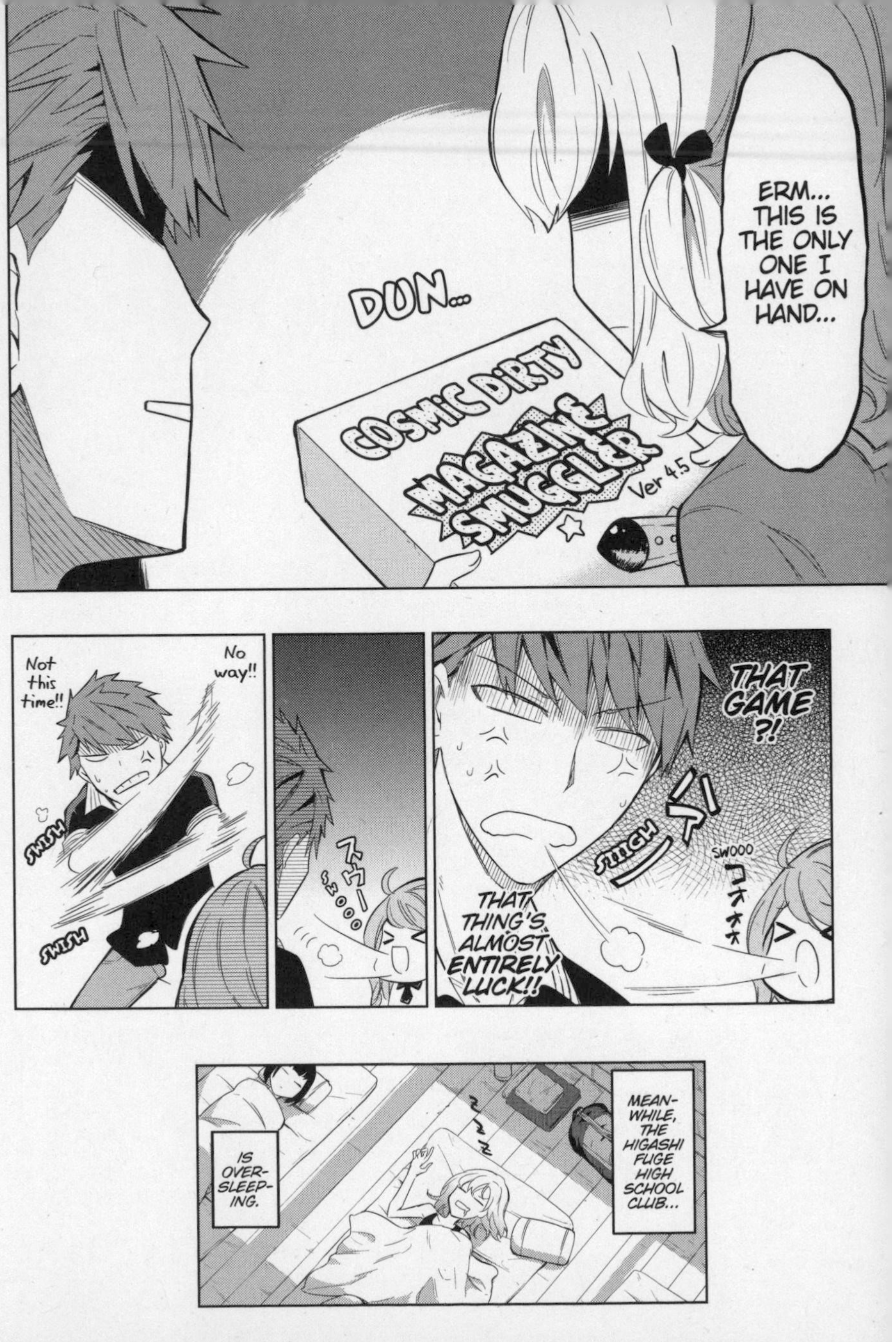
ERM... THIS IS THE ONLY ONE I HAVE ON HAND...
DUN...
COSMIC DIRTY
MAGAZINE SMUGGLER
Ver 4.5
THAT GAME?!
SIIIGH
SWOOO
コホホホ
THAT THING'S ALMOST ENTIRELY LUCK!!
スゥー
SWOOO
No way!!
Not this time!!
SWISH
SWISH
MEAN-WHILE, THE HIGASHI FUGE HIGH SCHOOL CLUB...
IS OVER-SLEEP-ING.

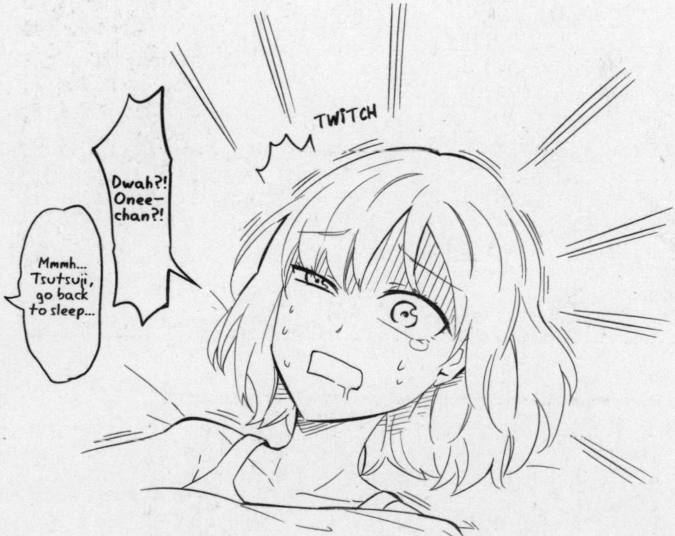
TWITCH
Dwah?! Onee-chan?!
Mmmh... Tsutsuji, go back to sleep...

D-FRAGMENTS

ディーふらぐ!

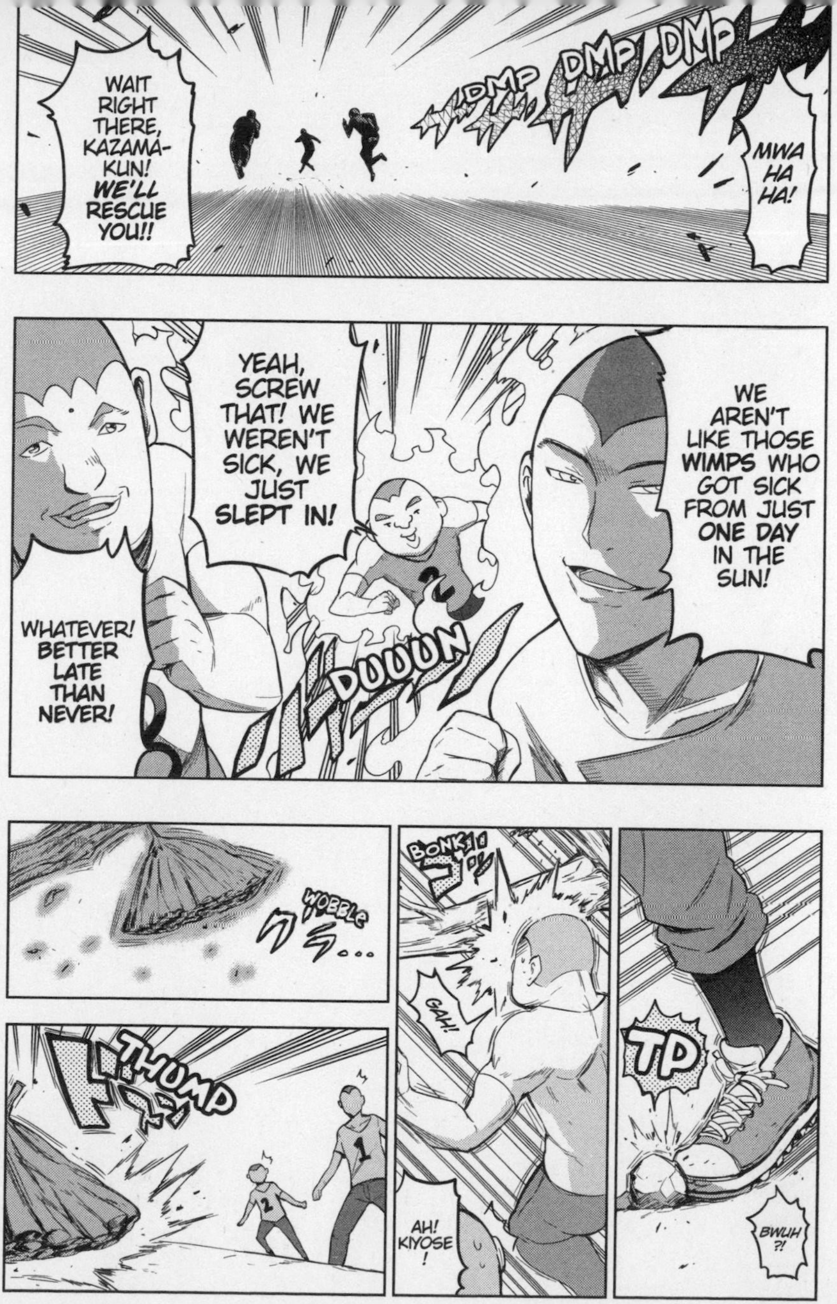
MWA HA HA!
DMP DMP DMP
WAIT RIGHT THERE, KAZAMA-KUN! WE'LL RESCUE YOU!!
WE AREN'T LIKE THOSE WIMPS WHO GOT SICK FROM JUST ONE DAY IN THE SUN!
YEAH, SCREW THAT! WE WEREN'T SICK, WE JUST SLEPT IN!
DUUUN
WHATEVER! BETTER LATE THAN NEVER!
TP
BWUH ?!
BONK
GAH!
AH! KIYOSE !
WOBBLE
THUMP

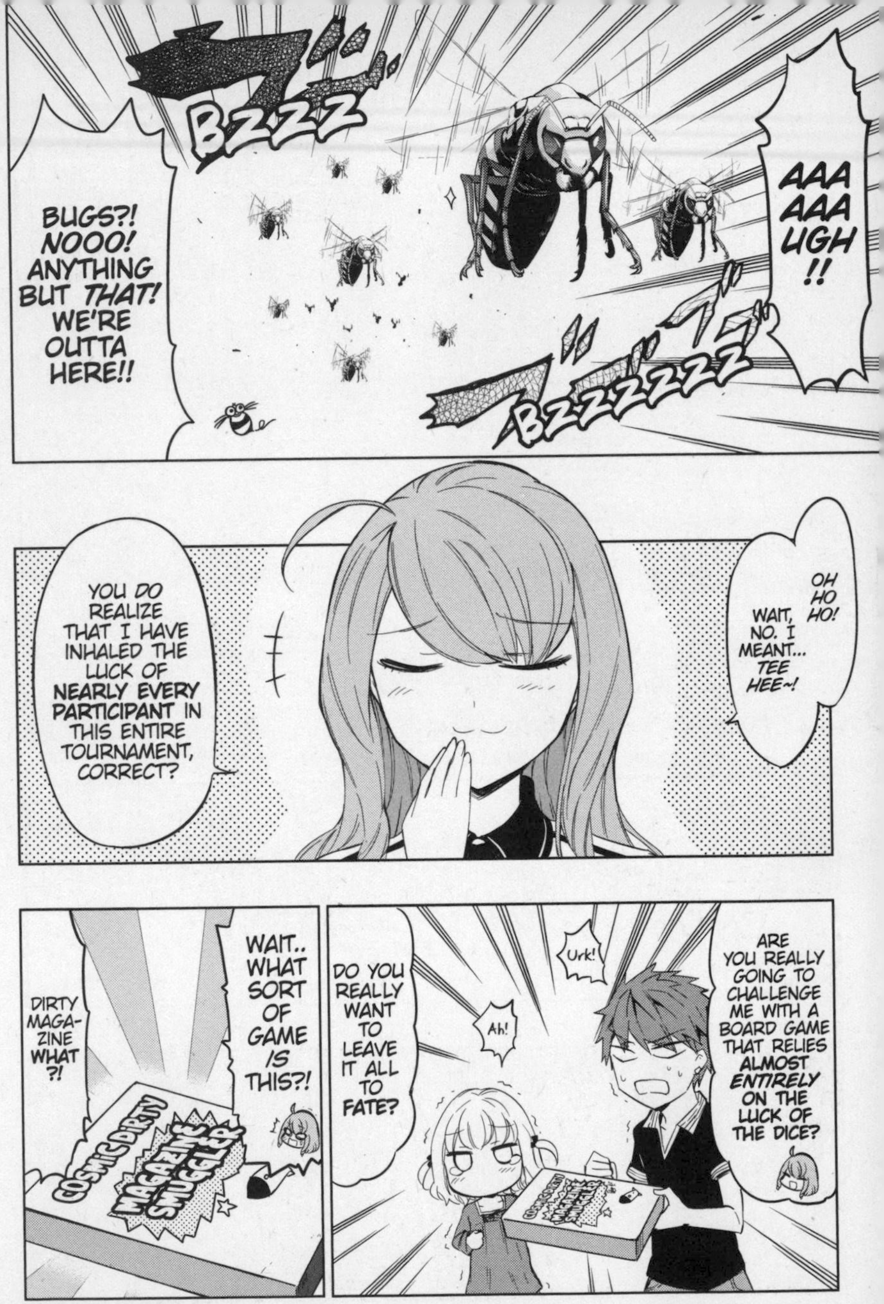
AAA AAA UGH !!
BZZZ
BUGS?! NOOO! ANYTHING BUT THAT! WE'RE OUTTA HERE!!
BZZZZZZZZ
OH HO HO! WAIT, NO. I MEANT... TEE HEE~!
YOU DO REALIZE THAT I HAVE INHALED THE LUCK OF NEARLY EVERY PARTICIPANT IN THIS ENTIRE TOURNAMENT, CORRECT?
ARE YOU REALLY GOING TO CHALLENGE ME WITH A BOARD GAME THAT RELIES ALMOST ENTIRELY ON THE LUCK OF THE DICE?
Urk!
Ah!
DO YOU REALLY WANT TO LEAVE IT ALL TO FATE?
WAIT.. WHAT SORT OF GAME IS THIS?!
DIRTY MAGAZINE WHAT?!
COSMIC DIRTY MAGAZINE SMUGGLER

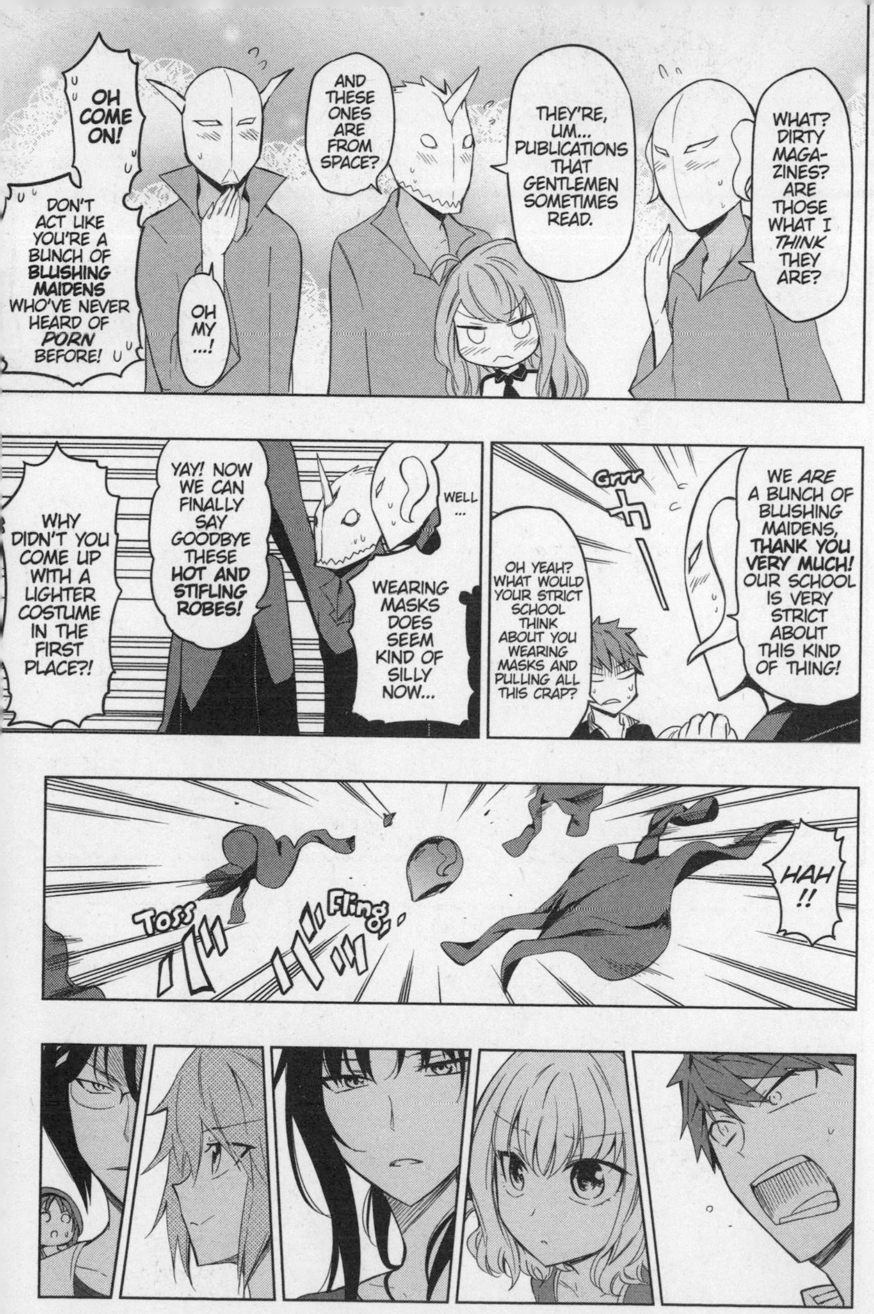
WHAT? DIRTY MAGA-ZINES? ARE THOSE WHAT I *THINK* THEY ARE?
THEY'RE, UM... PUBLICATIONS THAT GENTLEMEN SOMETIMES READ.
AND THESE ONES ARE FROM SPACE?
OH MY ...!
OH COME ON!
DON'T ACT LIKE YOU'RE A BUNCH OF **BLUSHING MAIDENS** WHO'VE NEVER HEARD OF ***PORN*** BEFORE!
WE *ARE* A BUNCH OF BLUSHING MAIDENS, **THANK YOU VERY MUCH!** OUR SCHOOL IS VERY STRICT ABOUT THIS KIND OF THING!
Grrr
OH YEAH? WHAT WOULD YOUR STRICT SCHOOL THINK ABOUT YOU WEARING MASKS AND PULLING ALL THIS CRAP?
WELL ...
WEARING MASKS DOES SEEM KIND OF SILLY NOW...
YAY! NOW WE CAN FINALLY SAY GOODBYE THESE **HOT AND STIFLING ROBES!**
WHY DIDN'T YOU COME UP WITH A LIGHTER COSTUME IN THE FIRST PLACE?!
HAH !!
Fling
Toss

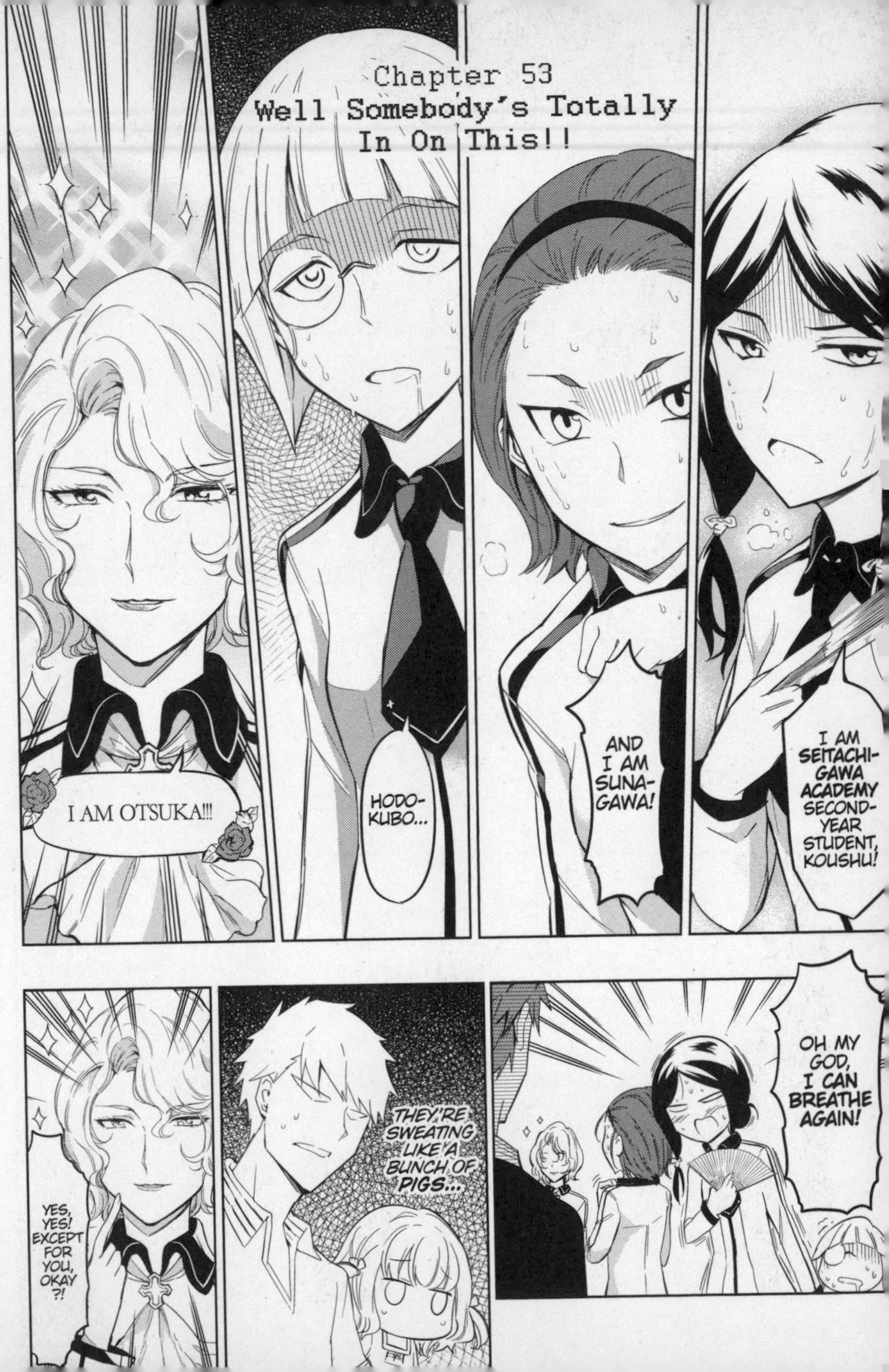
Chapter 53
Well Somebody's Totally In On This!!
I AM SEITACHIGAWA ACADEMY SECOND-YEAR STUDENT, KOUSHU!
AND I AM SUNAGAWA!
HODOKUBO...
I AM OTSUKA!!!
OH MY GOD, I CAN BREATHE AGAIN!
THEY'RE SWEATING LIKE A BUNCH OF PIGS...
YES, YES! EXCEPT FOR YOU, OKAY?!

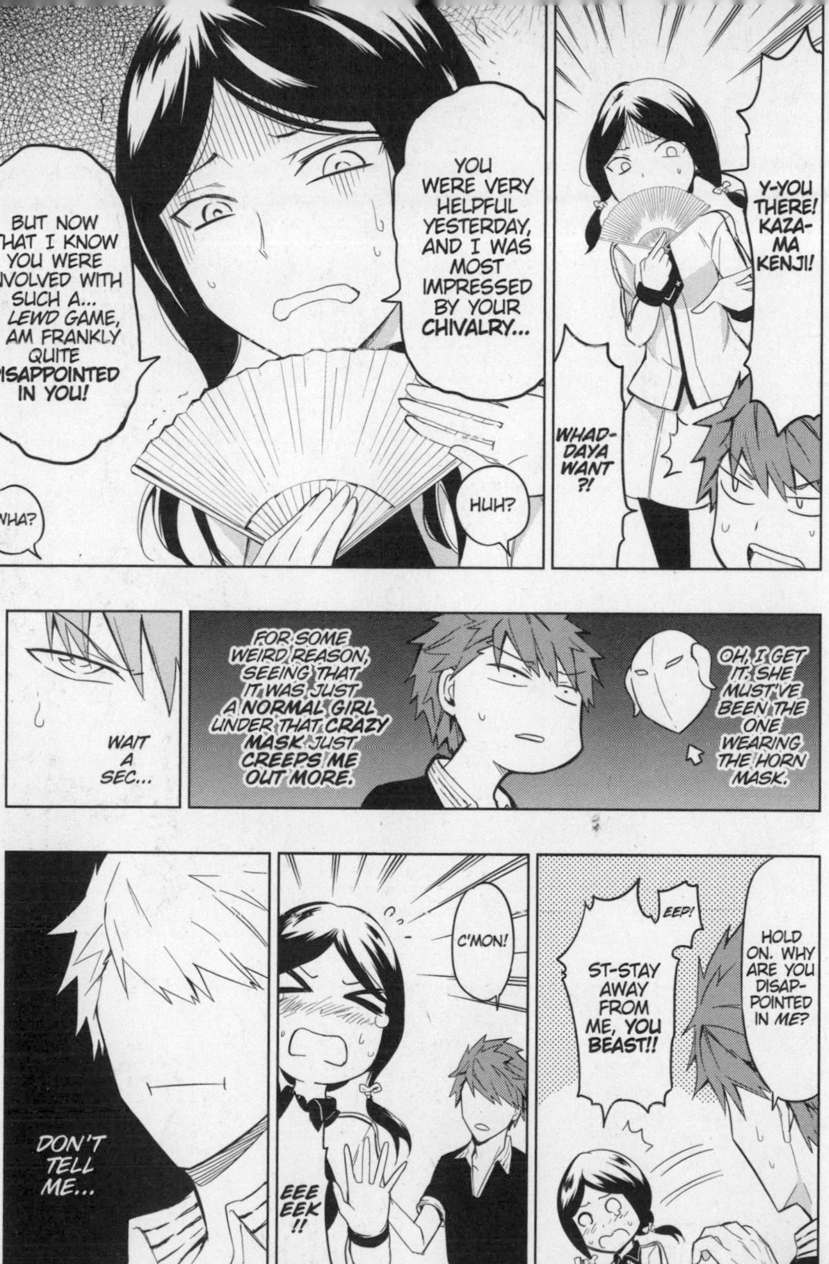
Y-YOU THERE! KAZAMA KENJI!
WHADDAYA WANT?!
YOU WERE VERY HELPFUL YESTERDAY, AND I WAS MOST IMPRESSED BY YOUR CHIVALRY...
HUH?
BUT NOW THAT I KNOW YOU WERE INVOLVED WITH SUCH A... A LEWD GAME, I AM FRANKLY QUITE DISAPPOINTED IN YOU!
WHA?
OH, I GET IT. SHE MUST'VE BEEN THE ONE WEARING THE HORN MASK.
FOR SOME WEIRD REASON, SEEING THAT IT WAS JUST A NORMAL GIRL UNDER THAT CRAZY MASK JUST CREEPS ME OUT MORE.
WAIT A SEC...
HOLD ON. WHY ARE YOU DISAPPOINTED IN ME?
EEP!
ST-STAY AWAY FROM ME, YOU BEAST!!
C'MON!
EEEEEK!!
DON'T TELL ME...

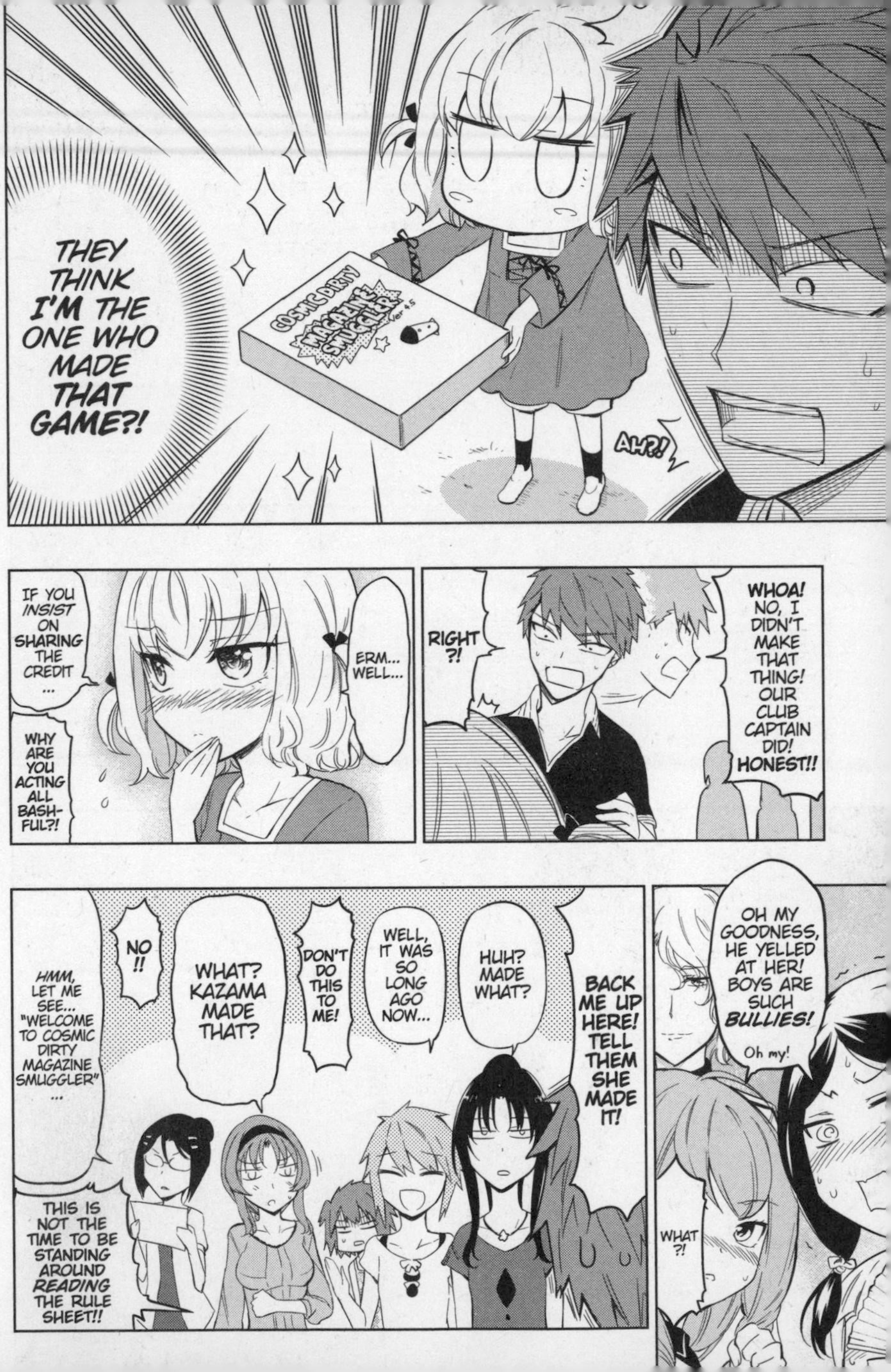
AH?!
THEY THINK I'M THE ONE WHO MADE THAT GAME?!
COSMIC DIRTY MAGAZINE SMUGGLER Ver 4.5
WHOA! NO, I DIDN'T MAKE THAT THING! OUR CLUB CAPTAIN DID! HONEST!!
RIGHT ?!
ERM... WELL...
IF YOU *INSIST* ON SHARING THE CREDIT ...
WHY ARE YOU ACTING ALL BASHFUL?!
OH MY GOODNESS, HE YELLED AT HER! BOYS ARE SUCH *BULLIES!*
Oh my!
WHAT ?!
BACK ME UP HERE! TELL THEM SHE MADE IT!
HUH? MADE WHAT?
WELL, IT WAS SO LONG AGO NOW...
DON'T DO THIS TO ME!
WHAT? KAZAMA MADE THAT?
NO !!
HMM, LET ME SEE... "WELCOME TO COSMIC DIRTY MAGAZINE SMUGGLER" ...
THIS IS NOT THE TIME TO BE STANDING AROUND *READING* THE RULE SHEET!!

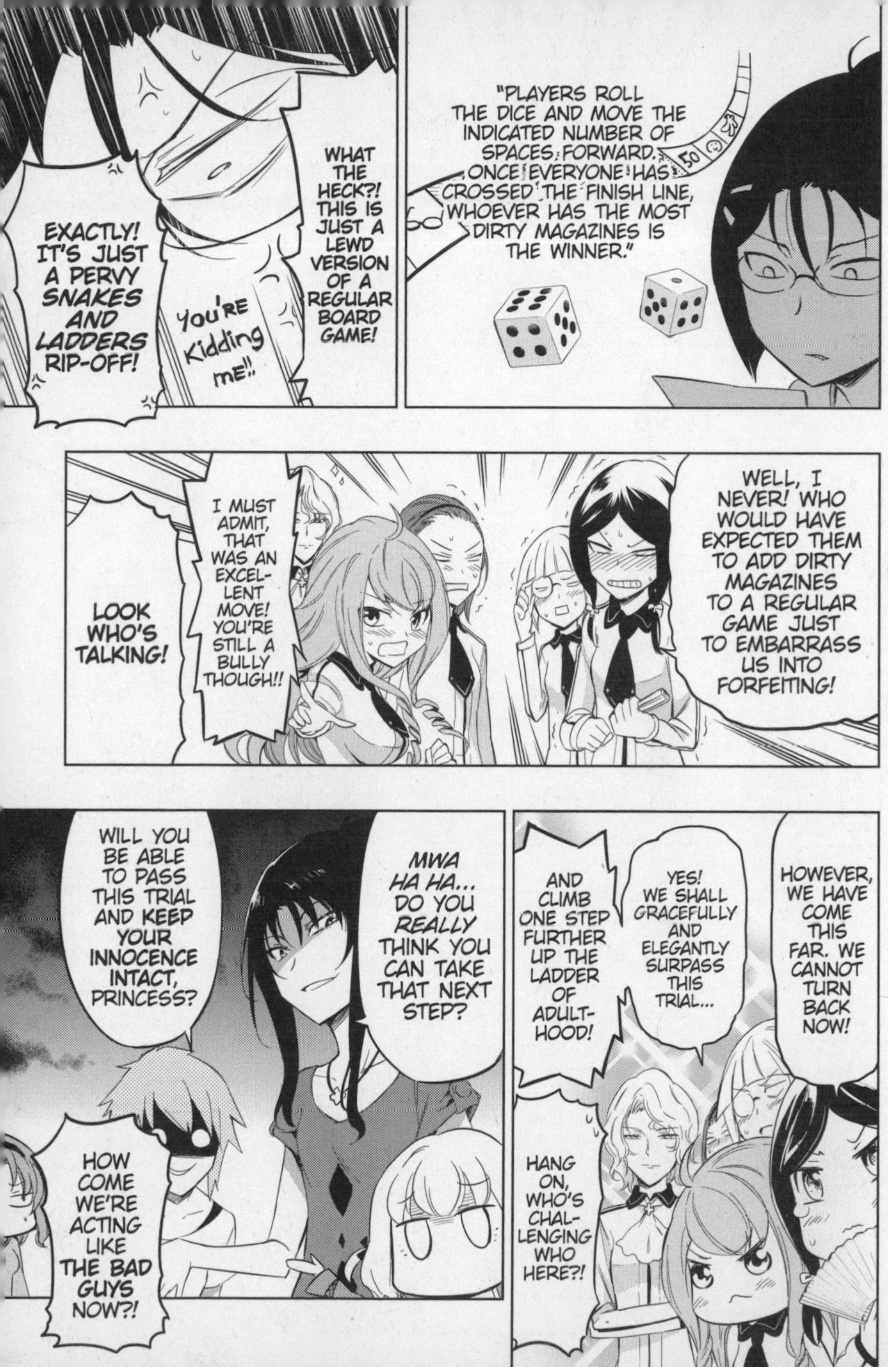
"PLAYERS ROLL THE DICE AND MOVE THE INDICATED NUMBER OF SPACES FORWARD. ONCE EVERYONE HAS CROSSED THE FINISH LINE, WHOEVER HAS THE MOST DIRTY MAGAZINES IS THE WINNER."
50
WHAT THE HECK?! THIS IS JUST A LEWD VERSION OF A REGULAR BOARD GAME!
You're Kidding me!!
EXACTLY! IT'S JUST A PERVY SNAKES AND LADDERS RIP-OFF!
WELL, I NEVER! WHO WOULD HAVE EXPECTED THEM TO ADD DIRTY MAGAZINES TO A REGULAR GAME JUST TO EMBARRASS US INTO FORFEITING!
I MUST ADMIT, THAT WAS AN EXCEL-LENT MOVE! YOU'RE STILL A BULLY THOUGH!!
LOOK WHO'S TALKING!
HOWEVER, WE HAVE COME THIS FAR. WE CANNOT TURN BACK NOW!
YES! WE SHALL GRACEFULLY AND ELEGANTLY SURPASS THIS TRIAL...
AND CLIMB ONE STEP FURTHER UP THE LADDER OF ADULT-HOOD!
HANG ON, WHO'S CHAL-LENGING WHO HERE?!
MWA HA HA... DO YOU REALLY THINK YOU CAN TAKE THAT NEXT STEP?
WILL YOU BE ABLE TO PASS THIS TRIAL AND KEEP YOUR INNOCENCE INTACT, PRINCESS?
HOW COME WE'RE ACTING LIKE THE BAD GUYS NOW?!

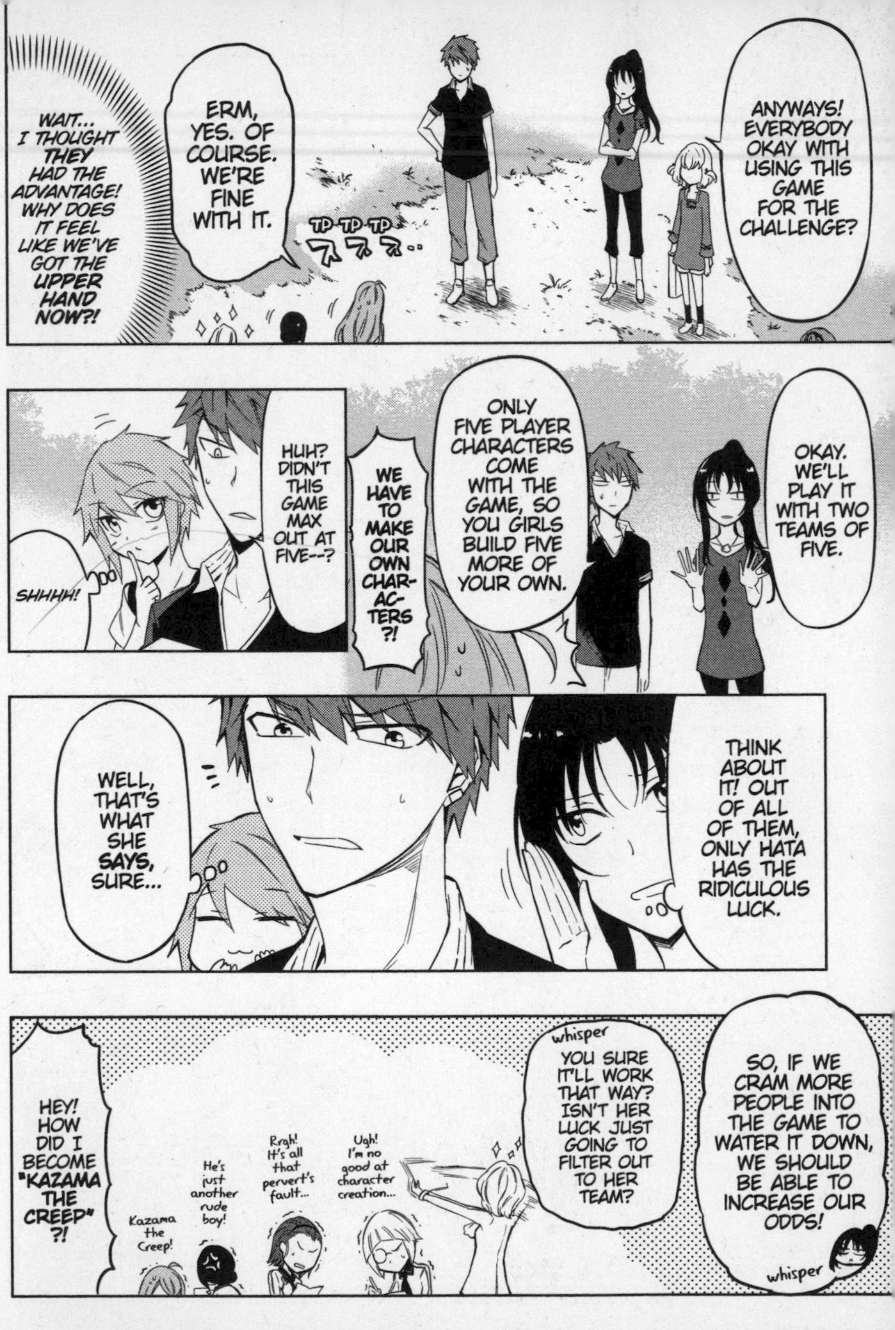
ANYWAYS! EVERYBODY OKAY WITH USING THIS GAME FOR THE CHALLENGE?
TP TP TP
ERM, YES. OF COURSE. WE'RE FINE WITH IT.
WAIT... I THOUGHT THEY HAD THE ADVANTAGE! WHY DOES IT FEEL LIKE WE'VE GOT THE UPPER HAND NOW?!
OKAY. WE'LL PLAY IT WITH TWO TEAMS OF FIVE.
ONLY FIVE PLAYER CHARACTERS COME WITH THE GAME, SO YOU GIRLS BUILD FIVE MORE OF YOUR OWN.
WE HAVE TO MAKE OUR OWN CHARACTERS?!
HUH? DIDN'T THIS GAME MAX OUT AT FIVE--?
SHHHH!
THINK ABOUT IT! OUT OF ALL OF THEM, ONLY HATA HAS THE RIDICULOUS LUCK.
WELL, THAT'S WHAT SHE SAYS, SURE...
SO, IF WE CRAM MORE PEOPLE INTO THE GAME TO WATER IT DOWN, WE SHOULD BE ABLE TO INCREASE OUR ODDS!
whisper
whisper
YOU SURE IT'LL WORK THAT WAY? ISN'T HER LUCK JUST GOING TO FILTER OUT TO HER TEAM?
Ugh! I'm no good at character creation...
Rrgh! It's all that pervert's fault...
He's just another rude boy!
Kazama the Creep!
HEY! HOW DID I BECOME "KAZAMA THE CREEP"?!

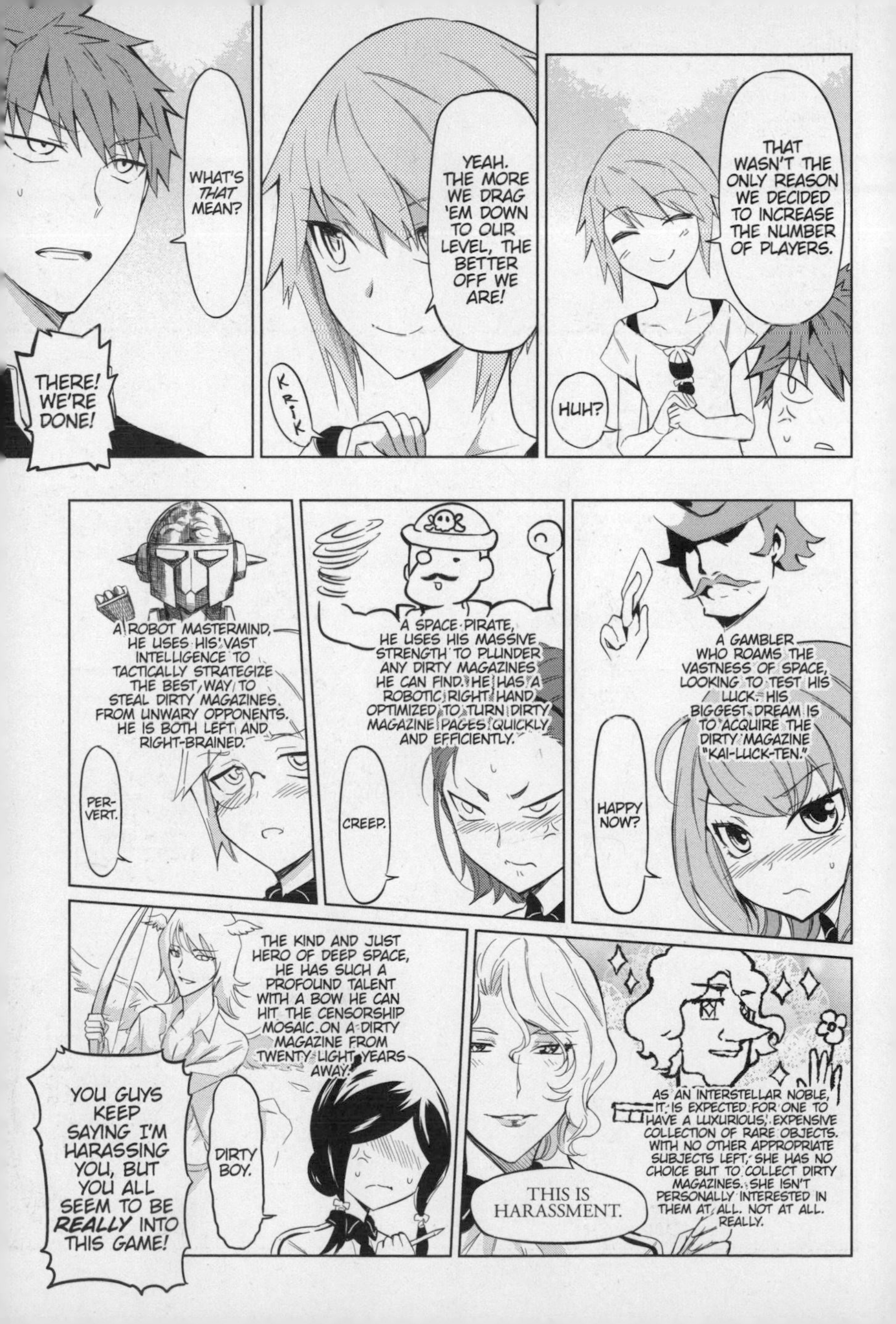
THAT WASN'T THE ONLY REASON WE DECIDED TO INCREASE THE NUMBER OF PLAYERS.
HUH?
YEAH. THE MORE WE DRAG 'EM DOWN TO OUR LEVEL, THE BETTER OFF WE ARE!
KRIK
WHAT'S THAT MEAN?
THERE! WE'RE DONE!
A GAMBLER WHO ROAMS THE VASTNESS OF SPACE, LOOKING TO TEST HIS LUCK. HIS BIGGEST DREAM IS TO ACQUIRE THE DIRTY MAGAZINE "KAI-LUCK-TEN."
HAPPY NOW?
A SPACE PIRATE, HE USES HIS MASSIVE STRENGTH TO PLUNDER ANY DIRTY MAGAZINES HE CAN FIND. HE HAS A ROBOTIC RIGHT HAND OPTIMIZED TO TURN DIRTY MAGAZINE PAGES QUICKLY AND EFFICIENTLY.
CREEP.
A ROBOT MASTERMIND, HE USES HIS VAST INTELLIGENCE TO TACTICALLY STRATEGIZE THE BEST WAY TO STEAL DIRTY MAGAZINES FROM UNWARY OPPONENTS. HE IS BOTH LEFT AND RIGHT-BRAINED.
PER-VERT.
AS AN INTERSTELLAR NOBLE, IT IS EXPECTED FOR ONE TO HAVE A LUXURIOUS, EXPENSIVE COLLECTION OF RARE OBJECTS. WITH NO OTHER APPROPRIATE SUBJECTS LEFT, SHE HAS NO CHOICE BUT TO COLLECT DIRTY MAGAZINES. SHE ISN'T PERSONALLY INTERESTED IN THEM AT ALL. NOT AT ALL. REALLY.
THIS IS HARASSMENT.
THE KIND AND JUST HERO OF DEEP SPACE, HE HAS SUCH A PROFOUND TALENT WITH A BOW HE CAN HIT THE CENSORSHIP MOSAIC ON A DIRTY MAGAZINE FROM TWENTY LIGHT YEARS AWAY.
DIRTY BOY.
YOU GUYS KEEP SAYING I'M HARASSING YOU, BUT YOU ALL SEEM TO BE REALLY INTO THIS GAME!

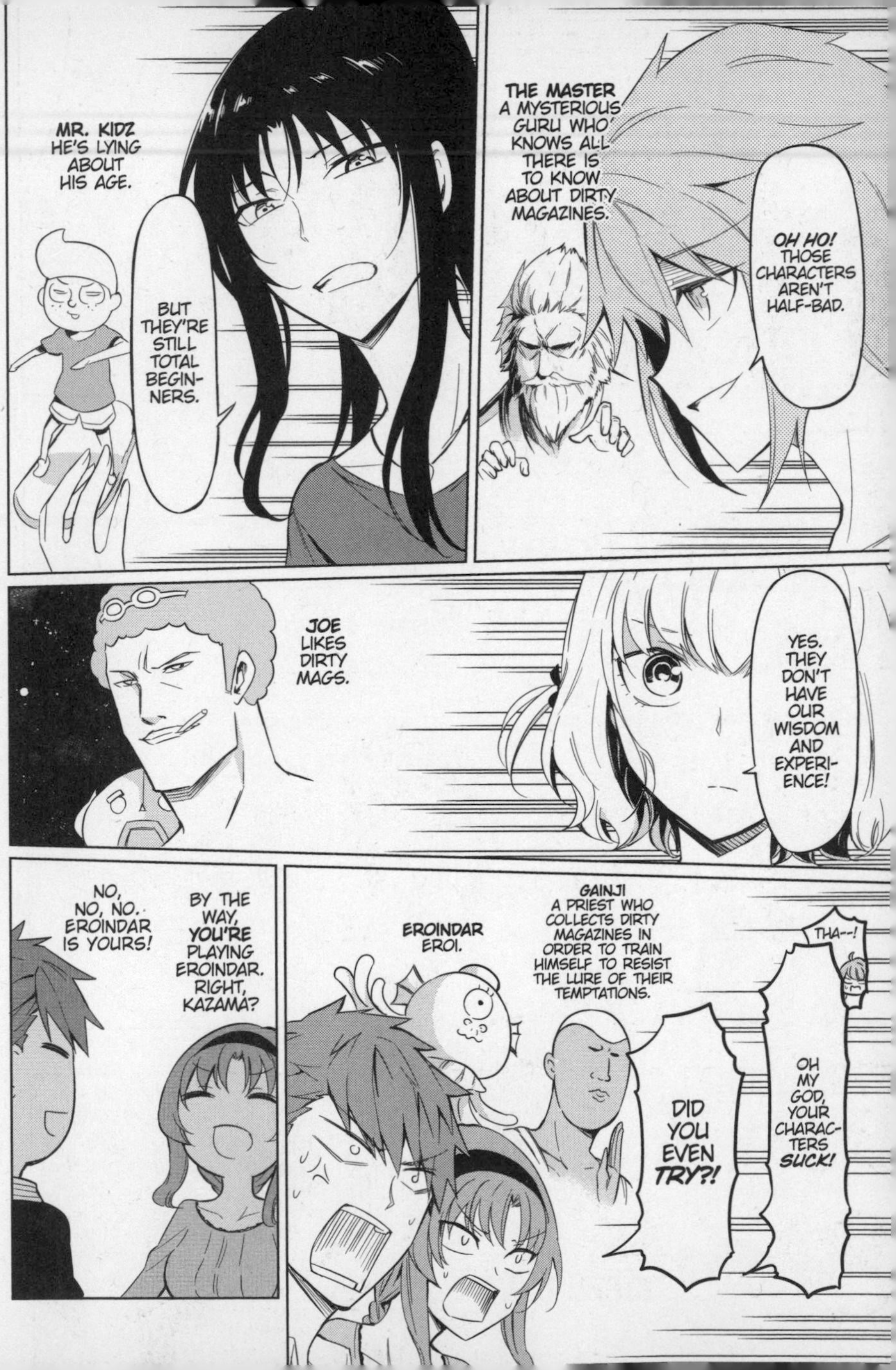
THE MASTER A MYSTERIOUS GURU WHO KNOWS ALL THERE IS TO KNOW ABOUT DIRTY MAGAZINES.
OH HO! THOSE CHARACTERS AREN'T HALF-BAD.
MR. KIDZ HE'S LYING ABOUT HIS AGE.
BUT THEY'RE STILL TOTAL BEGINNERS.
YES. THEY DON'T HAVE OUR WISDOM AND EXPERIENCE!
JOE LIKES DIRTY MAGS.
THA--!
OH MY GOD, YOUR CHARACTERS SUCK!
DID YOU EVEN TRY?!
GAINJI A PRIEST WHO COLLECTS DIRTY MAGAZINES IN ORDER TO TRAIN HIMSELF TO RESIST THE LURE OF THEIR TEMPTATIONS.
EROINDAR EROI.
BY THE WAY, YOU'RE PLAYING EROINDAR. RIGHT, KAZAMA?
NO, NO, NO. EROINDAR IS YOURS!

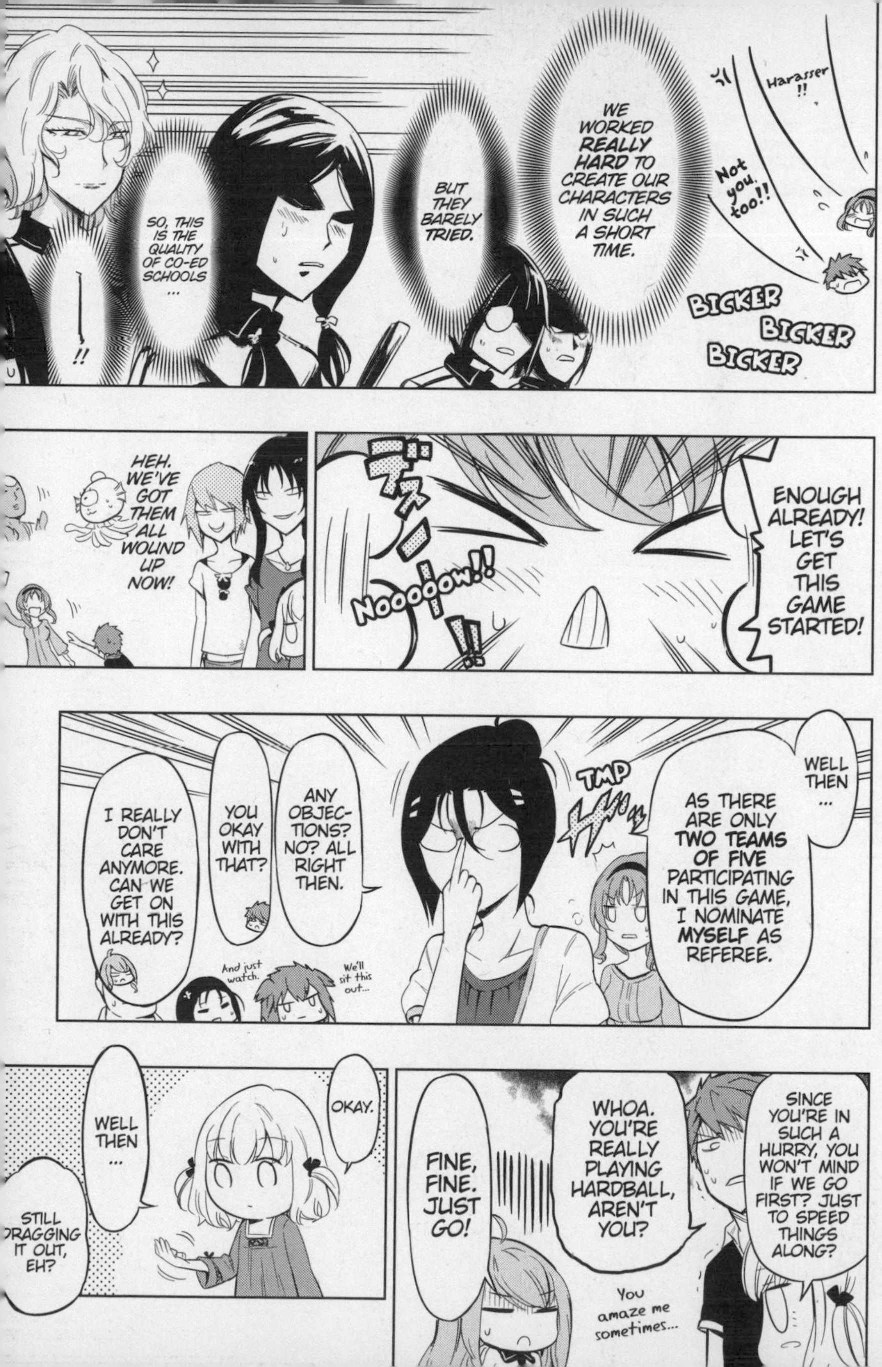
Harasser!!
Not you, too!!
WE WORKED REALLY HARD TO CREATE OUR CHARACTERS IN SUCH A SHORT TIME.
BUT THEY BARELY TRIED.
SO, THIS IS THE QUALITY OF CO-ED SCHOOLS...
!!
BICKER
BICKER
BICKER
ENOUGH ALREADY! LET'S GET THIS GAME STARTED!
Noooooow!!
HEH. WE'VE GOT THEM ALL WOUND UP NOW!
WELL THEN...
AS THERE ARE ONLY TWO TEAMS OF FIVE PARTICIPATING IN THIS GAME, I NOMINATE MYSELF AS REFEREE.
TMP
ANY OBJECTIONS? NO? ALL RIGHT THEN.
YOU OKAY WITH THAT?
I REALLY DON'T CARE ANYMORE. CAN WE GET ON WITH THIS ALREADY?
We'll sit this out...
And just watch.
SINCE YOU'RE IN SUCH A HURRY, YOU WON'T MIND IF WE GO FIRST? JUST TO SPEED THINGS ALONG?
WHOA. YOU'RE REALLY PLAYING HARDBALL, AREN'T YOU?
FINE, FINE. JUST GO!
You amaze me sometimes...
OKAY.
WELL THEN...
STILL DRAGGING IT OUT, EH?

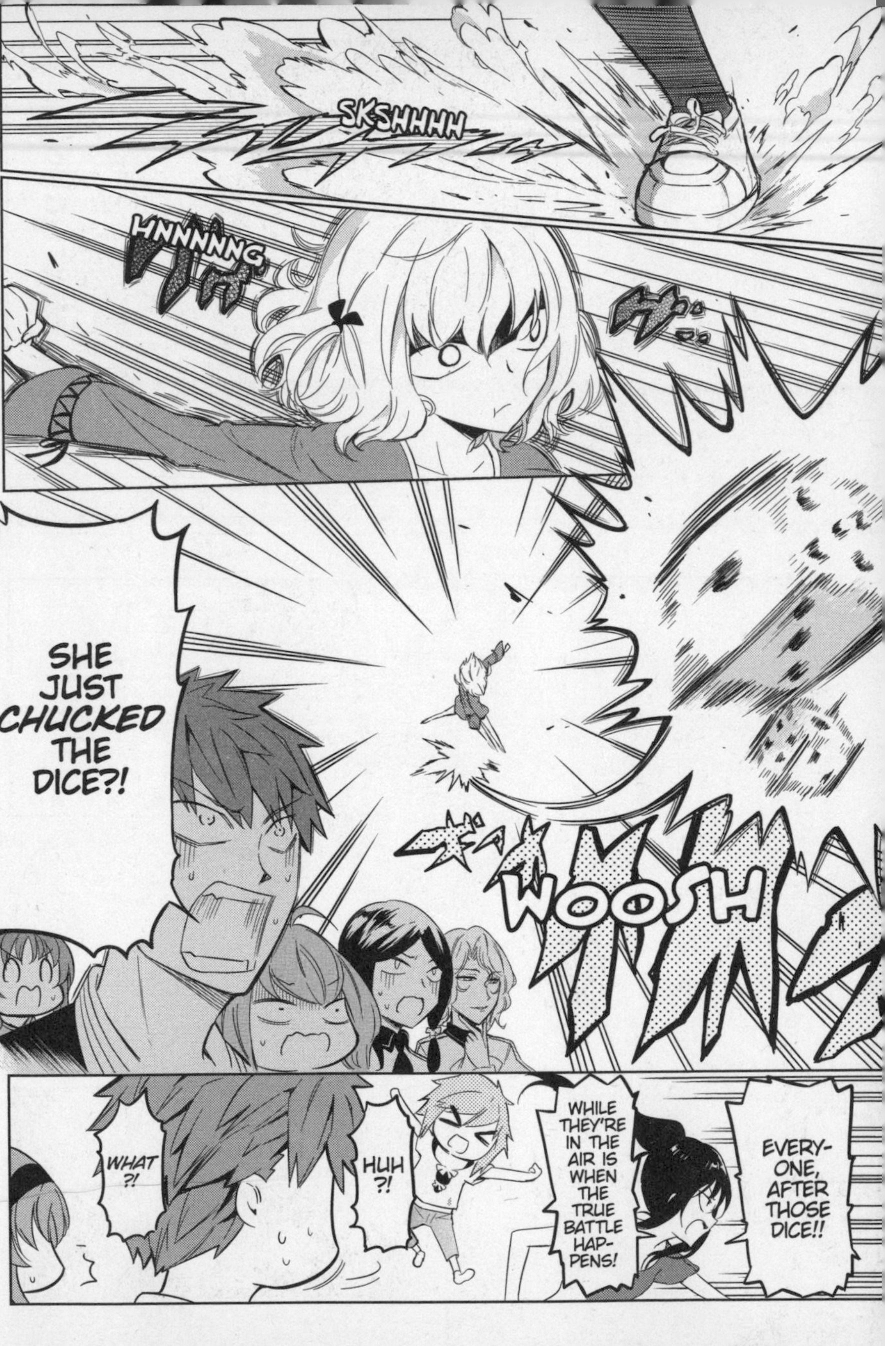
SKSHHHH
HNNNNNG
WOOSH
SHE JUST CHUCKED THE DICE?!
EVERY-ONE, AFTER THOSE DICE!!
WHILE THEY'RE IN THE AIR IS WHEN THE TRUE BATTLE HAP-PENS!
HUH?!
WHAT?!

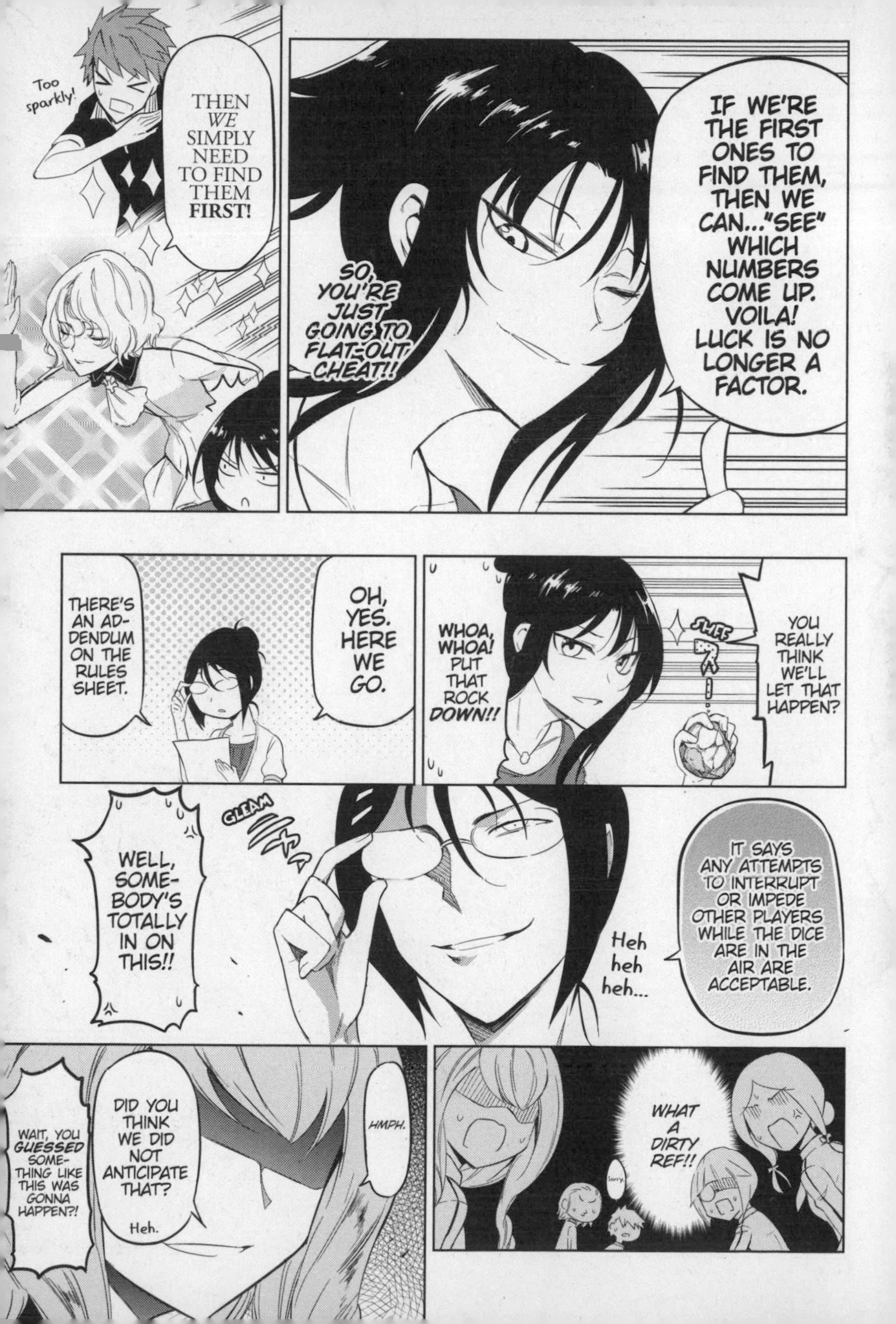
IF WE'RE THE FIRST ONES TO FIND THEM, THEN WE CAN..."SEE" WHICH NUMBERS COME UP. VOILA! LUCK IS NO LONGER A FACTOR.
SO, YOU'RE JUST GOING TO FLAT-OUT CHEAT!!
THEN *WE* SIMPLY NEED TO FIND THEM **FIRST!**
Too sparkly!
YOU REALLY THINK WE'LL LET THAT HAPPEN?
WHOA, WHOA! PUT THAT ROCK *DOWN!!*
OH, YES. HERE WE GO.
THERE'S AN ADDENDUM ON THE RULES SHEET.
IT SAYS ANY ATTEMPTS TO INTERRUPT OR IMPEDE OTHER PLAYERS WHILE THE DICE ARE IN THE AIR ARE ACCEPTABLE.
Heh heh heh...
GLEAM
WELL, SOMEBODY'S TOTALLY IN ON THIS!!
WHAT A DIRTY REF!!
Sorry.
HMPH.
DID YOU THINK WE DID NOT ANTICIPATE THAT?
Heh.
WAIT, YOU *GUESSED* SOMETHING LIKE THIS WAS GONNA HAPPEN?!

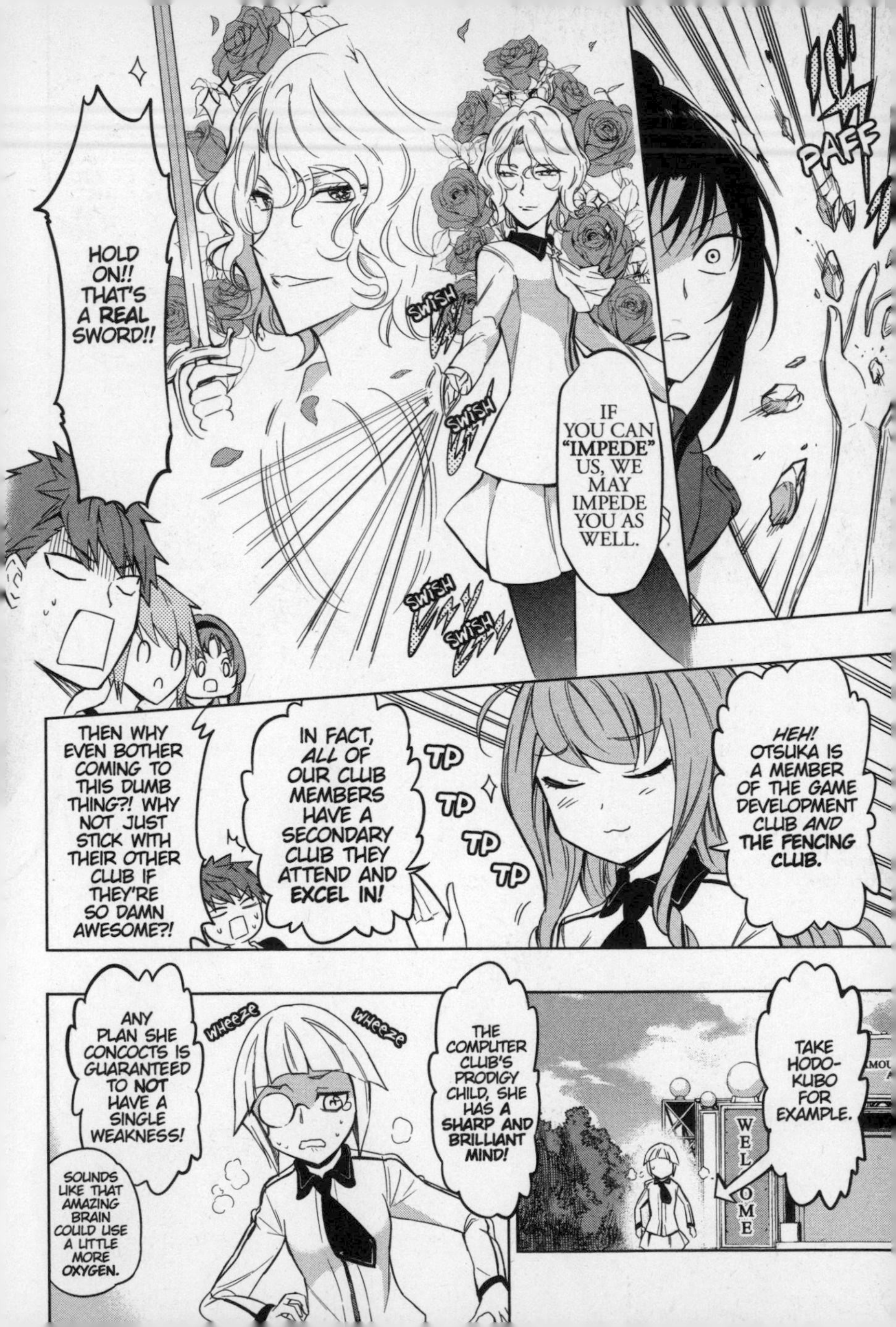
PAFF
SWISH
SWISH
IF YOU CAN "IMPEDE" US, WE MAY IMPEDE YOU AS WELL.
HOLD ON!! THAT'S A REAL SWORD!!
SWISH
SWISH
HEH! OTSUKA IS A MEMBER OF THE GAME DEVELOPMENT CLUB AND THE FENCING CLUB.
TP
TP
TP
TP
IN FACT, ALL OF OUR CLUB MEMBERS HAVE A SECONDARY CLUB THEY ATTEND AND EXCEL IN!
THEN WHY EVEN BOTHER COMING TO THIS DUMB THING?! WHY NOT JUST STICK WITH THEIR OTHER CLUB IF THEY'RE SO DAMN AWESOME?!
TAKE HODO-KUBO FOR EXAMPLE.
WEL
OME
THE COMPUTER CLUB'S PRODIGY CHILD, SHE HAS A SHARP AND BRILLIANT MIND!
WHEEZE
WHEEZE
ANY PLAN SHE CONCOCTS IS GUARANTEED TO NOT HAVE A SINGLE WEAKNESS!
SOUNDS LIKE THAT AMAZING BRAIN COULD USE A LITTLE MORE OXYGEN.

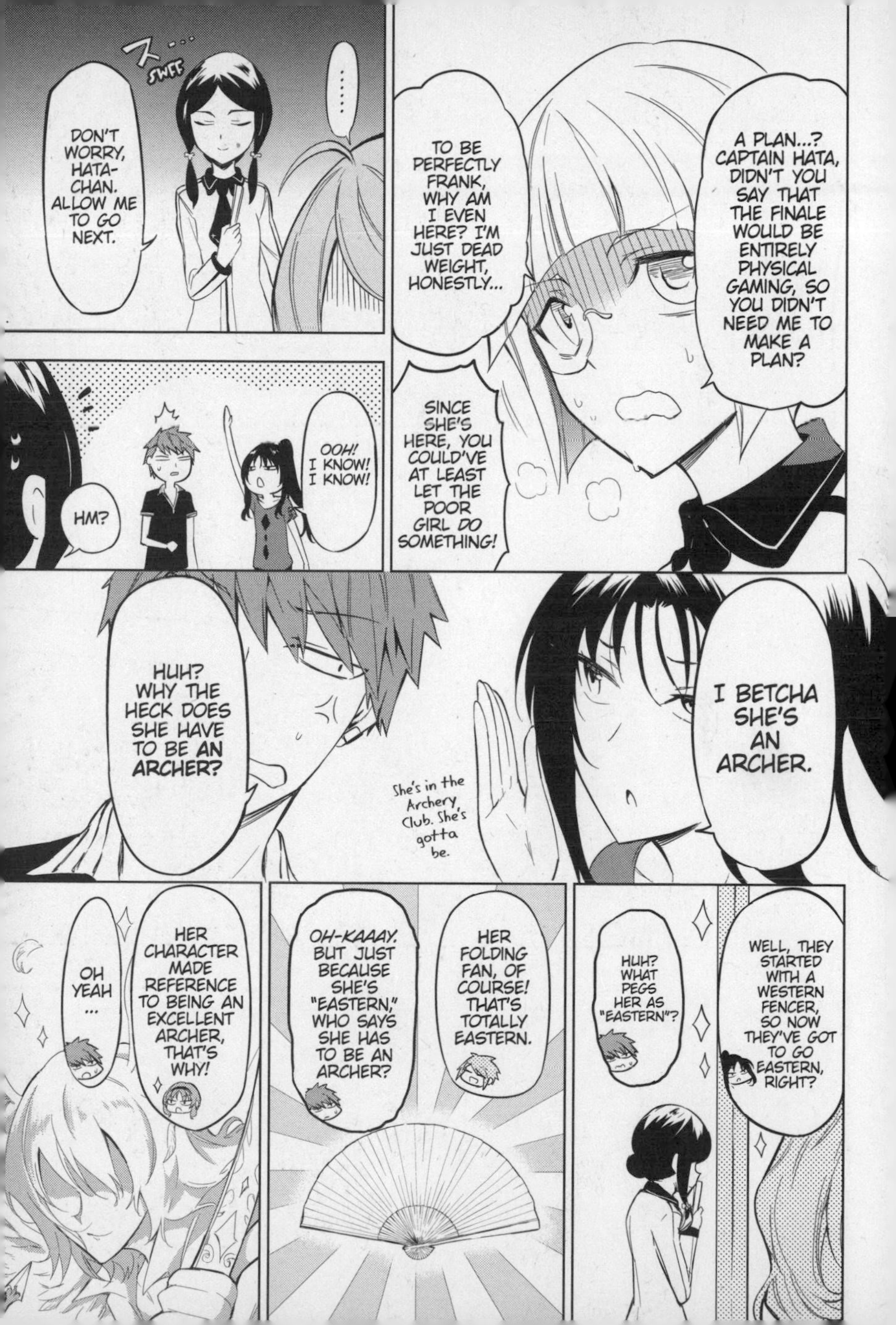
A PLAN...? CAPTAIN HATA, DIDN'T YOU SAY THAT THE FINALE WOULD BE ENTIRELY PHYSICAL GAMING, SO YOU DIDN'T NEED ME TO MAKE A PLAN?
TO BE PERFECTLY FRANK, WHY AM I EVEN HERE? I'M JUST DEAD WEIGHT, HONESTLY...
SINCE SHE'S HERE, YOU COULD'VE AT LEAST LET THE POOR GIRL *DO* SOMETHING!
......
ス...
SWFF
DON'T WORRY, HATA-CHAN. ALLOW ME TO GO NEXT.
OOH! I KNOW! I KNOW!
HM?
I BETCHA SHE'S AN ARCHER.
She's in the Archery Club. She's gotta be.
HUH? WHY THE HECK DOES SHE HAVE TO BE AN ARCHER?
WELL, THEY STARTED WITH A WESTERN FENCER, SO NOW THEY'VE GOT TO GO EASTERN, RIGHT?
HUH? WHAT PEGS HER AS "EASTERN"?
HER FOLDING FAN, OF COURSE! THAT'S TOTALLY EASTERN.
OH-KAAAY. BUT JUST BECAUSE SHE'S "EASTERN," WHO SAYS SHE HAS TO BE AN ARCHER?
HER CHARACTER MADE REFERENCE TO BEING AN EXCELLENT ARCHER, THAT'S WHY!
OH YEAH ...

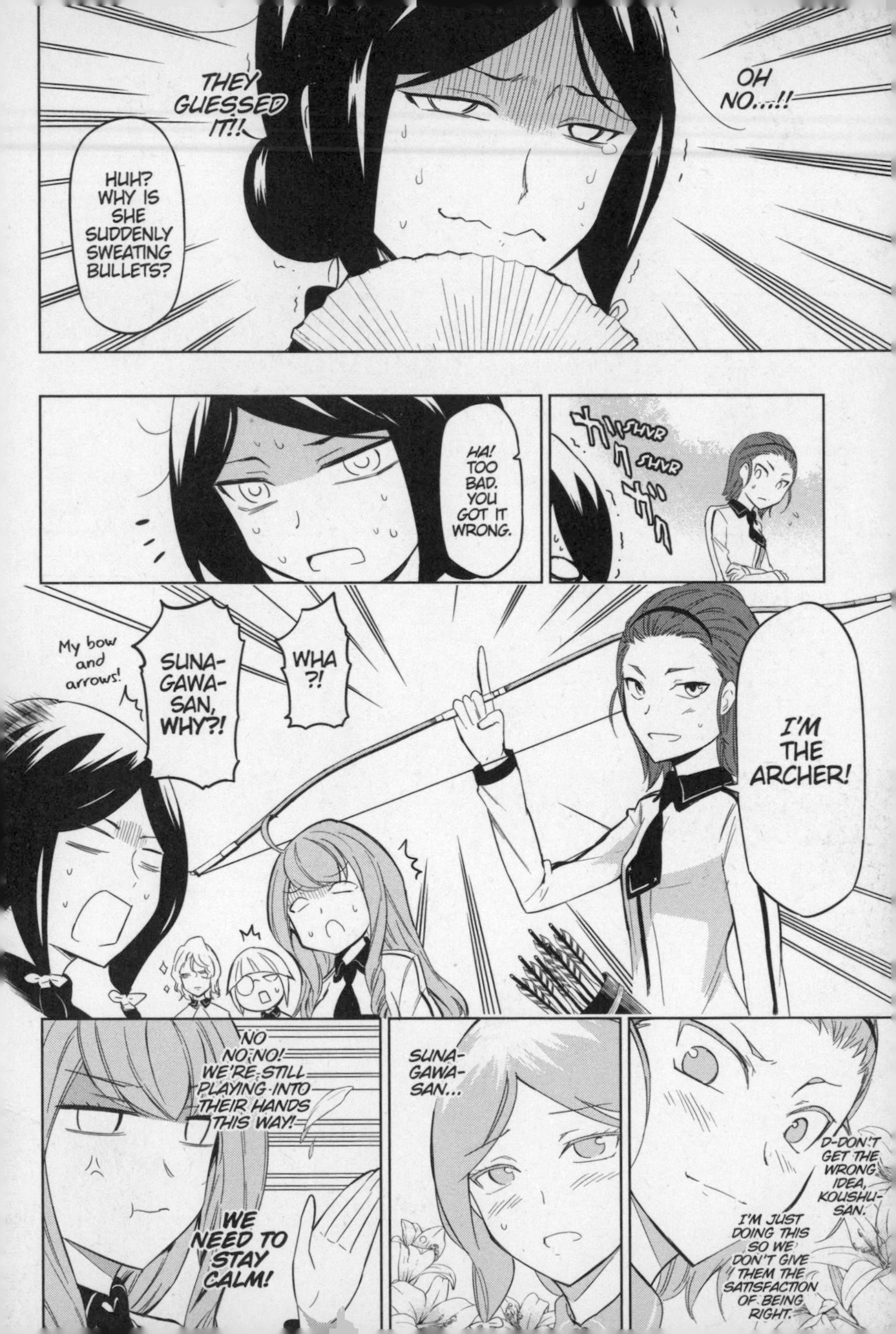
OH NO...!!
THEY GUESSED IT!!
HUH? WHY IS SHE SUDDENLY SWEATING BULLETS?
SHVR SHVR
HA! TOO BAD. YOU GOT IT WRONG.
I'M THE ARCHER!
WHA?!
SUNA-GAWA-SAN, WHY?!
My bow and arrows!
D-DON'T GET THE WRONG IDEA, KOUSHU-SAN.
I'M JUST DOING THIS SO WE DON'T GIVE THEM THE SATISFACTION OF BEING RIGHT.
SUNA-GAWA-SAN...
NO NO NO! WE'RE STILL PLAYING INTO THEIR HANDS THIS WAY!
WE NEED TO STAY CALM!

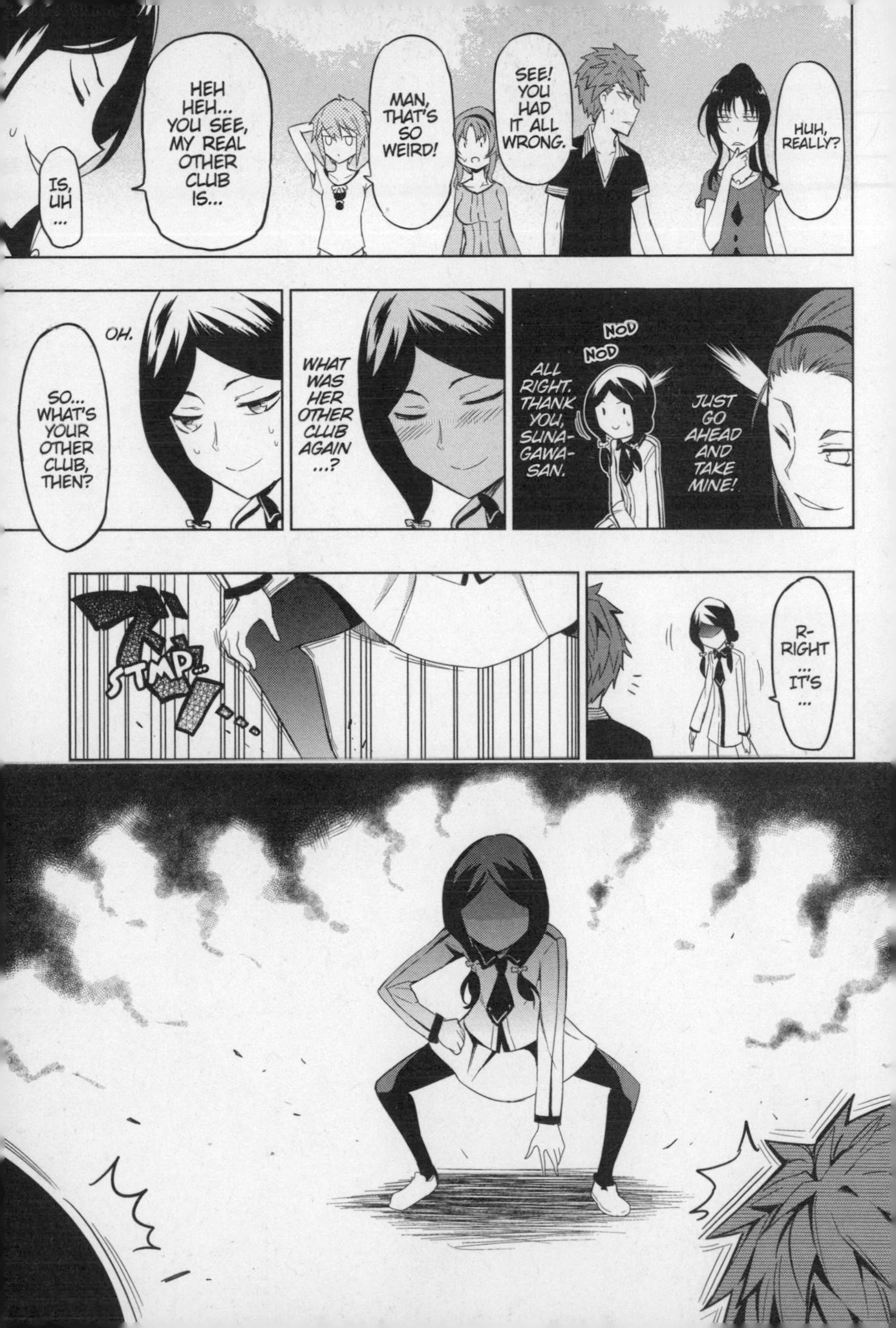
HUH, REALLY?
SEE! YOU HAD IT ALL WRONG.
MAN, THAT'S SO WEIRD!
HEH HEH... YOU SEE, MY REAL OTHER CLUB IS...
IS, UH ...
JUST GO AHEAD AND TAKE MINE!
NOD NOD
ALL RIGHT. THANK YOU, SUNAGAWA-SAN.
WHAT WAS HER OTHER CLUB AGAIN ...?
OH.
SO... WHAT'S YOUR OTHER CLUB, THEN?
R-RIGHT ... IT'S ...
STMP...

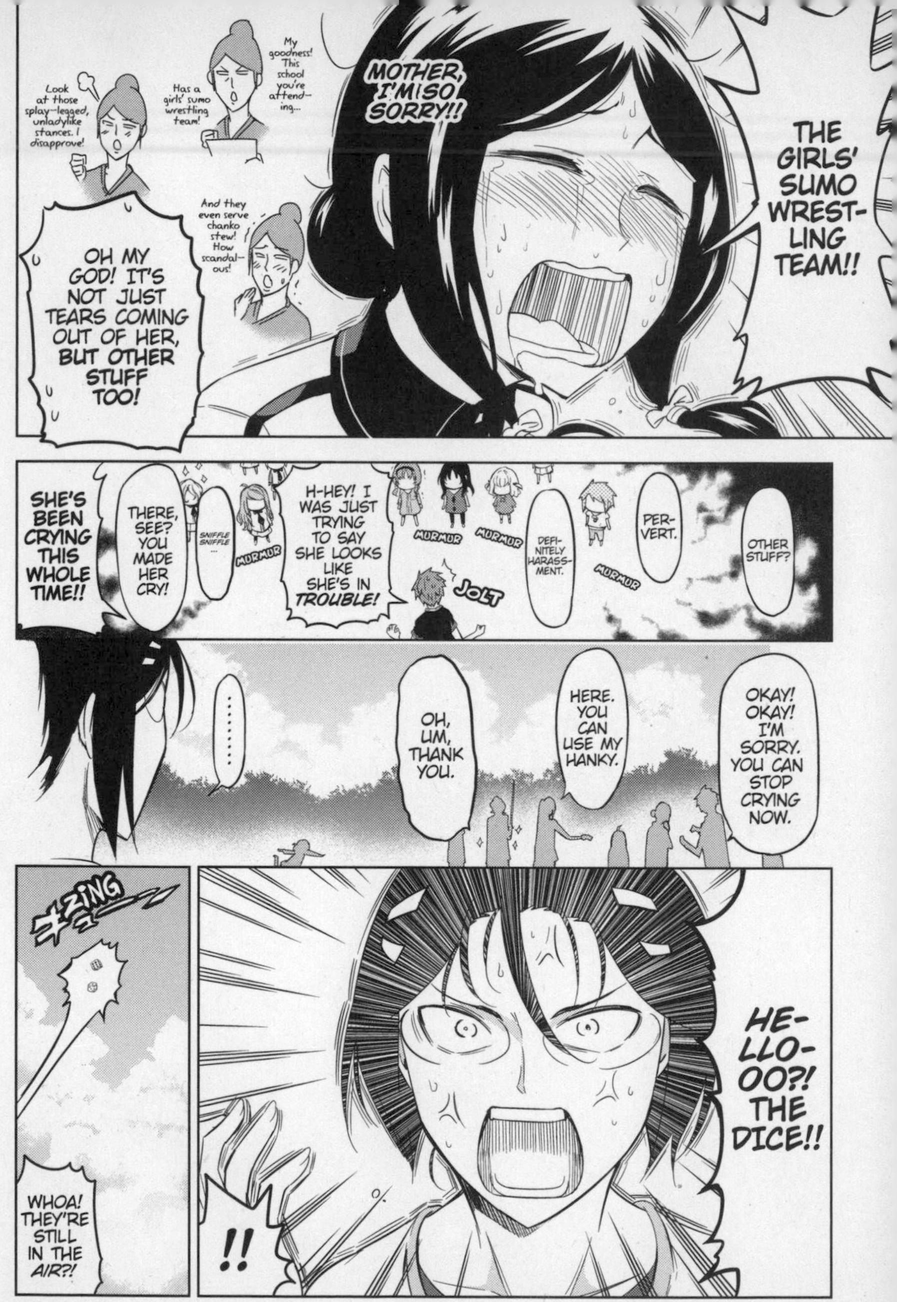
THE GIRLS' SUMO WREST-LING TEAM!!
MOTHER, I'M SO SORRY!!
My goodness! This school you're attend-ing...
Has a girls' sumo wrestling team!
Look at those splay-legged, unladylike stances. I disapprove!
And they even serve chanko stew! How scandal-ous!
OH MY GOD! IT'S NOT JUST TEARS COMING OUT OF HER, BUT OTHER STUFF TOO!
OTHER STUFF?
PER-VERT.
DEFI-NITELY HARASS-MENT.
MURMUR
MURMUR
MURMUR
JOLT
H-HEY! I WAS JUST TRYING TO SAY SHE LOOKS LIKE SHE'S IN TROUBLE!
MURMUR
SNIFFLE SNIFFLE...
THERE, SEE? YOU MADE HER CRY!
SHE'S BEEN CRYING THIS WHOLE TIME!!
OKAY! OKAY! I'M SORRY. YOU CAN STOP CRYING NOW.
HERE. YOU CAN USE MY HANKY.
OH, UM, THANK YOU.
......
HE-LLO-OO?! THE DICE!!
!!
ZING
WHOA! THEY'RE STILL IN THE AIR?!

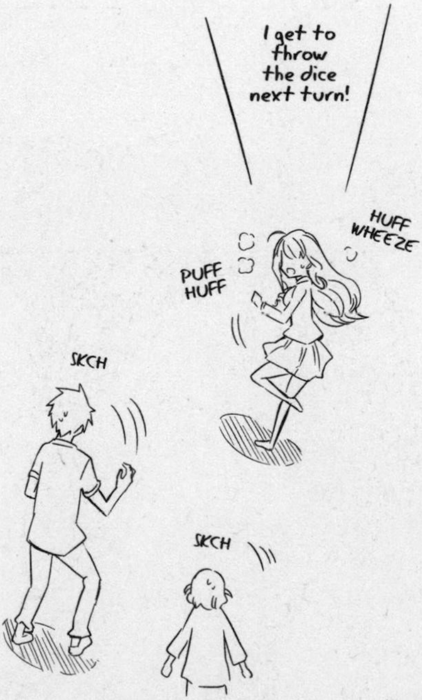
I get to throw the dice next turn!
HUFF WHEEZE
PUFF HUFF
SKCH
SKCH

ディーふらぐ!
D-FRAGMENTS

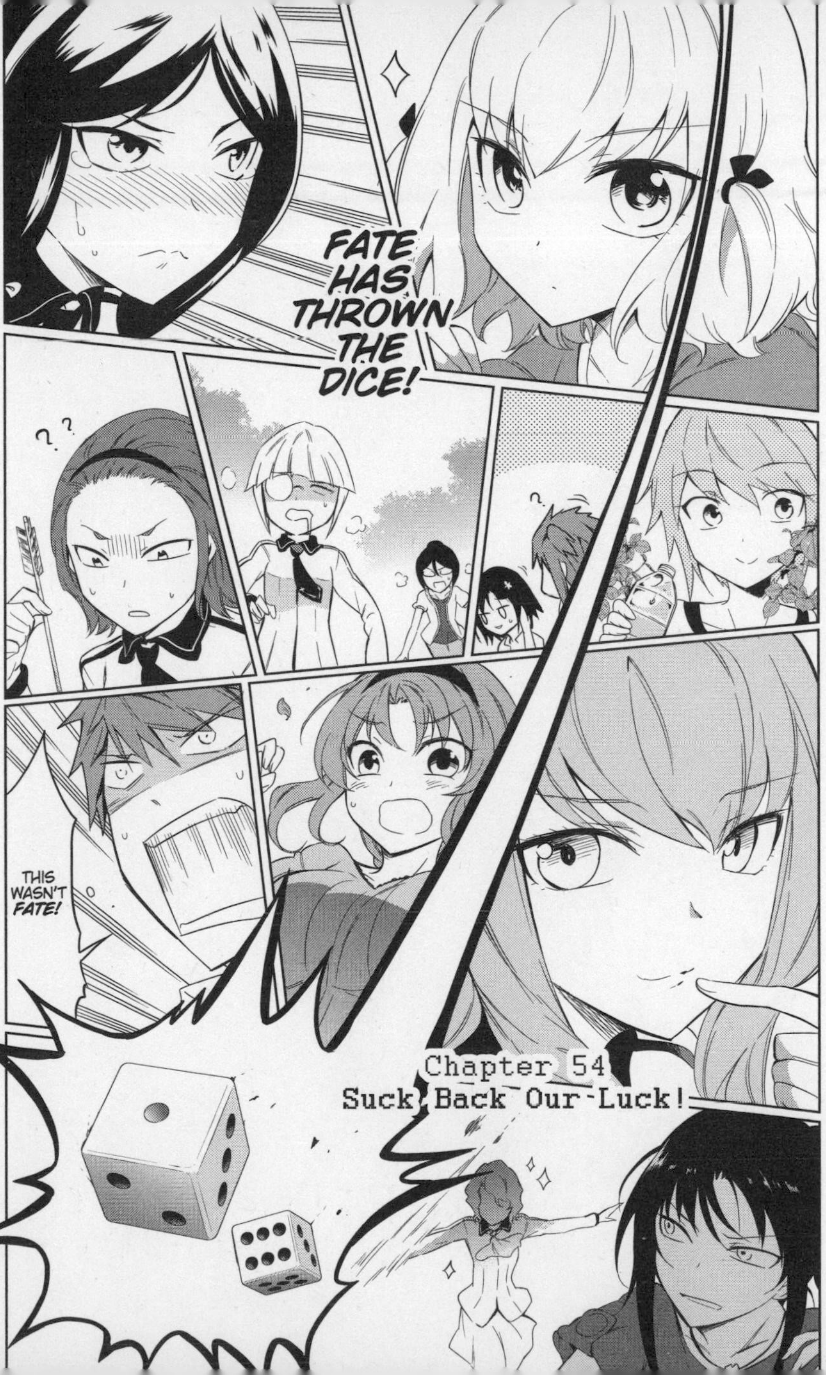
FATE HAS THROWN THE DICE!
??
THIS WASN'T FATE!
Chapter 54
Suck Back Our Luck!

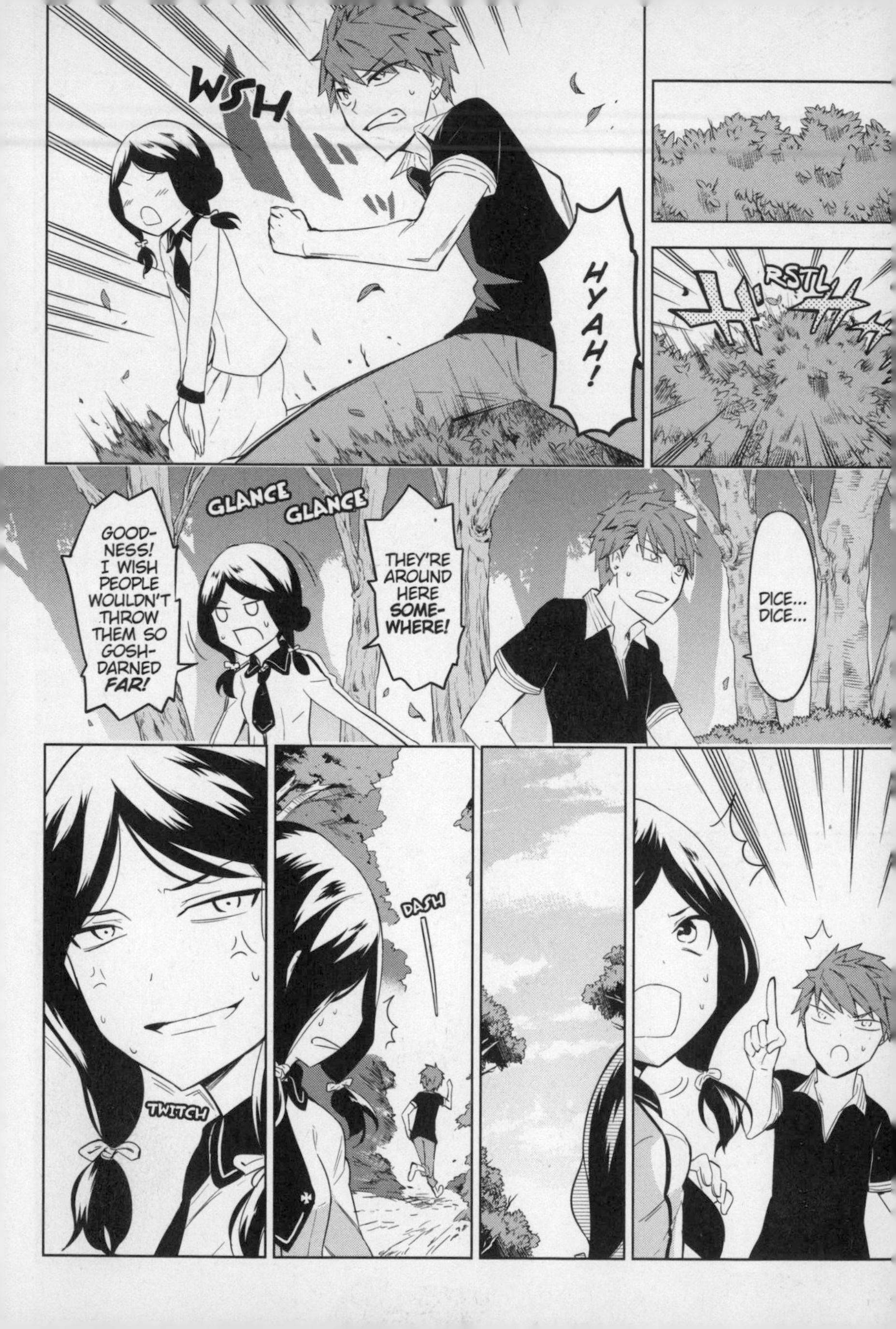
RSTL
WSH
HYAH!
DICE... DICE...
THEY'RE AROUND HERE SOME-WHERE!
GLANCE GLANCE
GOOD-NESS! I WISH PEOPLE WOULDN'T THROW THEM SO GOSH-DARNED FAR!
DASH
TWITCH

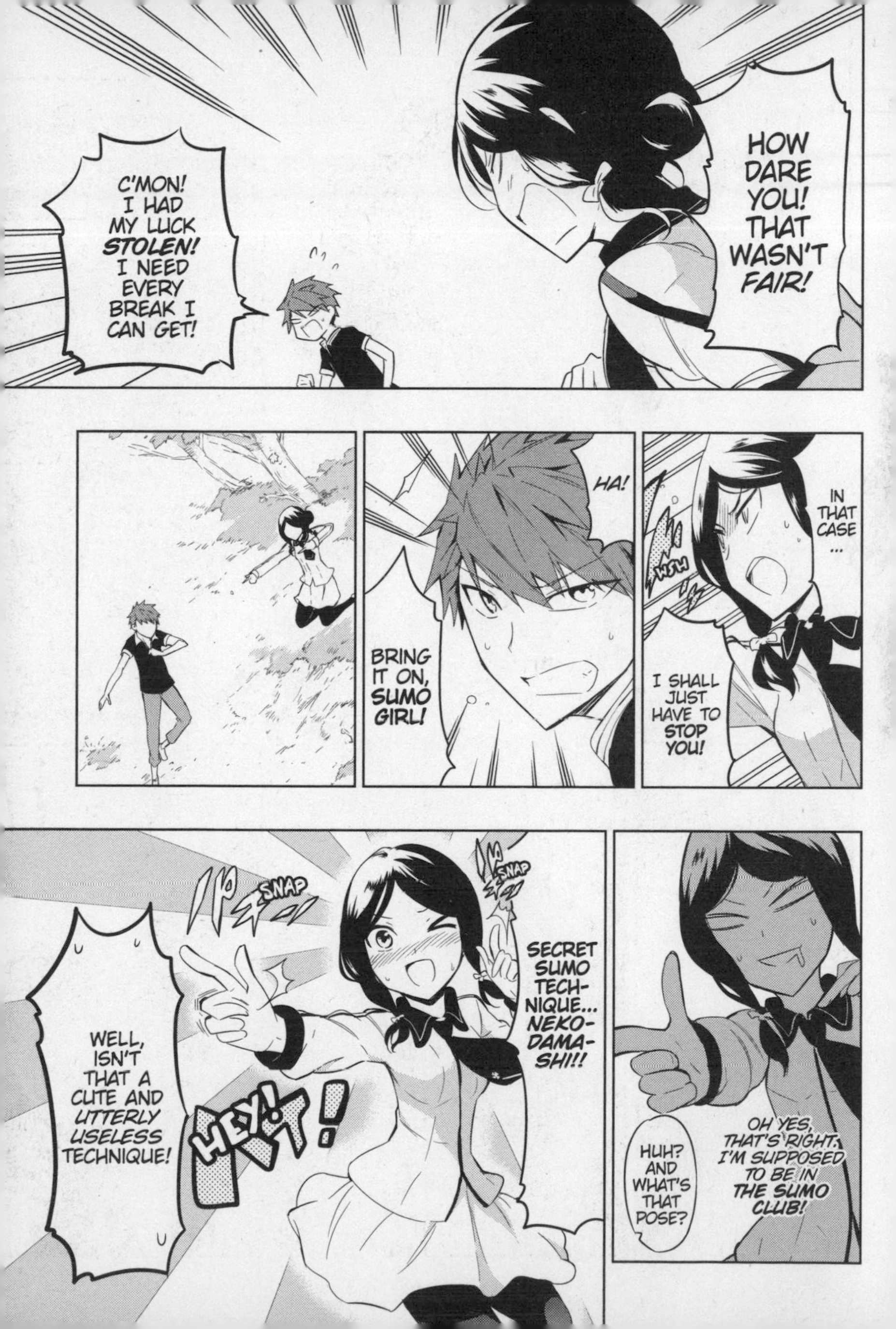
HOW DARE YOU! THAT WASN'T FAIR!
C'MON! I HAD MY LUCK STOLEN! I NEED EVERY BREAK I CAN GET!
IN THAT CASE ...
WSH
I SHALL JUST HAVE TO STOP YOU!
HA!
BRING IT ON, SUMO GIRL!
OH YES, THAT'S RIGHT. I'M SUPPOSED TO BE IN THE SUMO CLUB!
HUH? AND WHAT'S THAT POSE?
SNAP
SNAP
SECRET SUMO TECH-NIQUE... NEKO-DAMA-SHI!!
HEY!
WELL, ISN'T THAT A CUTE AND UTTERLY USELESS TECHNIQUE!

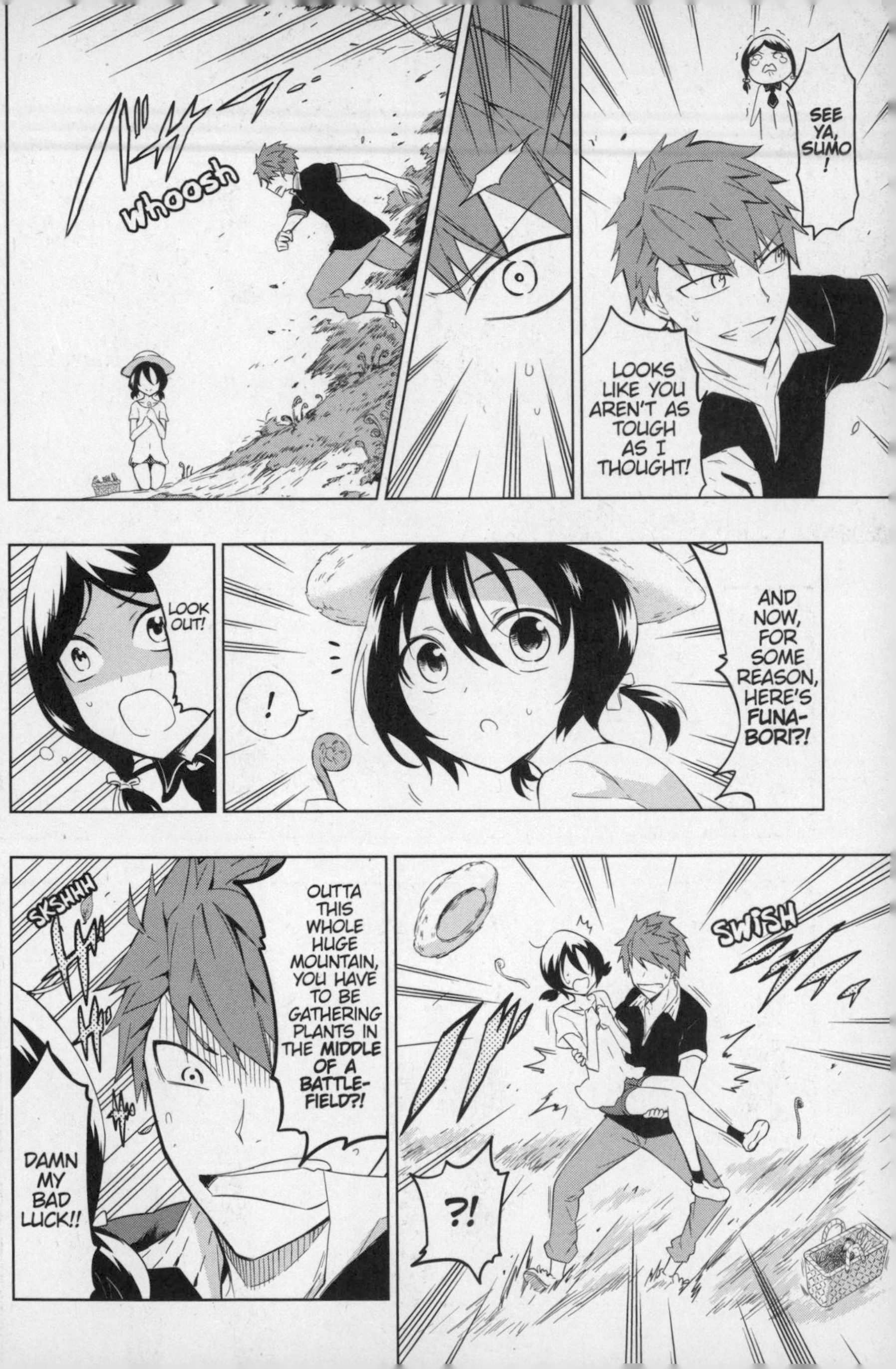
SEE YA, SUMO!
LOOKS LIKE YOU AREN'T AS TOUGH AS I THOUGHT!
whoosh
AND NOW, FOR SOME REASON, HERE'S FUNABORI?!
!
LOOK OUT!
SWISH
?!
OUTTA THIS WHOLE HUGE MOUNTAIN, YOU HAVE TO BE GATHERING PLANTS IN THE MIDDLE OF A BATTLEFIELD?!
SKSHHH
DAMN MY BAD LUCK!!

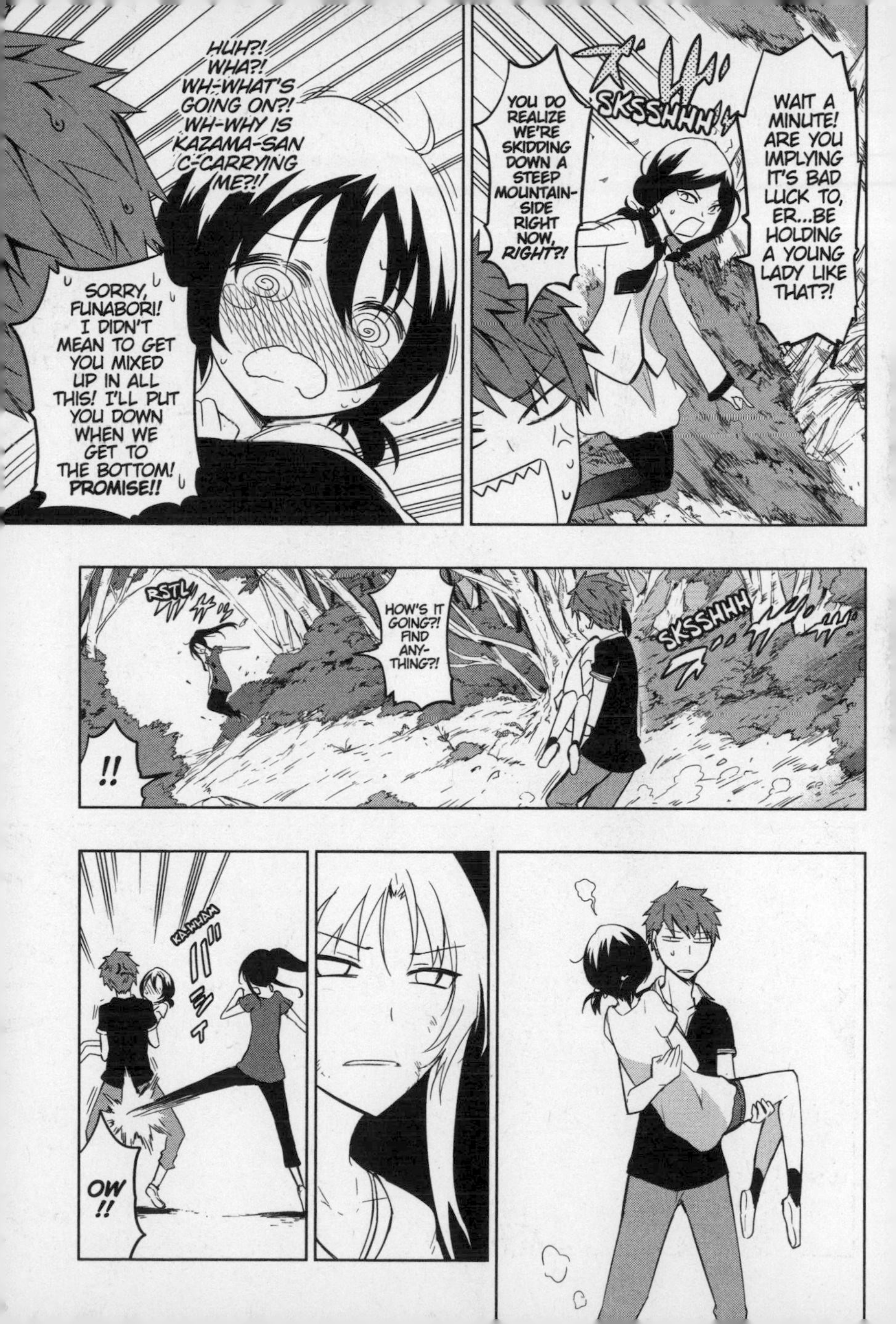
WAIT A MINUTE! ARE YOU IMPLYING IT'S BAD LUCK TO, ER...BE HOLDING A YOUNG LADY LIKE THAT?!
SKSSHHH
YOU DO REALIZE WE'RE SKIDDING DOWN A STEEP MOUNTAIN-SIDE RIGHT NOW, RIGHT?!
HUH?! WHA?! WH-WHAT'S GOING ON?! WH-WHY IS KAZAMA-SAN C-CARRYING ME?!
SORRY, FUNABORI! I DIDN'T MEAN TO GET YOU MIXED UP IN ALL THIS! I'LL PUT YOU DOWN WHEN WE GET TO THE BOTTOM! PROMISE!!
SKSSHHH
HOW'S IT GOING?! FIND ANYTHING?!
RSTL
!!
KA-WHAM
OW!!

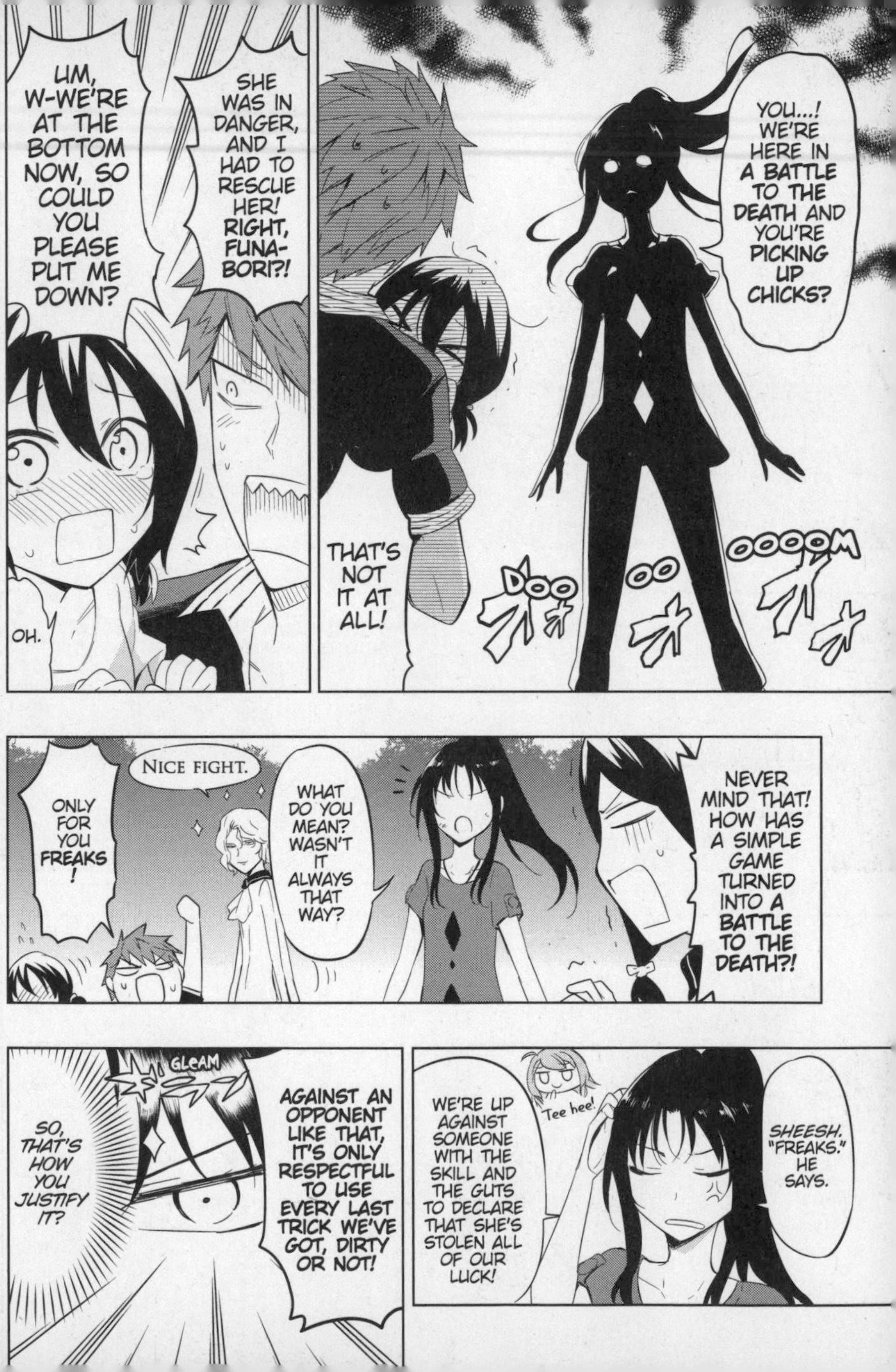
YOU...! WE'RE HERE IN A BATTLE TO THE DEATH AND YOU'RE PICKING UP CHICKS?
DOO
OO
OOOOM
THAT'S NOT IT AT ALL!
SHE WAS IN DANGER, AND I HAD TO RESCUE HER! RIGHT, FUNABORI?!
UM, W-WE'RE AT THE BOTTOM NOW, SO COULD YOU PLEASE PUT ME DOWN?
OH.
NEVER MIND THAT! HOW HAS A SIMPLE GAME TURNED INTO A BATTLE TO THE DEATH?!
WHAT DO YOU MEAN? WASN'T IT ALWAYS THAT WAY?
NICE FIGHT.
ONLY FOR YOU FREAKS!
SHEESH. "FREAKS." HE SAYS.
Tee hee!
WE'RE UP AGAINST SOMEONE WITH THE SKILL AND THE GUTS TO DECLARE THAT SHE'S STOLEN ALL OF OUR LUCK!
GLEAM
AGAINST AN OPPONENT LIKE THAT, IT'S ONLY RESPECTFUL TO USE EVERY LAST TRICK WE'VE GOT, DIRTY OR NOT!
SO, THAT'S HOW YOU JUSTIFY IT?

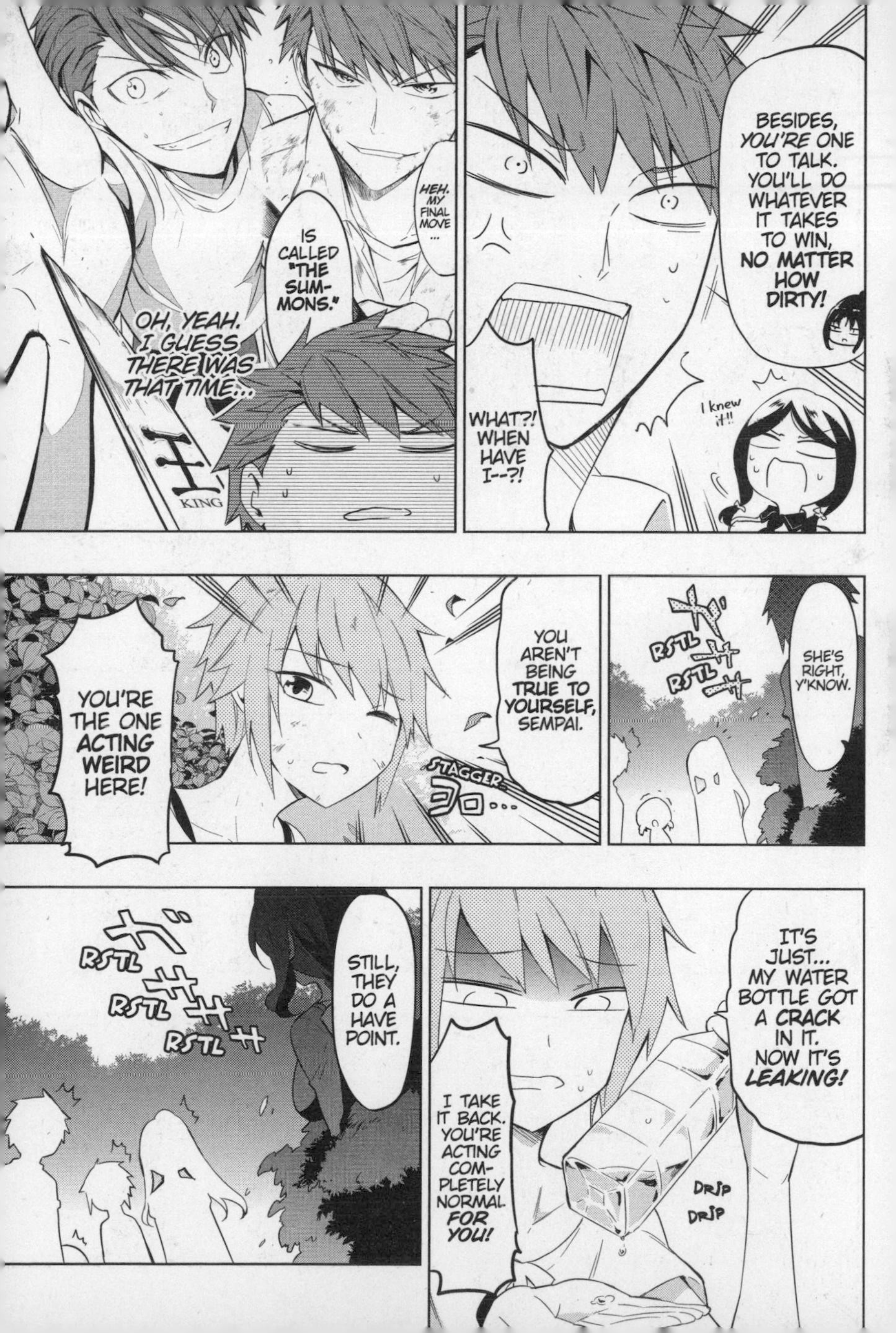
BESIDES, YOU'RE ONE TO TALK. YOU'LL DO WHATEVER IT TAKES TO WIN, NO MATTER HOW DIRTY!
WHAT?! WHEN HAVE I--?!
I knew it!!
HEH. MY FINAL MOVE ...
IS CALLED "THE SUMMONS."
OH, YEAH. I GUESS THERE WAS THAT TIME...
KING
SHE'S RIGHT, Y'KNOW.
RSTL
RSTL
YOU AREN'T BEING TRUE TO YOURSELF, SEMPAI.
STAGGER...
YOU'RE THE ONE ACTING WEIRD HERE!
IT'S JUST... MY WATER BOTTLE GOT A CRACK IN IT. NOW IT'S LEAKING!
DRIP
DRIP
I TAKE IT BACK. YOU'RE ACTING COM-PLETELY NORMAL FOR YOU!
STILL, THEY DO A HAVE POINT.
RSTL
RSTL
RSTL

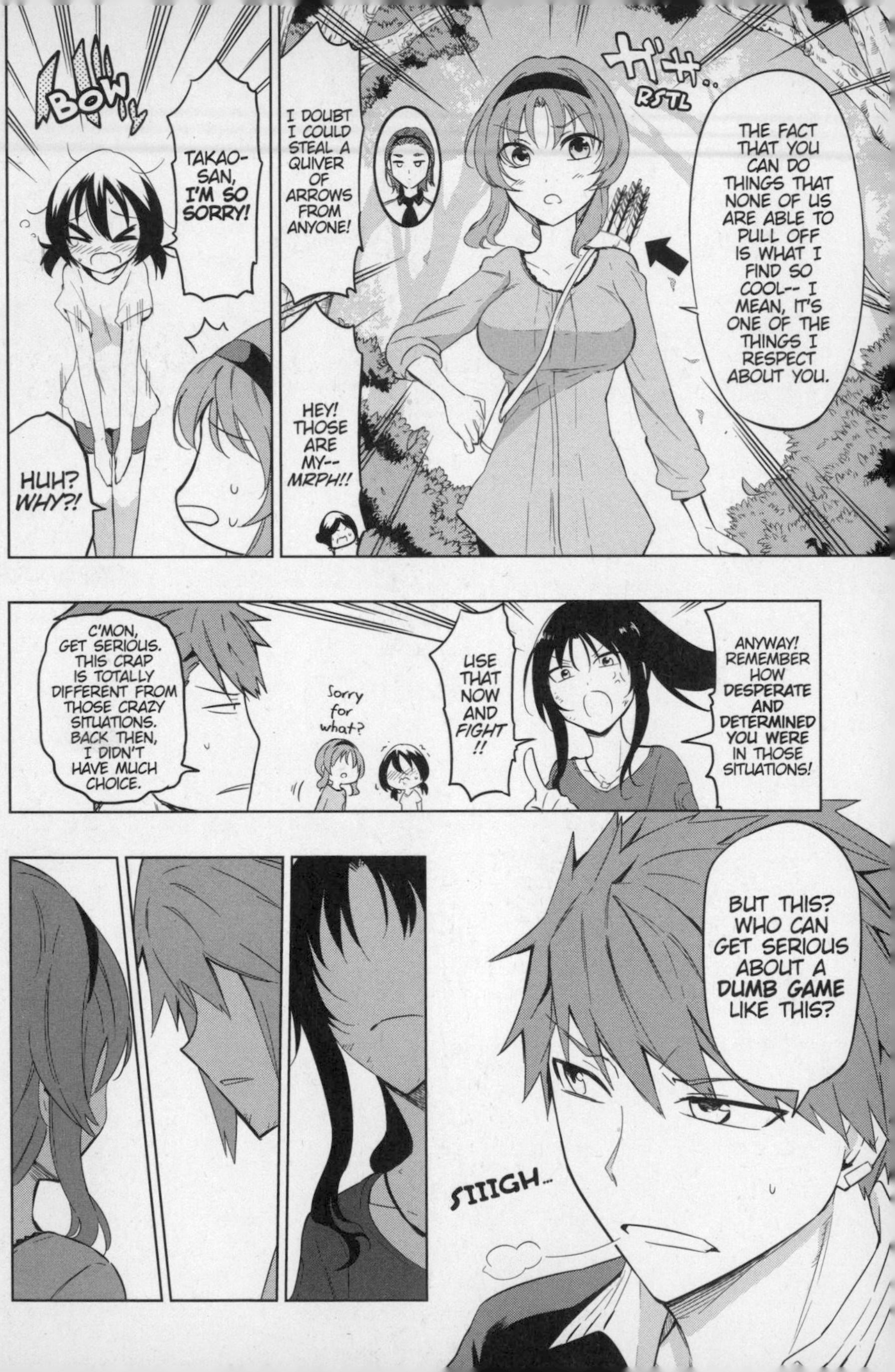
ガサ..
RSTL
THE FACT THAT YOU CAN DO THINGS THAT NONE OF US ARE ABLE TO PULL OFF IS WHAT I FIND SO COOL-- I MEAN, IT'S ONE OF THE THINGS I RESPECT ABOUT YOU.
I DOUBT I COULD STEAL A QUIVER OF ARROWS FROM ANYONE!
HEY! THOSE ARE MY-- MRPH!!
BOW
TAKAO-SAN, I'M SO SORRY!
HUH? WHY?!
ANYWAY! REMEMBER HOW DESPERATE AND DETERMINED YOU WERE IN THOSE SITUATIONS!
USE THAT NOW AND FIGHT!!
Sorry for what?
C'MON, GET SERIOUS. THIS CRAP IS TOTALLY DIFFERENT FROM THOSE CRAZY SITUATIONS. BACK THEN, I DIDN'T HAVE MUCH CHOICE.
BUT THIS? WHO CAN GET SERIOUS ABOUT A DUMB GAME LIKE THIS?
SIIIGH...

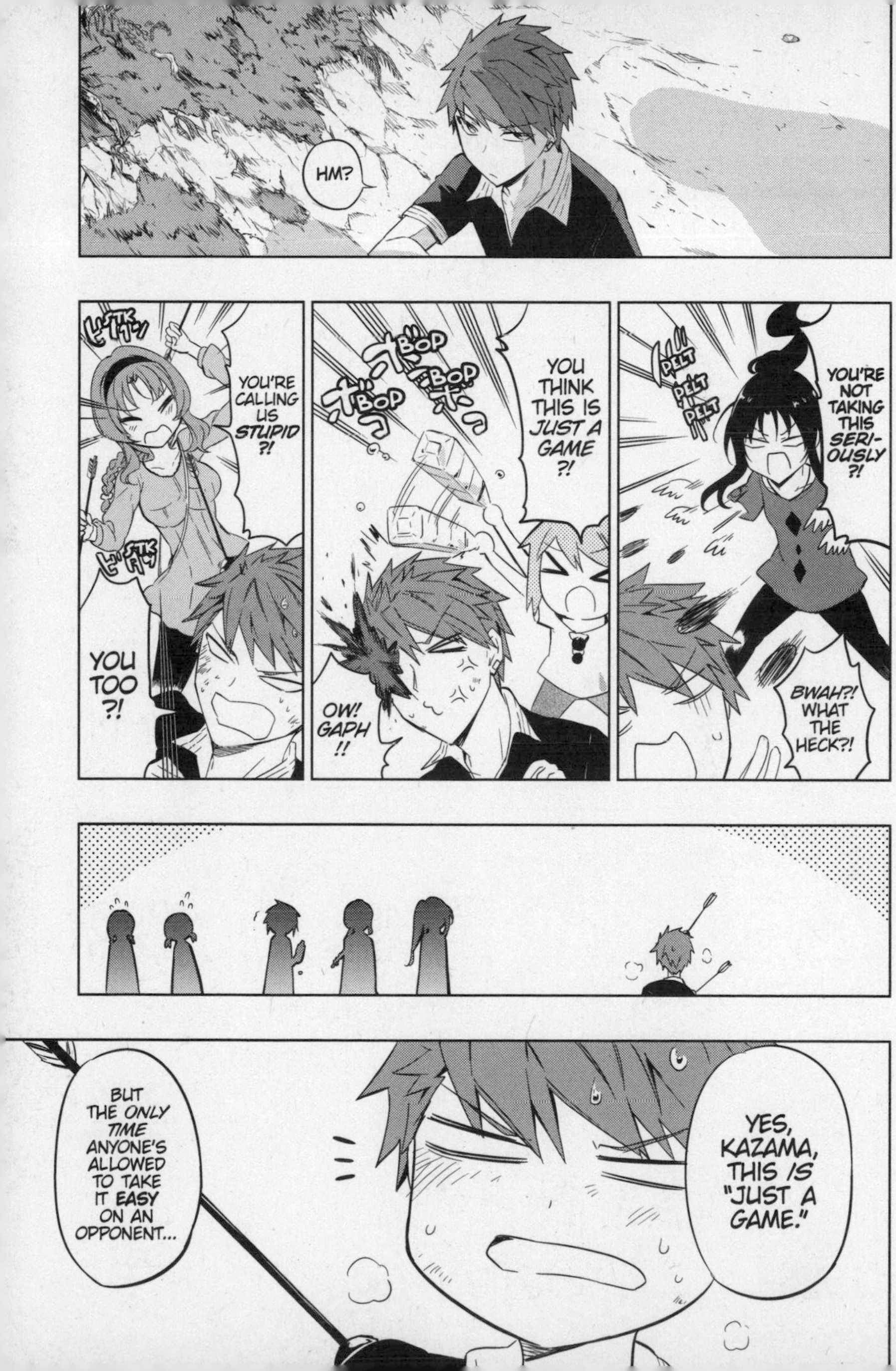
HM?
PELT
PELT
PELT
YOU'RE NOT TAKING THIS SERIOUSLY?!
BWAH?! WHAT THE HECK?!
BOP
BOP
BOP
YOU THINK THIS IS JUST A GAME?!
OW! GAPH!!
STK
STK
YOU'RE CALLING US STUPID?!
YOU TOO?!
YES, KAZAMA, THIS IS "JUST A GAME."
BUT THE ONLY TIME ANYONE'S ALLOWED TO TAKE IT EASY ON AN OPPONENT...

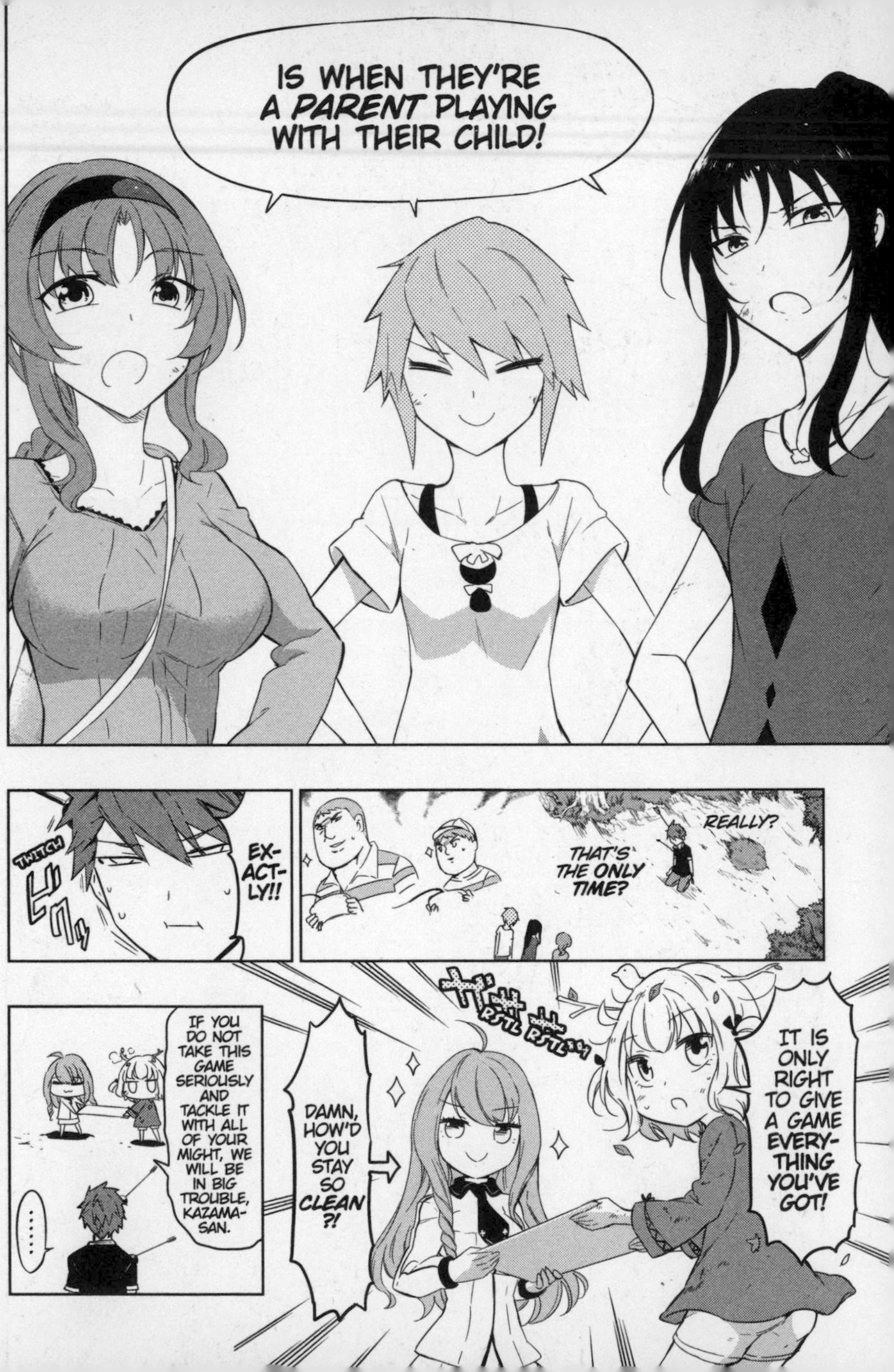
IS WHEN THEY'RE A *PARENT* PLAYING WITH THEIR CHILD!
REALLY?
THAT'S THE ONLY TIME?
EX-ACT-LY!!
TWITCH
IT IS ONLY RIGHT TO GIVE A GAME EVERY-THING YOU'VE GOT!
RSTL RSTL
DAMN, HOW'D YOU STAY SO *CLEAN*?!
IF YOU DO NOT TAKE THIS GAME SERIOUSLY AND TACKLE IT WITH ALL OF YOUR MIGHT, WE WILL BE IN BIG TROUBLE, KAZAMA-SAN.
......

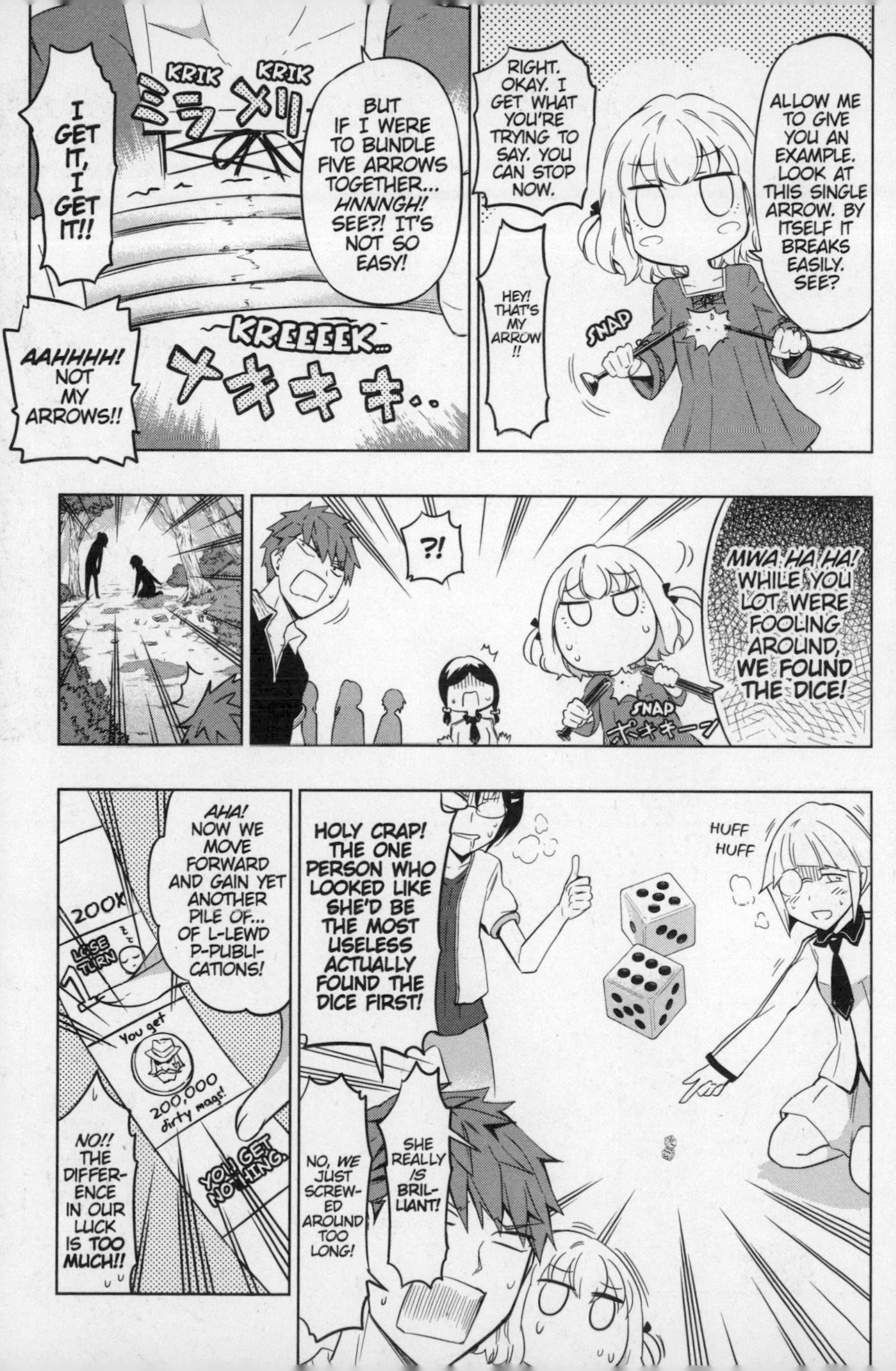
ALLOW ME TO GIVE YOU AN EXAMPLE. LOOK AT THIS SINGLE ARROW. BY ITSELF IT BREAKS EASILY. SEE?
SNAP
RIGHT. OKAY. I GET WHAT YOU'RE TRYING TO SAY. YOU CAN STOP NOW.
HEY! THAT'S MY ARROW!!
BUT IF I WERE TO BUNDLE FIVE ARROWS TOGETHER... HNNNGH! SEE?! IT'S NOT SO EASY!
KRIK KRIK
I GET IT, I GET IT!!
KREEEEK...
AAHHHH! NOT MY ARROWS!!
MWA HA HA! WHILE YOU LOT WERE FOOLING AROUND, WE FOUND THE DICE!
?!
SNAP
HUFF HUFF
HOLY CRAP! THE ONE PERSON WHO LOOKED LIKE SHE'D BE THE MOST USELESS ACTUALLY FOUND THE DICE FIRST!
SHE REALLY IS BRILLIANT!
NO, WE JUST SCREWED AROUND TOO LONG!
AHA! NOW WE MOVE FORWARD AND GAIN YET ANOTHER PILE OF... OF L-LEWD P-PUBLICATIONS!
200K
LOSE TURN
You get 200,000 dirty mags!
YOU GET NOTHING.
NO!! THE DIFFERENCE IN OUR LUCK IS TOO MUCH!!

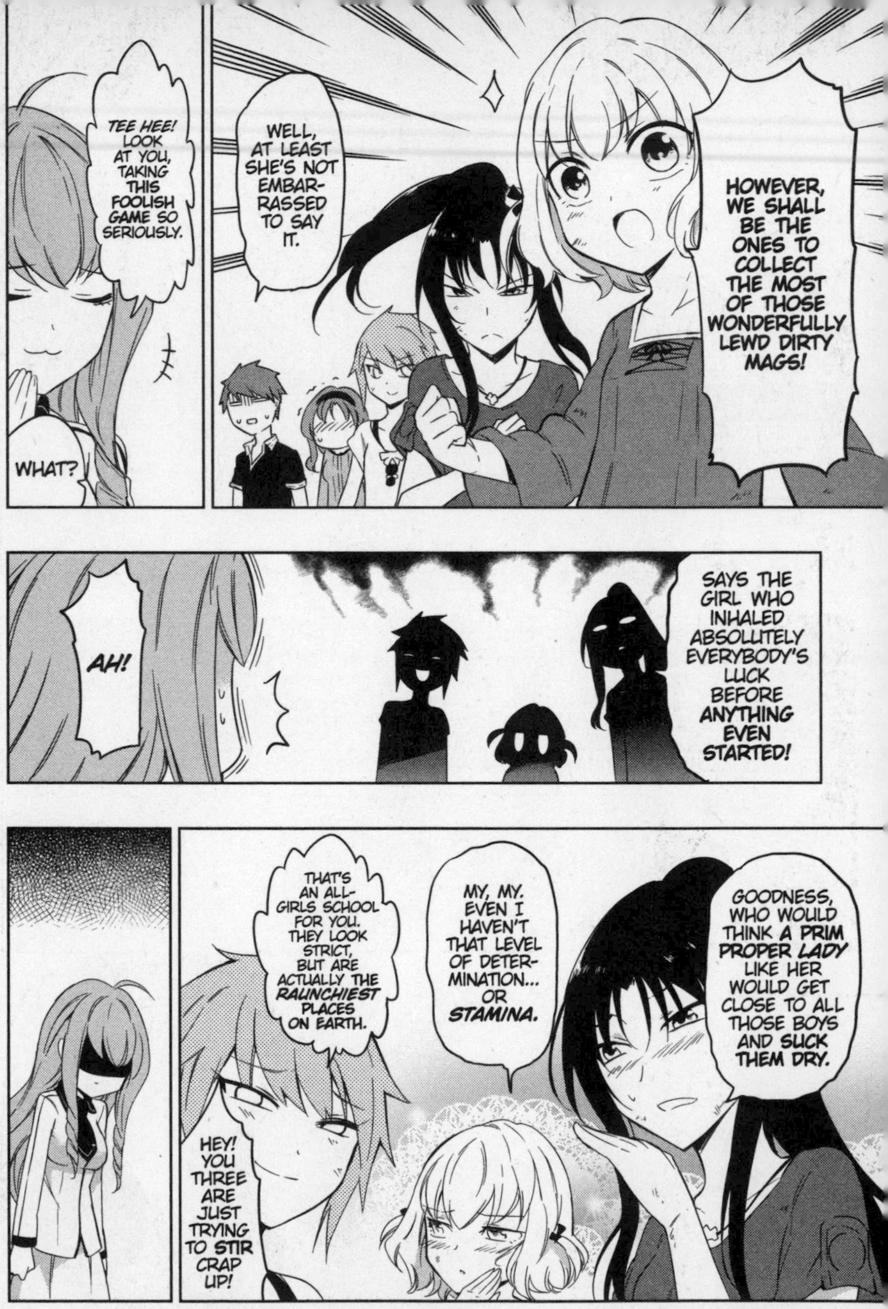
HOWEVER, WE SHALL BE THE ONES TO COLLECT THE MOST OF THOSE WONDERFULLY LEWD DIRTY MAGS!
WELL, AT LEAST SHE'S NOT EMBARRASSED TO SAY IT.
TEE HEE! LOOK AT YOU, TAKING THIS FOOLISH GAME SO SERIOUSLY.
WHAT?
SAYS THE GIRL WHO INHALED ABSOLUTELY EVERYBODY'S LUCK BEFORE ANYTHING EVEN STARTED!
AH!
GOODNESS, WHO WOULD THINK A PRIM PROPER LADY LIKE HER WOULD GET CLOSE TO ALL THOSE BOYS AND SUCK THEM DRY.
MY, MY. EVEN I HAVEN'T THAT LEVEL OF DETERMINATION... OR STAMINA.
THAT'S AN ALL-GIRLS SCHOOL FOR YOU. THEY LOOK STRICT, BUT ARE ACTUALLY THE RAUNCHIEST PLACES ON EARTH.
HEY! YOU THREE ARE JUST TRYING TO STIR CRAP UP!

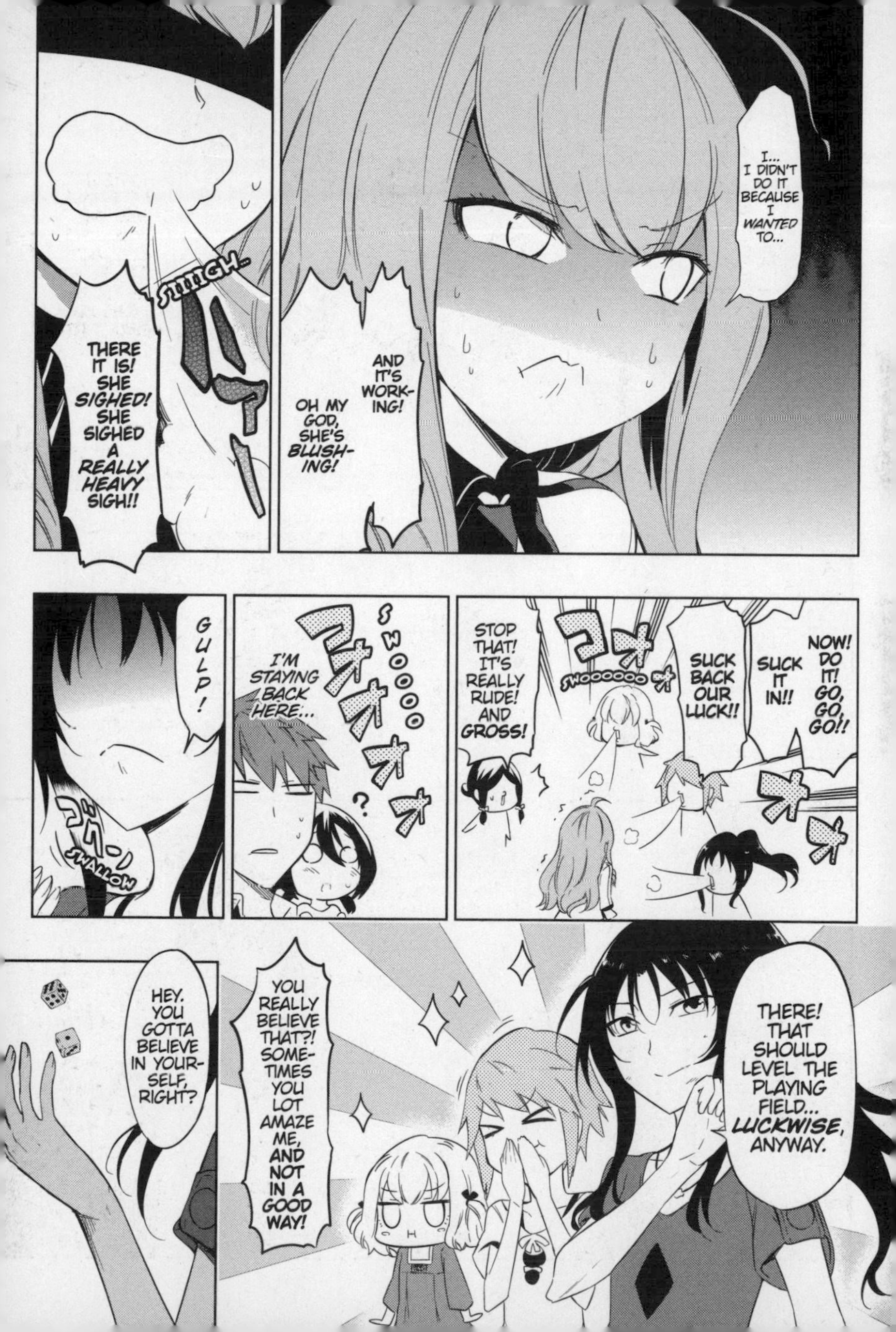
I... I DIDN'T DO IT BECAUSE I WANTED TO...
AND IT'S WORKING!
OH MY GOD, SHE'S BLUSHING!
SIIIGH..
THERE IT IS! SHE SIGHED! SHE SIGHED A REALLY HEAVY SIGH!!
NOW! DO IT! GO, GO, GO!!
SUCK IT IN!!
SUCK BACK OUR LUCK!!
SWOOOOOOO
STOP THAT! IT'S REALLY RUDE! AND GROSS!
SWOOOOO
I'M STAYING BACK HERE...
GULP!
SWALLOW
THERE! THAT SHOULD LEVEL THE PLAYING FIELD... LUCKWISE, ANYWAY.
YOU REALLY BELIEVE THAT?! SOMETIMES YOU LOT AMAZE ME, AND NOT IN A GOOD WAY!
HEY. YOU GOTTA BELIEVE IN YOURSELF, RIGHT?

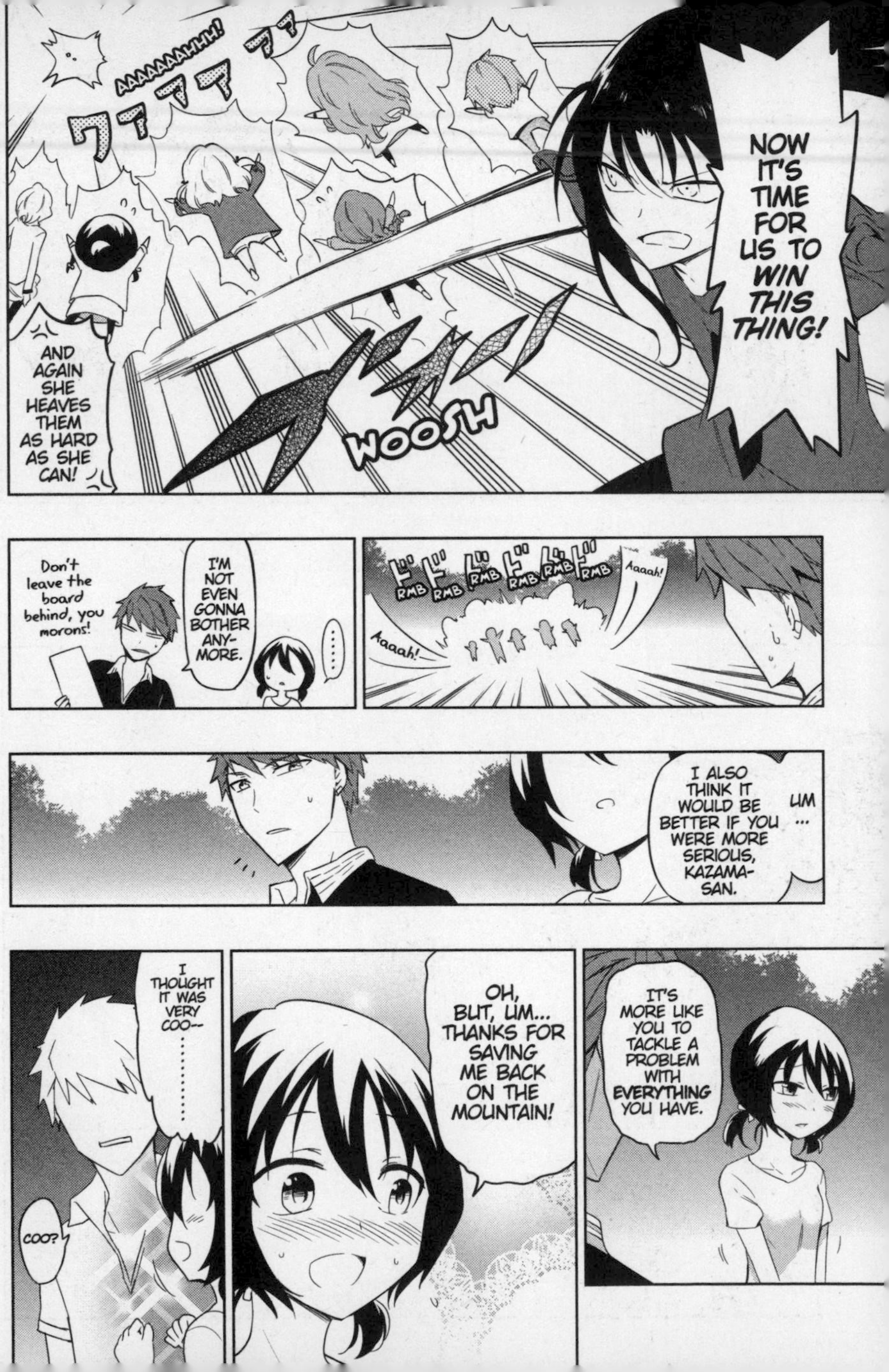
NOW IT'S TIME FOR US TO WIN THIS THING!
AAAAAAAHHH!
ワァァァ ァァ
AND AGAIN SHE HEAVES THEM AS HARD AS SHE CAN!
WOOSH
ドドドドドド
RMB RMB RMB RMB RMB RMB
Aaaah!
Aaaah!
I'M NOT EVEN GONNA BOTHER ANYMORE.
Don't leave the board behind, you morons!
......
UM ...
I ALSO THINK IT WOULD BE BETTER IF YOU WERE MORE SERIOUS, KAZAMA-SAN.
IT'S MORE LIKE YOU TO TACKLE A PROBLEM WITH EVERYTHING YOU HAVE.
OH, BUT, UM... THANKS FOR SAVING ME BACK ON THE MOUNTAIN!
I THOUGHT IT WAS VERY COO--
......
COO?

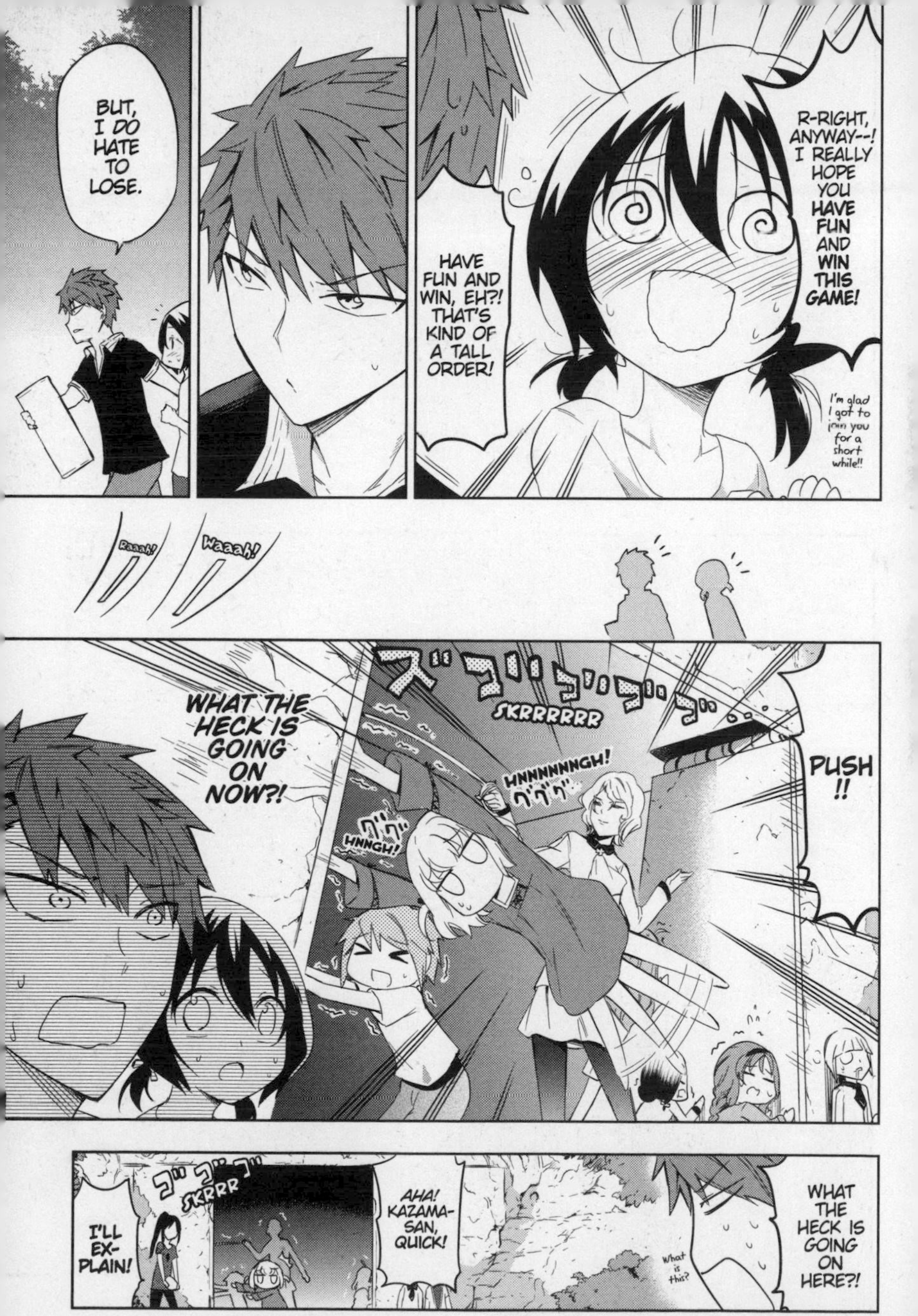
R-RIGHT, ANYWAY--! I REALLY HOPE YOU HAVE FUN AND WIN THIS GAME!
I'm glad I got to join you for a short while!!
HAVE FUN AND WIN, EH?! THAT'S KIND OF A TALL ORDER!
BUT, I DO HATE TO LOSE.
Waaah!
Raaah!
PUSH!!
SKRRRRRR
HNNNNNNGH!
HNNGH!
WHAT THE HECK IS GOING ON NOW?!
WHAT THE HECK IS GOING ON HERE?!
What is this?
AHA! KAZAMA-SAN, QUICK!
SKRRR
I'LL EX-PLAIN!

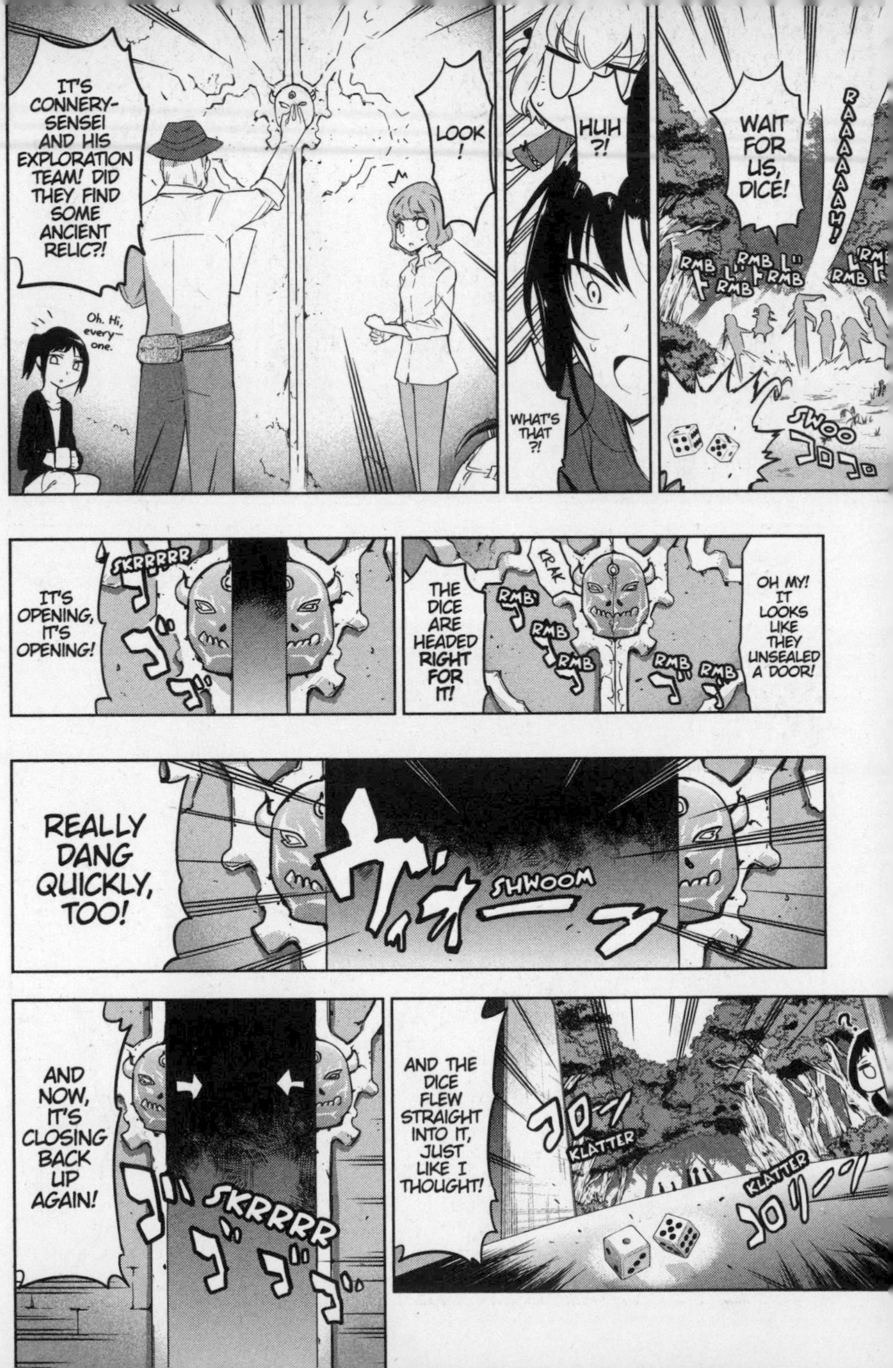
WAIT FOR US, DICE!
RAAAAAAAH!
RMB RMB RMB RMB RMB RMB
SWOO
HUH ?!
WHAT'S THAT ?!
LOOK !
IT'S CONNERY-SENSEI AND HIS EXPLORATION TEAM! DID THEY FIND SOME ANCIENT RELIC?!
Oh. Hi, every-one.
OH MY! IT LOOKS LIKE THEY UNSEALED A DOOR!
KRAK
RMB RMB RMB RMB RMB
THE DICE ARE HEADED RIGHT FOR IT!
SKRRRRR
IT'S OPENING, IT'S OPENING!
SHWOOM
REALLY DANG QUICKLY, TOO!
KLATTER
KLATTER
AND THE DICE FLEW STRAIGHT INTO IT, JUST LIKE I THOUGHT!
AND NOW, IT'S CLOSING BACK UP AGAIN!
SKRRRR

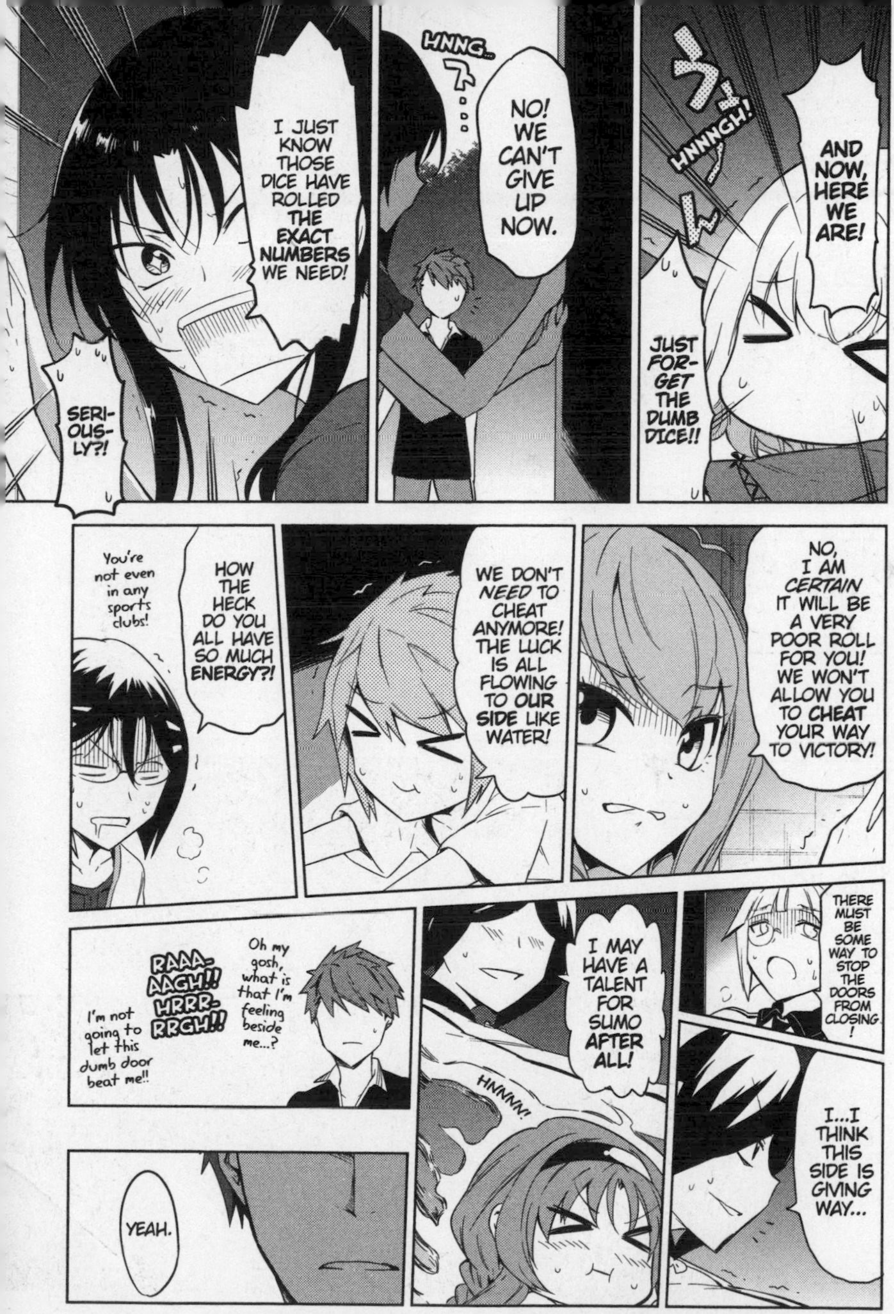
AND NOW, HERE WE ARE!
HNNNGH!
JUST FOR-GET THE DUMB DICE!!
HNNG...
NO! WE CAN'T GIVE UP NOW.
I JUST KNOW THOSE DICE HAVE ROLLED THE EXACT NUMBERS WE NEED!
SERI-OUSLY?!
NO, I AM *CERTAIN* IT WILL BE A VERY POOR ROLL FOR YOU! WE WON'T ALLOW YOU TO CHEAT YOUR WAY TO VICTORY!
WE DON'T *NEED* TO CHEAT ANYMORE! THE LUCK IS ALL FLOWING TO OUR SIDE LIKE WATER!
HOW THE HECK DO YOU ALL HAVE SO MUCH ENERGY?!
You're not even in any sports clubs!
THERE MUST BE SOME WAY TO STOP THE DOORS FROM CLOSING!
I...I THINK THIS SIDE IS GIVING WAY...
I MAY HAVE A TALENT FOR SUMO AFTER ALL!
HNNNN!
Oh my gosh, what is that I'm feeling beside me...?
RAAA-AAGH!! HRRR-RRGH!!
I'm not going to let this dumb door beat me!!
YEAH.

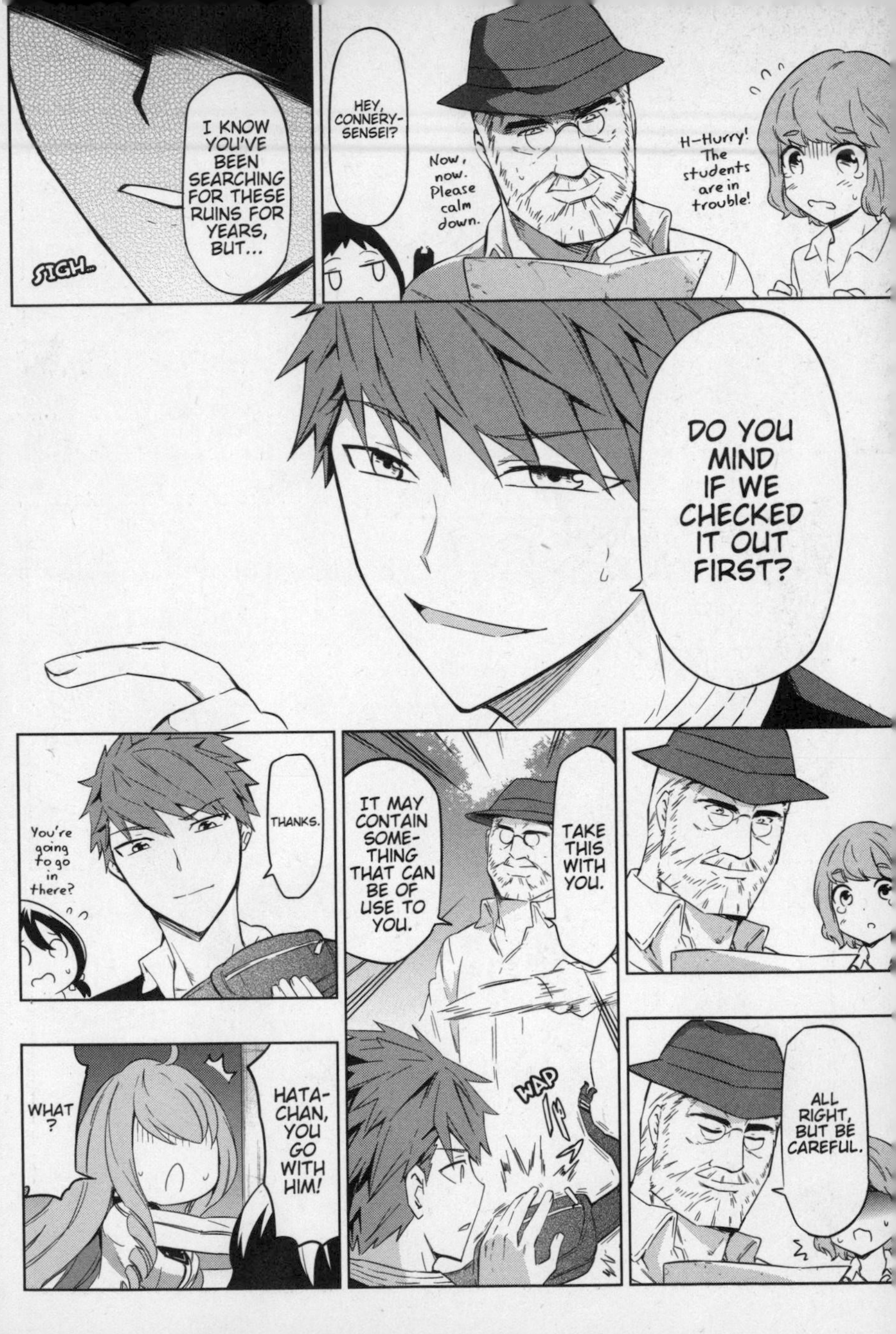
H-Hurry! The students are in trouble!
Now, now. Please calm down.
HEY, CONNERY-SENSEI?
I KNOW YOU'VE BEEN SEARCHING FOR THESE RUINS FOR YEARS, BUT...
SIGH...
DO YOU MIND IF WE CHECKED IT OUT FIRST?
TAKE THIS WITH YOU.
IT MAY CONTAIN SOME-THING THAT CAN BE OF USE TO YOU.
THANKS.
You're going to go in there?
ALL RIGHT, BUT BE CAREFUL.
WAP
HATA-CHAN, YOU GO WITH HIM!
WHAT?

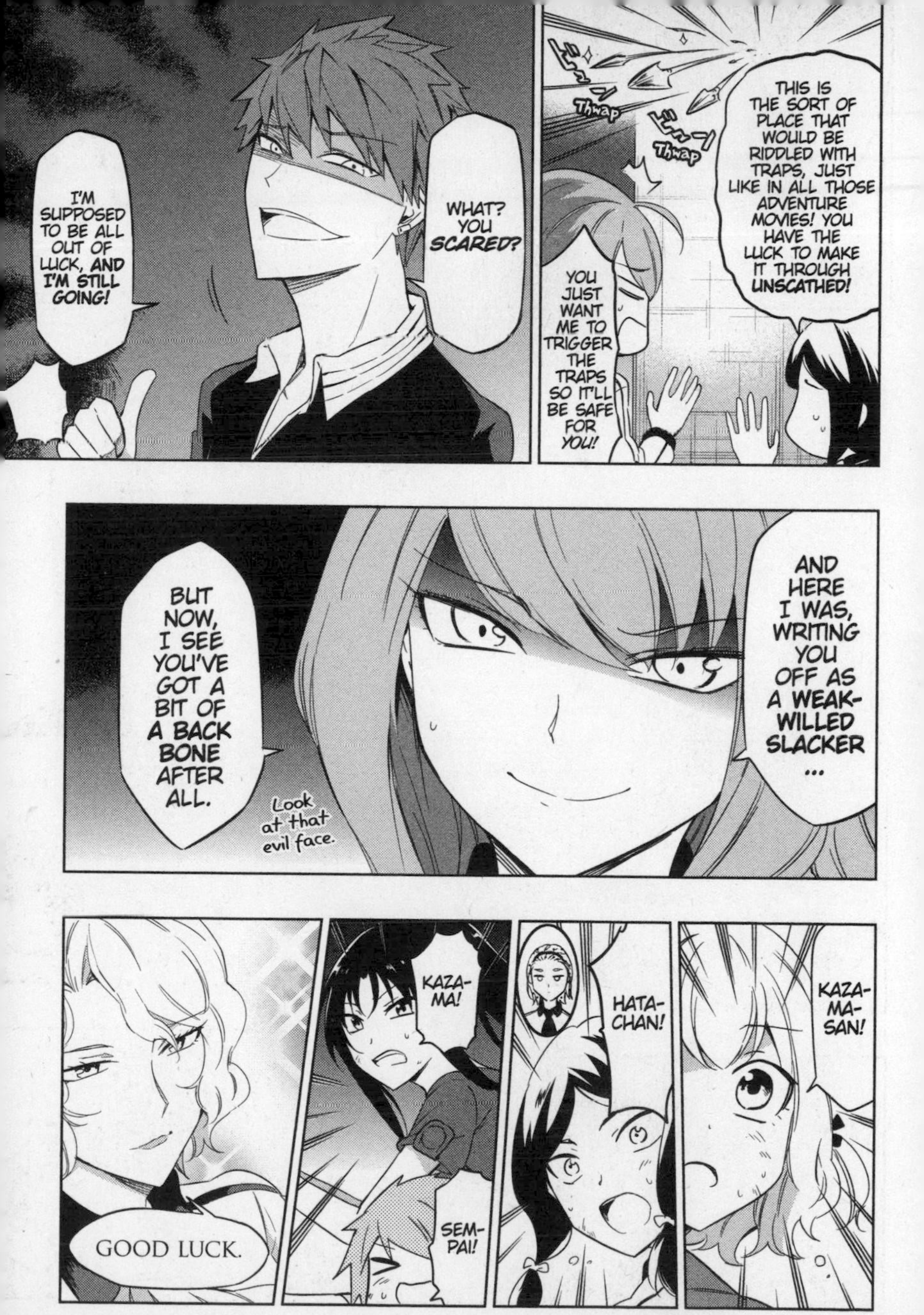
Thwap
Thwap
THIS IS THE SORT OF PLACE THAT WOULD BE RIDDLED WITH TRAPS, JUST LIKE IN ALL THOSE ADVENTURE MOVIES! YOU HAVE THE LUCK TO MAKE IT THROUGH UNSCATHED!
YOU JUST WANT ME TO TRIGGER THE TRAPS SO IT'LL BE SAFE FOR YOU!
WHAT? YOU SCARED?
I'M SUPPOSED TO BE ALL OUT OF LUCK, AND I'M STILL GOING!
AND HERE I WAS, WRITING YOU OFF AS A WEAK-WILLED SLACKER...
BUT NOW, I SEE YOU'VE GOT A BIT OF A BACK BONE AFTER ALL.
Look at that evil face.
KAZAMA-SAN!
HATA-CHAN!
KAZAMA!
SEMPAI!
GOOD LUCK.

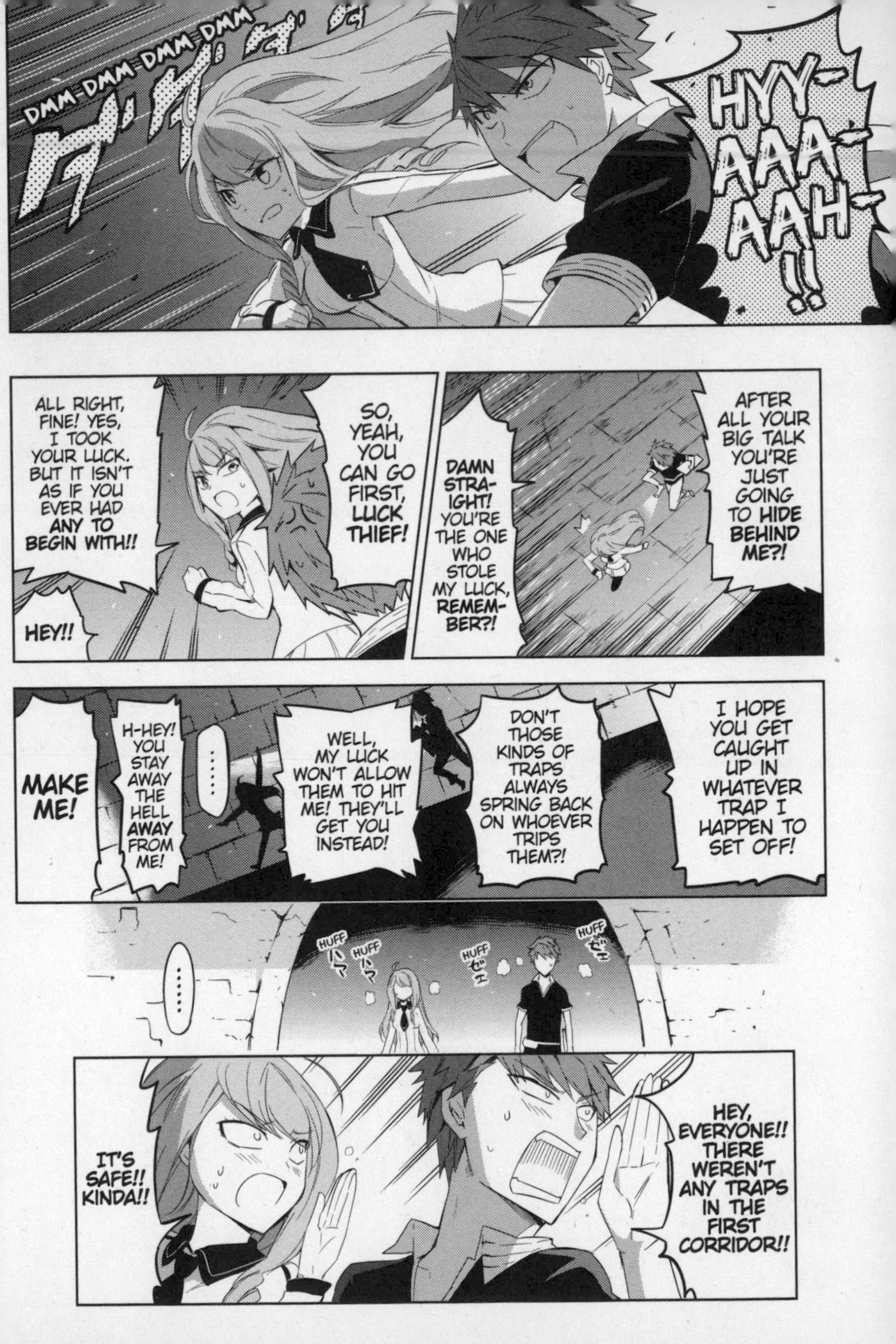
HYY-AAAA-AAH-!!
DMM DMM DMM DMM
AFTER ALL YOUR BIG TALK YOU'RE JUST GOING TO HIDE BEHIND ME?!
DAMN STRAIGHT! YOU'RE THE ONE WHO STOLE MY LUCK, REMEMBER?!
SO, YEAH, YOU CAN GO FIRST, LUCK THIEF!
ALL RIGHT, FINE! YES, I TOOK YOUR LUCK. BUT IT ISN'T AS IF YOU EVER HAD ANY TO BEGIN WITH!!
HEY!!
I HOPE YOU GET CAUGHT UP IN WHATEVER TRAP I HAPPEN TO SET OFF!
DON'T THOSE KINDS OF TRAPS ALWAYS SPRING BACK ON WHOEVER TRIPS THEM?!
WELL, MY LUCK WON'T ALLOW THEM TO HIT ME! THEY'LL GET YOU INSTEAD!
......
H-HEY! YOU STAY AWAY THE HELL AWAY FROM ME!
MAKE ME!
HUFF
HUFF
HUFF
HUFF
......
HEY, EVERYONE!! THERE WEREN'T ANY TRAPS IN THE FIRST CORRIDOR!!
IT'S SAFE!! KINDA!!

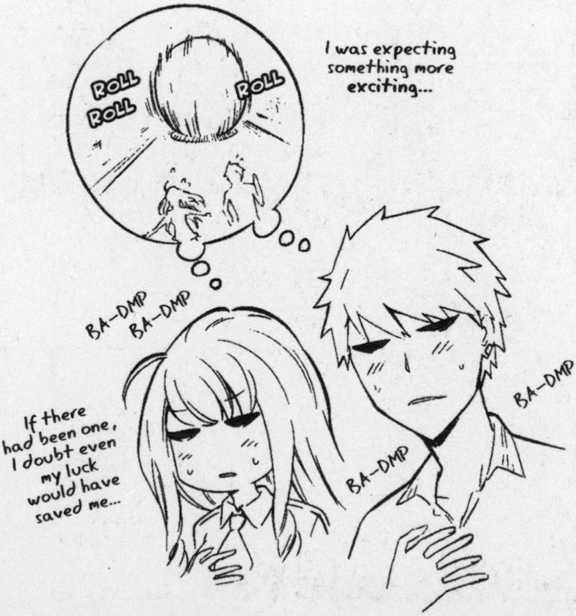
ROLL
ROLL
ROLL
I was expecting something more exciting...
BA-DMP
BA-DMP
BA-DMP
BA-DMP
If there had been one, I doubt even my luck would have saved me...

D-FRAGMENTS
ディーふらぐ!

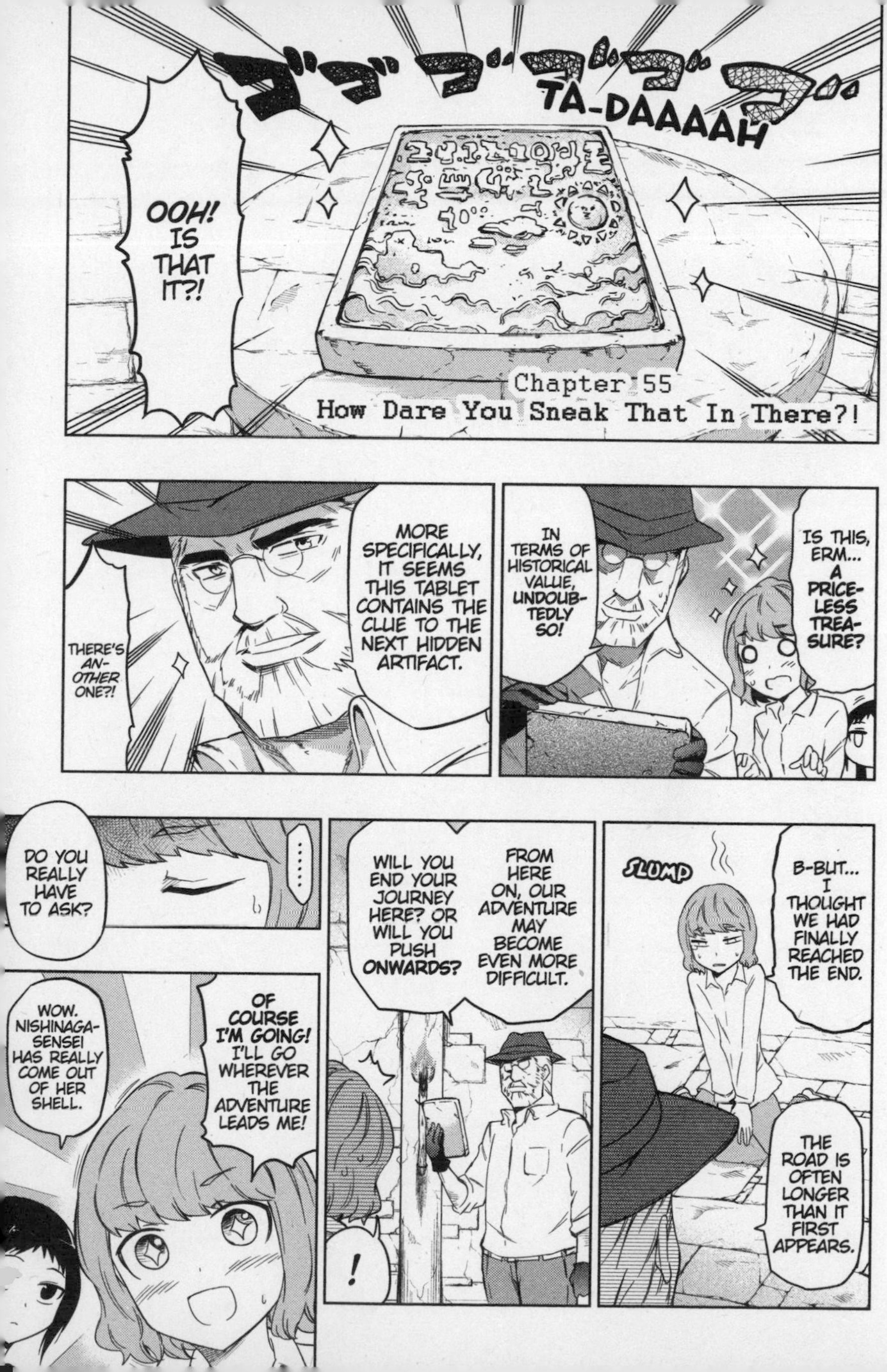
ゴゴゴゴゴゴ
TA-DAAAAH
OOH! IS THAT IT?!
Chapter 55
How Dare You Sneak That In There?!
IS THIS, ERM... A PRICELESS TREASURE?
IN TERMS OF HISTORICAL VALUE, UNDOUBTEDLY SO!
MORE SPECIFICALLY, IT SEEMS THIS TABLET CONTAINS THE CLUE TO THE NEXT HIDDEN ARTIFACT.
THERE'S ANOTHER ONE?!
SLUMP
B-BUT... I THOUGHT WE HAD FINALLY REACHED THE END.
THE ROAD IS OFTEN LONGER THAN IT FIRST APPEARS.
FROM HERE ON, OUR ADVENTURE MAY BECOME EVEN MORE DIFFICULT.
WILL YOU END YOUR JOURNEY HERE? OR WILL YOU PUSH ONWARDS?
!
......
DO YOU REALLY HAVE TO ASK?
OF COURSE I'M GOING! I'LL GO WHEREVER THE ADVENTURE LEADS ME!
WOW. NISHINAGA-SENSEI HAS REALLY COME OUT OF HER SHELL.

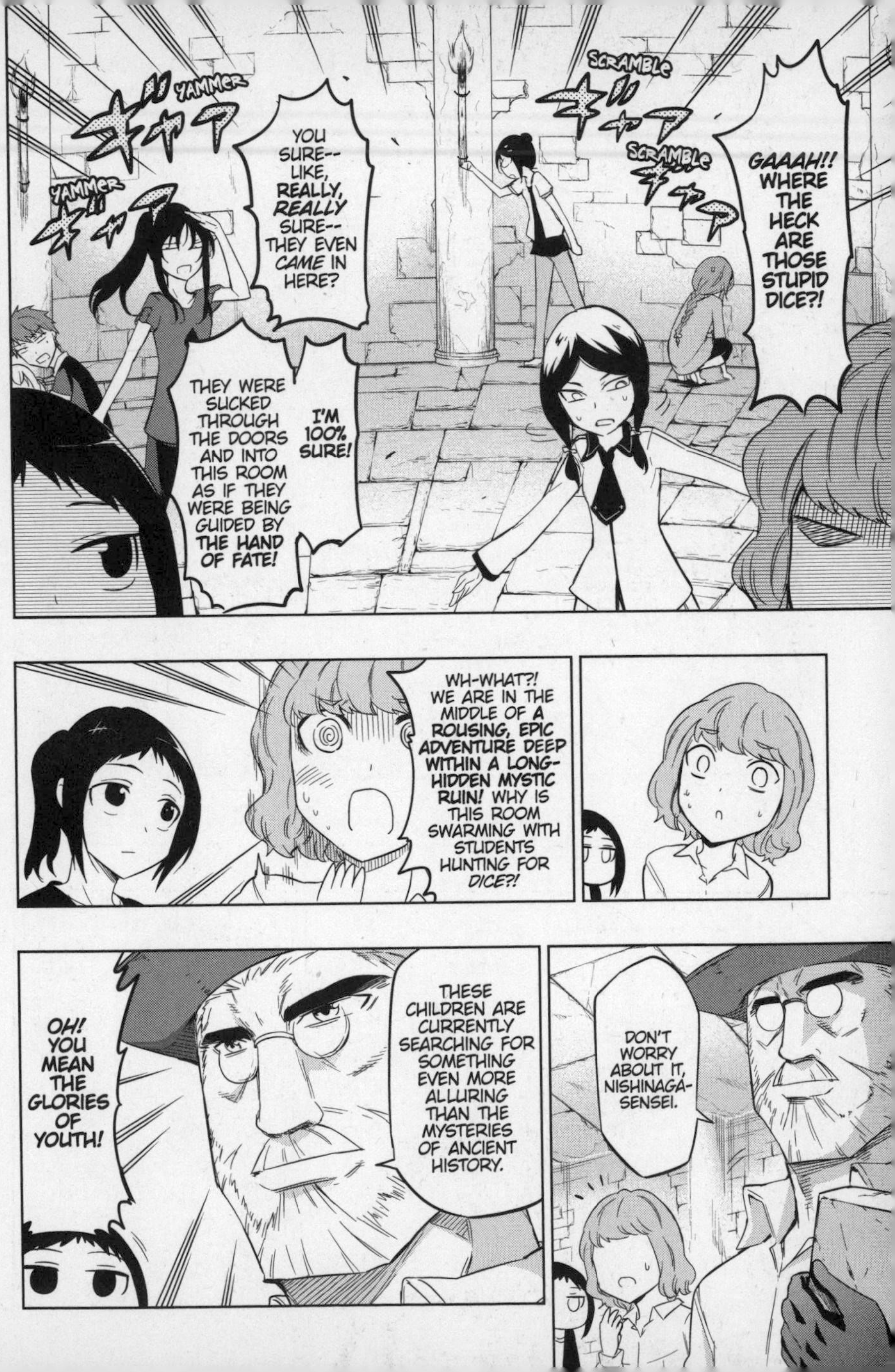
SCRAMBLE
SCRAMBLE
GAAAH!! WHERE THE HECK ARE THOSE STUPID DICE?!
YAMMER
YAMMER
YOU SURE-- LIKE, REALLY, REALLY SURE-- THEY EVEN CAME IN HERE?
I'M 100% SURE!
THEY WERE SUCKED THROUGH THE DOORS AND INTO THIS ROOM AS IF THEY WERE BEING GUIDED BY THE HAND OF FATE!
WH-WHAT?! WE ARE IN THE MIDDLE OF A ROUSING, EPIC ADVENTURE DEEP WITHIN A LONG-HIDDEN MYSTIC RUIN! WHY IS THIS ROOM SWARMING WITH STUDENTS HUNTING FOR DICE?!
DON'T WORRY ABOUT IT, NISHINAGA-SENSEI.
THESE CHILDREN ARE CURRENTLY SEARCHING FOR SOMETHING EVEN MORE ALLURING THAN THE MYSTERIES OF ANCIENT HISTORY.
OH! YOU MEAN THE GLORIES OF YOUTH!

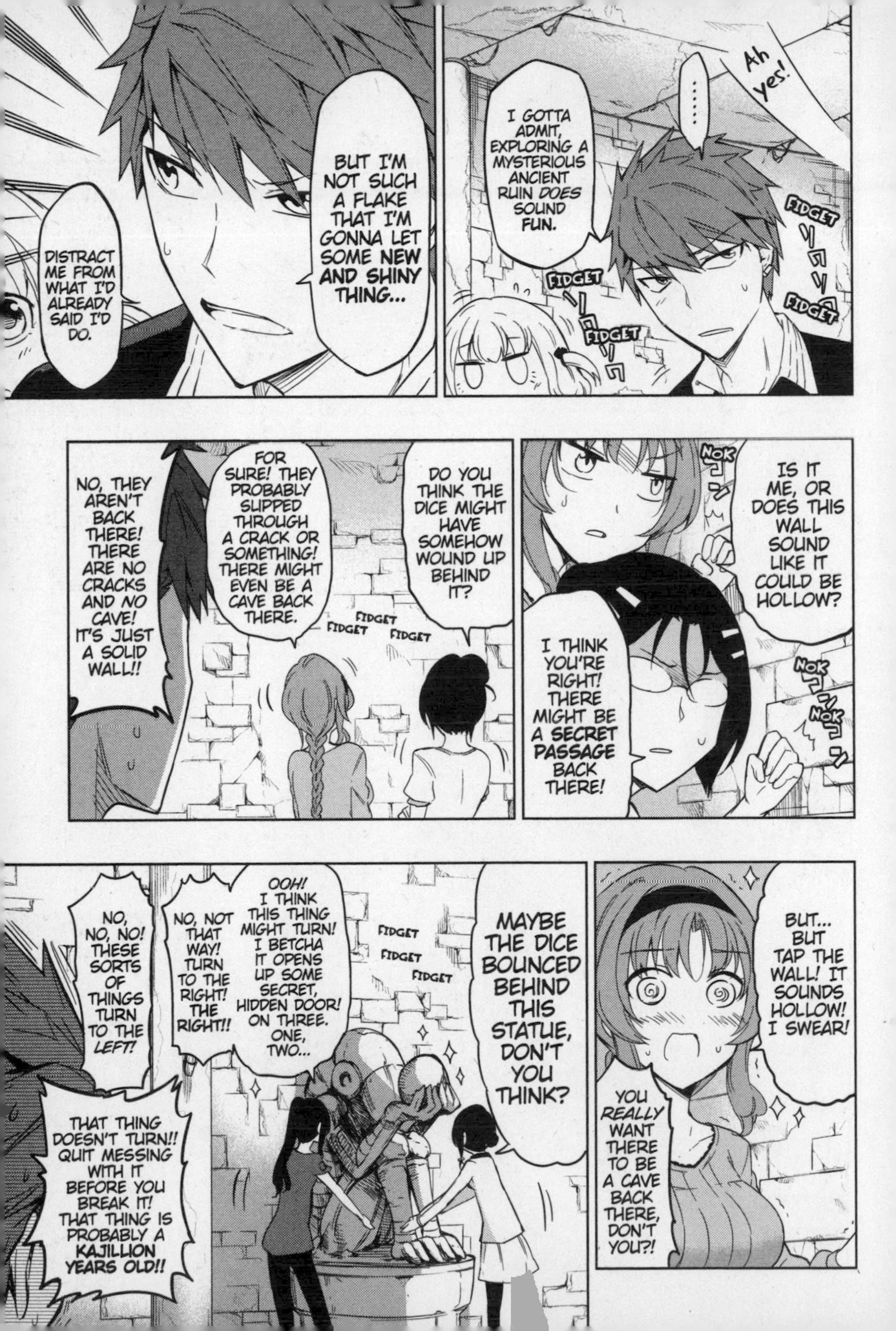
Ah yes!
......
I GOTTA ADMIT, EXPLORING A MYSTERIOUS ANCIENT RUIN DOES SOUND FUN.
FIDGET FIDGET FIDGET FIDGET
BUT I'M NOT SUCH A FLAKE THAT I'M GONNA LET SOME NEW AND SHINY THING...
DISTRACT ME FROM WHAT I'D ALREADY SAID I'D DO.
NOK
IS IT ME, OR DOES THIS WALL SOUND LIKE IT COULD BE HOLLOW?
I THINK YOU'RE RIGHT! THERE MIGHT BE A SECRET PASSAGE BACK THERE!
NOK NOK
DO YOU THINK THE DICE MIGHT HAVE SOMEHOW WOUND UP BEHIND IT?
FOR SURE! THEY PROBABLY SLIPPED THROUGH A CRACK OR SOMETHING! THERE MIGHT EVEN BE A CAVE BACK THERE.
FIDGET FIDGET FIDGET
NO, THEY AREN'T BACK THERE! THERE ARE NO CRACKS AND NO CAVE! IT'S JUST A SOLID WALL!!
BUT... BUT TAP THE WALL! IT SOUNDS HOLLOW! I SWEAR!
YOU REALLY WANT THERE TO BE A CAVE BACK THERE, DON'T YOU?!
MAYBE THE DICE BOUNCED BEHIND THIS STATUE, DON'T YOU THINK?
OOH! I THINK THIS THING MIGHT TURN! I BETCHA IT OPENS UP SOME SECRET, HIDDEN DOOR! ON THREE. ONE, TWO...
FIDGET FIDGET FIDGET
NO, NOT THAT WAY! TURN TO THE RIGHT! THE RIGHT!!
NO, NO, NO! THESE SORTS OF THINGS TURN TO THE LEFT!
THAT THING DOESN'T TURN!! QUIT MESSING WITH IT BEFORE YOU BREAK IT! THAT THING IS PROBABLY A KAJILLION YEARS OLD!!

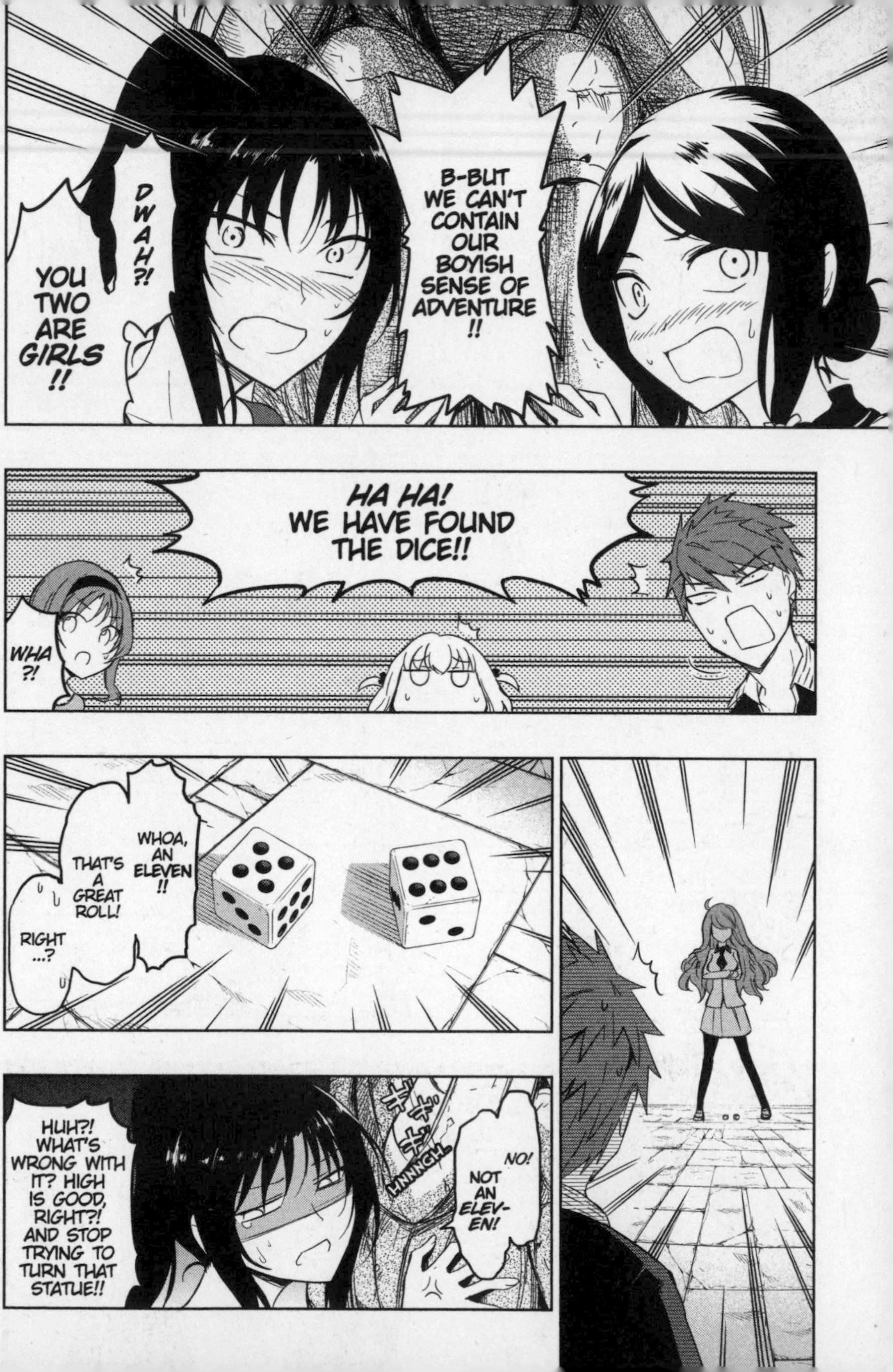
B-BUT WE CAN'T CONTAIN OUR BOYISH SENSE OF ADVENTURE!!
DWAH?!
YOU TWO ARE GIRLS!!
HA HA! WE HAVE FOUND THE DICE!!
WHA?!
WHOA, AN ELEVEN!!
THAT'S A GREAT ROLL!
RIGHT ...?
NO! NOT AN ELEV-EN!
MNNNGH
HUH?! WHAT'S WRONG WITH IT? HIGH IS GOOD, RIGHT?! AND STOP TRYING TO TURN THAT STATUE!!

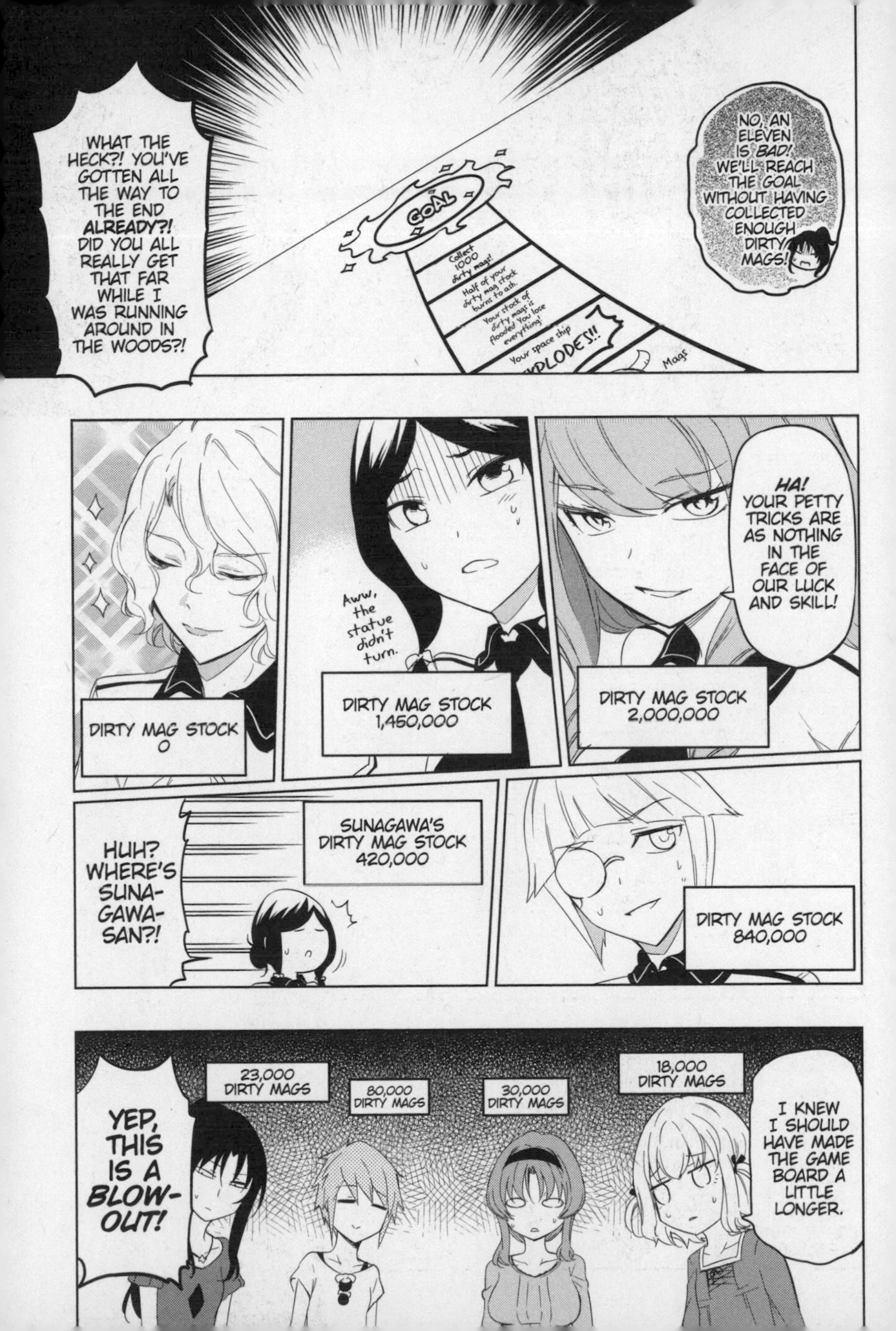
NO, AN ELEVEN IS BAD! WE'LL REACH THE GOAL WITHOUT HAVING COLLECTED ENOUGH DIRTY MAGS!
GOAL
Collect 1000 dirty mags!
Half of your dirty mag stock burns to ash.
Your stock of dirty mags is flooded! You lose everything!
Your space ship
XPLODES!!
Mags
WHAT THE HECK?! YOU'VE GOTTEN ALL THE WAY TO THE END ALREADY?! DID YOU ALL REALLY GET THAT FAR WHILE I WAS RUNNING AROUND IN THE WOODS?!
HA! YOUR PETTY TRICKS ARE AS NOTHING IN THE FACE OF OUR LUCK AND SKILL!
DIRTY MAG STOCK 2,000,000
Aww, the statue didn't turn.
DIRTY MAG STOCK 1,450,000
DIRTY MAG STOCK 0
DIRTY MAG STOCK 840,000
SUNAGAWA'S DIRTY MAG STOCK 420,000
HUH? WHERE'S SUNA-GAWA-SAN?!
I KNEW I SHOULD HAVE MADE THE GAME BOARD A LITTLE LONGER.
18,000 DIRTY MAGS
30,000 DIRTY MAGS
80,000 DIRTY MAGS
23,000 DIRTY MAGS
YEP, THIS IS A BLOW-OUT!

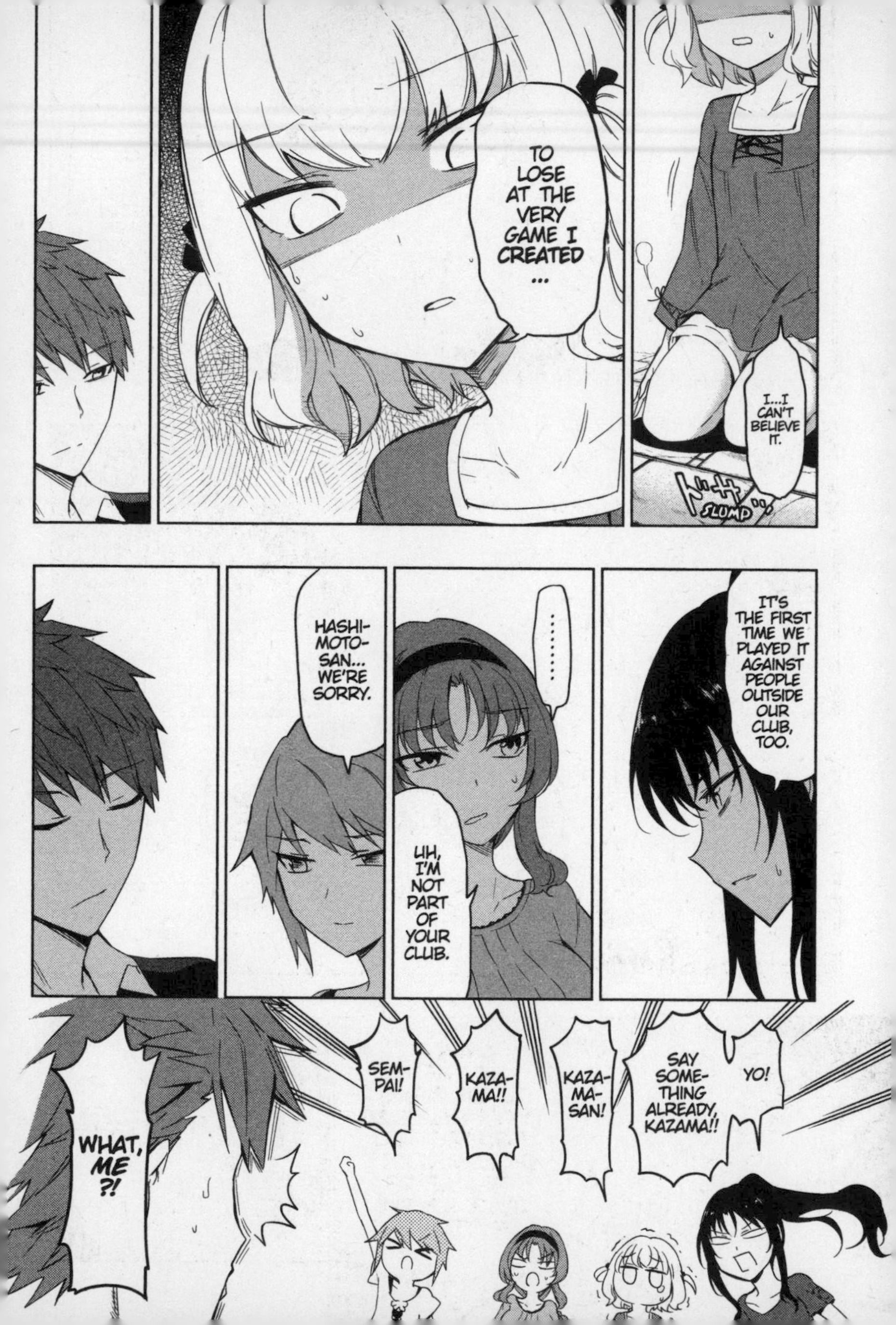
I...I CAN'T BELIEVE IT.
SLUMP
TO LOSE AT THE VERY GAME I CREATED ...
IT'S THE FIRST TIME WE PLAYED IT AGAINST PEOPLE OUTSIDE OUR CLUB, TOO.
......
HASHI-MOTO-SAN... WE'RE SORRY.
UH, I'M NOT PART OF YOUR CLUB.
YO!
SAY SOME-THING ALREADY, KAZAMA!!
KAZA-MA-SAN!
KAZA-MA!!
SEM-PAI!
WHAT, ME?!

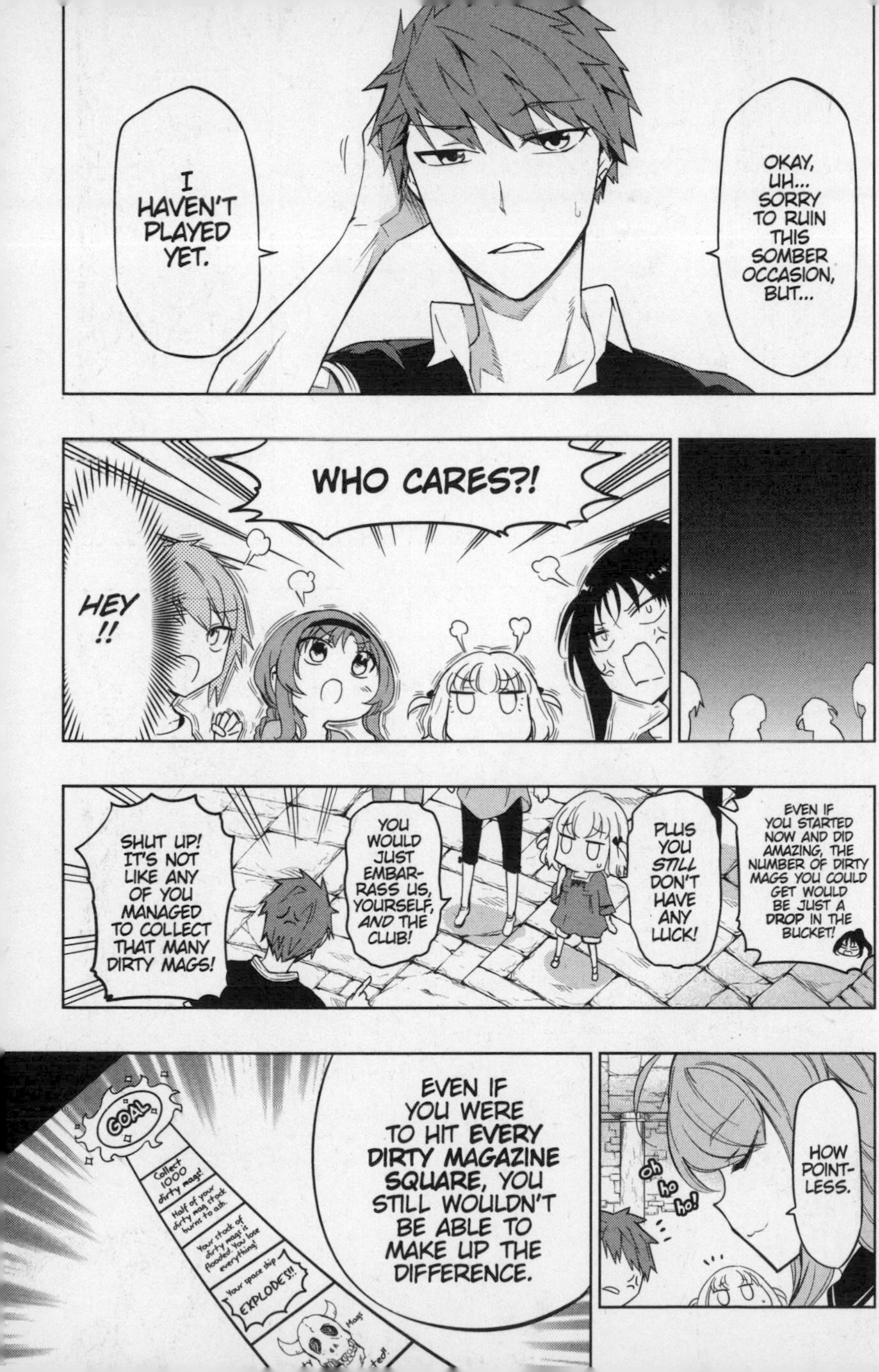
OKAY, UH... SORRY TO RUIN THIS SOMBER OCCASION, BUT...
I HAVEN'T PLAYED YET.
WHO CARES?!
HEY !!
EVEN IF YOU STARTED NOW AND DID AMAZING, THE NUMBER OF DIRTY MAGS YOU COULD GET WOULD BE JUST A DROP IN THE BUCKET!
PLUS YOU STILL DON'T HAVE ANY LUCK!
YOU WOULD JUST EMBAR-RASS US, YOURSELF, AND THE CLUB!
SHUT UP! IT'S NOT LIKE ANY OF YOU MANAGED TO COLLECT THAT MANY DIRTY MAGS!
HOW POINT-LESS.
oh ho ho!
EVEN IF YOU WERE TO HIT EVERY DIRTY MAGAZINE SQUARE, YOU STILL WOULDN'T BE ABLE TO MAKE UP THE DIFFERENCE.
GOAL
Collect 1000 dirty mags!
Half of your dirty mag stock burns to ash.
Your stock of dirty mags is flooded. You lose everything!
Your space ship EXPLODES!!

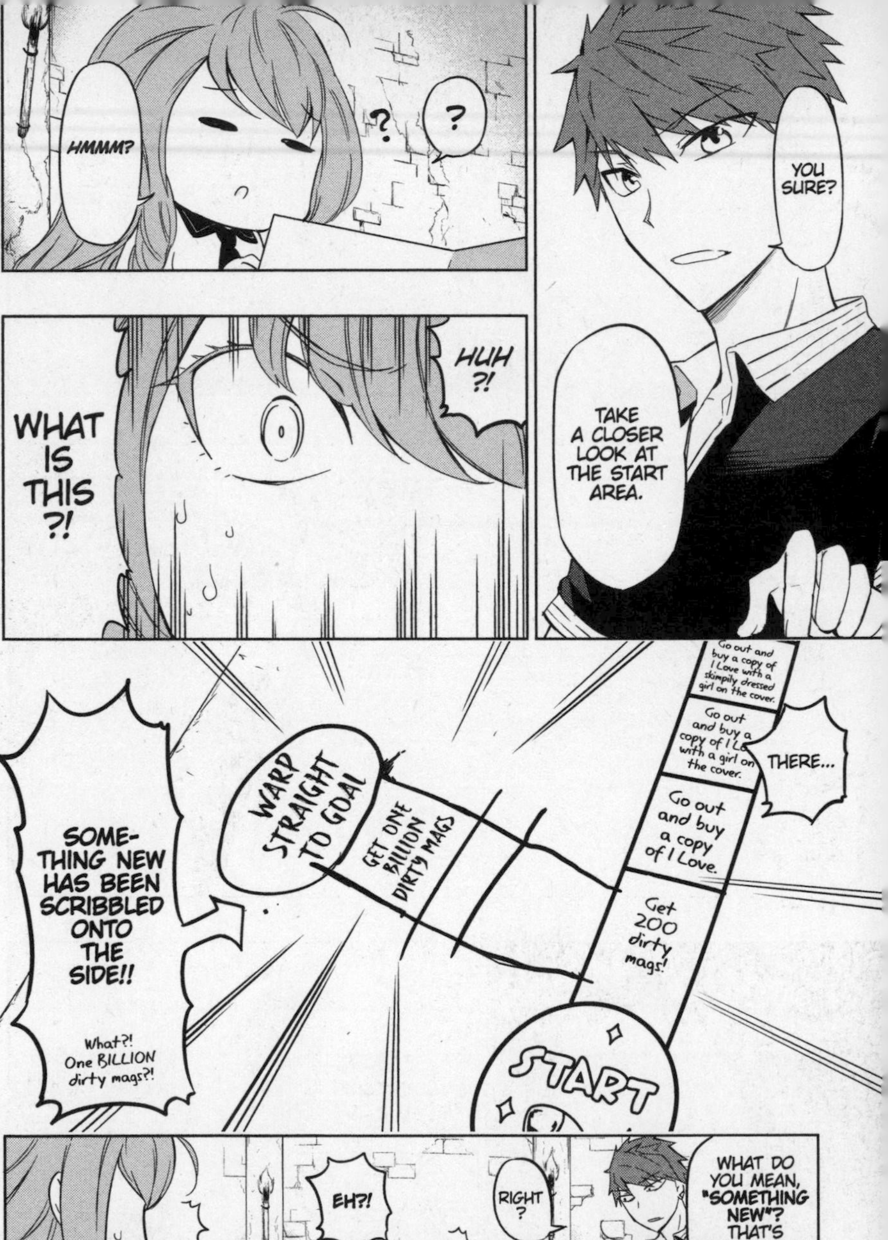
YOU SURE?
?
?
HMMM?
TAKE A CLOSER LOOK AT THE START AREA.
HUH?!
WHAT IS THIS?!
THERE...
Go out and buy a copy of I Love with a skimpily dressed girl on the cover.
Go out and buy a copy of I Love with a girl on the cover.
Go out and buy a copy of I Love.
Get 200 dirty mags!
START
GET ONE BILLION DIRTY MAGS
WARP STRAIGHT TO GOAL
SOMETHING NEW HAS BEEN SCRIBBLED ONTO THE SIDE!!
What?! One BILLION dirty mags?!
WHAT DO YOU MEAN, "SOMETHING NEW"? THAT'S BEEN THERE FROM THE BEGINNING.
RIGHT?
EH?!

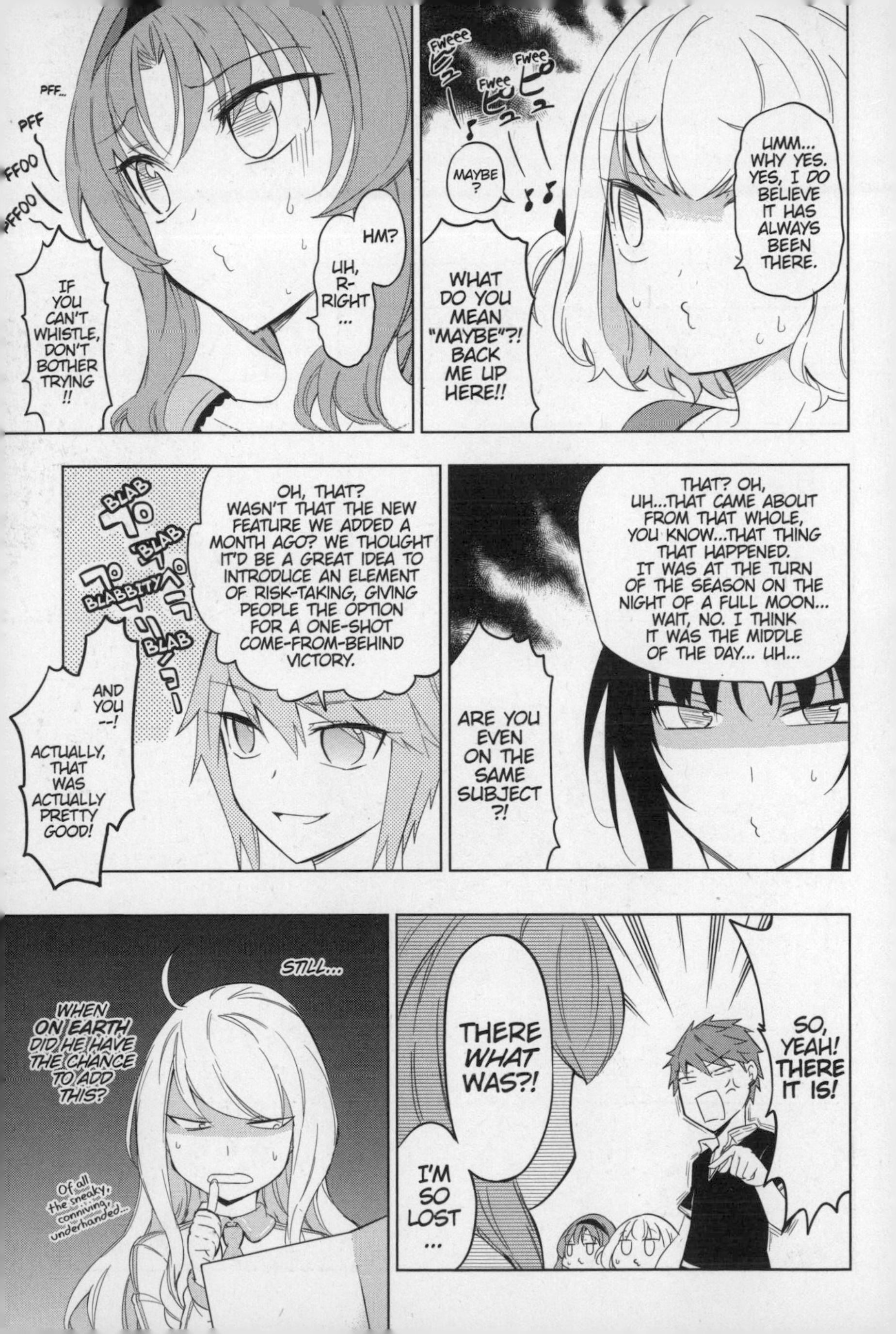
Fwee
Fwee
Fwee
UMM... WHY YES. YES, I DO BELIEVE IT HAS ALWAYS BEEN THERE.
MAYBE?
WHAT DO YOU MEAN "MAYBE"?! BACK ME UP HERE!!
HM?
UH, R-RIGHT...
PFF...
PFF
FFOO
FFOO
IF YOU CAN'T WHISTLE, DON'T BOTHER TRYING!!
THAT? OH, UH...THAT CAME ABOUT FROM THAT WHOLE, YOU KNOW...THAT THING THAT HAPPENED. IT WAS AT THE TURN OF THE SEASON ON THE NIGHT OF A FULL MOON... WAIT, NO. I THINK IT WAS THE MIDDLE OF THE DAY... UH...
ARE YOU EVEN ON THE SAME SUBJECT?!
OH, THAT? WASN'T THAT THE NEW FEATURE WE ADDED A MONTH AGO? WE THOUGHT IT'D BE A GREAT IDEA TO INTRODUCE AN ELEMENT OF RISK-TAKING, GIVING PEOPLE THE OPTION FOR A ONE-SHOT COME-FROM-BEHIND VICTORY.
BLAB
BLAB
BLABBITY
BLAB
AND YOU--!
ACTUALLY, THAT WAS ACTUALLY PRETTY GOOD!
SO, YEAH! THERE IT IS!
THERE WHAT WAS?!
I'M SO LOST...
STILL...
WHEN ON EARTH DID HE HAVE THE CHANCE TO ADD THIS?
Of all the sneaky, conniving, underhanded...

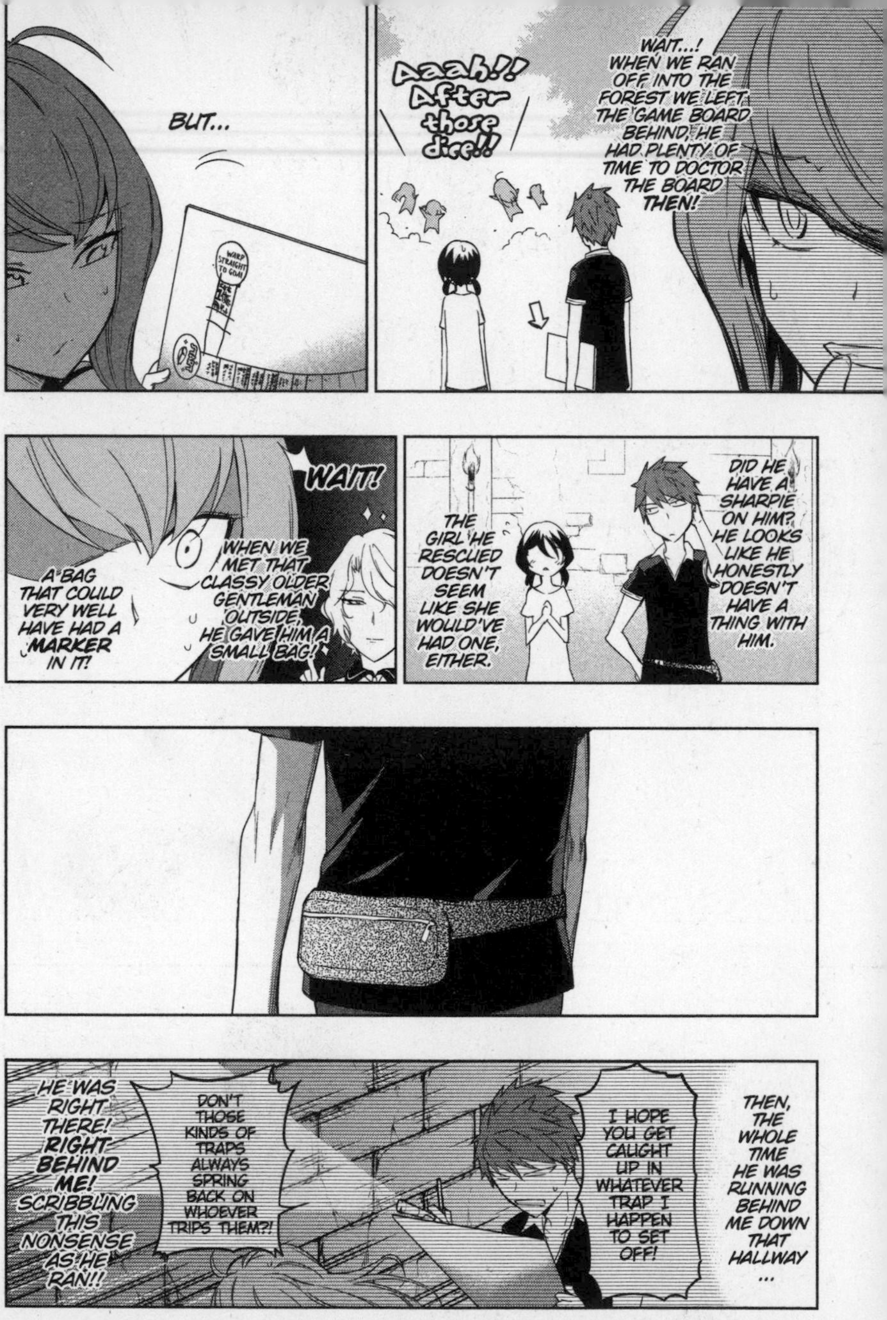
WAIT...! WHEN WE RAN OFF INTO THE FOREST WE LEFT THE GAME BOARD BEHIND, HE HAD PLENTY OF TIME TO DOCTOR THE BOARD THEN!
Aaah!! After those dice!!
BUT...
WARP STRAIGHT TO GOAL
DID HE HAVE A SHARPIE ON HIM? HE LOOKS LIKE HE HONESTLY DOESN'T HAVE A THING WITH HIM.
THE GIRL HE RESCUED DOESN'T SEEM LIKE SHE WOULD'VE HAD ONE, EITHER.
WAIT!
WHEN WE MET THAT CLASSY OLDER GENTLEMAN OUTSIDE, HE GAVE HIM A SMALL BAG!
A BAG THAT COULD VERY WELL HAVE HAD A MARKER IN IT!
THEN, THE WHOLE TIME HE WAS RUNNING BEHIND ME DOWN THAT HALLWAY...
I HOPE YOU GET CAUGHT UP IN WHATEVER TRAP I HAPPEN TO SET OFF!
DON'T THOSE KINDS OF TRAPS ALWAYS SPRING BACK ON WHOEVER TRIPS THEM?!
HE WAS RIGHT THERE! RIGHT BEHIND ME! SCRIBBLING THIS NONSENSE AS HE RAN!!

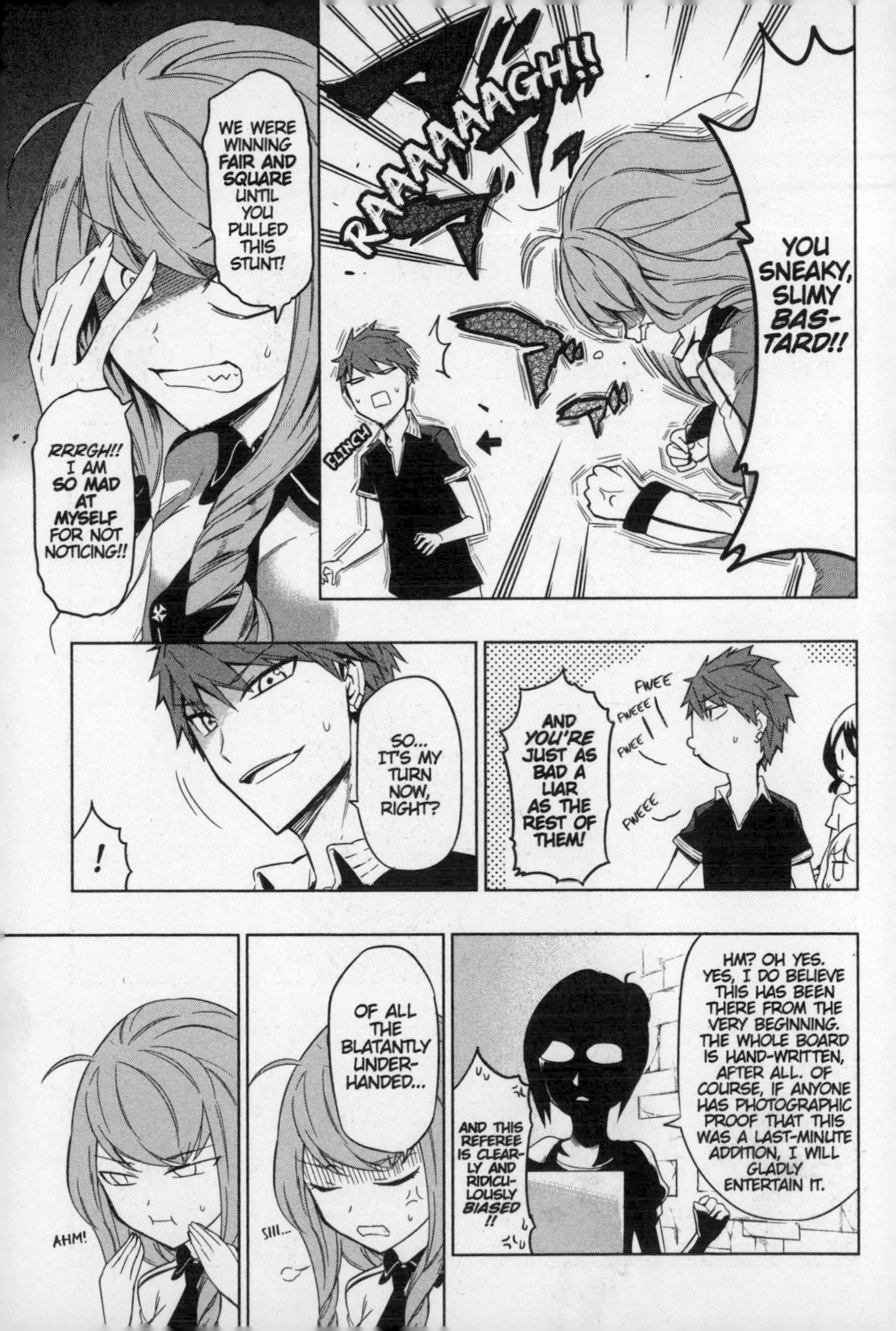
RAAAAAGH!!
YOU SNEAKY, SLIMY BASTARD!!
FLINCH
WE WERE WINNING FAIR AND SQUARE UNTIL YOU PULLED THIS STUNT!
RRRGH!! I AM SO MAD AT MYSELF FOR NOT NOTICING!!
FWEE
FWEEE
FWEE
FWEEE
AND YOU'RE JUST AS BAD A LIAR AS THE REST OF THEM!
SO... IT'S MY TURN NOW, RIGHT?
!
HM? OH YES. YES, I DO BELIEVE THIS HAS BEEN THERE FROM THE VERY BEGINNING. THE WHOLE BOARD IS HAND-WRITTEN, AFTER ALL. OF COURSE, IF ANYONE HAS PHOTOGRAPHIC PROOF THAT THIS WAS A LAST-MINUTE ADDITION, I WILL GLADLY ENTERTAIN IT.
AND THIS REFEREE IS CLEARLY AND RIDICULOUSLY BIASED!!
OF ALL THE BLATANTLY UNDER-HANDED...
SIII...
AHM!

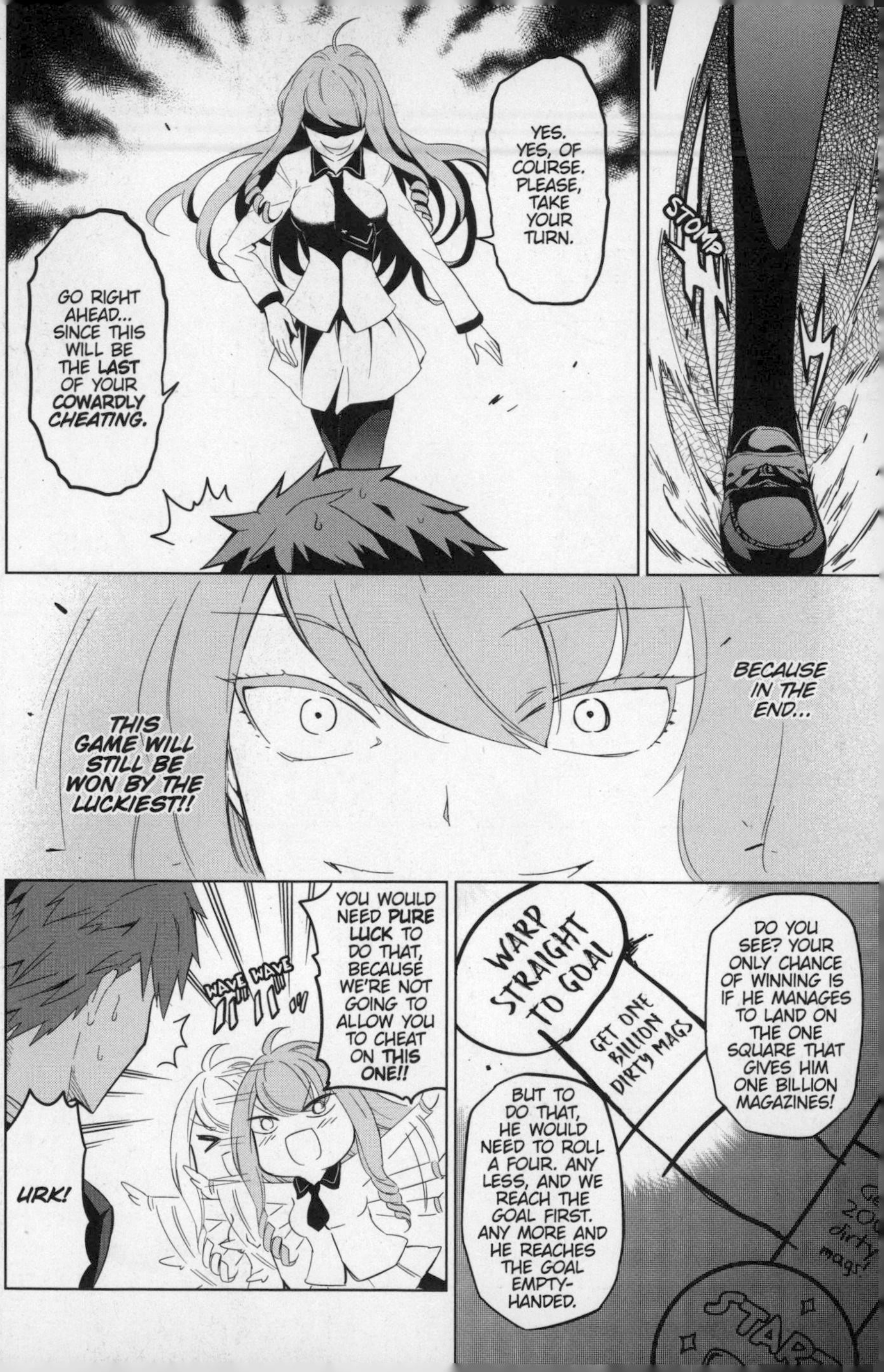
STOMP
YES. YES, OF COURSE. PLEASE, TAKE YOUR TURN.
GO RIGHT AHEAD... SINCE THIS WILL BE THE LAST OF YOUR COWARDLY CHEATING.
BECAUSE IN THE END...
THIS GAME WILL STILL BE WON BY THE LUCKIEST!!
DO YOU SEE? YOUR ONLY CHANCE OF WINNING IS IF HE MANAGES TO LAND ON THE ONE SQUARE THAT GIVES HIM ONE BILLION MAGAZINES!
WARP STRAIGHT TO GOAL
GET ONE BILLION DIRTY MAGS
BUT TO DO THAT, HE WOULD NEED TO ROLL A FOUR. ANY LESS, AND WE REACH THE GOAL FIRST. ANY MORE AND HE REACHES THE GOAL EMPTY-HANDED.
YOU WOULD NEED PURE LUCK TO DO THAT, BECAUSE WE'RE NOT GOING TO ALLOW YOU TO CHEAT ON THIS ONE!!
WAVE WAVE
URK!

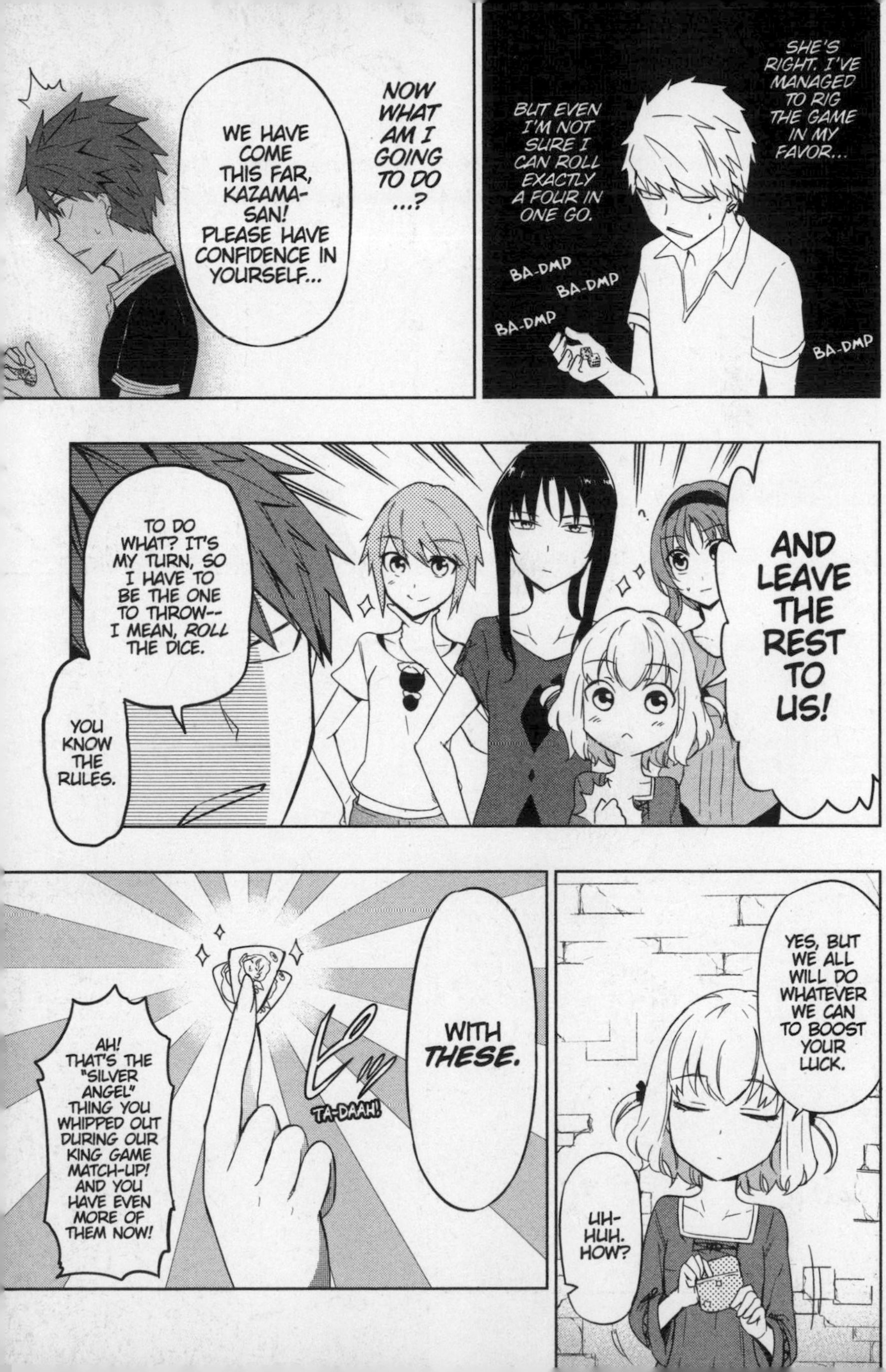
SHE'S RIGHT. I'VE MANAGED TO RIG THE GAME IN MY FAVOR...
BUT EVEN I'M NOT SURE I CAN ROLL EXACTLY A FOUR IN ONE GO.
BA-DMP
BA-DMP
BA-DMP
BA-DMP
NOW WHAT AM I GOING TO DO ...?
WE HAVE COME THIS FAR, KAZAMA-SAN! PLEASE HAVE CONFIDENCE IN YOURSELF...
AND LEAVE THE REST TO US!
TO DO WHAT? IT'S MY TURN, SO I HAVE TO BE THE ONE TO THROW-- I MEAN, *ROLL* THE DICE.
YOU KNOW THE RULES.
YES, BUT WE ALL WILL DO WHATEVER WE CAN TO BOOST YOUR LUCK.
UH-HUH. HOW?
WITH *THESE.*
TA-DAAH!
AH! THAT'S THE "SILVER ANGEL" THING YOU WHIPPED OUT DURING OUR KING GAME MATCH-UP! AND YOU HAVE EVEN MORE OF THEM NOW!

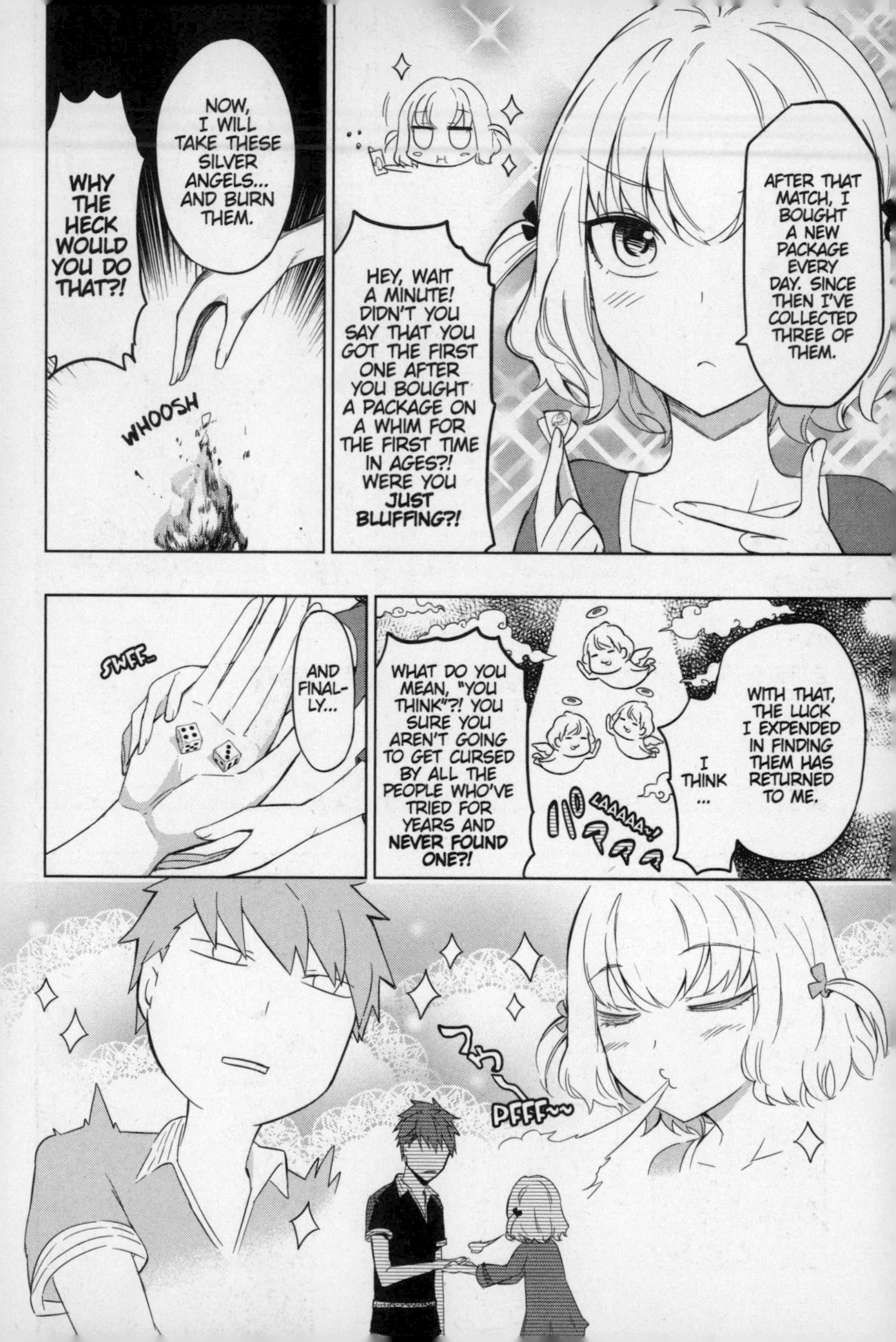
AFTER THAT MATCH, I BOUGHT A NEW PACKAGE EVERY DAY. SINCE THEN I'VE COLLECTED THREE OF THEM.
HEY, WAIT A MINUTE! DIDN'T YOU SAY THAT YOU GOT THE FIRST ONE AFTER YOU BOUGHT A PACKAGE ON A WHIM FOR THE FIRST TIME IN AGES?! WERE YOU JUST BLUFFING?!
NOW, I WILL TAKE THESE SILVER ANGELS... AND BURN THEM.
WHY THE HECK WOULD YOU DO THAT?!
WHOOSH
WITH THAT, THE LUCK I EXPENDED IN FINDING THEM HAS RETURNED TO ME.
I THINK...
LAAAAA~!
WHAT DO YOU MEAN, "YOU THINK"?! YOU SURE YOU AREN'T GOING TO GET CURSED BY ALL THE PEOPLE WHO'VE TRIED FOR YEARS AND NEVER FOUND ONE?!
AND FINALLY...
SWFF...
PFFF~~

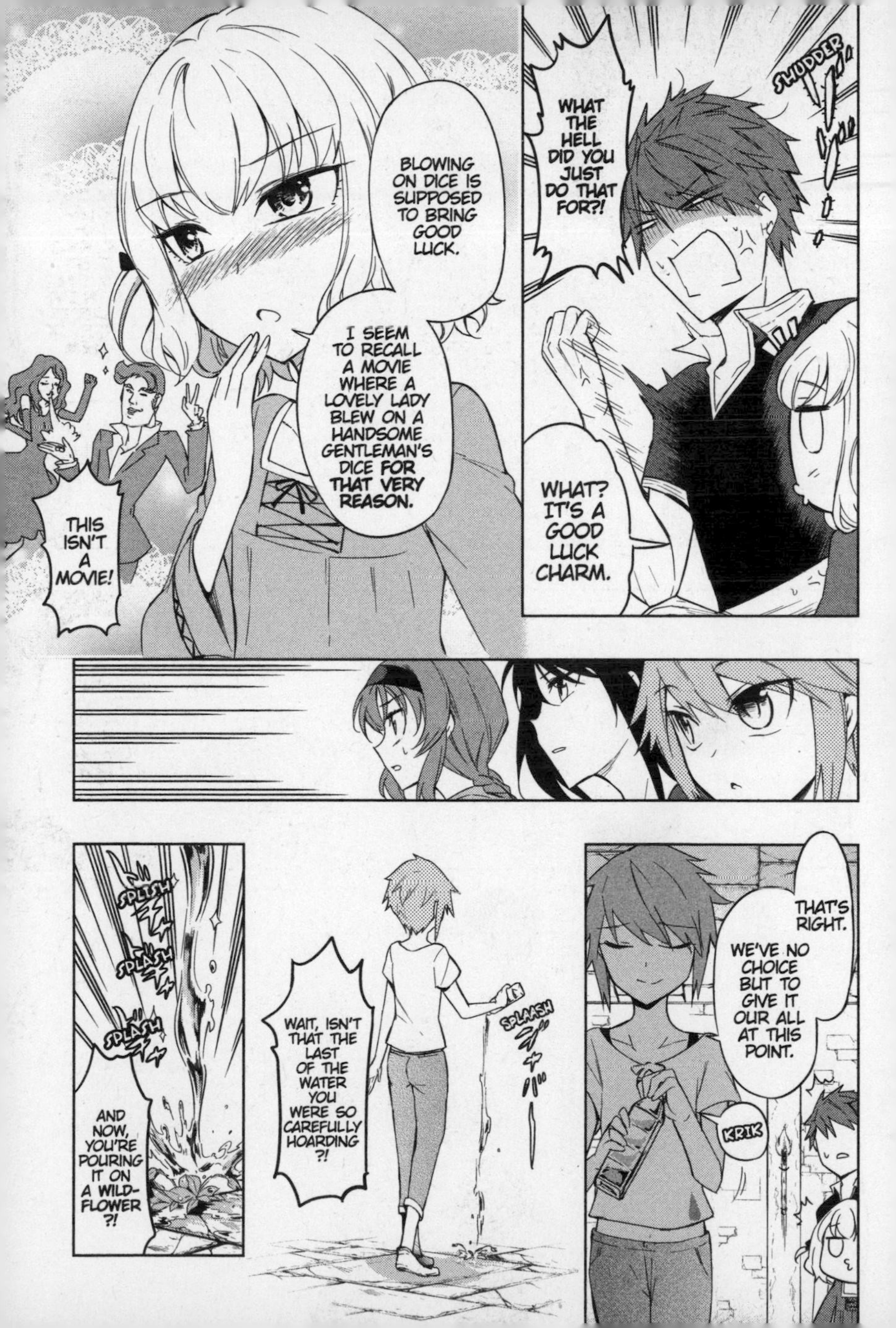
SHUDDER
WHAT THE HELL DID YOU JUST DO THAT FOR?!
WHAT? IT'S A GOOD LUCK CHARM.
BLOWING ON DICE IS SUPPOSED TO BRING GOOD LUCK.
I SEEM TO RECALL A MOVIE WHERE A LOVELY LADY BLEW ON A HANDSOME GENTLEMAN'S DICE FOR THAT VERY REASON.
THIS ISN'T A MOVIE!
THAT'S RIGHT.
WE'VE NO CHOICE BUT TO GIVE IT OUR ALL AT THIS POINT.
KRIK
SPLAASH
WAIT, ISN'T THAT THE LAST OF THE WATER YOU WERE SO CAREFULLY HOARDING?!
SPLISH
SPLASH
SPLASH
AND NOW, YOU'RE POURING IT ON A WILD-FLOWER?!

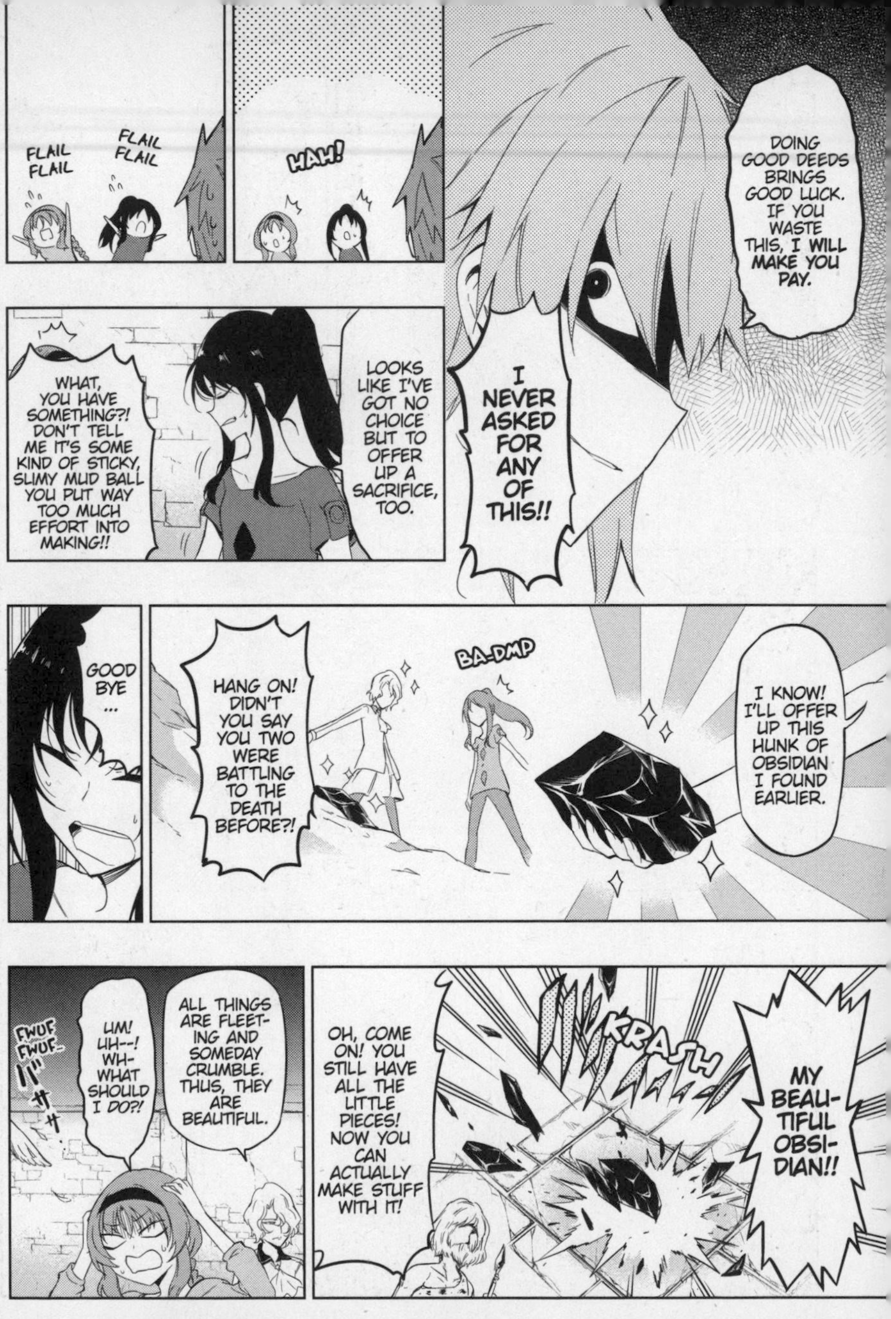

DOING GOOD DEEDS BRINGS GOOD LUCK. IF YOU WASTE THIS, I WILL MAKE YOU PAY.
I NEVER ASKED FOR ANY OF THIS!!
HAH!
FLAIL FLAIL
FLAIL FLAIL
LOOKS LIKE I'VE GOT NO CHOICE BUT TO OFFER UP A SACRIFICE, TOO.
WHAT, YOU HAVE SOMETHING?! DON'T TELL ME IT'S SOME KIND OF STICKY, SLIMY MUD BALL YOU PUT WAY TOO MUCH EFFORT INTO MAKING!!
I KNOW! I'LL OFFER UP THIS HUNK OF OBSIDIAN I FOUND EARLIER.
BA-DMP
HANG ON! DIDN'T YOU SAY YOU TWO WERE BATTLING TO THE DEATH BEFORE?!
GOOD BYE ...
MY BEAUTIFUL OBSIDIAN!!
KRASH
OH, COME ON! YOU STILL HAVE ALL THE LITTLE PIECES! NOW YOU CAN ACTUALLY MAKE STUFF WITH IT!
ALL THINGS ARE FLEETING AND SOMEDAY CRUMBLE. THUS, THEY ARE BEAUTIFUL.
UM! UH--! WH-WHAT SHOULD I DO?!
FWUF FWUF

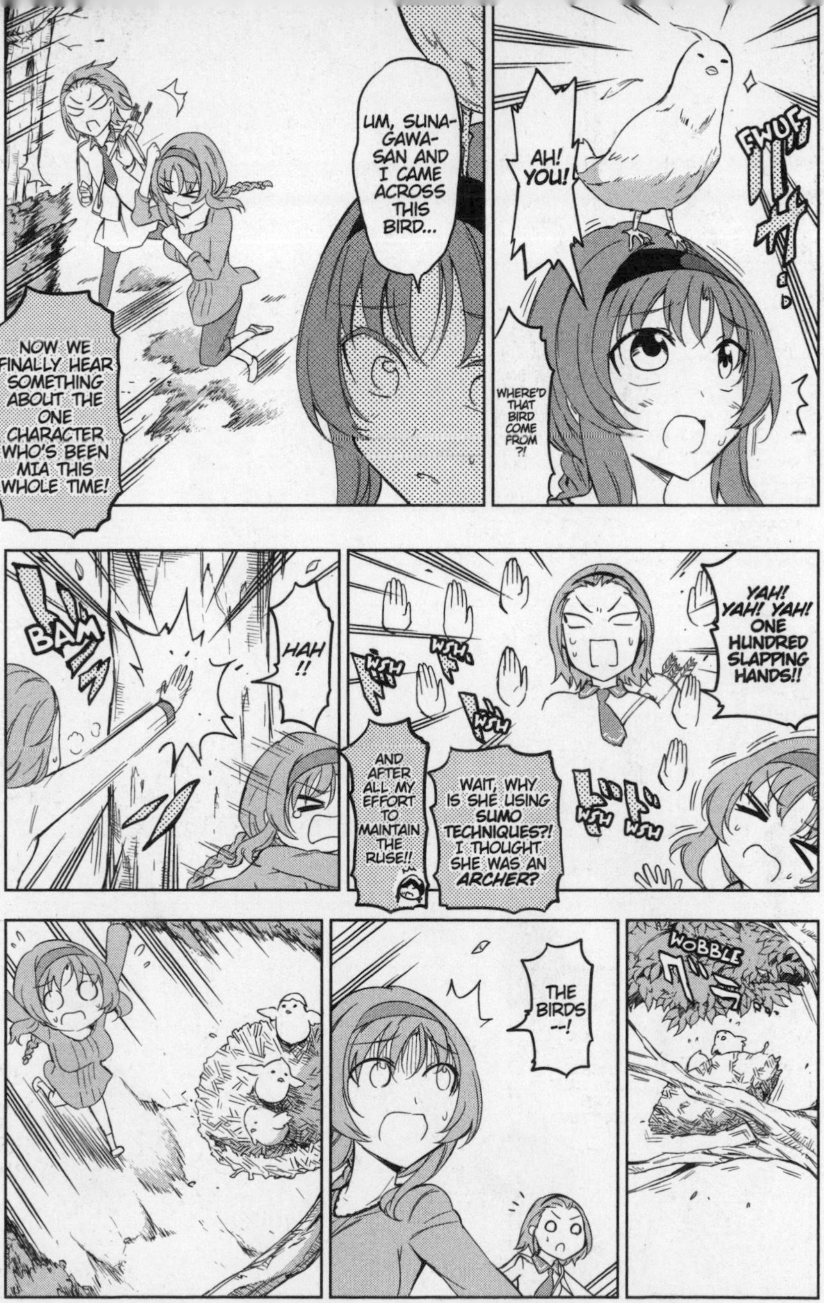
AH! YOU!
FWUF
WHERE'D THAT BIRD COME FROM?!
UM, SUNA-GAWA-SAN AND I CAME ACROSS THIS BIRD...
NOW WE FINALLY HEAR SOMETHING ABOUT THE ONE CHARACTER WHO'S BEEN MIA THIS WHOLE TIME!
YAH! YAH! YAH! ONE HUNDRED SLAPPING HANDS!!
WSH
WSH
WSH
WSH
WSH
WSH
WAIT, WHY IS SHE USING SUMO TECHNIQUES?! I THOUGHT SHE WAS AN ARCHER?
AND AFTER ALL MY EFFORT TO MAINTAIN THE RUSE!!
HAH!!
BAM
WOBBLE
THE BIRDS--!

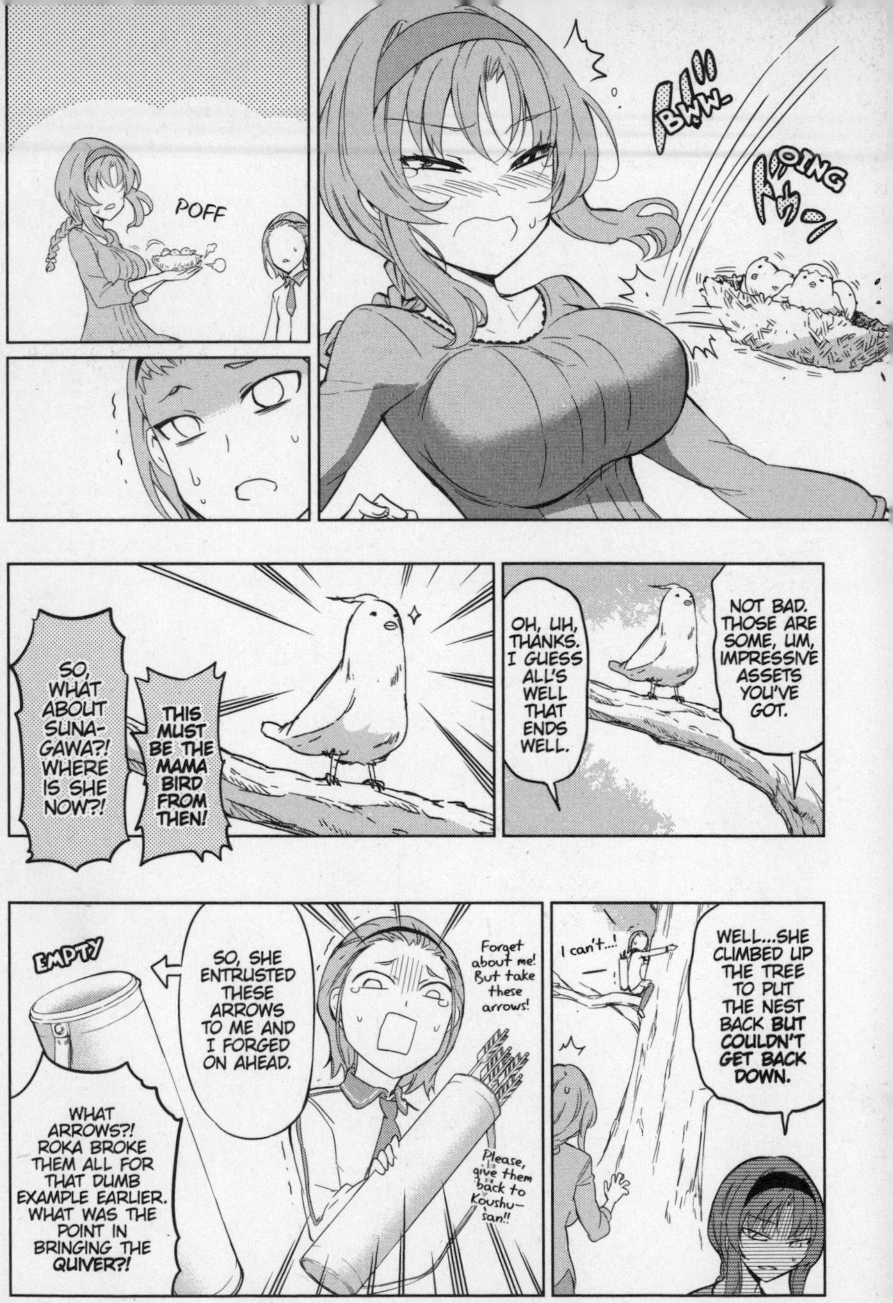
BWW!!
KOING
POFF
NOT BAD. THOSE ARE SOME, UM, IMPRESSIVE ASSETS YOU'VE GOT.
OH, UH, THANKS. I GUESS ALL'S WELL THAT ENDS WELL.
THIS MUST BE THE MAMA BIRD FROM THEN!
SO, WHAT ABOUT SUNA-GAWA?! WHERE IS SHE NOW?!
WELL...SHE CLIMBED UP THE TREE TO PUT THE NEST BACK BUT COULDN'T GET BACK DOWN.
I can't...!
Forget about me! But take these arrows!
SO, SHE ENTRUSTED THESE ARROWS TO ME AND I FORGED ON AHEAD.
EMPTY
Please, give them back to Koushu-san!!
WHAT ARROWS?! ROKA BROKE THEM ALL FOR THAT DUMB EXAMPLE EARLIER. WHAT WAS THE POINT IN BRINGING THE QUIVER?!

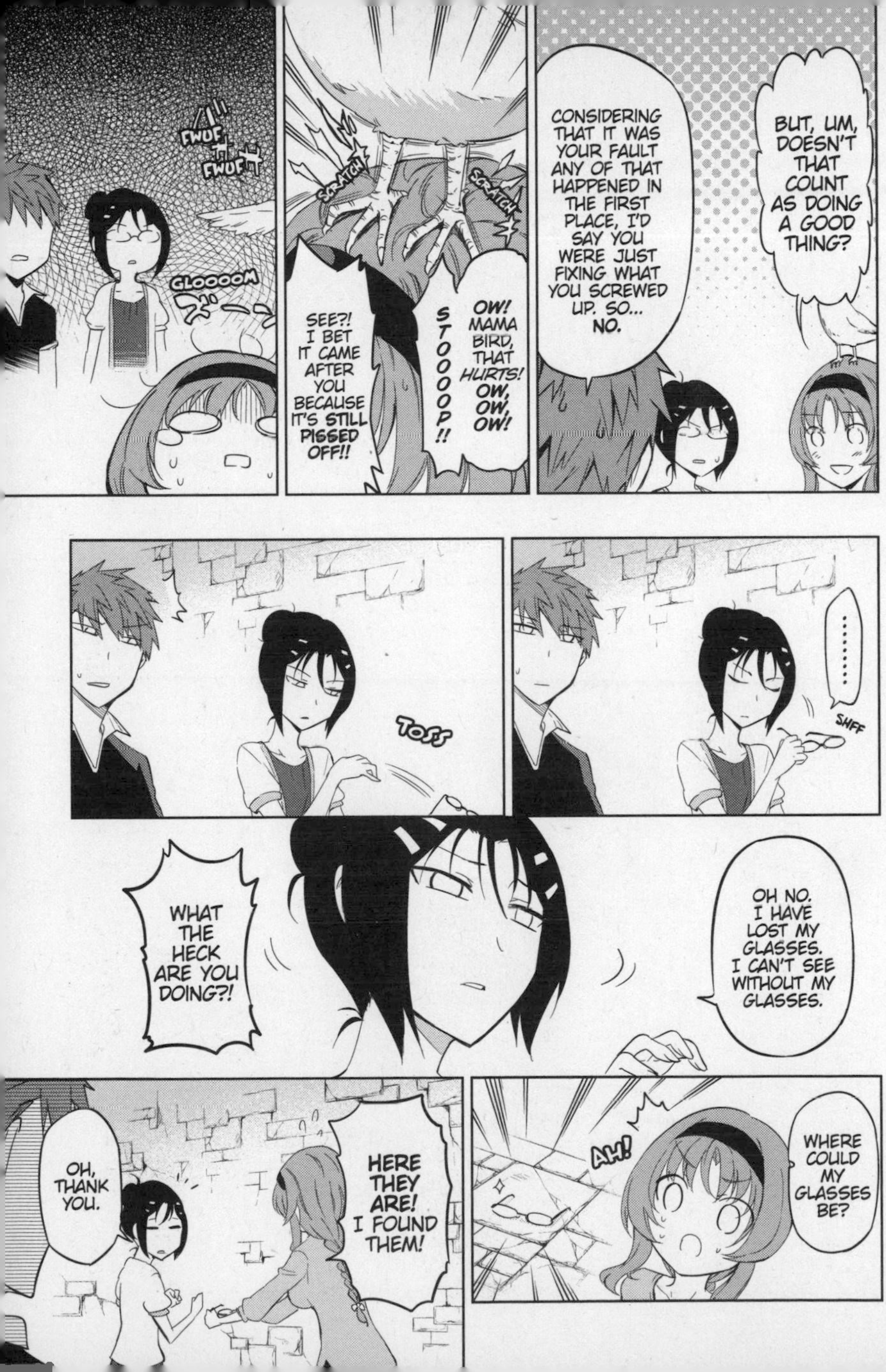
BUT, UM, DOESN'T THAT COUNT AS DOING A GOOD THING?
CONSIDERING THAT IT WAS YOUR FAULT ANY OF THAT HAPPENED IN THE FIRST PLACE, I'D SAY YOU WERE JUST FIXING WHAT YOU SCREWED UP. SO... NO.
SCRATCH
SCRATCH
OW! MAMA BIRD, THAT HURTS! OW, OW, OW!
STOOOOOP!!
SEE?! I BET IT CAME AFTER YOU BECAUSE IT'S STILL PISSED OFF!!
FWUF FWUF
GLOOOOM
......
SHFF
TOSS
OH NO. I HAVE LOST MY GLASSES. I CAN'T SEE WITHOUT MY GLASSES.
WHAT THE HECK ARE YOU DOING?!
WHERE COULD MY GLASSES BE?
AH!
HERE THEY ARE! I FOUND THEM!
OH, THANK YOU.

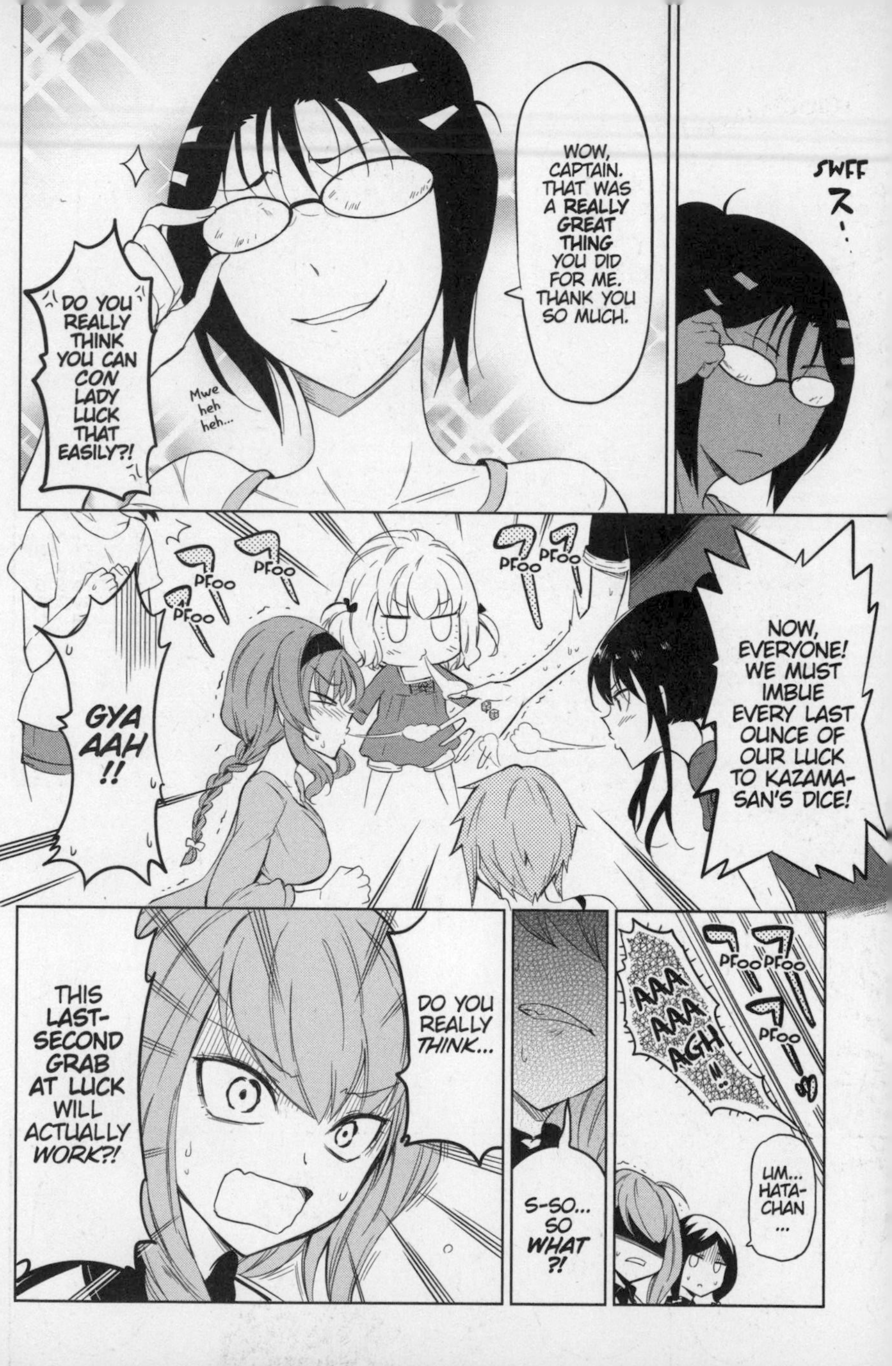

SWFF
ス
WOW, CAPTAIN. THAT WAS A REALLY GREAT THING YOU DID FOR ME. THANK YOU SO MUCH.
DO YOU REALLY THINK YOU CAN CON LADY LUCK THAT EASILY?!
Mwe heh heh...
NOW, EVERYONE! WE MUST IMBUE EVERY LAST OUNCE OF OUR LUCK TO KAZAMA-SAN'S DICE!
PFOO PFOO
PFOO
PFOO
GYA AAH!!
PFOO PFOO
AAAAAAAGH!!
PFOO
UM... HATA-CHAN...
DO YOU REALLY THINK...
S-SO... SO WHAT?!
THIS LAST-SECOND GRAB AT LUCK WILL ACTUALLY WORK?!

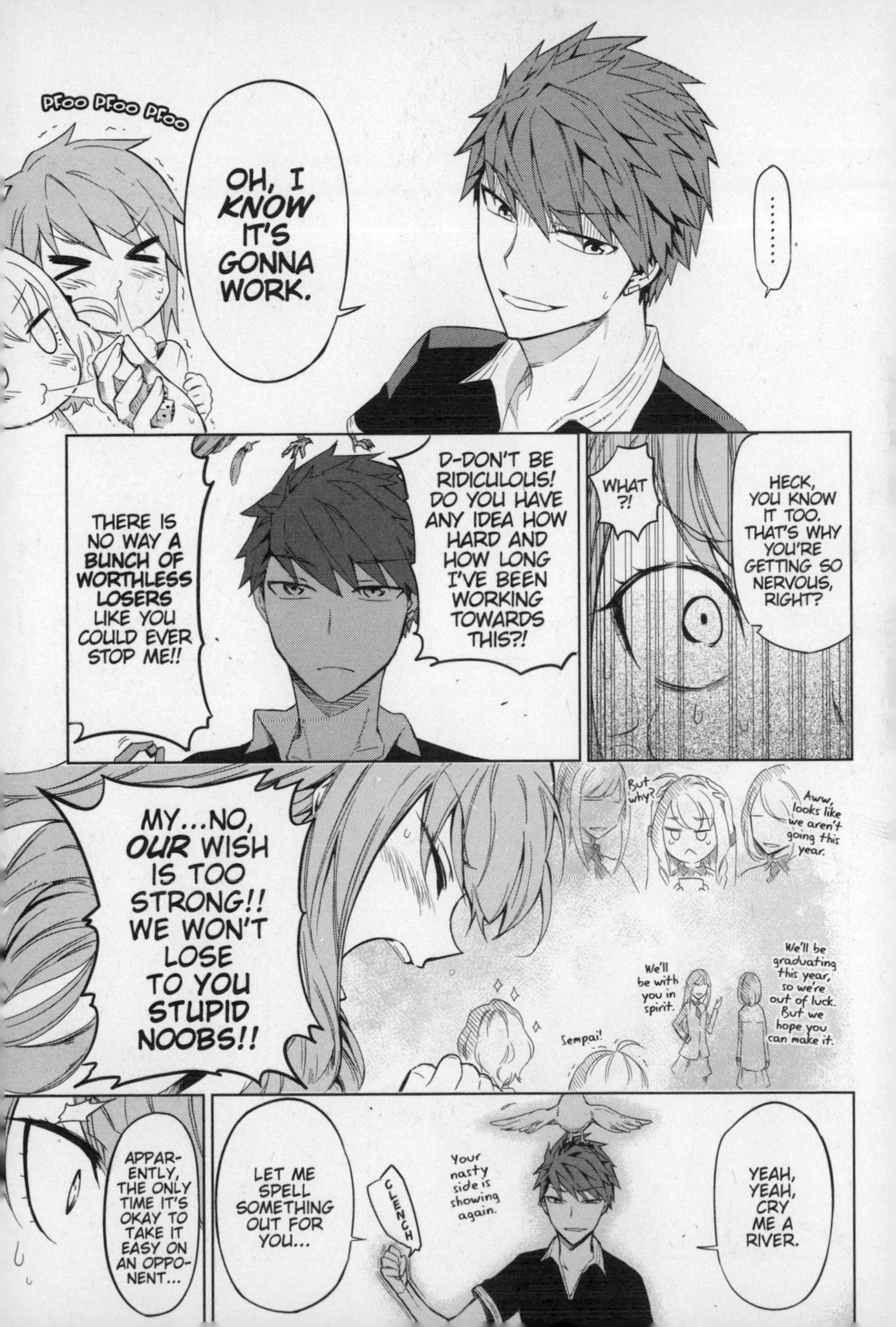
……
OH, I KNOW IT'S GONNA WORK.
PFOO PFOO PFOO
HECK, YOU KNOW IT TOO. THAT'S WHY YOU'RE GETTING SO NERVOUS, RIGHT?
WHAT?!
D-DON'T BE RIDICULOUS! DO YOU HAVE ANY IDEA HOW HARD AND HOW LONG I'VE BEEN WORKING TOWARDS THIS?!
THERE IS NO WAY A BUNCH OF WORTHLESS LOSERS LIKE YOU COULD EVER STOP ME!!
Aww, looks like we aren't going this year.
But why?
We'll be graduating this year, so we're out of luck. But we hope you can make it.
We'll be with you in spirit.
Sempai!
MY…NO, OUR WISH IS TOO STRONG!! WE WON'T LOSE TO YOU STUPID NOOBS!!
YEAH, YEAH, CRY ME A RIVER.
Your nasty side is showing again.
CLENCH
LET ME SPELL SOMETHING OUT FOR YOU…
APPARENTLY, THE ONLY TIME IT'S OKAY TO TAKE IT EASY ON AN OPPONENT…

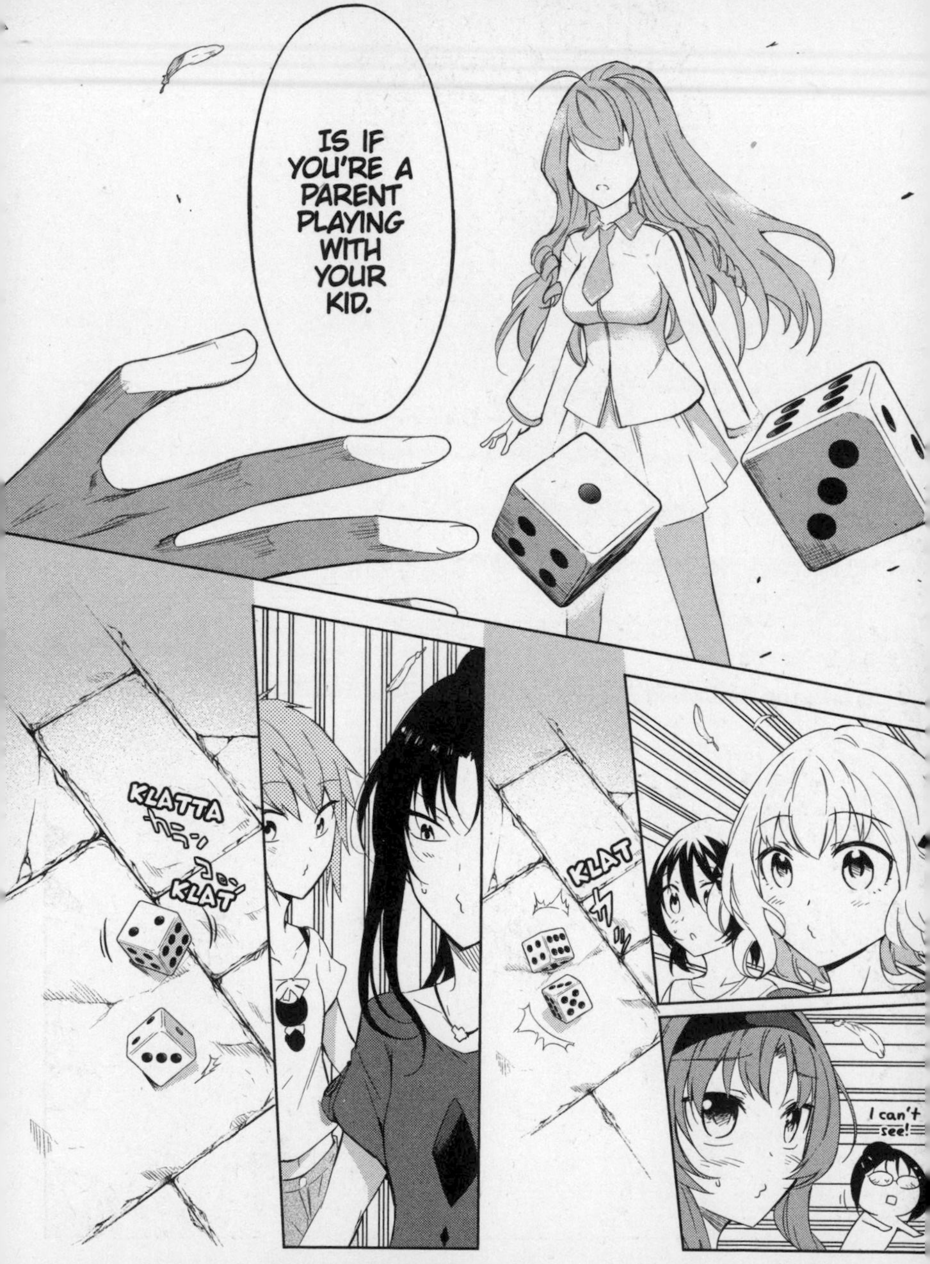
IS IF YOU'RE A PARENT PLAYING WITH YOUR KID.
KLAT
I can't see!
KLATTA
KLAT

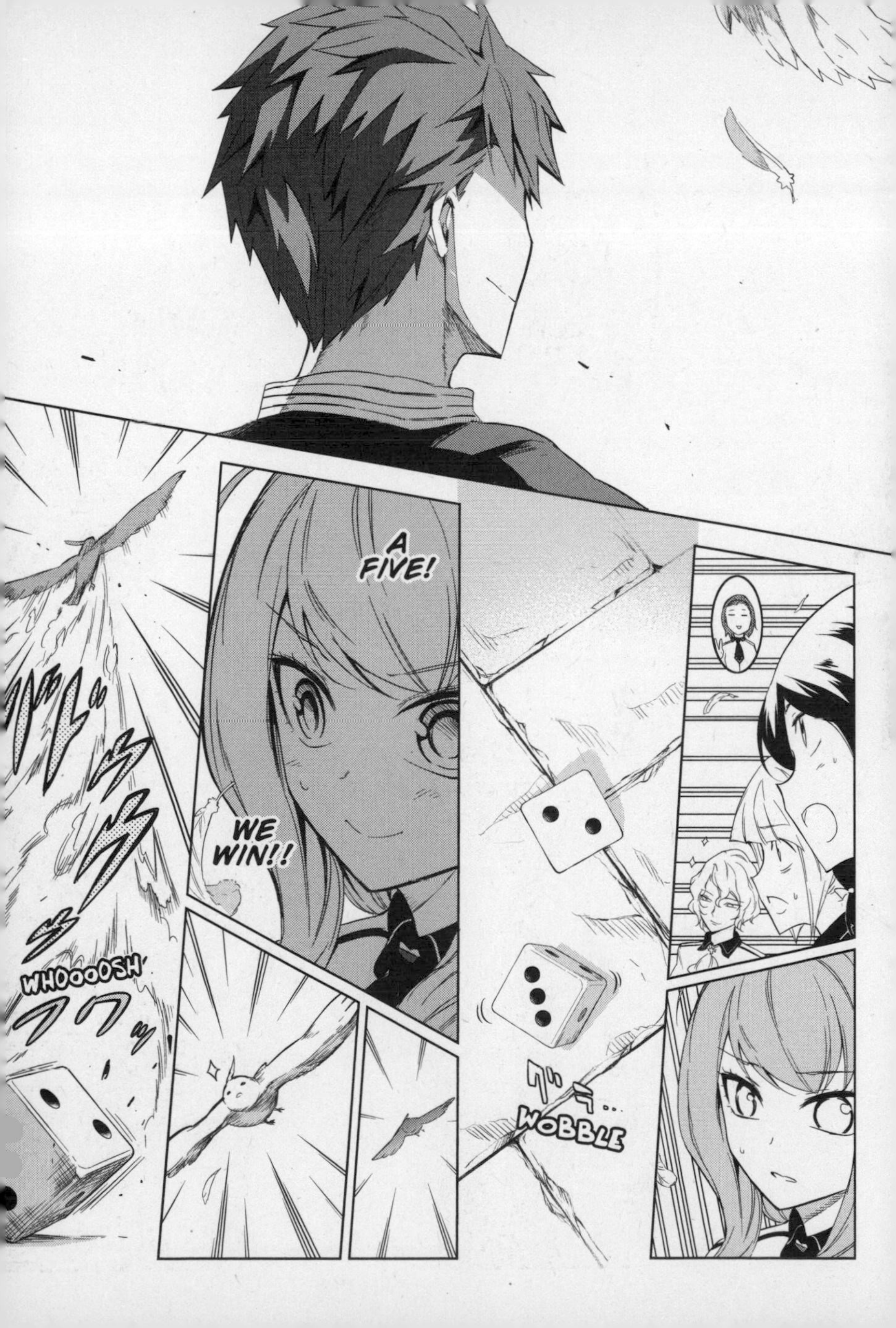

WOBBLE
A FIVE!
WE WIN!!
WHOOOOSH

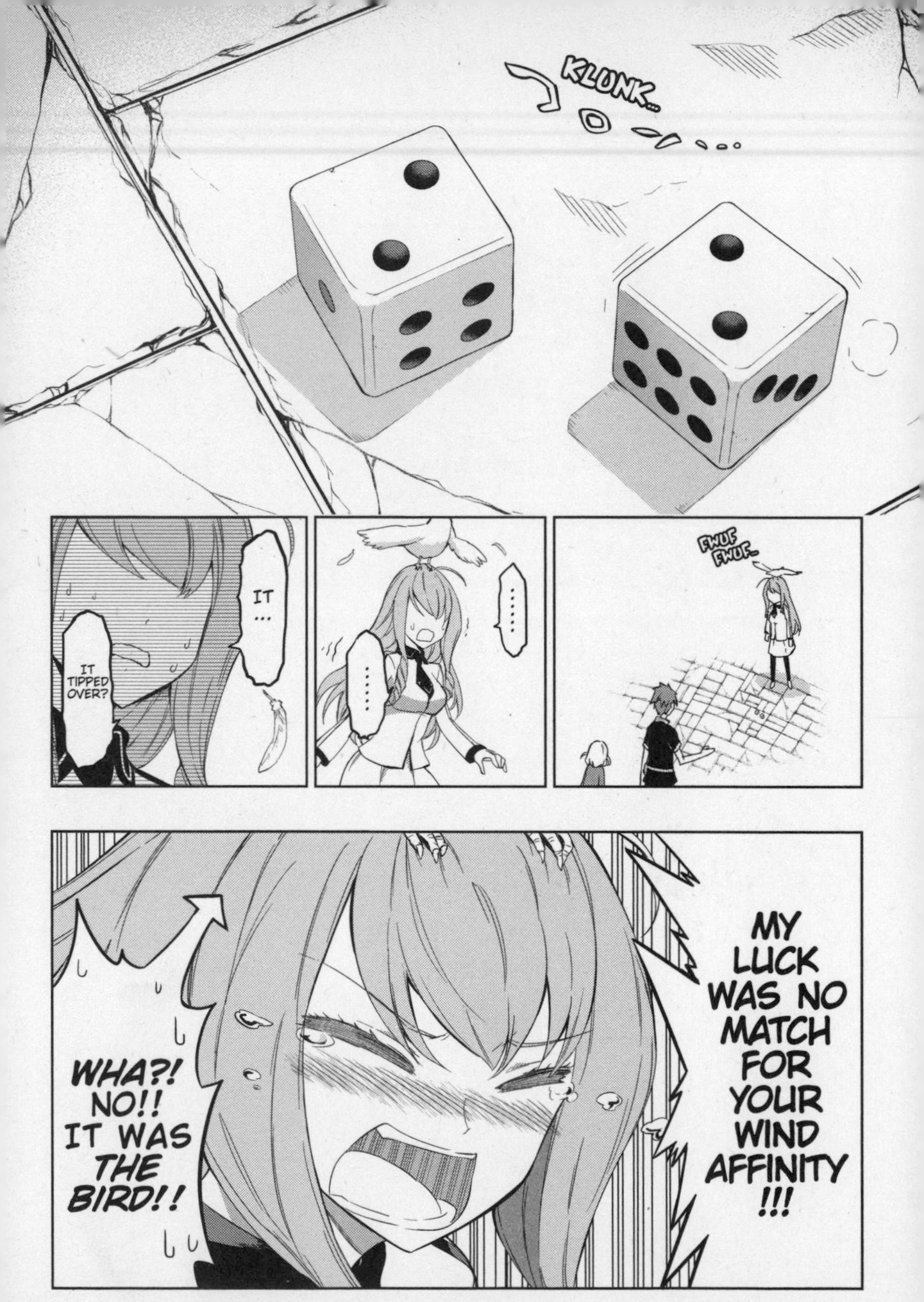
KLUNK...
FWUF FWUF..
......
......
IT ...
IT TIPPED OVER?
MY LUCK WAS NO MATCH FOR YOUR WIND AFFINITY !!!
WHA?! NO!! IT WAS THE BIRD!!

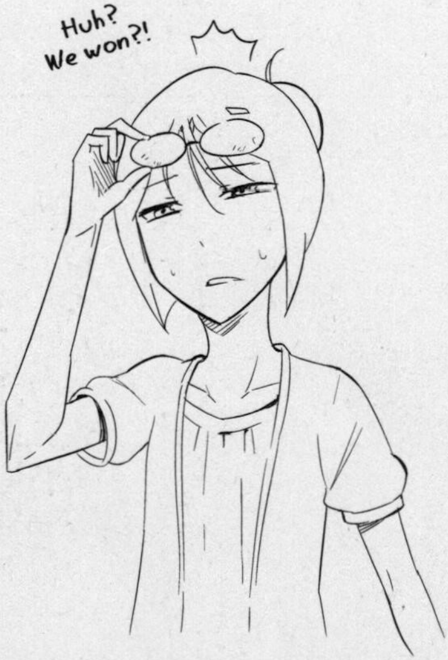
Huh?
We won?!

D-FRAGMENTS

ディーふらぐ!

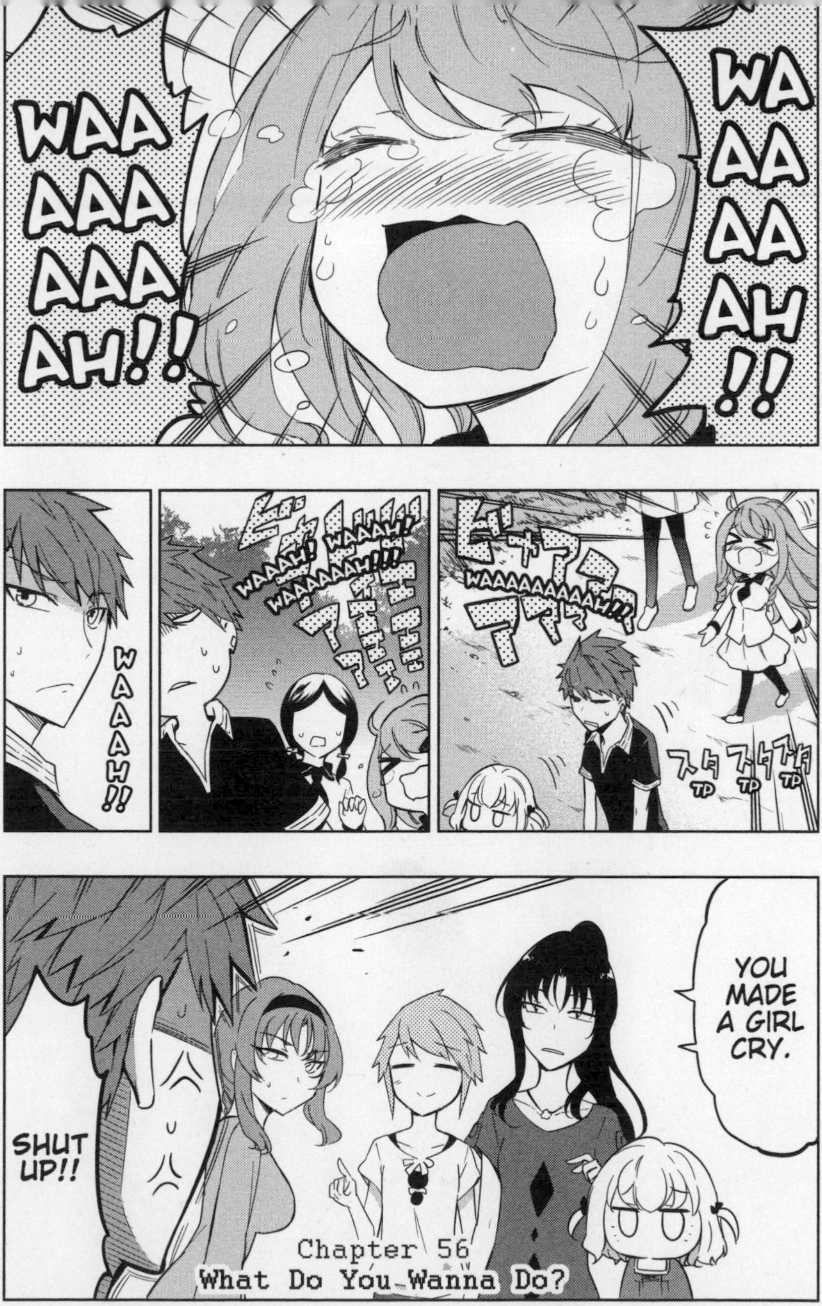
WAAAAAAAH!!
WAAAAAAAAAAH!!
WAAAAAAAAAAH!!!
TP TP TP
WAAAH! WAAAH!
WAAAAAAH!!!
WAAAAH!!
YOU MADE A GIRL CRY.
SHUT UP!!
Chapter 56
What Do You Wanna Do?

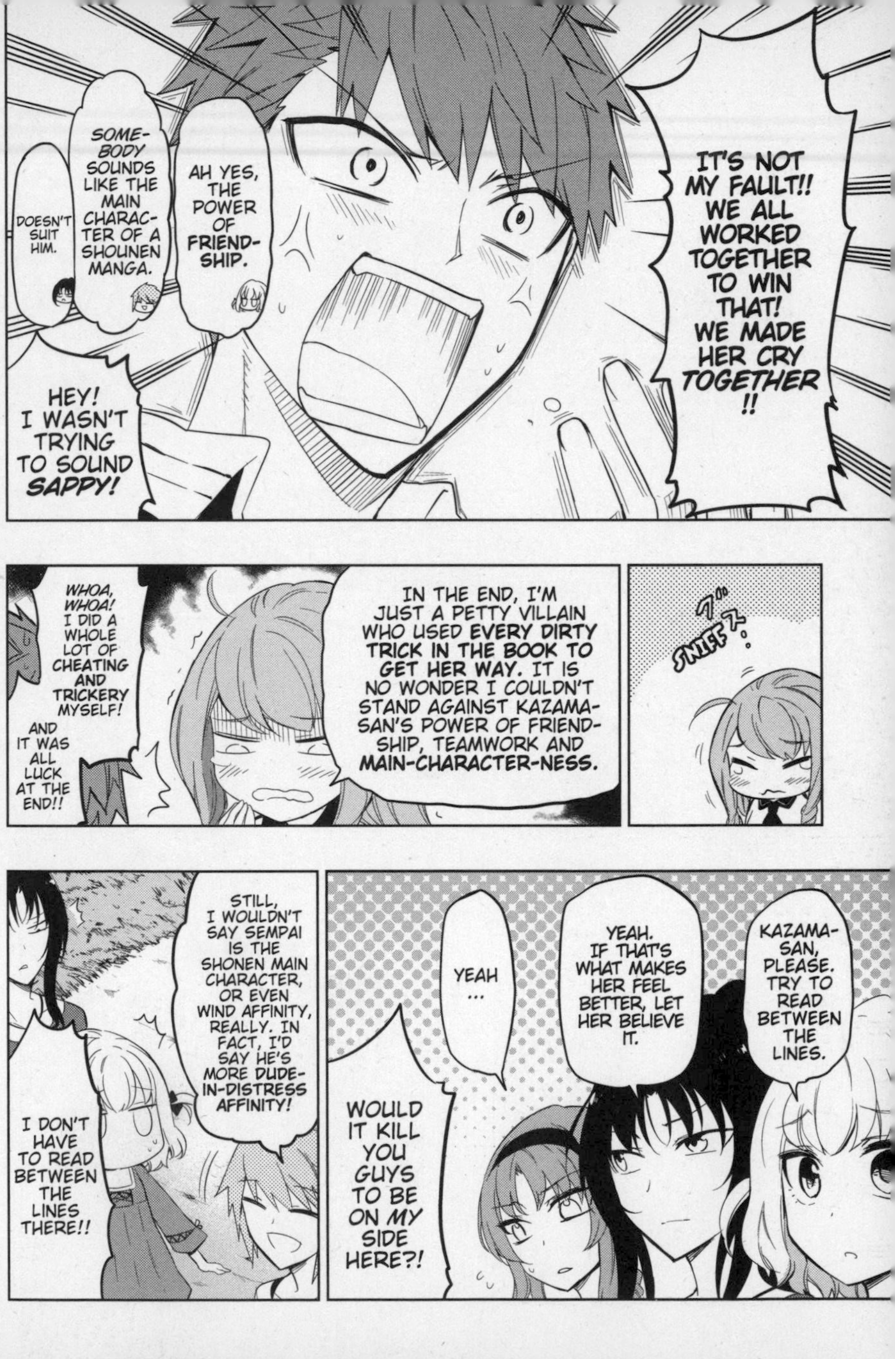
IT'S NOT MY FAULT!! WE ALL WORKED TOGETHER TO WIN THAT! WE MADE HER CRY TOGETHER!!
AH YES, THE POWER OF FRIENDSHIP.
SOMEBODY SOUNDS LIKE THE MAIN CHARACTER OF A SHOUNEN MANGA.
DOESN'T SUIT HIM.
HEY! I WASN'T TRYING TO SOUND SAPPY!
SNIFF
IN THE END, I'M JUST A PETTY VILLAIN WHO USED EVERY DIRTY TRICK IN THE BOOK TO GET HER WAY. IT IS NO WONDER I COULDN'T STAND AGAINST KAZAMA-SAN'S POWER OF FRIENDSHIP, TEAMWORK AND MAIN-CHARACTER-NESS.
WHOA, WHOA! I DID A WHOLE LOT OF CHEATING AND TRICKERY MYSELF!
AND IT WAS ALL LUCK AT THE END!!
KAZAMA-SAN, PLEASE. TRY TO READ BETWEEN THE LINES.
YEAH. IF THAT'S WHAT MAKES HER FEEL BETTER, LET HER BELIEVE IT.
YEAH ...
WOULD IT KILL YOU GUYS TO BE ON MY SIDE HERE?!
STILL, I WOULDN'T SAY SEMPAI IS THE SHONEN MAIN CHARACTER, OR EVEN WIND AFFINITY, REALLY. IN FACT, I'D SAY HE'S MORE DUDE-IN-DISTRESS AFFINITY!
I DON'T HAVE TO READ BETWEEN THE LINES THERE!!

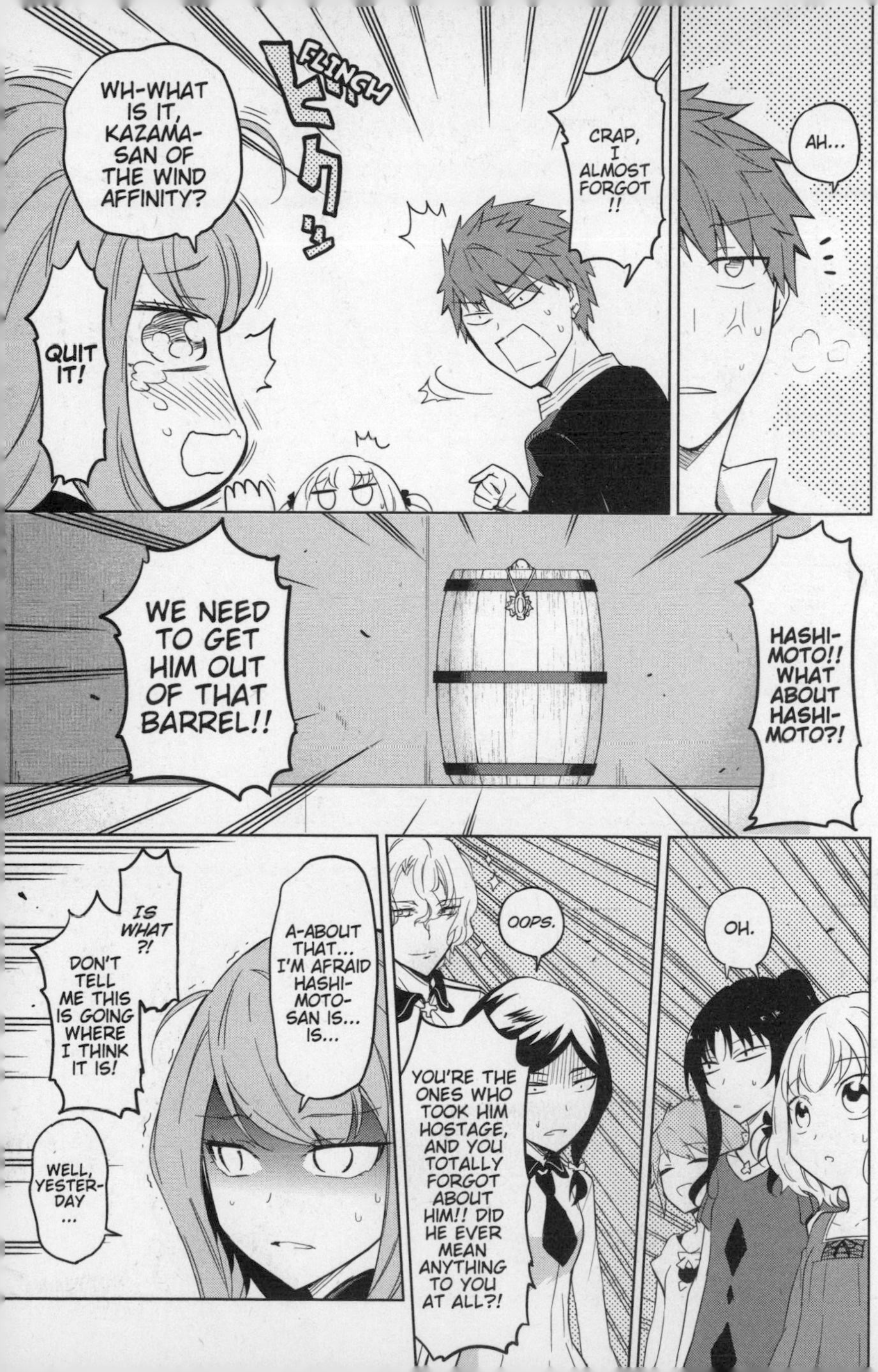
AH...
CRAP, I ALMOST FORGOT!!
FLINCH
WH-WHAT IS IT, KAZAMA-SAN OF THE WIND AFFINITY?
QUIT IT!
HASHI-MOTO!! WHAT ABOUT HASHI-MOTO?!
WE NEED TO GET HIM OUT OF THAT BARREL!!
OH.
OOPS.
YOU'RE THE ONES WHO TOOK HIM HOSTAGE, AND YOU TOTALLY FORGOT ABOUT HIM!! DID HE EVER MEAN ANYTHING TO YOU AT ALL?!
A-ABOUT THAT... I'M AFRAID HASHI-MOTO-SAN IS... IS...
IS WHAT?! DON'T TELL ME THIS IS GOING WHERE I THINK IT IS!
WELL, YESTER-DAY...

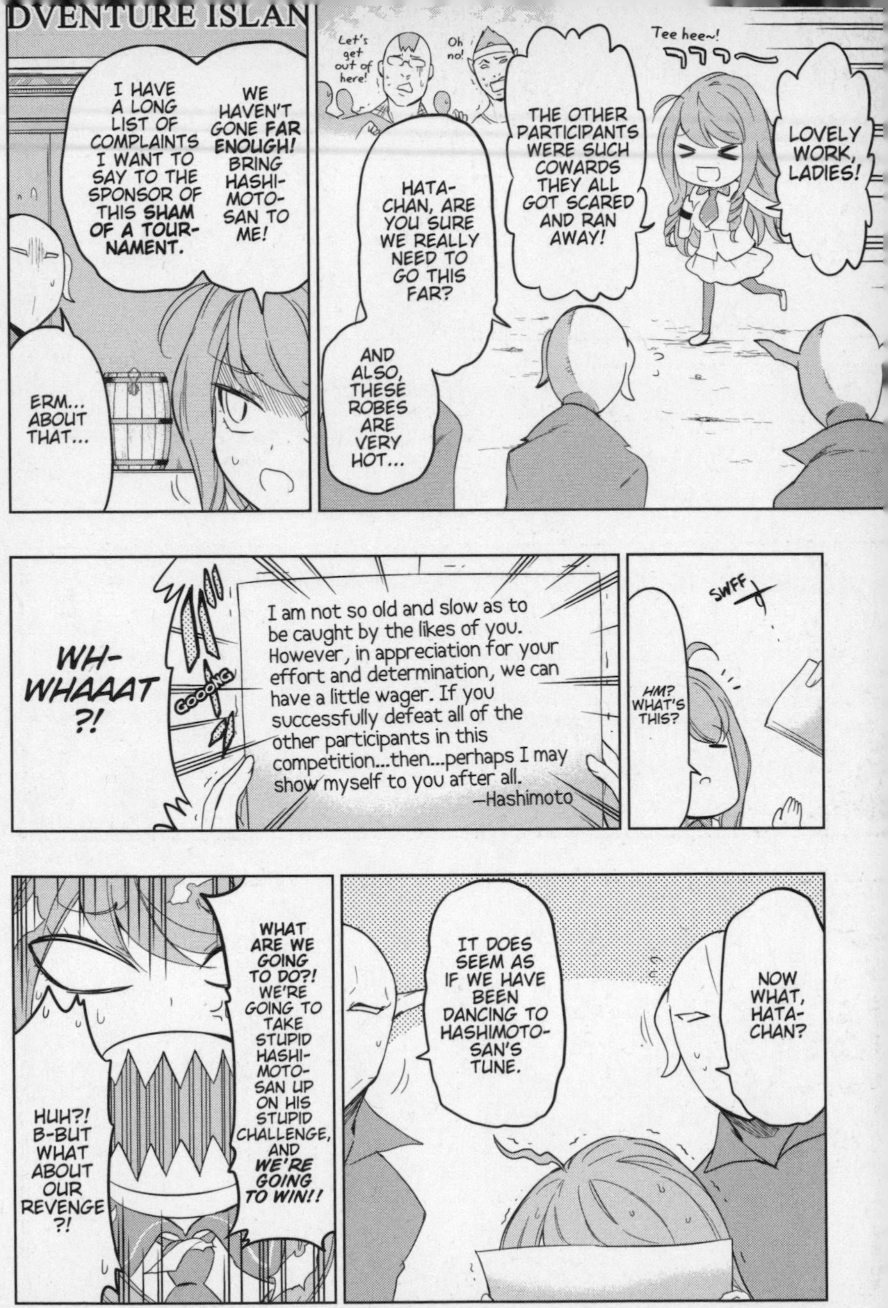
Tee hee~!
LOVELY WORK, LADIES!
THE OTHER PARTICIPANTS WERE SUCH COWARDS THEY ALL GOT SCARED AND RAN AWAY!
Oh no!
Let's get out of here!
HATA-CHAN, ARE YOU SURE WE REALLY NEED TO GO THIS FAR?
AND ALSO, THESE ROBES ARE VERY HOT...
DVENTURE ISLAN
WE HAVEN'T GONE FAR ENOUGH! BRING HASHIMOTO-SAN TO ME!
I HAVE A LONG LIST OF COMPLAINTS I WANT TO SAY TO THE SPONSOR OF THIS SHAM OF A TOURNAMENT.
ERM... ABOUT THAT...
SWFF
HM? WHAT'S THIS?
I am not so old and slow as to be caught by the likes of you. However, in appreciation for your effort and determination, we can have a little wager. If you successfully defeat all of the other participants in this competition...then...perhaps I may show myself to you after all.
—Hashimoto
GOOONG
WH-WHAAAT?!
NOW WHAT, HATA-CHAN?
IT DOES SEEM AS IF WE HAVE BEEN DANCING TO HASHIMOTO-SAN'S TUNE.
WHAT ARE WE GOING TO DO?! WE'RE GOING TO TAKE STUPID HASHIMOTO-SAN UP ON HIS STUPID CHALLENGE, AND WE'RE GOING TO WIN!!
HUH?! B-BUT WHAT ABOUT OUR REVENGE?!

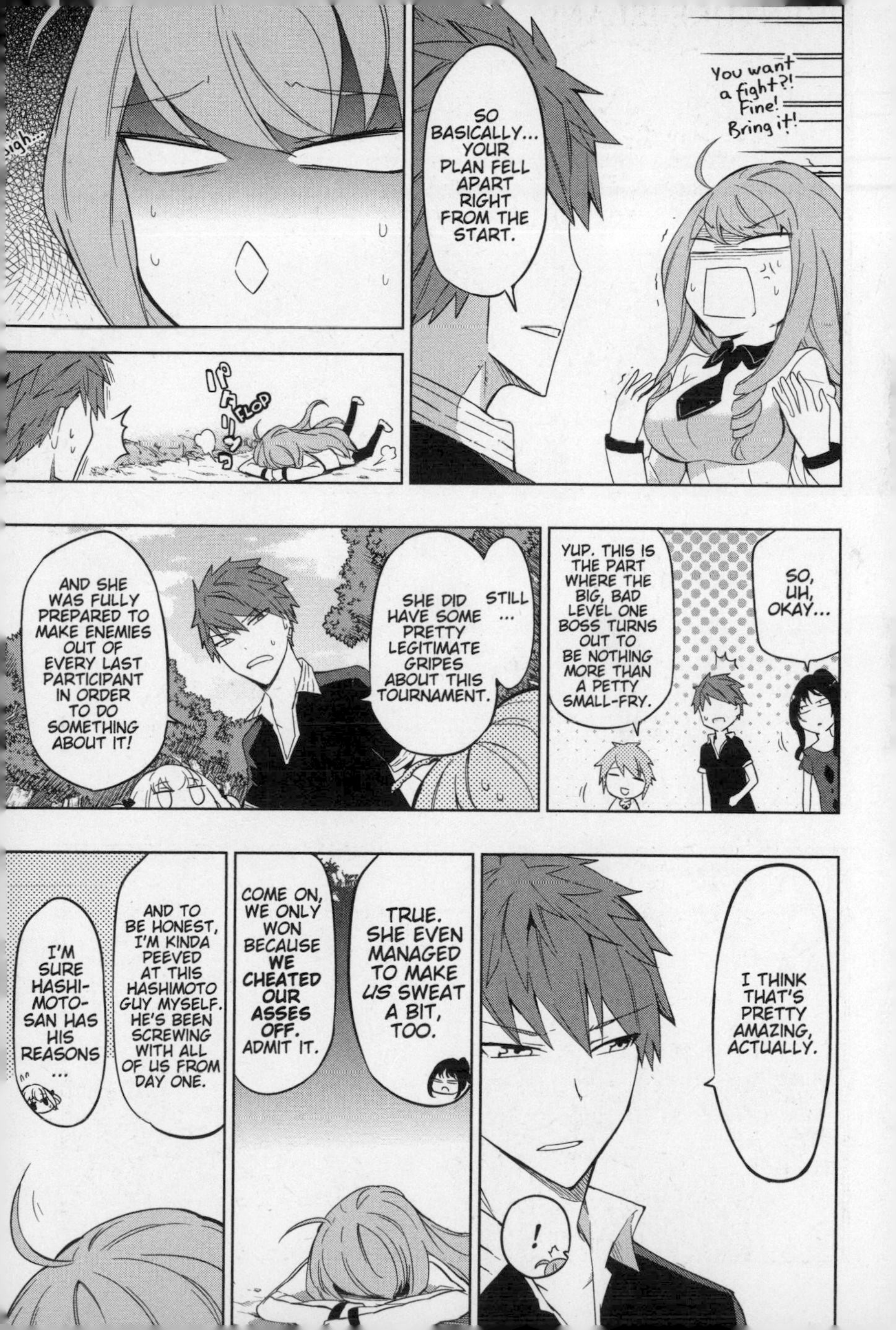
You want a fight?! Fine! Bring it!
SO BASICALLY... YOUR PLAN FELL APART RIGHT FROM THE START.
sigh...
FLOP
SO, UH, OKAY...
YUP. THIS IS THE PART WHERE THE BIG, BAD LEVEL ONE BOSS TURNS OUT TO BE NOTHING MORE THAN A PETTY SMALL-FRY.
STILL...
SHE DID HAVE SOME PRETTY LEGITIMATE GRIPES ABOUT THIS TOURNAMENT.
AND SHE WAS FULLY PREPARED TO MAKE ENEMIES OUT OF EVERY LAST PARTICIPANT IN ORDER TO DO SOMETHING ABOUT IT!
I THINK THAT'S PRETTY AMAZING, ACTUALLY.
TRUE. SHE EVEN MANAGED TO MAKE US SWEAT A BIT, TOO.
COME ON, WE ONLY WON BECAUSE WE CHEATED OUR ASSES OFF. ADMIT IT.
AND TO BE HONEST, I'M KINDA PEEVED AT THIS HASHIMOTO GUY MYSELF. HE'S BEEN SCREWING WITH ALL OF US FROM DAY ONE.
I'M SURE HASHIMOTO-SAN HAS HIS REASONS...

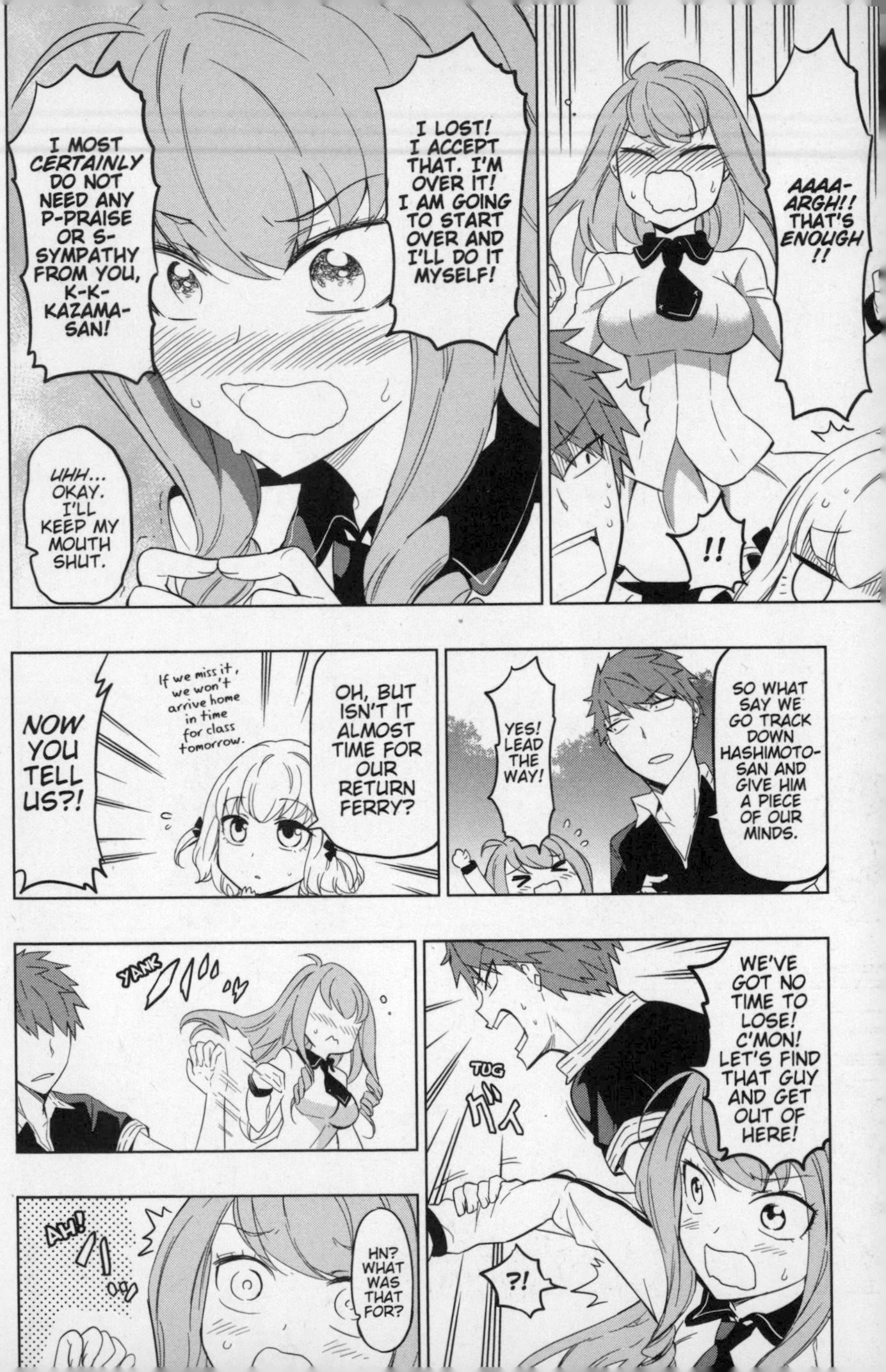
AAAA-ARGH!! THAT'S ENOUGH!!
!!
I LOST! I ACCEPT THAT. I'M OVER IT! I AM GOING TO START OVER AND I'LL DO IT MYSELF!
I MOST CERTAINLY DO NOT NEED ANY P-PRAISE OR S-SYMPATHY FROM YOU, K-K-KAZAMA-SAN!
UHH... OKAY. I'LL KEEP MY MOUTH SHUT.
SO WHAT SAY WE GO TRACK DOWN HASHIMOTO-SAN AND GIVE HIM A PIECE OF OUR MINDS.
YES! LEAD THE WAY!
OH, BUT ISN'T IT ALMOST TIME FOR OUR RETURN FERRY?
If we miss it, we won't arrive home in time for class tomorrow.
NOW YOU TELL US?!
WE'VE GOT NO TIME TO LOSE! C'MON! LET'S FIND THAT GUY AND GET OUT OF HERE!
TUG
?!
YANK
HN? WHAT WAS THAT FOR?
AH!

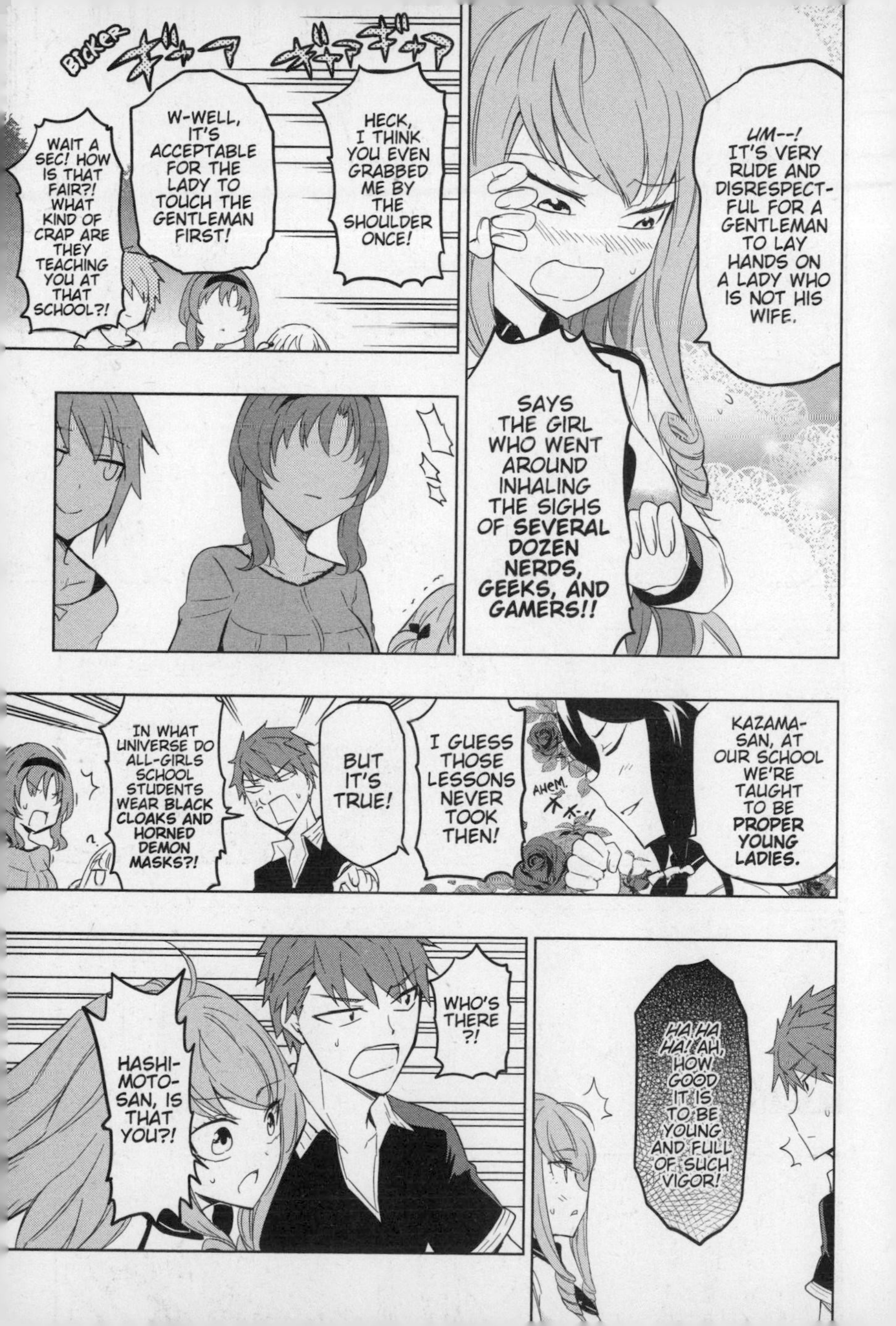
UM--! IT'S VERY RUDE AND DISRESPECTFUL FOR A GENTLEMAN TO LAY HANDS ON A LADY WHO IS NOT HIS WIFE.
SAYS THE GIRL WHO WENT AROUND INHALING THE SIGHS OF SEVERAL DOZEN NERDS, GEEKS, AND GAMERS!!
BICKER
HECK, I THINK YOU EVEN GRABBED ME BY THE SHOULDER ONCE!
W-WELL, IT'S ACCEPTABLE FOR THE LADY TO TOUCH THE GENTLEMAN FIRST!
WAIT A SEC! HOW IS THAT FAIR?! WHAT KIND OF CRAP ARE THEY TEACHING YOU AT THAT SCHOOL?!
KAZAMA-SAN, AT OUR SCHOOL WE'RE TAUGHT TO BE PROPER YOUNG LADIES.
AHEM.
I GUESS THOSE LESSONS NEVER TOOK THEN!
BUT IT'S TRUE!
IN WHAT UNIVERSE DO ALL-GIRLS SCHOOL STUDENTS WEAR BLACK CLOAKS AND HORNED DEMON MASKS?!
HA HA HA! AH, HOW GOOD IT IS TO BE YOUNG AND FULL OF SUCH VIGOR!
WHO'S THERE?!
HASHIMOTO-SAN, IS THAT YOU?!

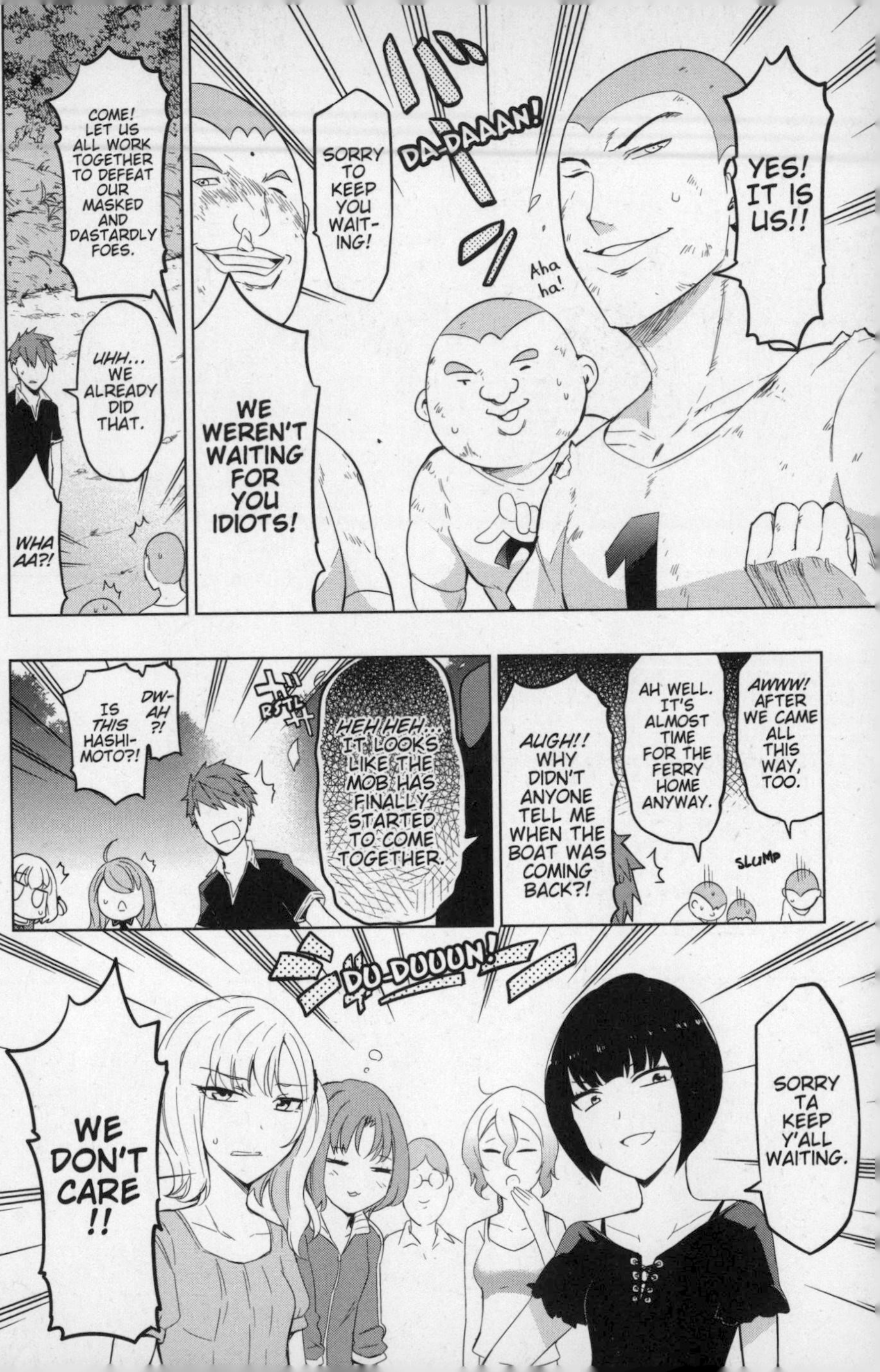
YES! IT IS US!!
DA-DAAAN!
Aha ha!
SORRY TO KEEP YOU WAIT-ING!
WE WEREN'T WAITING FOR YOU IDIOTS!
COME! LET US ALL WORK TOGETHER TO DEFEAT OUR MASKED AND DASTARDLY FOES.
UHH... WE ALREADY DID THAT.
WHAAA?!
AWWW! AFTER WE CAME ALL THIS WAY, TOO.
AH WELL. IT'S ALMOST TIME FOR THE FERRY HOME ANYWAY.
AUGH!! WHY DIDN'T ANYONE TELL ME WHEN THE BOAT WAS COMING BACK?!
SLUMP
HEH HEH... IT LOOKS LIKE THE MOB HAS FINALLY STARTED TO COME TOGETHER.
RSTL
DWAH?!
IS THIS HASHI-MOTO?!
DU-DUUUN!
SORRY TA KEEP Y'ALL WAITING.
WE DON'T CARE!!

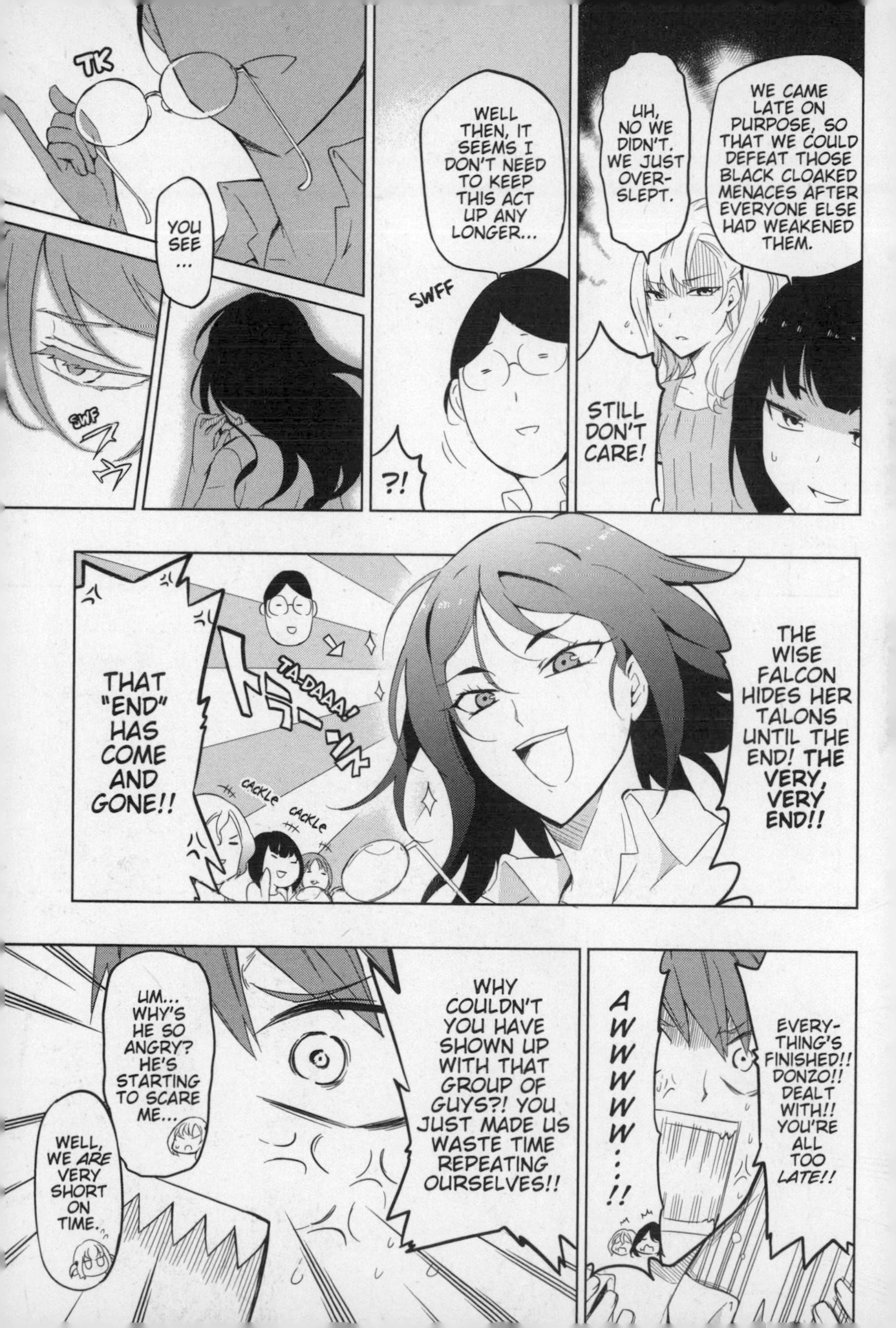
WE CAME LATE ON PURPOSE, SO THAT WE COULD DEFEAT THOSE BLACK CLOAKED MENACES AFTER EVERYONE ELSE HAD WEAKENED THEM.
UH, NO WE DIDN'T. WE JUST OVER-SLEPT.
STILL DON'T CARE!
WELL THEN, IT SEEMS I DON'T NEED TO KEEP THIS ACT UP ANY LONGER...
SWFF
?!
TK
YOU SEE ...
SWF
THE WISE FALCON HIDES HER TALONS UNTIL THE END! THE VERY, VERY END!!
TA-DAAA!
THAT "END" HAS COME AND GONE!!
CACKLE
CACKLE
EVERY-THING'S FINISHED!! DONZO!! DEALT WITH!! YOU'RE ALL TOO LATE!!
AWWWWWW...!!
WHY COULDN'T YOU HAVE SHOWN UP WITH THAT GROUP OF GUYS?! YOU JUST MADE US WASTE TIME REPEATING OURSELVES!!
UM... WHY'S HE SO ANGRY? HE'S STARTING TO SCARE ME...
WELL, WE *ARE* VERY SHORT ON TIME.

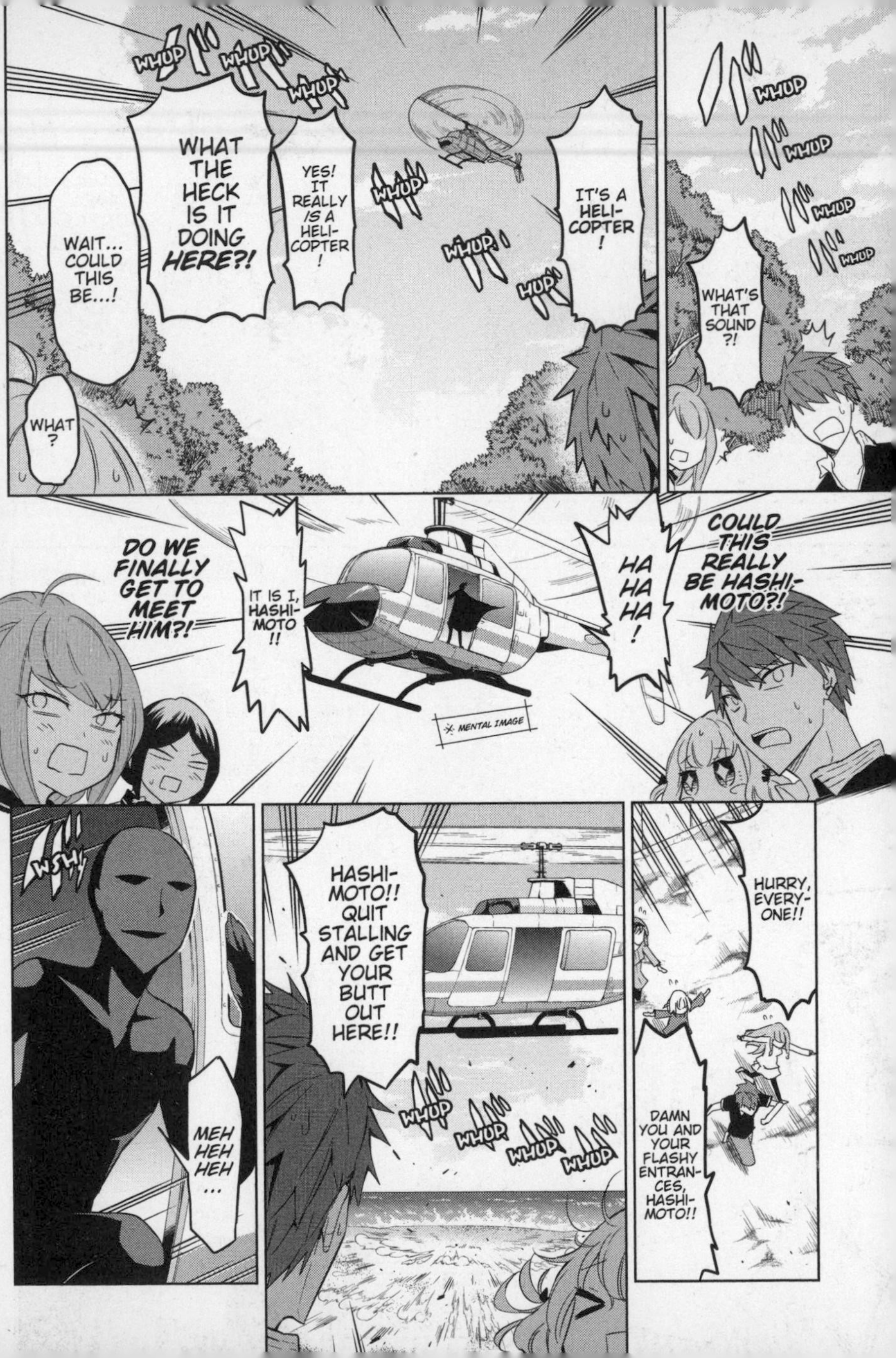
WHUP
WHUP
WHUP
WHUP
WHAT'S THAT SOUND?!
IT'S A HELI-COPTER!
WHUP WHUP WHUP
WHUP
HUP
YES! IT REALLY IS A HELI-COPTER!
WHAT THE HECK IS IT DOING HERE?!
WAIT... COULD THIS BE...!
WHAT?
COULD THIS REALLY BE HASHI-MOTO?!
HA HA HA!
IT IS I, HASHI-MOTO!!
DO WE FINALLY GET TO MEET HIM?!
※ MENTAL IMAGE
HURRY, EVERY-ONE!!
DAMN YOU AND YOUR FLASHY ENTRAN-CES, HASHI-MOTO!!
HASHI-MOTO!! QUIT STALLING AND GET YOUR BUTT OUT HERE!!
WHUP
WHUP
WHUP
WHUP
WSH
MEH HEH HEH ...

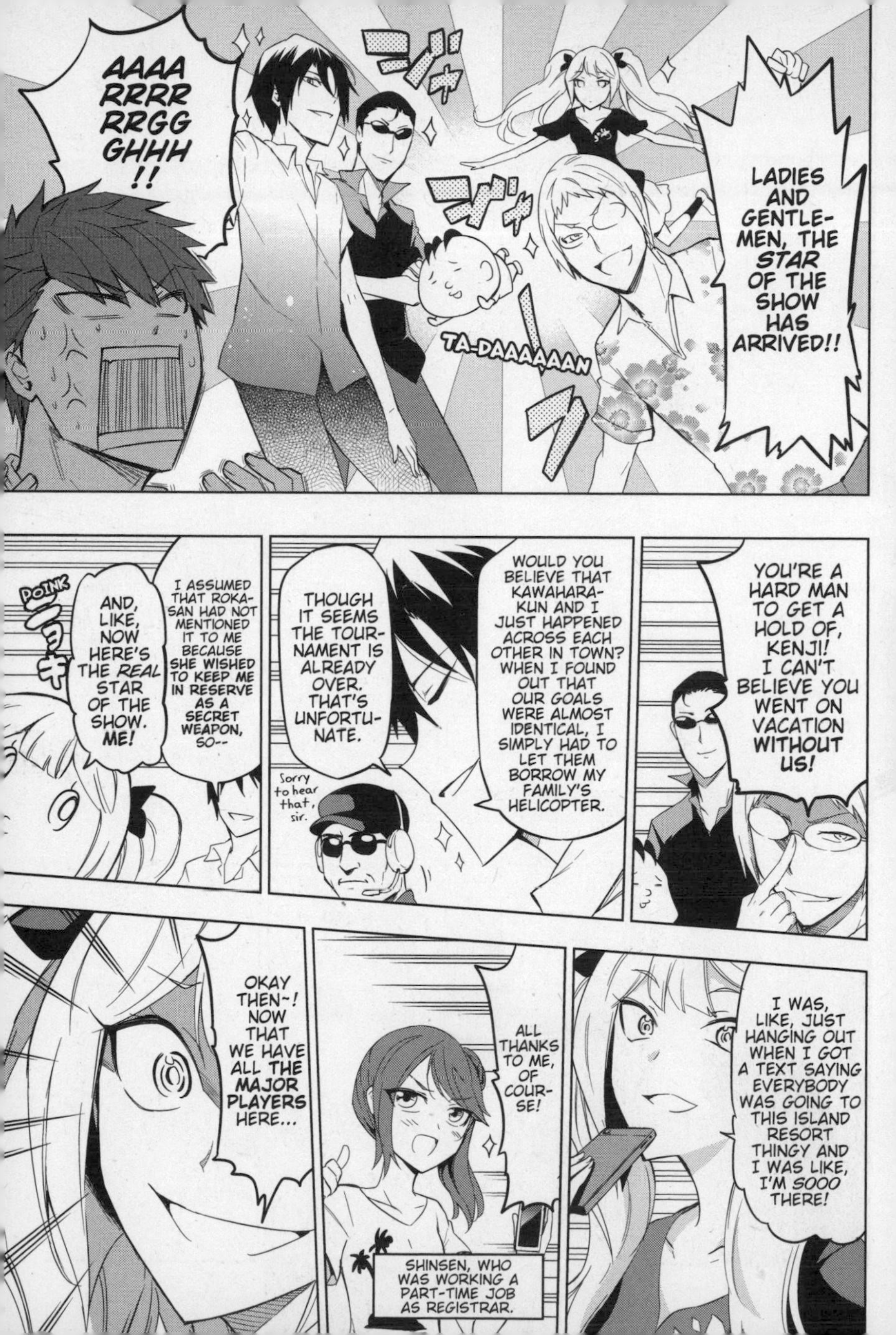

LADIES AND GENTLEMEN, THE STAR OF THE SHOW HAS ARRIVED!!
TA-DAAAAAAN
AAAA RRRR RRGG GHHH!!
YOU'RE A HARD MAN TO GET A HOLD OF, KENJI! I CAN'T BELIEVE YOU WENT ON VACATION WITHOUT US!
WOULD YOU BELIEVE THAT KAWAHARA-KUN AND I JUST HAPPENED ACROSS EACH OTHER IN TOWN? WHEN I FOUND OUT THAT OUR GOALS WERE ALMOST IDENTICAL, I SIMPLY HAD TO LET THEM BORROW MY FAMILY'S HELICOPTER.
THOUGH IT SEEMS THE TOURNAMENT IS ALREADY OVER. THAT'S UNFORTUNATE.
Sorry to hear that, sir.
I ASSUMED THAT ROKA-SAN HAD NOT MENTIONED IT TO ME BECAUSE SHE WISHED TO KEEP ME IN RESERVE AS A SECRET WEAPON, SO--
POINK
AND, LIKE, NOW HERE'S THE REAL STAR OF THE SHOW. ME!
I WAS, LIKE, JUST HANGING OUT WHEN I GOT A TEXT SAYING EVERYBODY WAS GOING TO THIS ISLAND RESORT THINGY AND I WAS LIKE, I'M SOOO THERE!
ALL THANKS TO ME, OF COURSE!
SHINSEN, WHO WAS WORKING A PART-TIME JOB AS REGISTRAR.
OKAY THEN~! NOW THAT WE HAVE ALL THE MAJOR PLAYERS HERE...

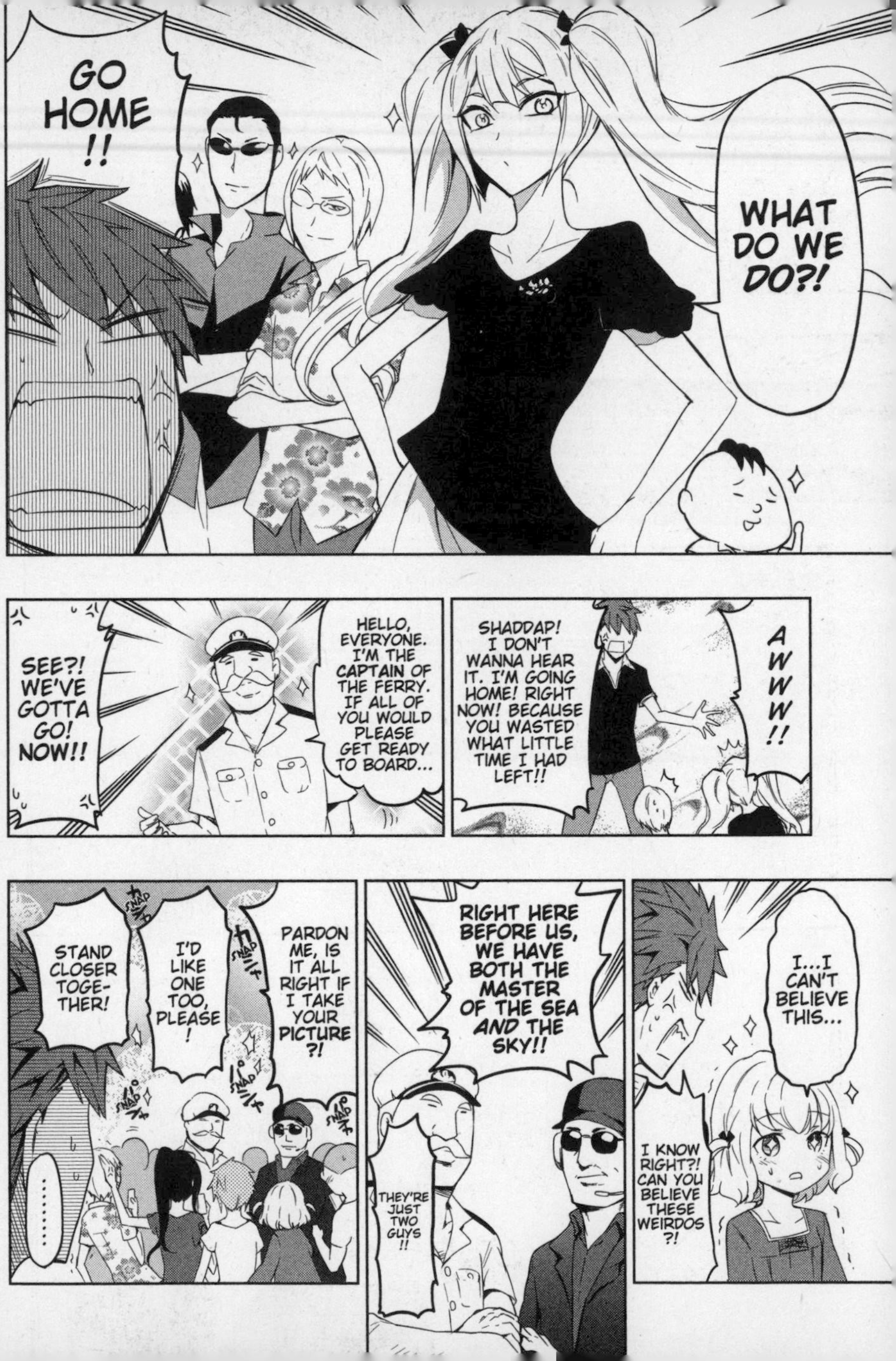
WHAT DO WE DO?!
GO HOME!!
AWWW!!
SHADDAP! I DON'T WANNA HEAR IT. I'M GOING HOME! RIGHT NOW! BECAUSE YOU WASTED WHAT LITTLE TIME I HAD LEFT!!
HELLO, EVERYONE. I'M THE CAPTAIN OF THE FERRY. IF ALL OF YOU WOULD PLEASE GET READY TO BOARD...
SEE?! WE'VE GOTTA GO! NOW!!
I...I CAN'T BELIEVE THIS...
I KNOW RIGHT?! CAN YOU BELIEVE THESE WEIRDOS?!
RIGHT HERE BEFORE US, WE HAVE BOTH THE MASTER OF THE SEA AND THE SKY!!
THEY'RE JUST TWO GUYS!!
SNAP
PARDON ME, IS IT ALL RIGHT IF I TAKE YOUR PICTURE?!
SNAP
I'D LIKE ONE TOO, PLEASE!
SNAP
STAND CLOSER TOGE-THER!
SNAP
SNAP
......

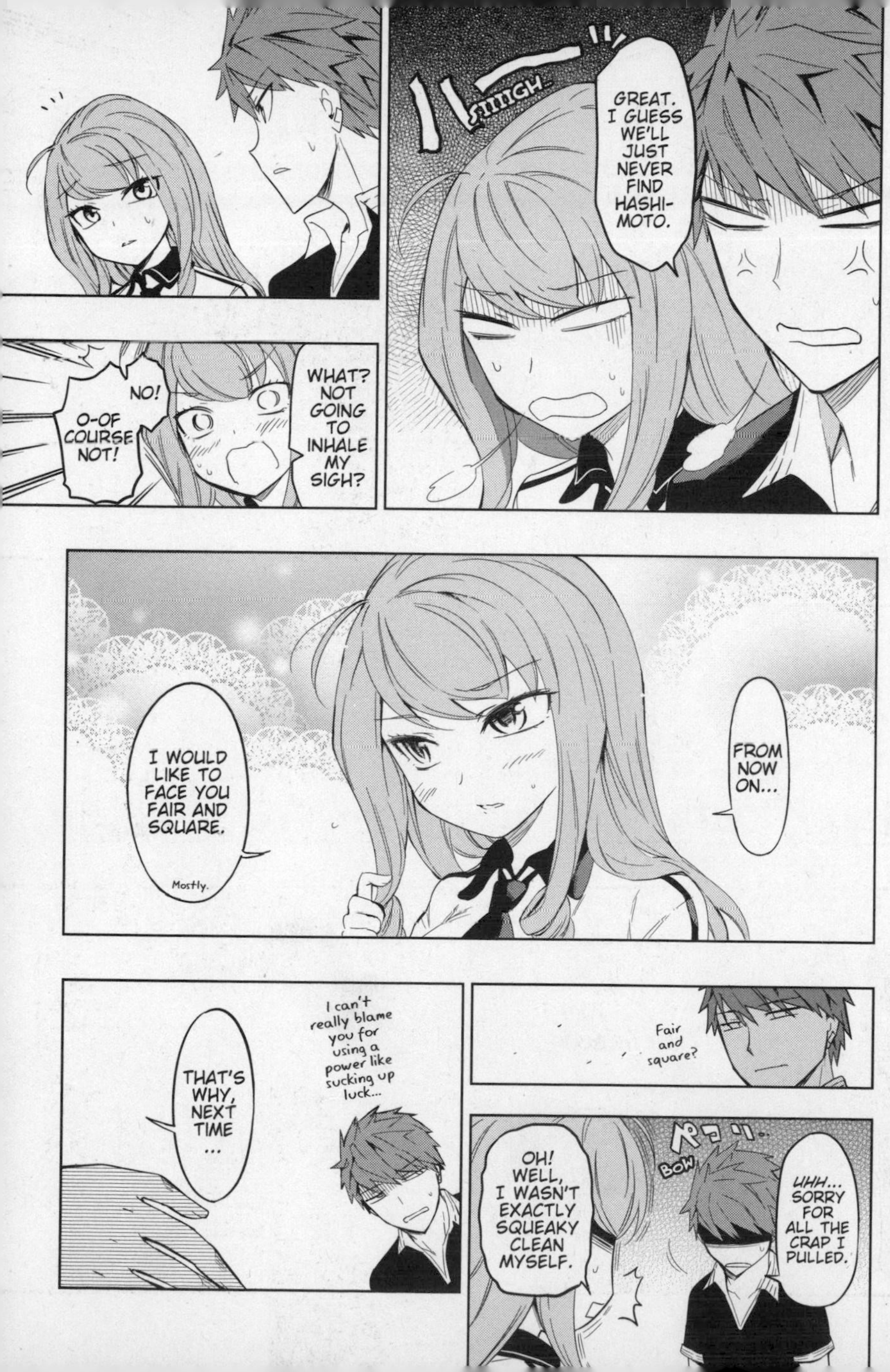
SIIIIGH
GREAT. I GUESS WE'LL JUST NEVER FIND HASHI-MOTO.
WHAT? NOT GOING TO INHALE MY SIGH?
NO!
O-OF COURSE NOT!
FROM NOW ON...
I WOULD LIKE TO FACE YOU FAIR AND SQUARE.
Mostly.
Fair and square?
BOW
UHH... SORRY FOR ALL THE CRAP I PULLED.
OH! WELL, I WASN'T EXACTLY SQUEAKY CLEAN MYSELF.
I can't really blame you for using a power like sucking up luck...
THAT'S WHY, NEXT TIME...

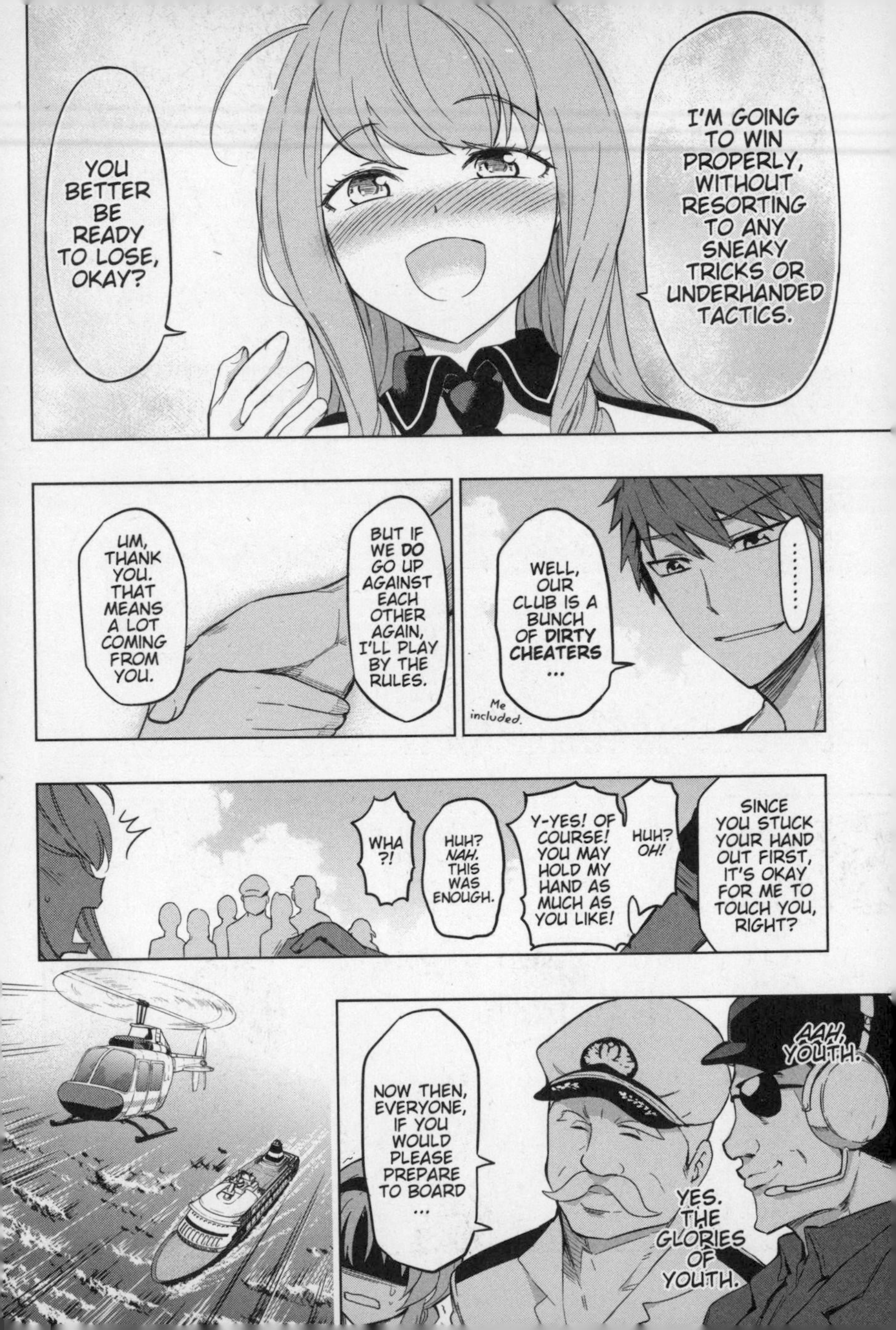
I'M GOING TO WIN PROPERLY, WITHOUT RESORTING TO ANY SNEAKY TRICKS OR UNDERHANDED TACTICS.
YOU BETTER BE READY TO LOSE, OKAY?
....
WELL, OUR CLUB IS A BUNCH OF DIRTY CHEATERS ...
Me included.
BUT IF WE DO GO UP AGAINST EACH OTHER AGAIN, I'LL PLAY BY THE RULES.
UM, THANK YOU. THAT MEANS A LOT COMING FROM YOU.
SINCE YOU STUCK YOUR HAND OUT FIRST, IT'S OKAY FOR ME TO TOUCH YOU, RIGHT?
HUH? OH!
Y-YES! OF COURSE! YOU MAY HOLD MY HAND AS MUCH AS YOU LIKE!
HUH? NAH. THIS WAS ENOUGH.
WHA ?!
AAH, YOUTH.
NOW THEN, EVERYONE, IF YOU WOULD PLEASE PREPARE TO BOARD ...
YES. THE GLORIES OF YOUTH.

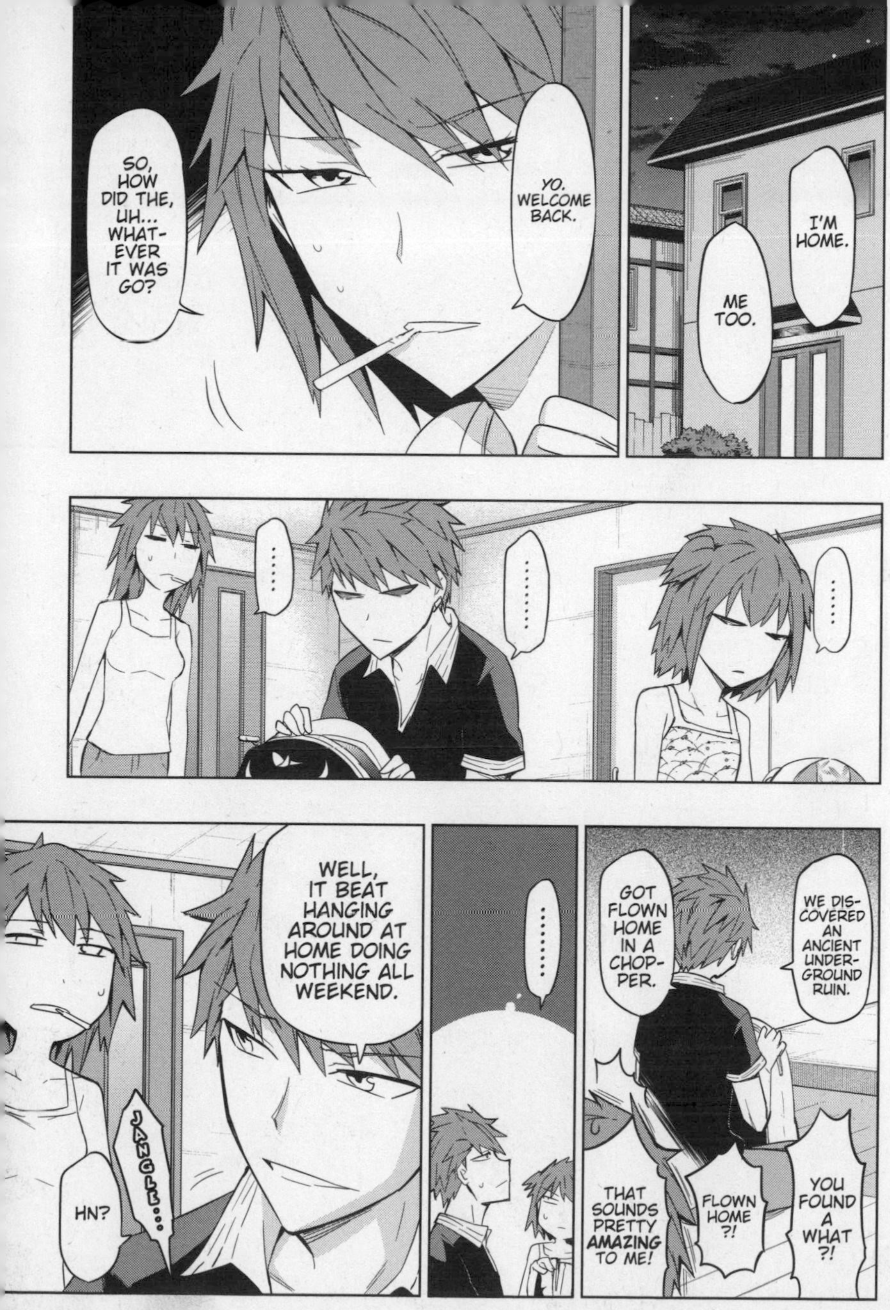
I'M HOME.
ME TOO.
YO. WELCOME BACK.
SO, HOW DID THE, UH... WHATEVER IT WAS GO?
......
......
......
WE DISCOVERED AN ANCIENT UNDERGROUND RUIN.
GOT FLOWN HOME IN A CHOPPER.
YOU FOUND A WHAT?!
FLOWN HOME?!
THAT SOUNDS PRETTY **AMAZING** TO ME!
......
WELL, IT BEAT HANGING AROUND AT HOME DOING NOTHING ALL WEEKEND.
JANGLE...
HN?

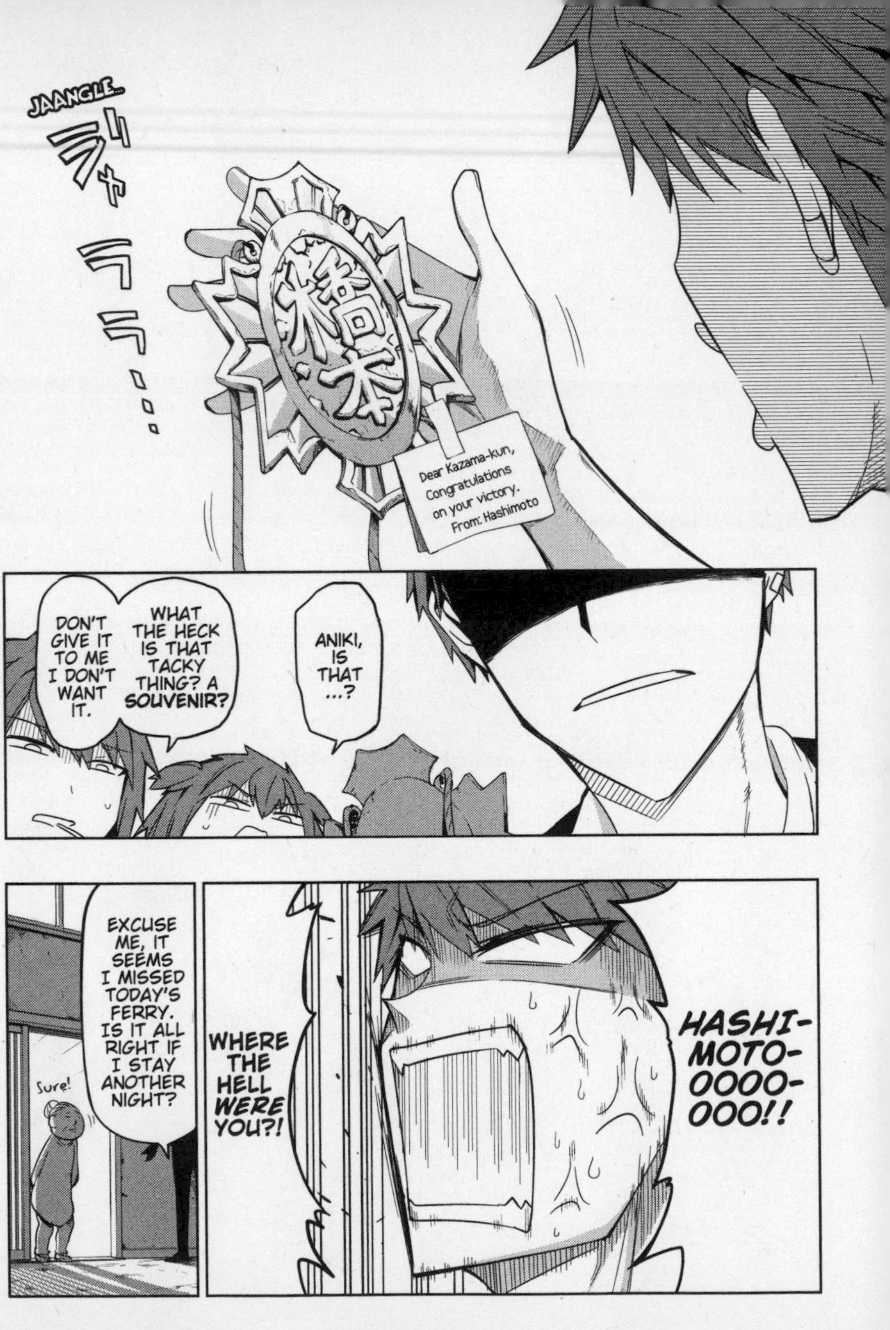
JAANGLE...
Dear Kazama-kun, Congratulations on your victory. From: Hashimoto
ANIKI, IS THAT ...?
WHAT THE HECK IS THAT TACKY THING? A SOUVENIR?
DON'T GIVE IT TO ME I DON'T WANT IT.
HASHI-MOTO-OOOO-OOO!!
WHERE THE HELL WERE YOU?!
EXCUSE ME, IT SEEMS I MISSED TODAY'S FERRY. IS IT ALL RIGHT IF I STAY ANOTHER NIGHT?
Sure!

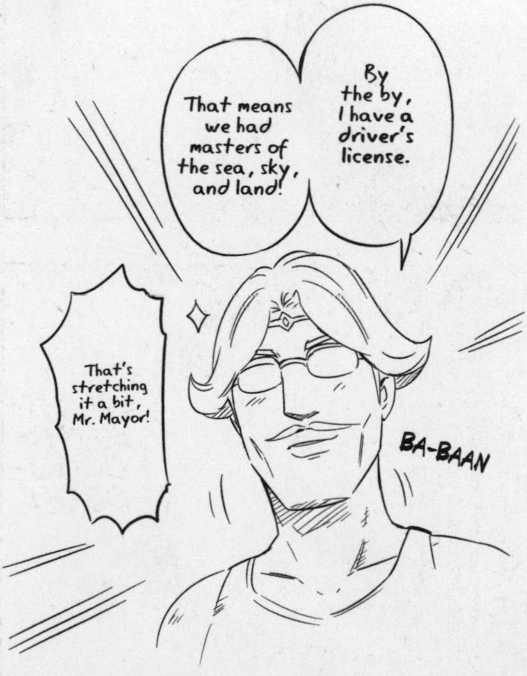
By the by, I have a driver's license.
That means we had masters of the sea, sky, and land!
BA-BAAN
That's stretching it a bit, Mr. Mayor!

D-FRAGMENTS

ディーふらぐ!

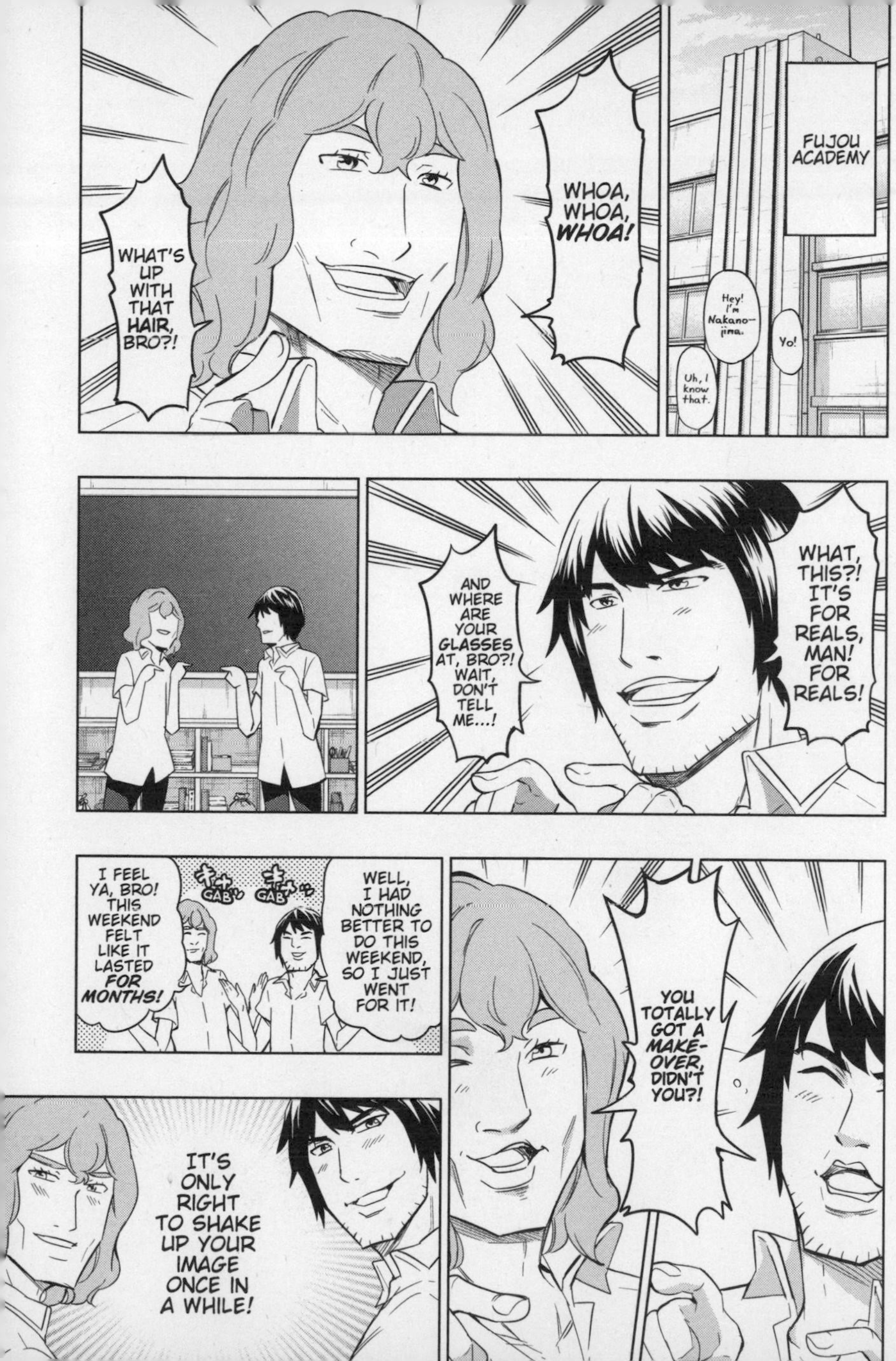
FUJOU ACADEMY
Hey! I'm Nakano-jima.
Yo!
Uh, I know that.
WHOA, WHOA, WHOA!
WHAT'S UP WITH THAT HAIR, BRO?!
WHAT, THIS?! IT'S FOR REALS, MAN! FOR REALS!
AND WHERE ARE YOUR GLASSES AT, BRO?! WAIT, DON'T TELL ME...!
YOU TOTALLY GOT A MAKE-OVER, DIDN'T YOU?!
WELL, I HAD NOTHING BETTER TO DO THIS WEEKEND, SO I JUST WENT FOR IT!
GAB
GAB
I FEEL YA, BRO! THIS WEEKEND FELT LIKE IT LASTED FOR MONTHS!
IT'S ONLY RIGHT TO SHAKE UP YOUR IMAGE ONCE IN A WHILE!

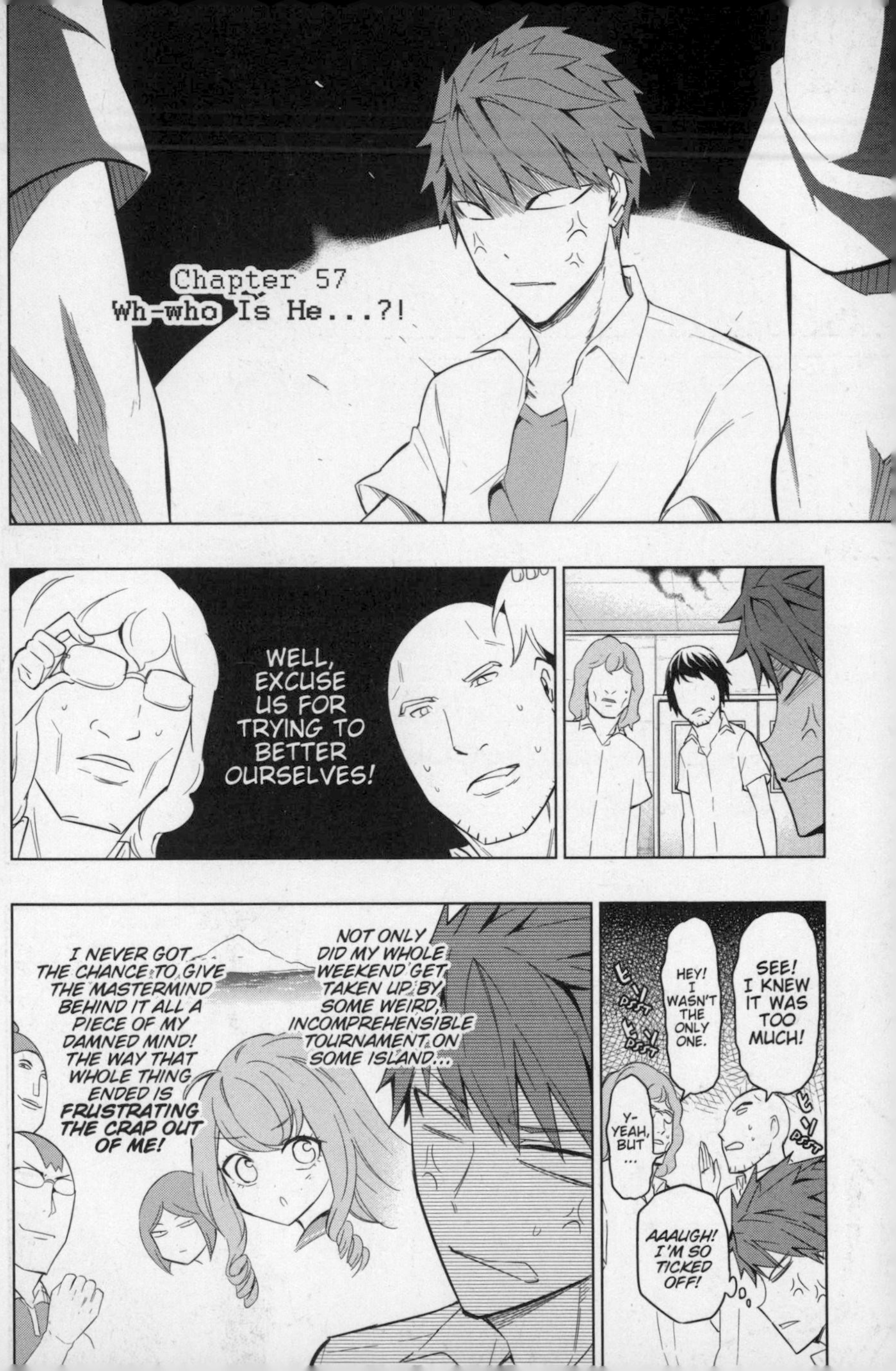
Chapter 57
Wh-who Is He...?!
WELL, EXCUSE US FOR TRYING TO BETTER OURSELVES!
SEE! I KNEW IT WAS TOO MUCH!
HEY! I WASN'T THE ONLY ONE.
Y-YEAH, BUT ...
AAAUGH! I'M SO TICKED OFF!
NOT ONLY DID MY WHOLE WEEKEND GET TAKEN UP BY SOME WEIRD, INCOMPREHENSIBLE TOURNAMENT ON SOME ISLAND...
I NEVER GOT THE CHANCE TO GIVE THE MASTERMIND BEHIND IT ALL A PIECE OF MY DAMNED MIND! THE WAY THAT WHOLE THING ENDED IS FRUSTRATING THE CRAP OUT OF ME!

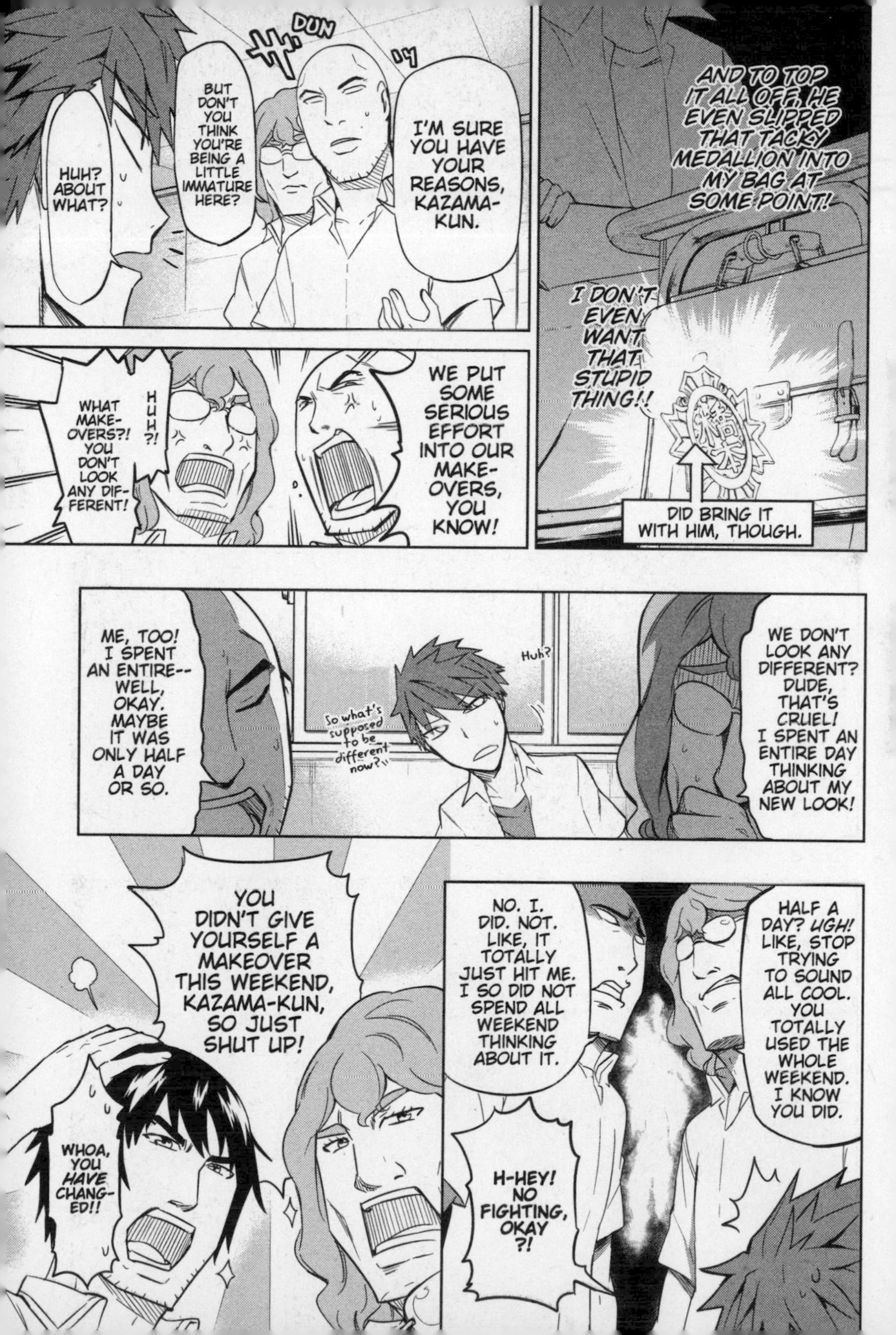
AND TO TOP IT ALL OFF, HE EVEN SLIPPED THAT TACKY MEDALLION INTO MY BAG AT SOME POINT!
I DON'T EVEN WANT THAT STUPID THING!!
DID BRING IT WITH HIM, THOUGH.
I'M SURE YOU HAVE YOUR REASONS, KAZAMA-KUN.
DUN
BUT DON'T YOU THINK YOU'RE BEING A LITTLE IMMATURE HERE?
HUH? ABOUT WHAT?
WE PUT SOME SERIOUS EFFORT INTO OUR MAKE-OVERS, YOU KNOW!
HUH?!
WHAT MAKE-OVERS?! YOU DON'T LOOK ANY DIF-FERENT!
WE DON'T LOOK ANY DIFFERENT? DUDE, THAT'S CRUEL! I SPENT AN ENTIRE DAY THINKING ABOUT MY NEW LOOK!
Huh?
So what's supposed to be different now?!
ME, TOO! I SPENT AN ENTIRE-- WELL, OKAY. MAYBE IT WAS ONLY HALF A DAY OR SO.
HALF A DAY? UGH! LIKE, STOP TRYING TO SOUND ALL COOL. YOU TOTALLY USED THE WHOLE WEEKEND. I KNOW YOU DID.
NO. I. DID. NOT. LIKE, IT TOTALLY JUST HIT ME. I SO DID NOT SPEND ALL WEEKEND THINKING ABOUT IT.
H-HEY! NO FIGHTING, OKAY?!
YOU DIDN'T GIVE YOURSELF A MAKEOVER THIS WEEKEND, KAZAMA-KUN, SO JUST SHUT UP!
WHOA, YOU HAVE CHANGED!!

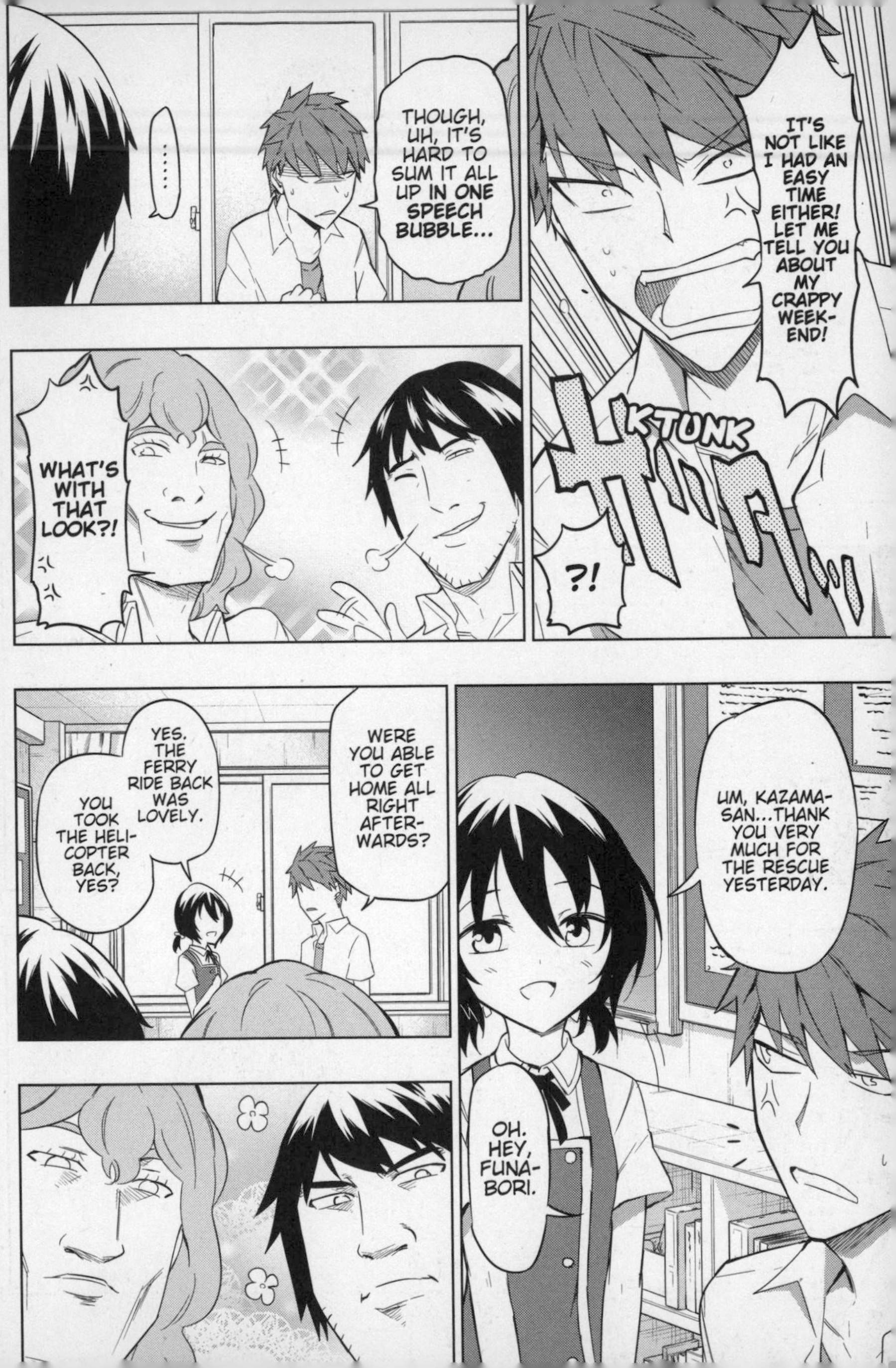
IT'S NOT LIKE I HAD AN EASY TIME EITHER! LET ME TELL YOU ABOUT MY CRAPPY WEEK-END!
KTUNK
?!
THOUGH, UH, IT'S HARD TO SUM IT ALL UP IN ONE SPEECH BUBBLE...
......
WHAT'S WITH THAT LOOK?!
UM, KAZAMA-SAN...THANK YOU VERY MUCH FOR THE RESCUE YESTERDAY.
OH. HEY, FUNA-BORI.
WERE YOU ABLE TO GET HOME ALL RIGHT AFTER-WARDS?
YES. THE FERRY RIDE BACK WAS LOVELY.
YOU TOOK THE HELI-COPTER BACK, YES?

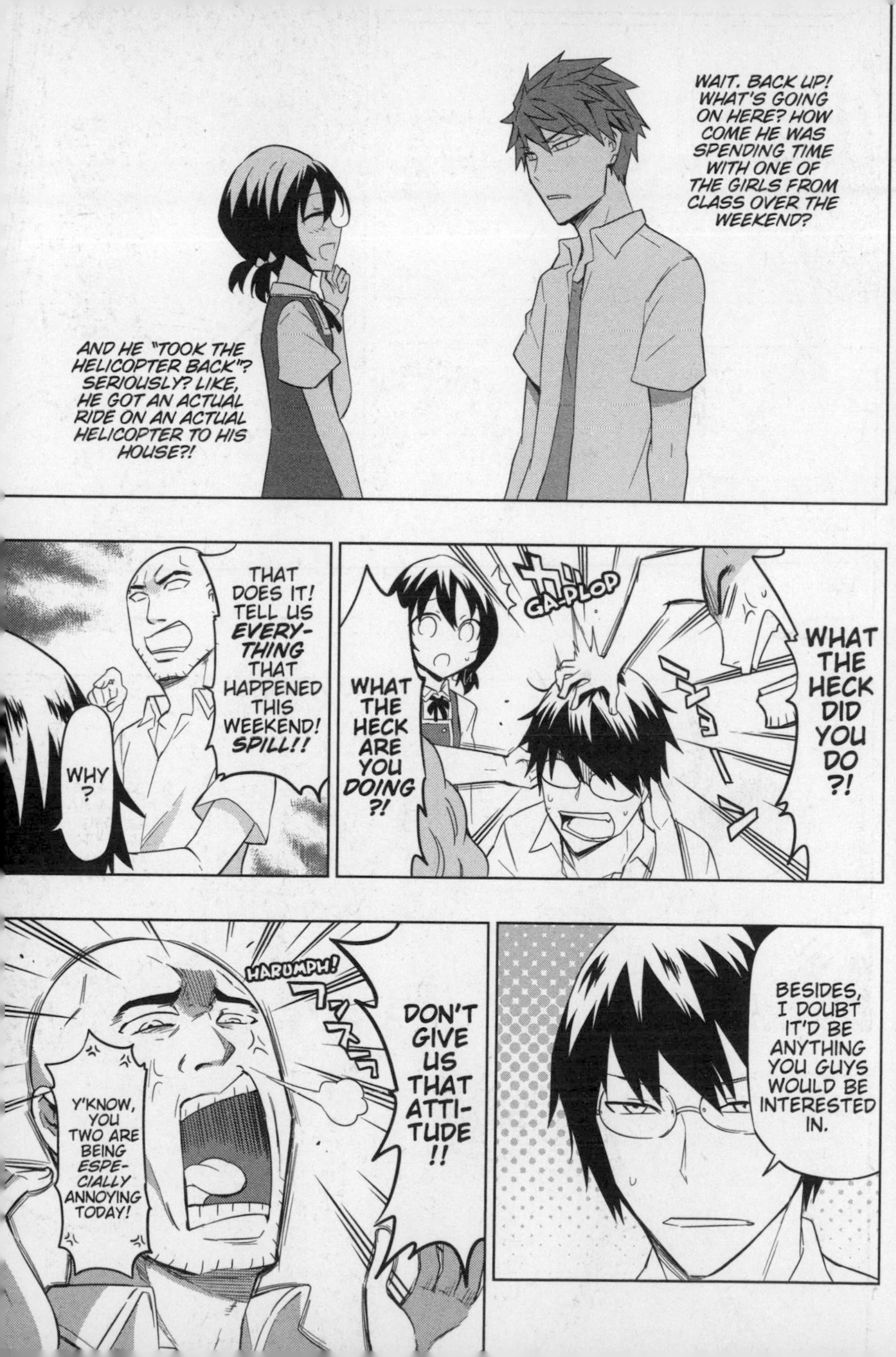
WAIT. BACK UP! WHAT'S GOING ON HERE? HOW COME HE WAS SPENDING TIME WITH ONE OF THE GIRLS FROM CLASS OVER THE WEEKEND?
AND HE "TOOK THE HELICOPTER BACK"? SERIOUSLY? LIKE, HE GOT AN ACTUAL RIDE ON AN ACTUAL HELICOPTER TO HIS HOUSE?!
GA-PLOP
WHAT THE HECK DID YOU DO?!
WHAT THE HECK ARE YOU DOING?!
THAT DOES IT! TELL US EVERYTHING THAT HAPPENED THIS WEEKEND! SPILL!!
WHY?
BESIDES, I DOUBT IT'D BE ANYTHING YOU GUYS WOULD BE INTERESTED IN.
HARUMPH!
DON'T GIVE US THAT ATTITUDE!!
Y'KNOW, YOU TWO ARE BEING ESPECIALLY ANNOYING TODAY!

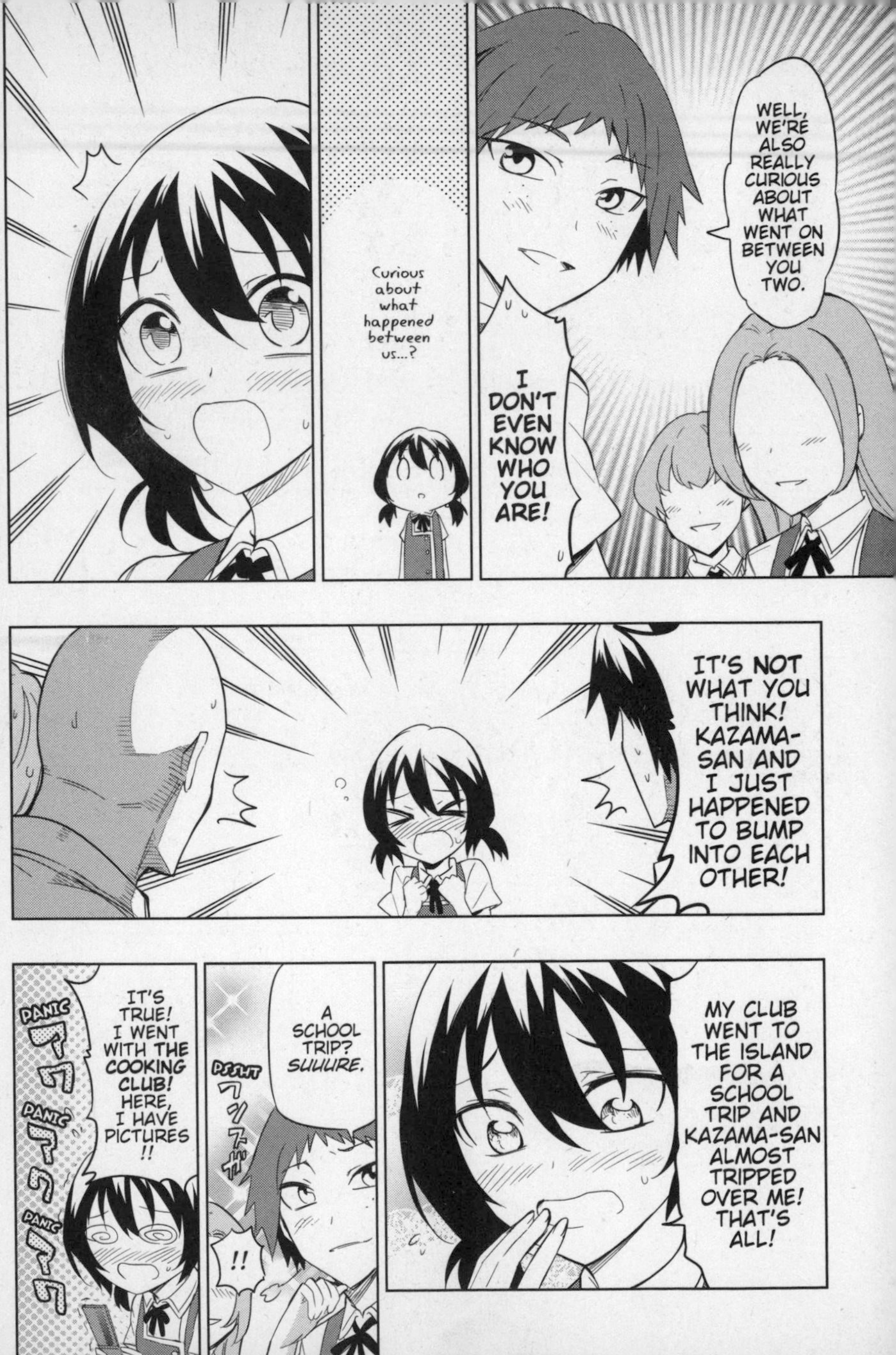

WELL, WE'RE ALSO REALLY CURIOUS ABOUT WHAT WENT ON BETWEEN YOU TWO.
I DON'T EVEN KNOW WHO YOU ARE!
Curious about what happened between us...?
IT'S NOT WHAT YOU THINK! KAZAMA-SAN AND I JUST HAPPENED TO BUMP INTO EACH OTHER!
MY CLUB WENT TO THE ISLAND FOR A SCHOOL TRIP AND KAZAMA-SAN ALMOST TRIPPED OVER ME! THAT'S ALL!
A SCHOOL TRIP? SUUURE.
PSSHT
!!
IT'S TRUE! I WENT WITH THE COOKING CLUB! HERE, I HAVE PICTURES!!
PANIC
PANIC
PANIC

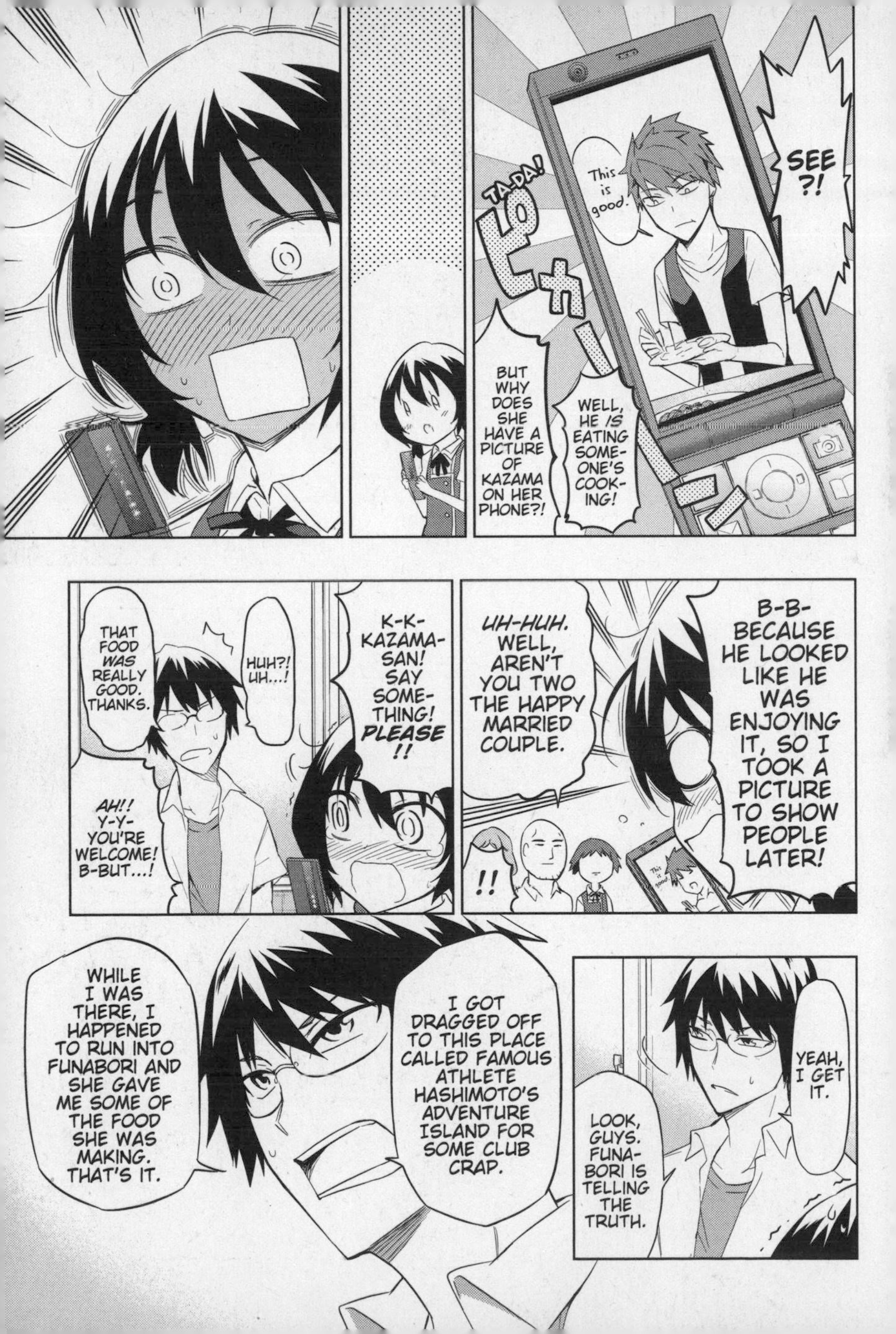
SEE ?!
This is good.
TA-DA!
WELL, HE *IS* EATING SOME-ONE'S COOK-ING!
BUT WHY DOES SHE HAVE A PICTURE OF KAZAMA ON HER PHONE?!
B-B-BECAUSE HE LOOKED LIKE HE WAS ENJOYING IT, SO I TOOK A PICTURE TO SHOW PEOPLE LATER!
UH-HUH. WELL, AREN'T YOU TWO THE HAPPY MARRIED COUPLE.
!!
K-K-KAZAMA-SAN! SAY SOME-THING! *PLEASE!!*
HUH?! UH...!
THAT FOOD *WAS* REALLY GOOD. THANKS.
AH!! Y-Y-YOU'RE WELCOME! B-BUT...!
YEAH, I GET IT.
LOOK, GUYS. FUNA-BORI IS TELLING THE TRUTH.
I GOT DRAGGED OFF TO THIS PLACE CALLED FAMOUS ATHLETE HASHIMOTO'S ADVENTURE ISLAND FOR SOME CLUB CRAP.
WHILE I WAS THERE, I HAPPENED TO RUN INTO FUNABORI AND SHE GAVE ME SOME OF THE FOOD SHE WAS MAKING. THAT'S IT.

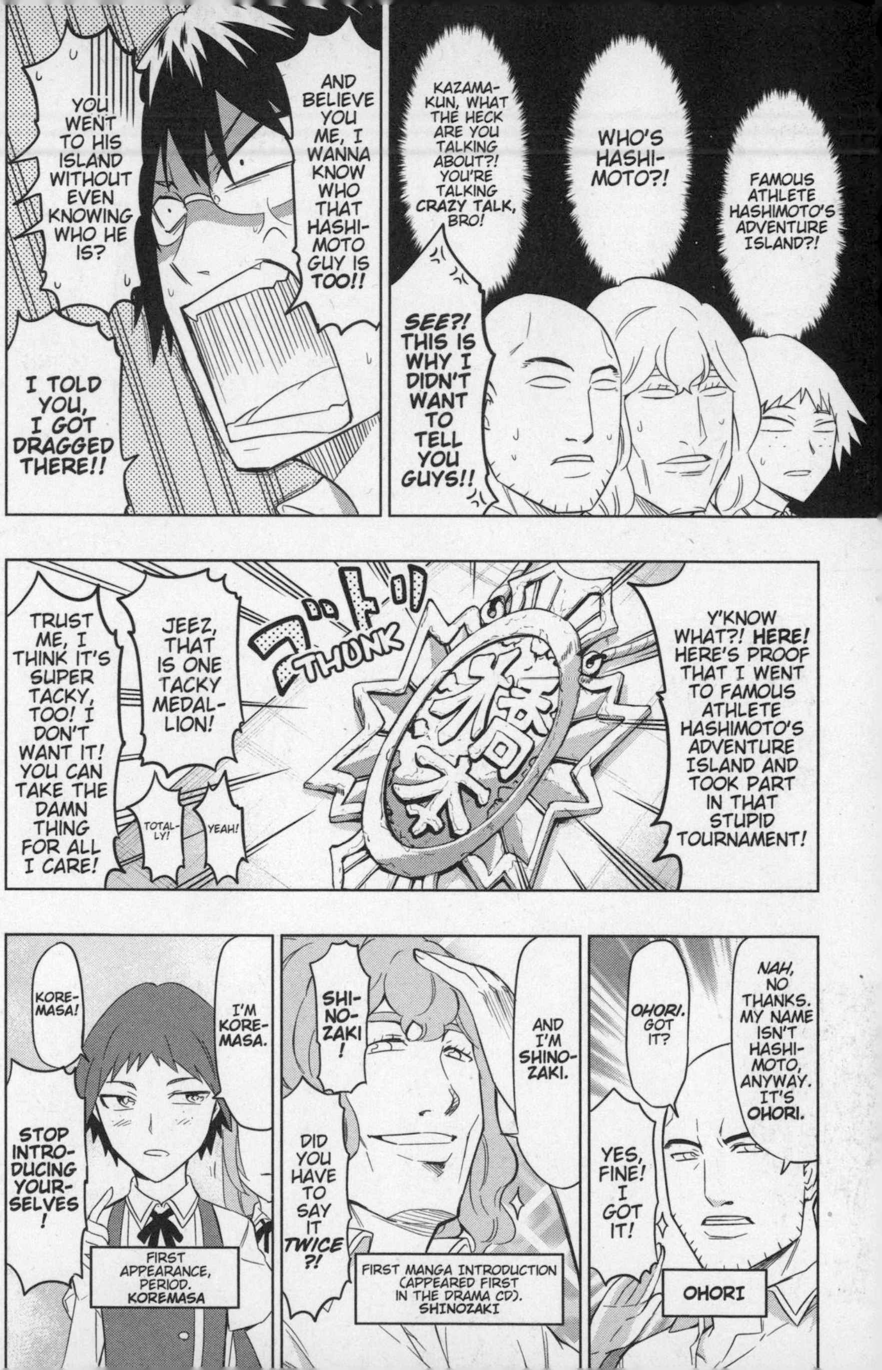
FAMOUS ATHLETE HASHIMOTO'S ADVENTURE ISLAND?!
WHO'S HASHIMOTO?!
KAZAMA-KUN, WHAT THE HECK ARE YOU TALKING ABOUT?! YOU'RE TALKING CRAZY TALK, BRO!
SEE?! THIS IS WHY I DIDN'T WANT TO TELL YOU GUYS!!
AND BELIEVE YOU ME, I WANNA KNOW WHO THAT HASHIMOTO GUY IS TOO!!
YOU WENT TO HIS ISLAND WITHOUT EVEN KNOWING WHO HE IS?
I TOLD YOU, I GOT DRAGGED THERE!!
Y'KNOW WHAT?! HERE! HERE'S PROOF THAT I WENT TO FAMOUS ATHLETE HASHIMOTO'S ADVENTURE ISLAND AND TOOK PART IN THAT STUPID TOURNAMENT!
ゴトッ
THUNK
橋本
JEEZ, THAT IS ONE TACKY MEDALLION!
TRUST ME, I THINK IT'S SUPER TACKY, TOO! I DON'T WANT IT! YOU CAN TAKE THE DAMN THING FOR ALL I CARE!
YEAH!
TOTALLY!
NAH, NO THANKS. MY NAME ISN'T HASHIMOTO, ANYWAY. IT'S OHORI.
OHORI. GOT IT?
YES, FINE! I GOT IT!
OHORI
AND I'M SHINOZAKI.
SHINOZAKI!
DID YOU HAVE TO SAY IT TWICE?!
FIRST MANGA INTRODUCTION (APPEARED FIRST IN THE DRAMA CD). SHINOZAKI
I'M KOREMASA.
KOREMASA!
STOP INTRODUCING YOURSELVES!
FIRST APPEARANCE, PERIOD. KOREMASA

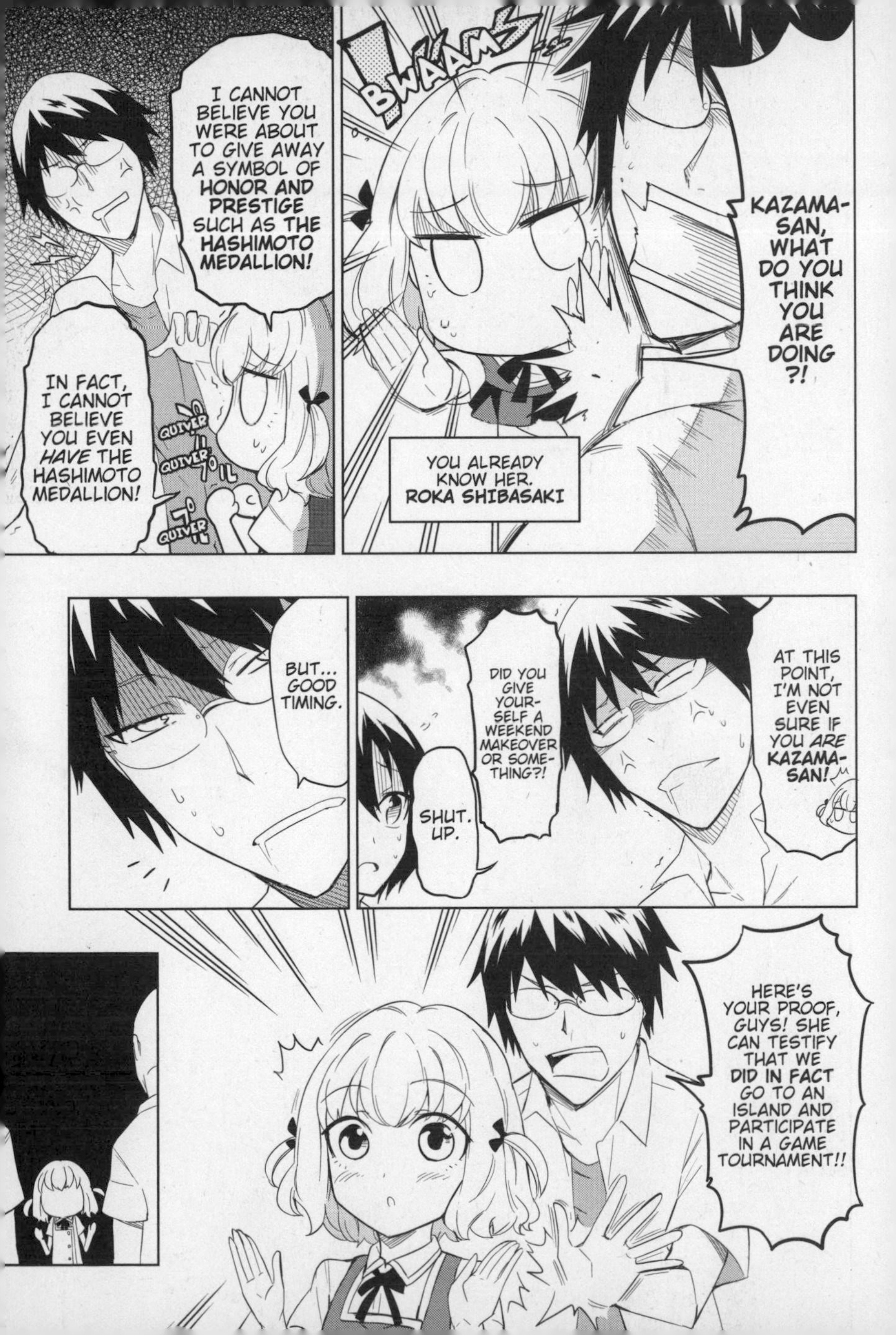
BWAAMS
KAZAMA-SAN, WHAT DO YOU THINK YOU ARE DOING?!
YOU ALREADY KNOW HER. ROKA SHIBASAKI
I CANNOT BELIEVE YOU WERE ABOUT TO GIVE AWAY A SYMBOL OF HONOR AND PRESTIGE SUCH AS THE HASHIMOTO MEDALLION!
IN FACT, I CANNOT BELIEVE YOU EVEN HAVE THE HASHIMOTO MEDALLION!
QUIVER
QUIVER
QUIVER
AT THIS POINT, I'M NOT EVEN SURE IF YOU ARE KAZAMA-SAN!
DID YOU GIVE YOURSELF A WEEKEND MAKEOVER OR SOMETHING?!
SHUT. UP.
BUT... GOOD TIMING.
HERE'S YOUR PROOF, GUYS! SHE CAN TESTIFY THAT WE DID IN FACT GO TO AN ISLAND AND PARTICIPATE IN A GAME TOURNAMENT!!

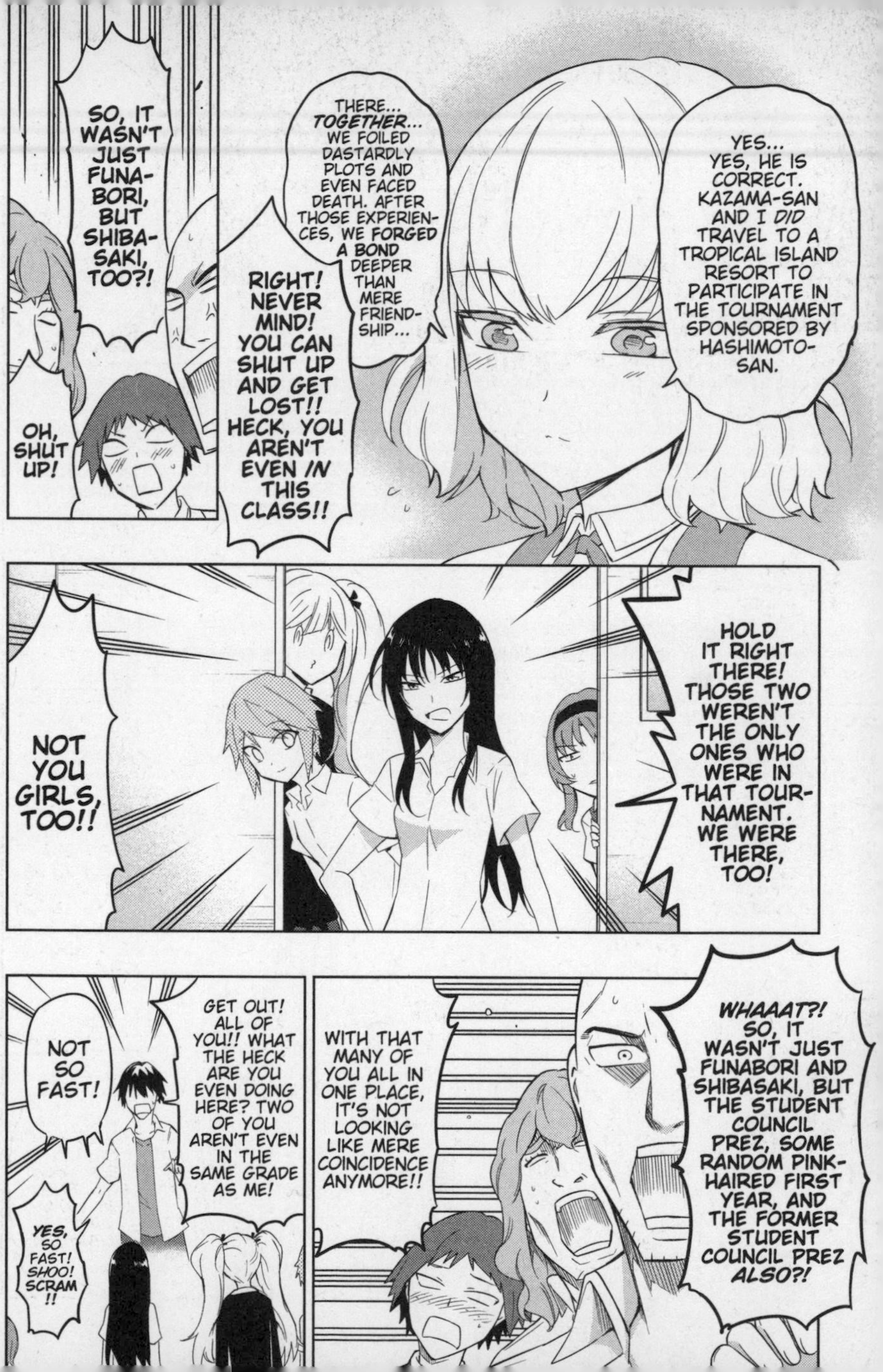
YES... YES, HE IS CORRECT. KAZAMA-SAN AND I *DID* TRAVEL TO A TROPICAL ISLAND RESORT TO PARTICIPATE IN THE TOURNAMENT SPONSORED BY HASHIMOTO-SAN.
THERE... *TOGETHER*... WE FOILED DASTARDLY PLOTS AND EVEN FACED DEATH. AFTER THOSE EXPERIENCES, WE FORGED A BOND DEEPER THAN MERE FRIENDSHIP...
RIGHT! NEVER MIND! YOU CAN SHUT UP AND GET LOST!! HECK, YOU AREN'T EVEN *IN* THIS CLASS!!
SO, IT WASN'T JUST FUNABORI, BUT SHIBASAKI, TOO?!
OH, SHUT UP!
HOLD IT RIGHT THERE! THOSE TWO WEREN'T THE ONLY ONES WHO WERE IN THAT TOURNAMENT. WE WERE THERE, TOO!
NOT YOU GIRLS, TOO!!
WHAAAT?! SO, IT WASN'T JUST FUNABORI AND SHIBASAKI, BUT THE STUDENT COUNCIL PREZ, SOME RANDOM PINK-HAIRED FIRST YEAR, AND THE FORMER STUDENT COUNCIL PREZ *ALSO?!*
WITH THAT MANY OF YOU ALL IN ONE PLACE, IT'S NOT LOOKING LIKE MERE COINCIDENCE ANYMORE!!
GET OUT! ALL OF YOU!! WHAT THE HECK ARE YOU EVEN DOING HERE? TWO OF YOU AREN'T EVEN IN THE SAME GRADE AS ME!
NOT SO FAST!
YES, SO FAST! SHOO! SCRAM!!

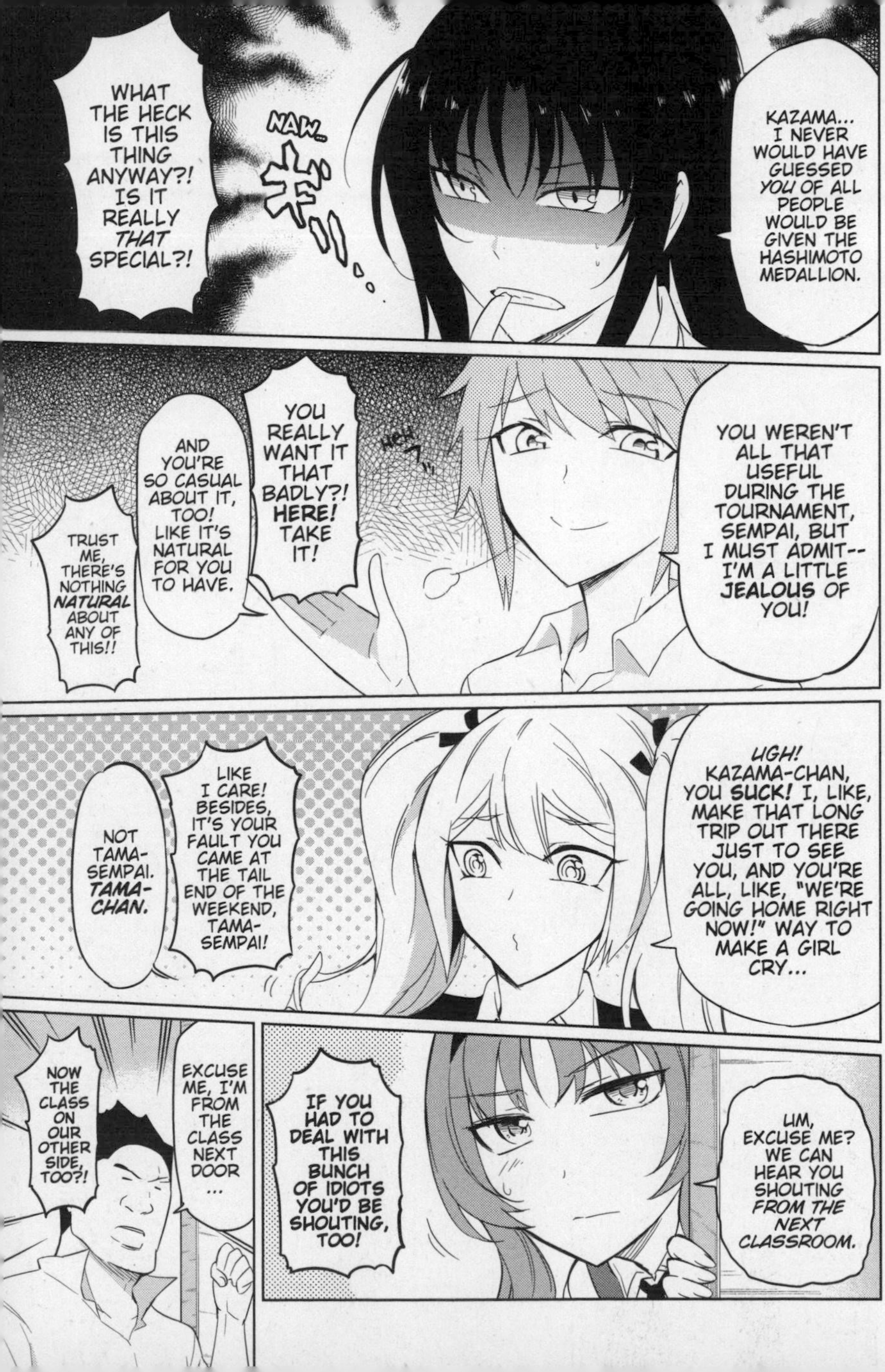
KAZAMA... I NEVER WOULD HAVE GUESSED YOU OF ALL PEOPLE WOULD BE GIVEN THE HASHIMOTO MEDALLION.
NAW...
WHAT THE HECK IS THIS THING ANYWAY?! IS IT REALLY THAT SPECIAL?!
YOU WEREN'T ALL THAT USEFUL DURING THE TOURNAMENT, SEMPAI, BUT I MUST ADMIT-- I'M A LITTLE JEALOUS OF YOU!
HEH
YOU REALLY WANT IT THAT BADLY?! HERE! TAKE IT!
AND YOU'RE SO CASUAL ABOUT IT, TOO! LIKE IT'S NATURAL FOR YOU TO HAVE.
TRUST ME, THERE'S NOTHING NATURAL ABOUT ANY OF THIS!!
UGH! KAZAMA-CHAN, YOU SUCK! I, LIKE, MAKE THAT LONG TRIP OUT THERE JUST TO SEE YOU, AND YOU'RE ALL, LIKE, "WE'RE GOING HOME RIGHT NOW!" WAY TO MAKE A GIRL CRY...
LIKE I CARE! BESIDES, IT'S YOUR FAULT YOU CAME AT THE TAIL END OF THE WEEKEND, TAMA-SEMPAI!
NOT TAMA-SEMPAI. TAMA-CHAN.
UM, EXCUSE ME? WE CAN HEAR YOU SHOUTING FROM THE NEXT CLASSROOM.
IF YOU HAD TO DEAL WITH THIS BUNCH OF IDIOTS YOU'D BE SHOUTING, TOO!
EXCUSE ME, I'M FROM THE CLASS NEXT DOOR...
NOW THE CLASS ON OUR OTHER SIDE, TOO?!

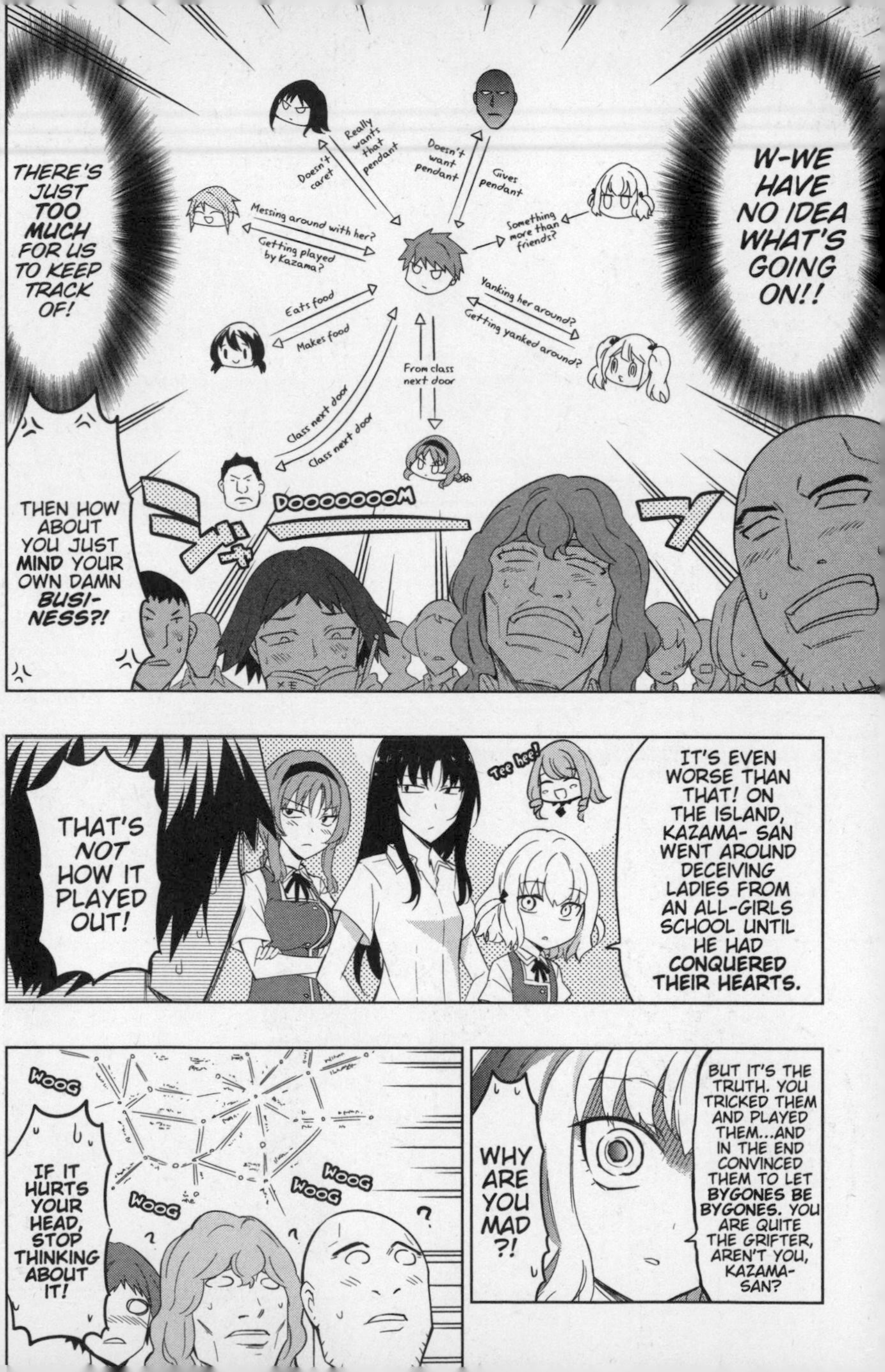
W-WE HAVE NO IDEA WHAT'S GOING ON!!
THERE'S JUST TOO MUCH FOR US TO KEEP TRACK OF!
Doesn't want pendant
Gives pendant
Really wants that pendant
Doesn't care!
Something more than friends?
Messing around with her?
Getting played by Kazama?
Yanking her around?
Getting yanked around?
Eats food
Makes food
From class next door
Class next door
Class next door
DOOOOOOOM
THEN HOW ABOUT YOU JUST MIND YOUR OWN DAMN BUSINESS?!
IT'S EVEN WORSE THAN THAT! ON THE ISLAND, KAZAMA- SAN WENT AROUND DECEIVING LADIES FROM AN ALL-GIRLS SCHOOL UNTIL HE HAD CONQUERED THEIR HEARTS.
Tee hee!
THAT'S NOT HOW IT PLAYED OUT!
BUT IT'S THE TRUTH. YOU TRICKED THEM AND PLAYED THEM...AND IN THE END CONVINCED THEM TO LET BYGONES BE BYGONES. YOU ARE QUITE THE GRIFTER, AREN'T YOU, KAZAMA-SAN?
WHY ARE YOU MAD?!
WOOG
WOOG
WOOG
WOOG
IF IT HURTS YOUR HEAD, STOP THINKING ABOUT IT!

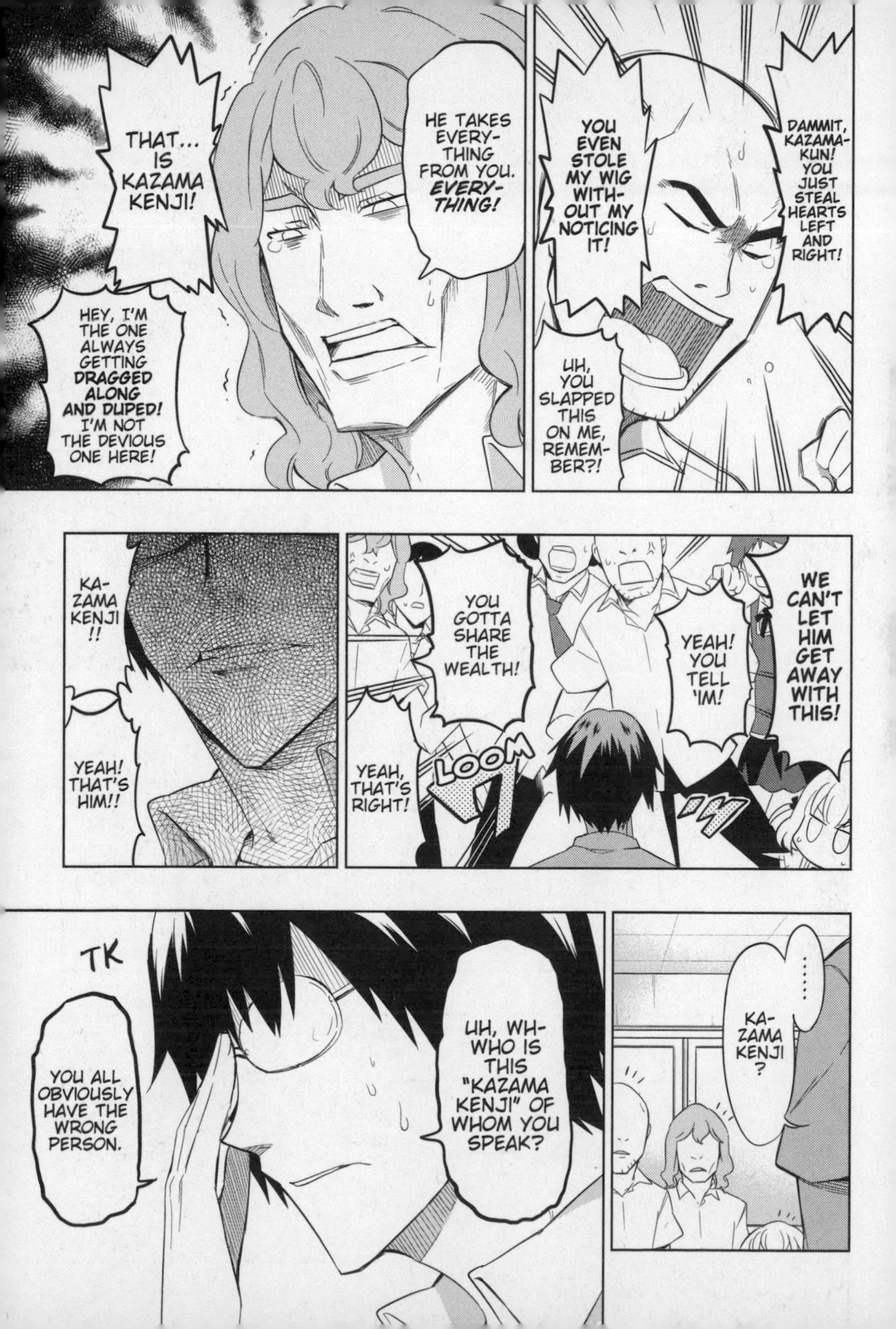
DAMMIT, KAZAMA-KUN! YOU JUST STEAL HEARTS LEFT AND RIGHT!
YOU EVEN STOLE MY WIG WITHOUT MY NOTICING IT!
UH, YOU SLAPPED THIS ON ME, REMEMBER?!
HE TAKES EVERYTHING FROM YOU. EVERYTHING!
THAT... IS KAZAMA KENJI!
HEY, I'M THE ONE ALWAYS GETTING DRAGGED ALONG AND DUPED! I'M NOT THE DEVIOUS ONE HERE!
WE CAN'T LET HIM GET AWAY WITH THIS!
YEAH! YOU TELL 'IM!
YOU GOTTA SHARE THE WEALTH!
LOOM
YEAH, THAT'S RIGHT!
KAZAMA KENJI!!
YEAH! THAT'S HIM!!
......
KAZAMA KENJI?
TK
UH, WH-WHO IS THIS "KAZAMA KENJI" OF WHOM YOU SPEAK?
YOU ALL OBVIOUSLY HAVE THE WRONG PERSON.

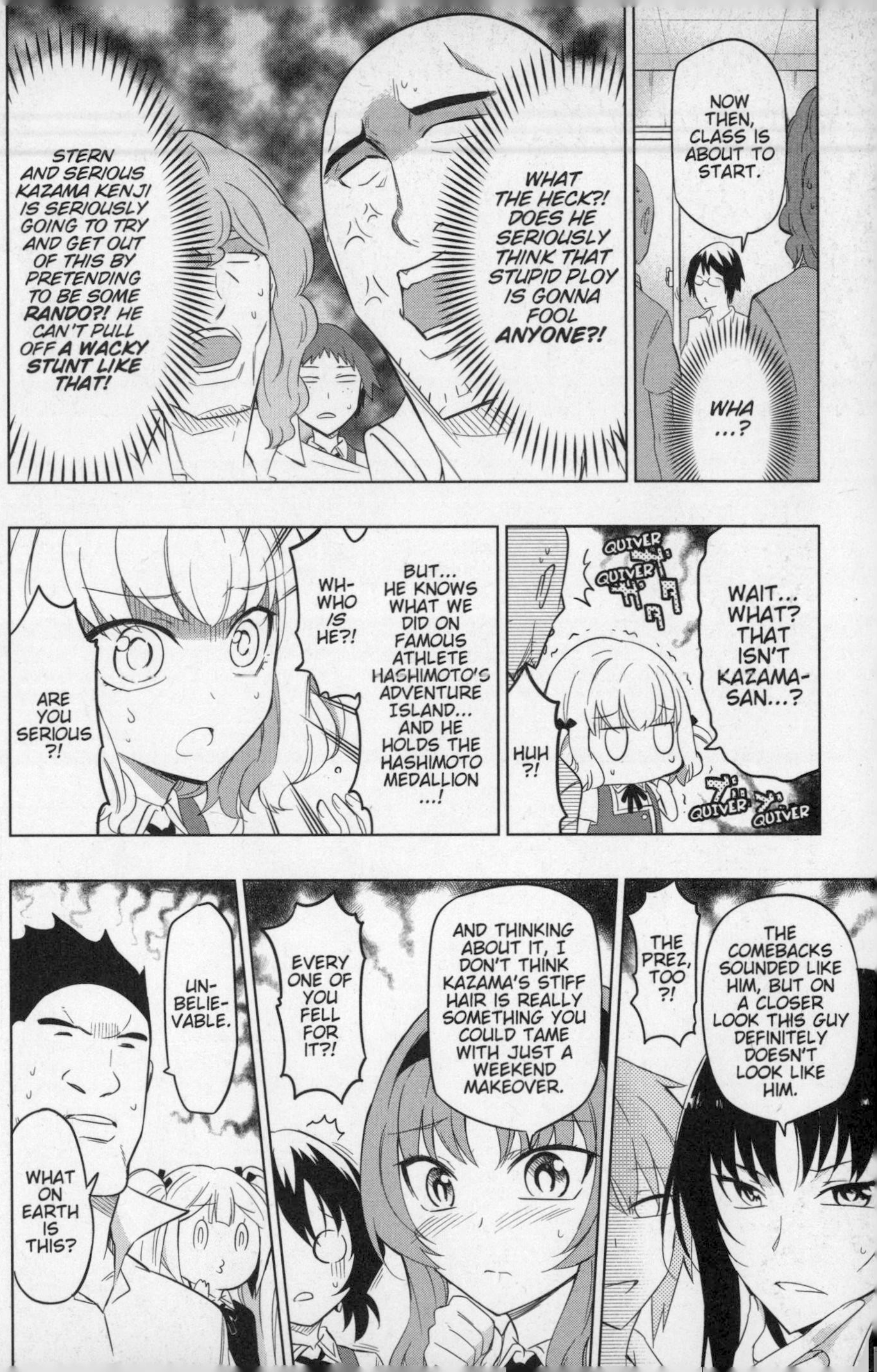
NOW THEN, CLASS IS ABOUT TO START.
WHA ...?
WHAT THE HECK?! DOES HE SERIOUSLY THINK THAT STUPID PLOY IS GONNA FOOL ANYONE?!
STERN AND SERIOUS KAZAMA KENJI IS SERIOUSLY GOING TO TRY AND GET OUT OF THIS BY PRETENDING TO BE SOME RANDO?! HE CAN'T PULL OFF A WACKY STUNT LIKE THAT!
QUIVER
QUIVER
WAIT... WHAT? THAT ISN'T KAZAMA-SAN...?
HUH ?!
QUIVER
QUIVER
BUT... HE KNOWS WHAT WE DID ON FAMOUS ATHLETE HASHIMOTO'S ADVENTURE ISLAND... AND HE HOLDS THE HASHIMOTO MEDALLION ...!
WH-WHO IS HE?!
ARE YOU SERIOUS ?!
THE COMEBACKS SOUNDED LIKE HIM, BUT ON A CLOSER LOOK THIS GUY DEFINITELY DOESN'T LOOK LIKE HIM.
THE PREZ, TOO ?!
AND THINKING ABOUT IT, I DON'T THINK KAZAMA'S STIFF HAIR IS REALLY SOMETHING YOU COULD TAME WITH JUST A WEEKEND MAKEOVER.
EVERY ONE OF YOU FELL FOR IT?!
UN-BELIE-VABLE.
WHAT ON EARTH IS THIS?

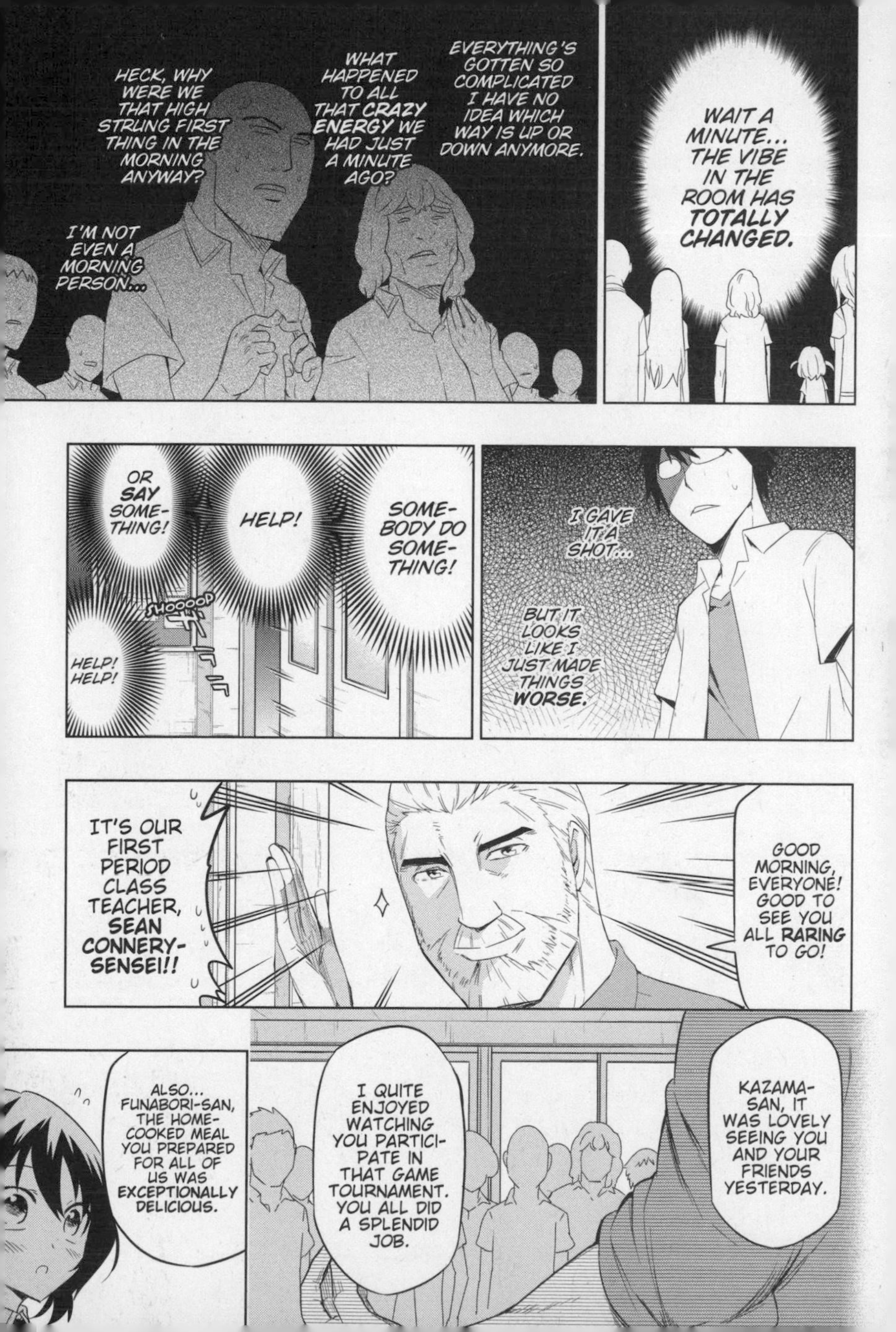
WAIT A MINUTE... THE VIBE IN THE ROOM HAS TOTALLY CHANGED.
EVERYTHING'S GOTTEN SO COMPLICATED I HAVE NO IDEA WHICH WAY IS UP OR DOWN ANYMORE.
WHAT HAPPENED TO ALL THAT CRAZY ENERGY WE HAD JUST A MINUTE AGO?
HECK, WHY WERE WE THAT HIGH STRUNG FIRST THING IN THE MORNING ANYWAY?
I'M NOT EVEN A MORNING PERSON...
I GAVE IT A SHOT...
BUT IT LOOKS LIKE I JUST MADE THINGS WORSE.
SOME-BODY DO SOME-THING!
HELP!
OR SAY SOME-THING!
SHOOOOOD
HELP! HELP!
GOOD MORNING, EVERYONE! GOOD TO SEE YOU ALL RARING TO GO!
IT'S OUR FIRST PERIOD CLASS TEACHER, SEAN CONNERY-SENSEI!!
KAZAMA-SAN, IT WAS LOVELY SEEING YOU AND YOUR FRIENDS YESTERDAY.
I QUITE ENJOYED WATCHING YOU PARTICI-PATE IN THAT GAME TOURNAMENT. YOU ALL DID A SPLENDID JOB.
ALSO... FUNABORI-SAN, THE HOME-COOKED MEAL YOU PREPARED FOR ALL OF US WAS EXCEPTIONALLY DELICIOUS.

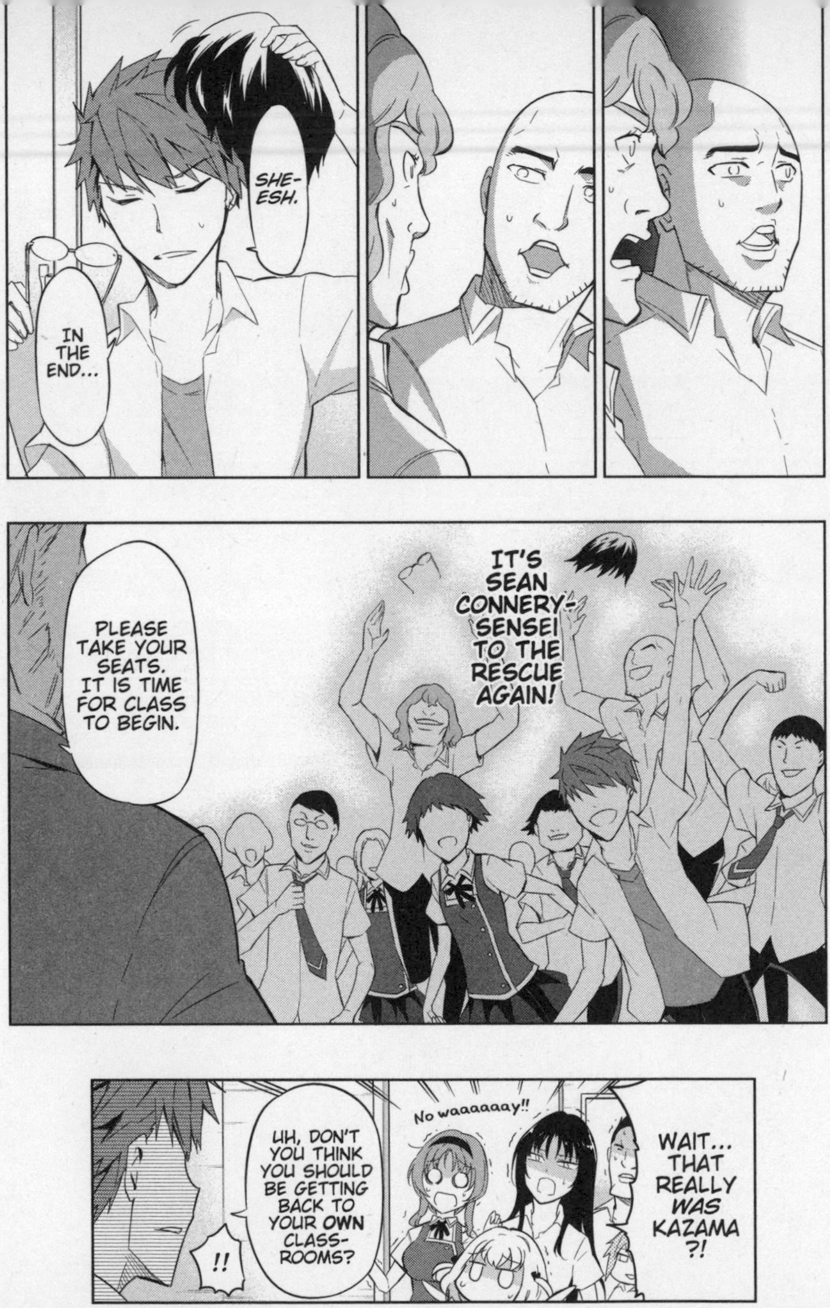
SHE-ESH.
IN THE END...
IT'S SEAN CONNERY-SENSEI TO THE RESCUE AGAIN!
PLEASE TAKE YOUR SEATS. IT IS TIME FOR CLASS TO BEGIN.
WAIT... THAT REALLY WAS KAZAMA?!
No waaaaaay!!
UH, DON'T YOU THINK YOU SHOULD BE GETTING BACK TO YOUR OWN CLASS-ROOMS?
!!

TOSS
My wig!!
My glass-es!!

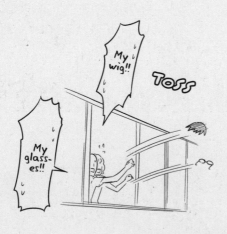

D-FRAGMENTS

ディーふらぐ!

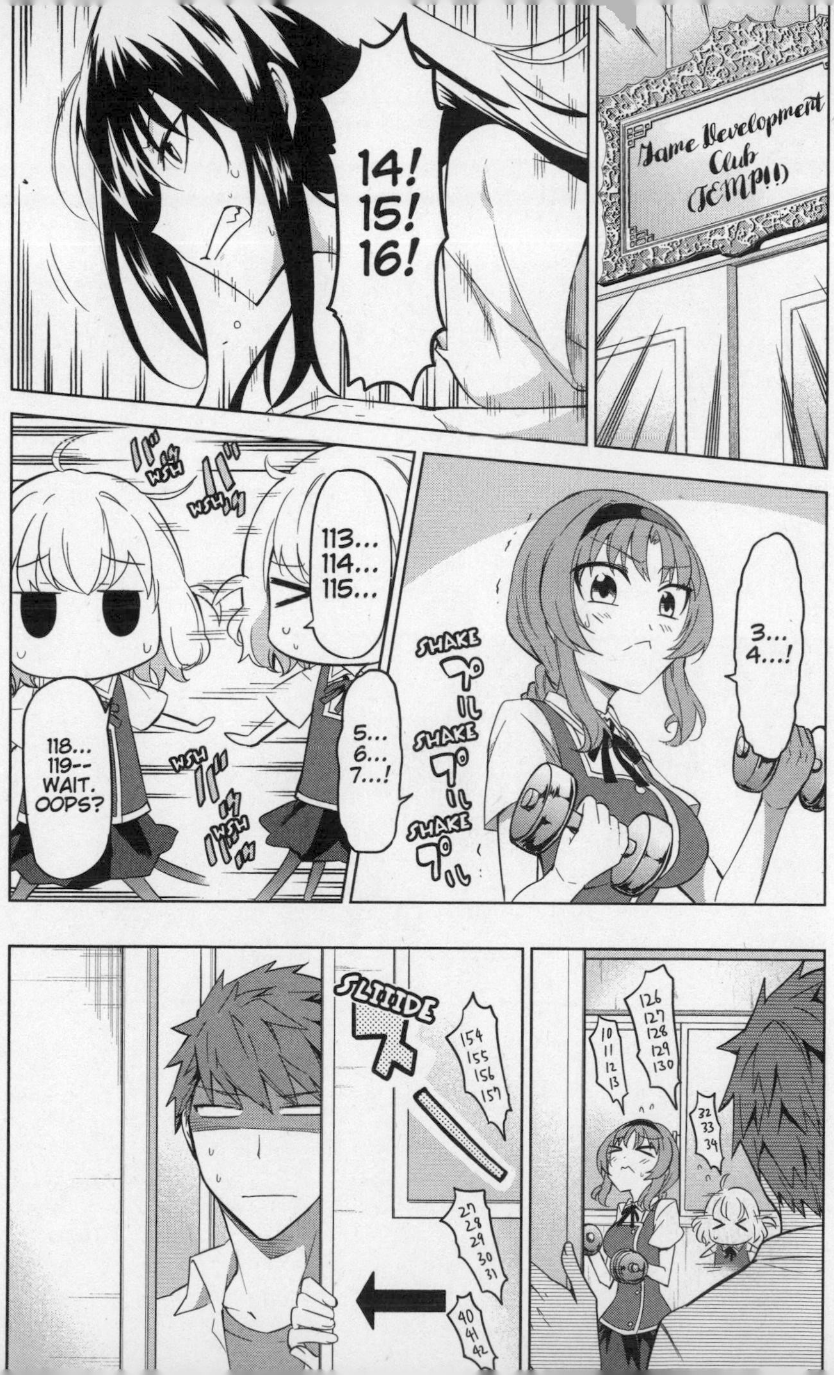
Game Development Club (TEMP!!)
14! 15! 16!
3... 4...!
SHAKE
SHAKE
SHAKE
113... 114... 115...
5... 6... 7...!
WSH
WSH
118... 119-- WAIT. OOPS?
WSH
WSH
126 127 128 129 130
10 11 12 13
32 33 34
SLIIIDE
154 155 156 157
27 28 29 30 31
40 41 42

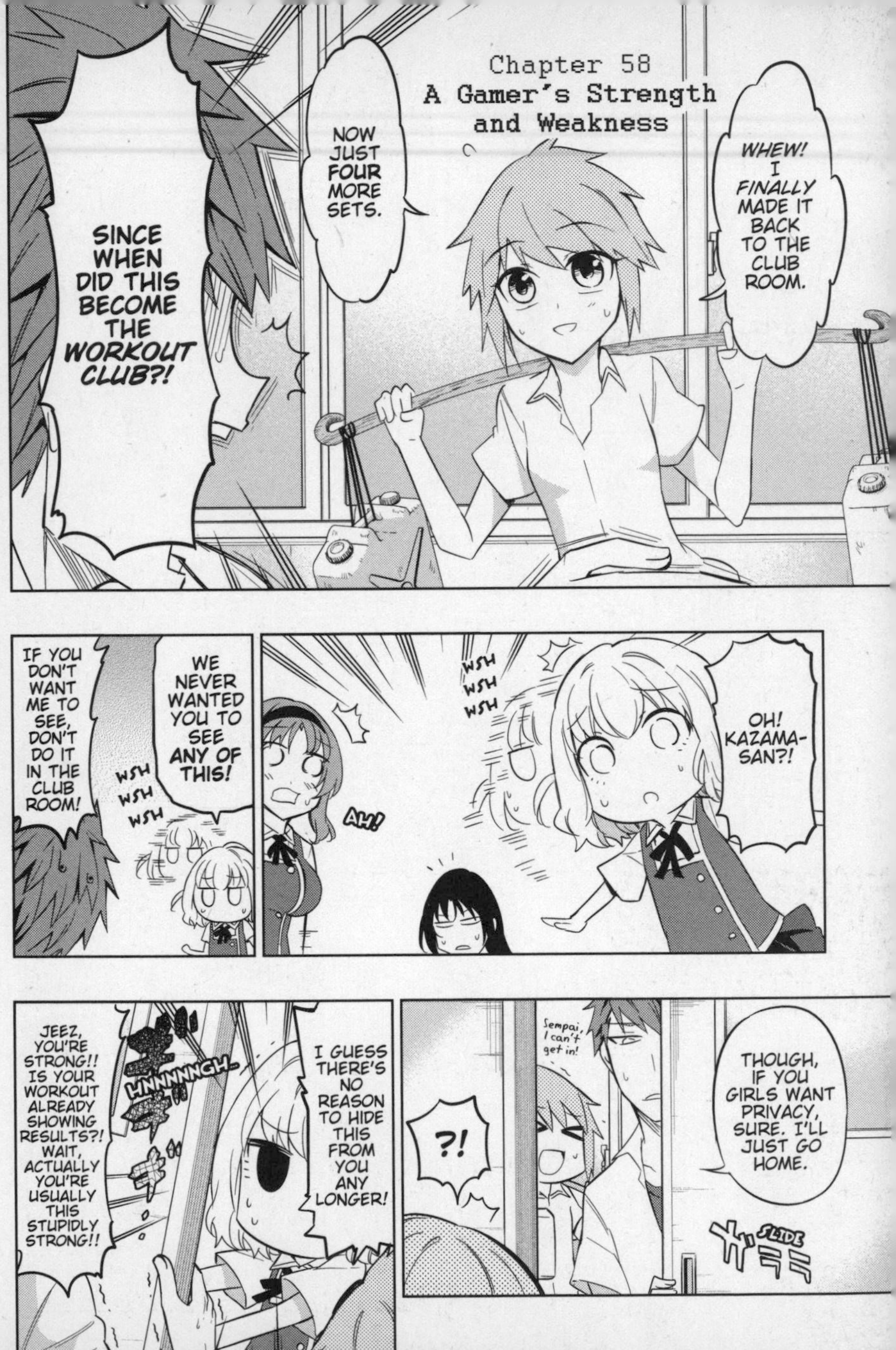
Chapter 58
A Gamer's Strength and Weakness
WHEW! I FINALLY MADE IT BACK TO THE CLUB ROOM.
NOW JUST FOUR MORE SETS.
SINCE WHEN DID THIS BECOME THE WORKOUT CLUB?!
WSH WSH WSH
OH! KAZAMA-SAN?!
AH!
WE NEVER WANTED YOU TO SEE ANY OF THIS!
IF YOU DON'T WANT ME TO SEE, DON'T DO IT IN THE CLUB ROOM!
WSH WSH WSH
Sempai, I can't get in!
THOUGH, IF YOU GIRLS WANT PRIVACY, SURE. I'LL JUST GO HOME.
?!
SLIDE
I GUESS THERE'S NO REASON TO HIDE THIS FROM YOU ANY LONGER!
HNNNNNGH...
JEEZ, YOU'RE STRONG!! IS YOUR WORKOUT ALREADY SHOWING RESULTS?! WAIT, ACTUALLY YOU'RE USUALLY THIS STUPIDLY STRONG!!

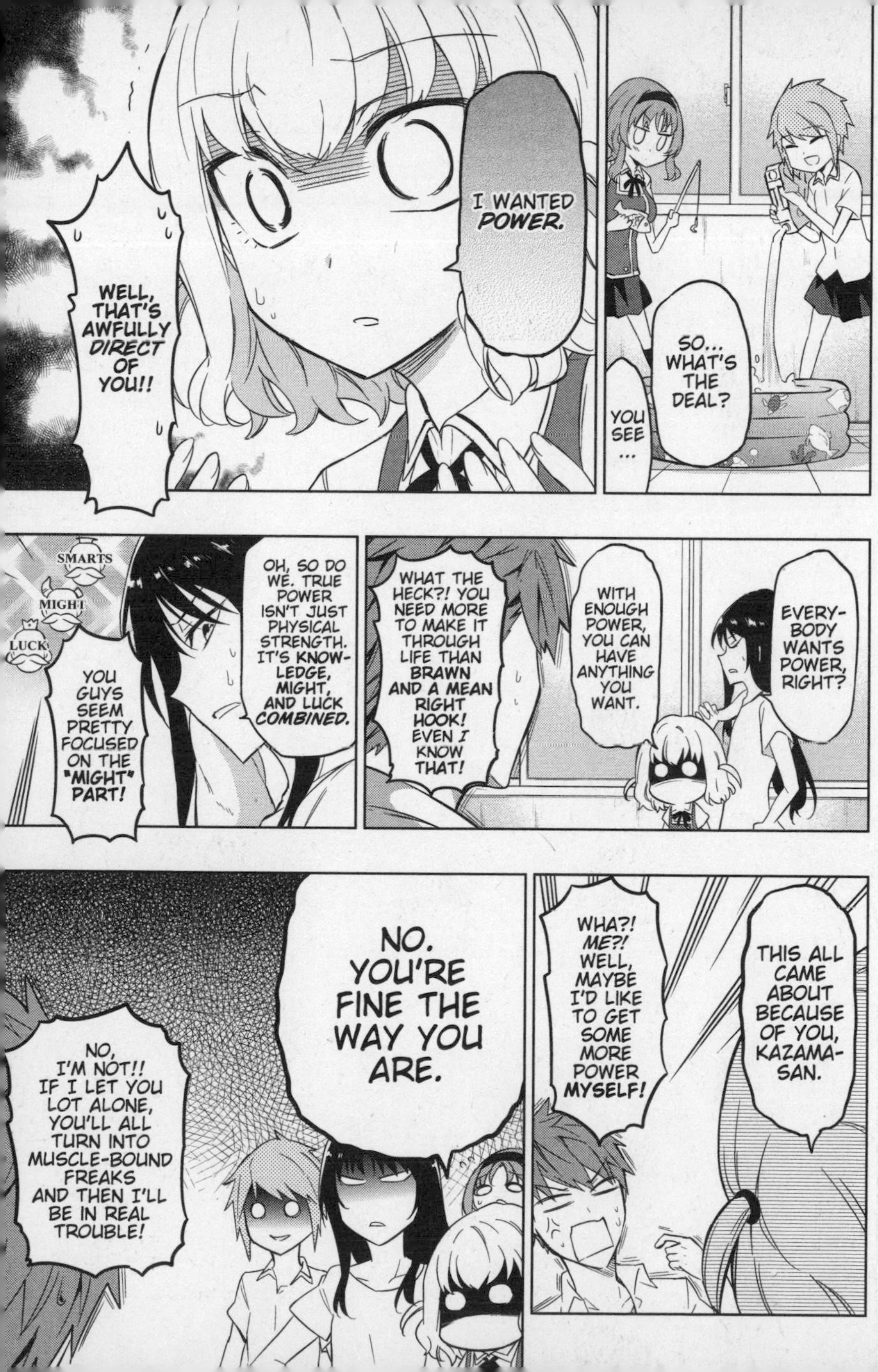

SO... WHAT'S THE DEAL?
YOU SEE ...
I WANTED POWER.
WELL, THAT'S AWFULLY DIRECT OF YOU!!
EVERY-BODY WANTS POWER, RIGHT?
WITH ENOUGH POWER, YOU CAN HAVE ANYTHING YOU WANT.
WHAT THE HECK?! YOU NEED MORE TO MAKE IT THROUGH LIFE THAN BRAWN AND A MEAN RIGHT HOOK! EVEN I KNOW THAT!
OH, SO DO WE. TRUE POWER ISN'T JUST PHYSICAL STRENGTH. IT'S KNOW-LEDGE, MIGHT, AND LUCK COMBINED.
SMARTS
MIGHT
LUCK
YOU GUYS SEEM PRETTY FOCUSED ON THE "MIGHT" PART!
THIS ALL CAME ABOUT BECAUSE OF YOU, KAZAMA-SAN.
WHA?! ME?! WELL, MAYBE I'D LIKE TO GET SOME MORE POWER MYSELF!
NO. YOU'RE FINE THE WAY YOU ARE.
NO, I'M NOT!! IF I LET YOU LOT ALONE, YOU'LL ALL TURN INTO MUSCLE-BOUND FREAKS AND THEN I'LL BE IN REAL TROUBLE!

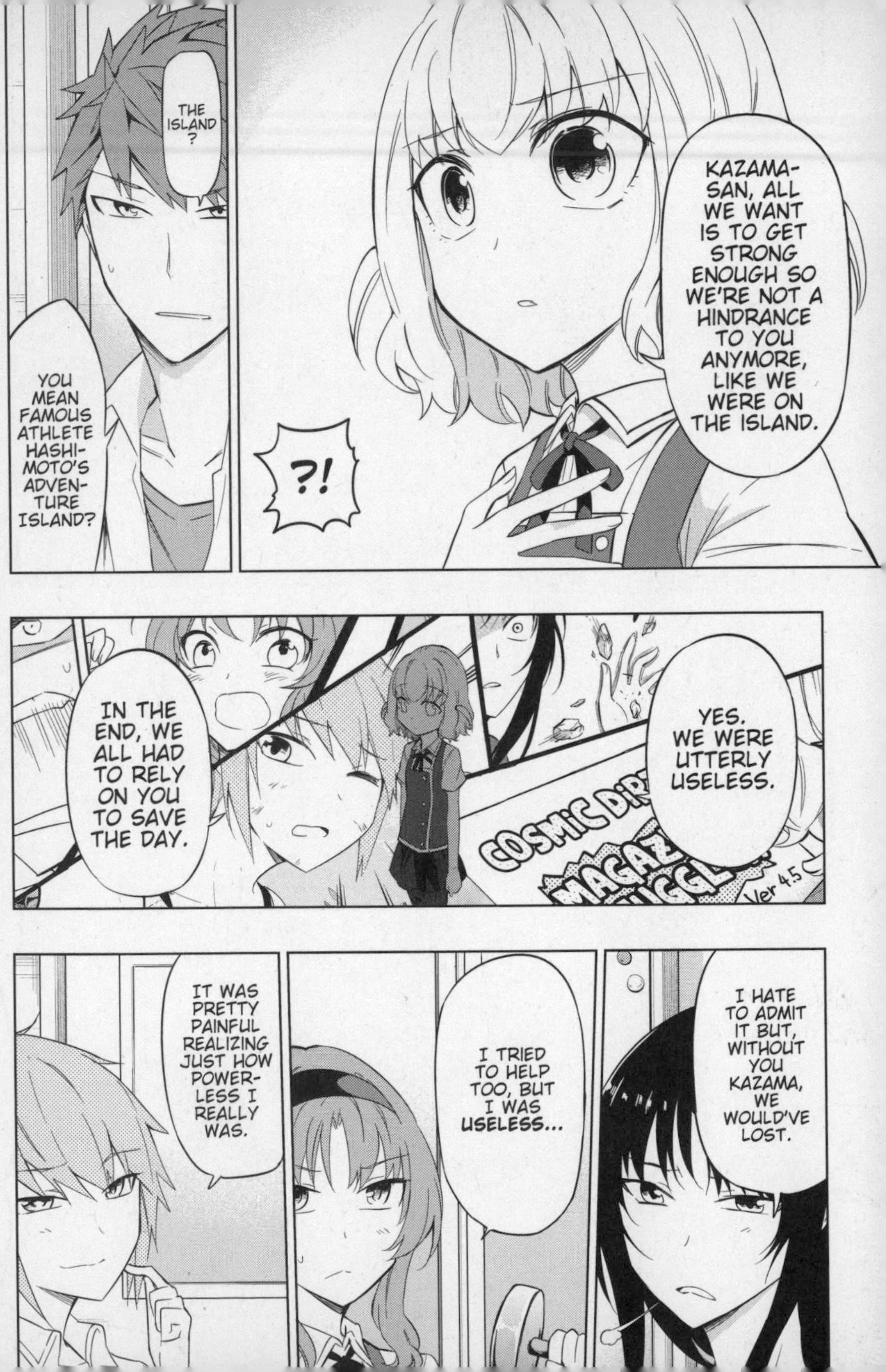
KAZAMA-SAN, ALL WE WANT IS TO GET STRONG ENOUGH SO WE'RE NOT A HINDRANCE TO YOU ANYMORE, LIKE WE WERE ON THE ISLAND.
?!
THE ISLAND?
YOU MEAN FAMOUS ATHLETE HASHIMOTO'S ADVENTURE ISLAND?
YES. WE WERE UTTERLY USELESS.
Ver 4.5
IN THE END, WE ALL HAD TO RELY ON YOU TO SAVE THE DAY.
I HATE TO ADMIT IT BUT, WITHOUT YOU KAZAMA, WE WOULD'VE LOST.
I TRIED TO HELP TOO, BUT I WAS USELESS...
IT WAS PRETTY PAINFUL REALIZING JUST HOW POWERLESS I REALLY WAS.

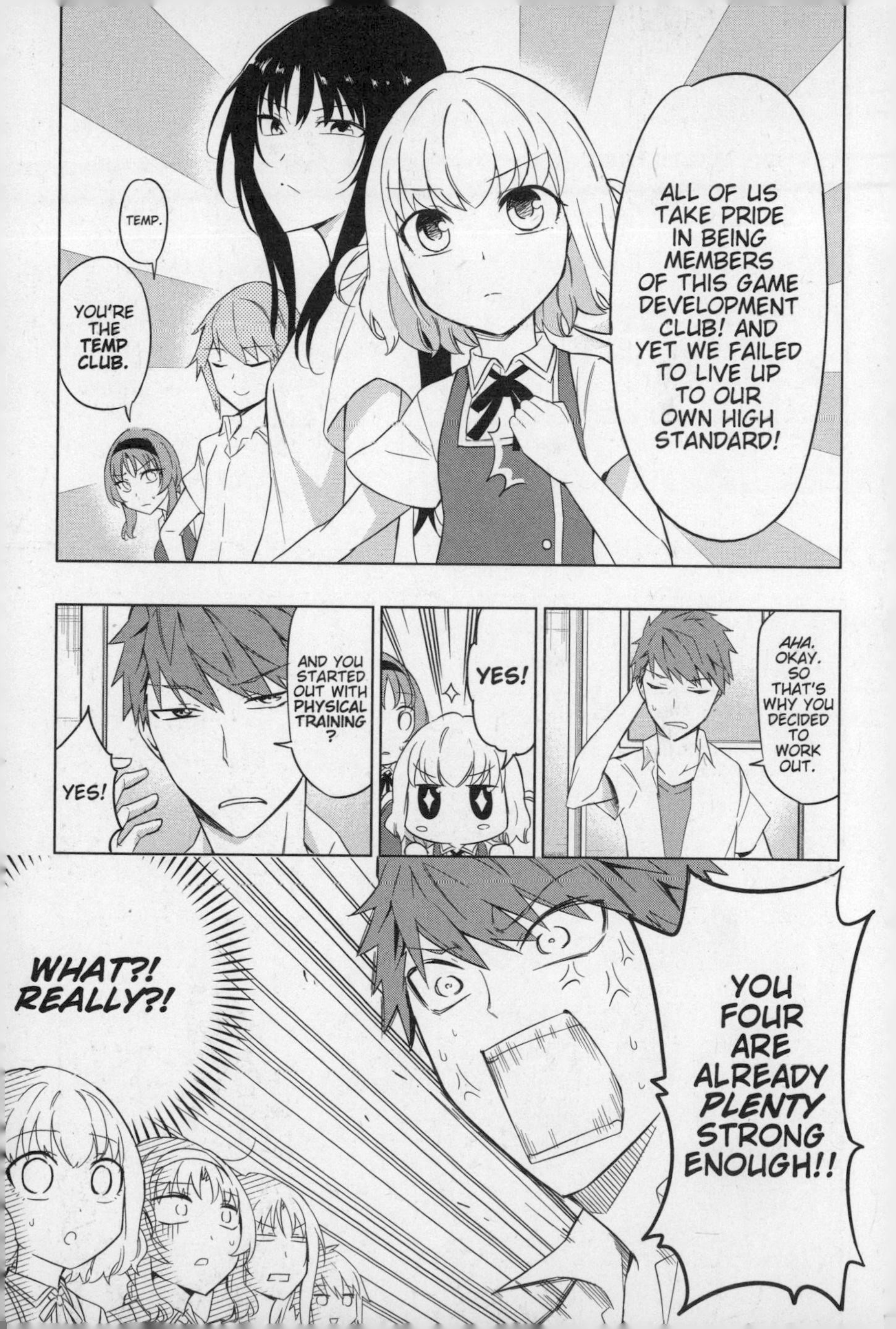
ALL OF US TAKE PRIDE IN BEING MEMBERS OF THIS GAME DEVELOPMENT CLUB! AND YET WE FAILED TO LIVE UP TO OUR OWN HIGH STANDARD!
TEMP.
YOU'RE THE TEMP CLUB.
AHA. OKAY. SO THAT'S WHY YOU DECIDED TO WORK OUT.
YES!
AND YOU STARTED OUT WITH PHYSICAL TRAINING?
YES!
YOU FOUR ARE ALREADY PLENTY STRONG ENOUGH!!
WHAT?! REALLY?!

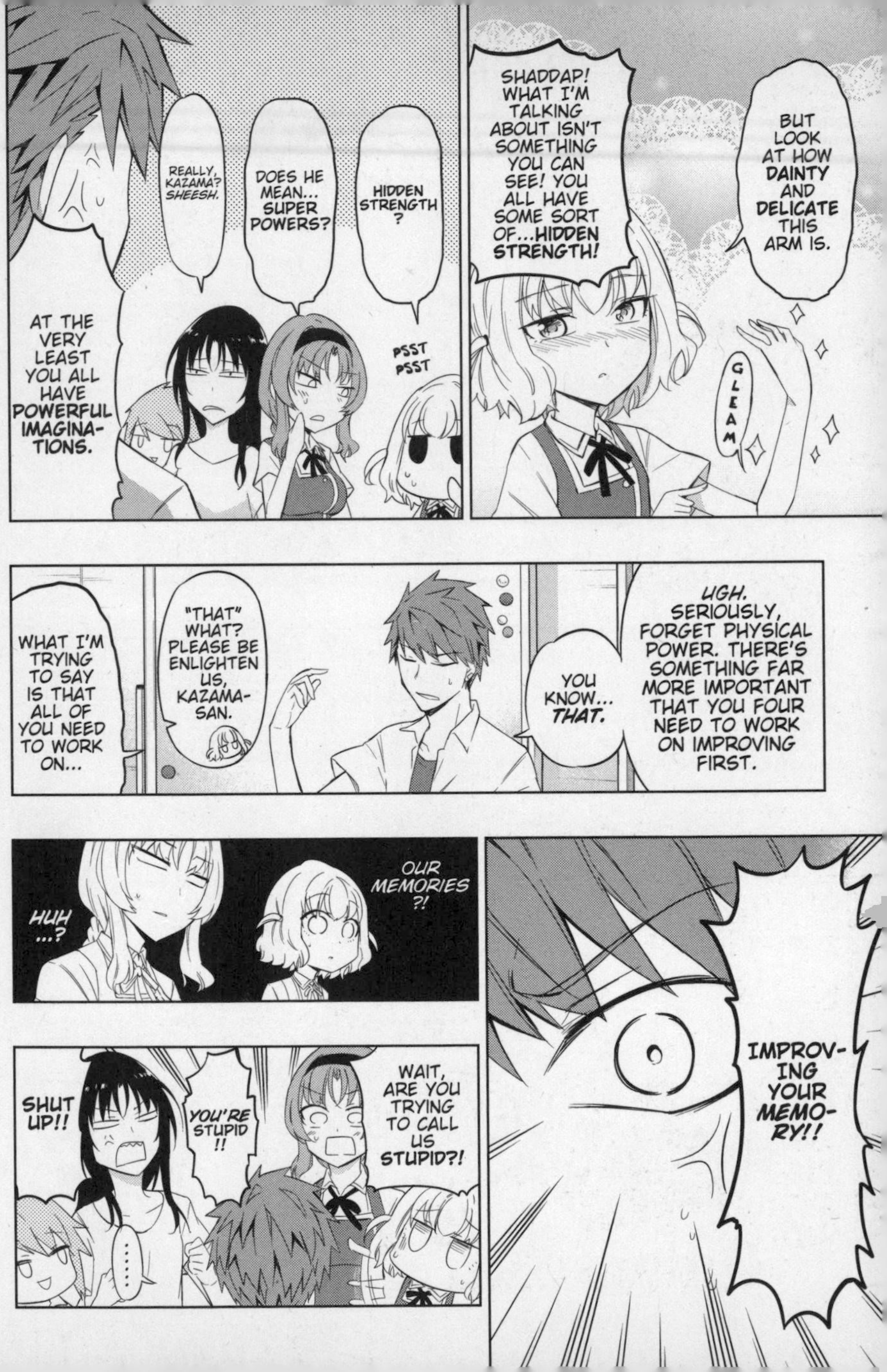
BUT LOOK AT HOW DAINTY AND DELICATE THIS ARM IS.
GLEAM
SHADDAP! WHAT I'M TALKING ABOUT ISN'T SOMETHING YOU CAN SEE! YOU ALL HAVE SOME SORT OF...HIDDEN STRENGTH!
HIDDEN STRENGTH?
PSST PSST
DOES HE MEAN... SUPER POWERS?
REALLY, KAZAMA? SHEESH.
AT THE VERY LEAST YOU ALL HAVE POWERFUL IMAGINATIONS.
UGH. SERIOUSLY, FORGET PHYSICAL POWER. THERE'S SOMETHING FAR MORE IMPORTANT THAT YOU FOUR NEED TO WORK ON IMPROVING FIRST.
YOU KNOW... THAT.
"THAT" WHAT? PLEASE BE ENLIGHTEN US, KAZAMA-SAN.
WHAT I'M TRYING TO SAY IS THAT ALL OF YOU NEED TO WORK ON...
IMPROVING YOUR MEMORY!!
OUR MEMORIES?!
HUH...?
WAIT, ARE YOU TRYING TO CALL US STUPID?!
YOU'RE STUPID!!
SHUT UP!!
......

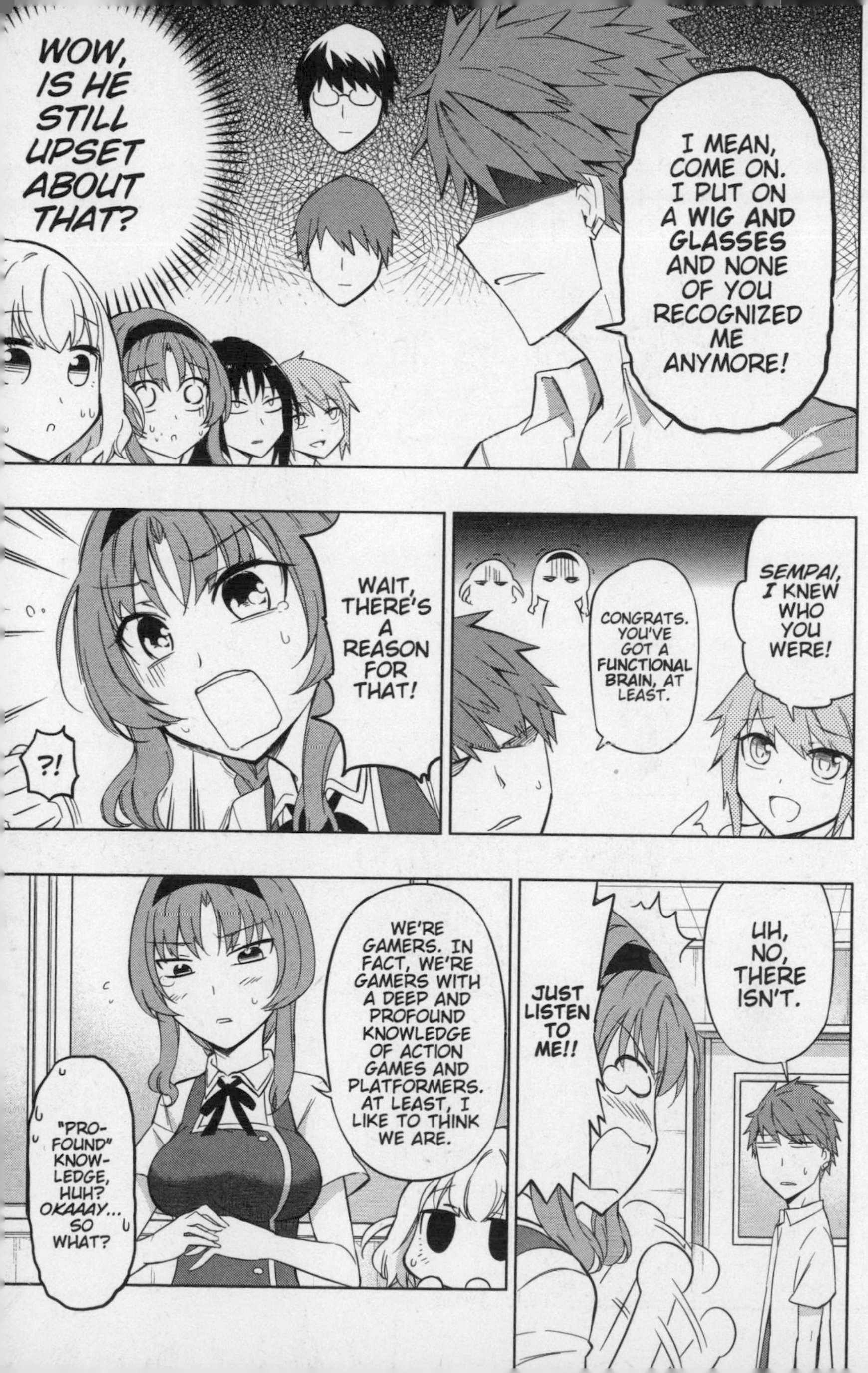
I MEAN, COME ON. I PUT ON A WIG AND GLASSES AND NONE OF YOU RECOGNIZED ME ANYMORE!
WOW, IS HE STILL UPSET ABOUT THAT?
SEMPAI, I KNEW WHO YOU WERE!
CONGRATS. YOU'VE GOT A FUNCTIONAL BRAIN, AT LEAST.
WAIT, THERE'S A REASON FOR THAT!
?!
UH, NO, THERE ISN'T.
JUST LISTEN TO ME!!
WE'RE GAMERS. IN FACT, WE'RE GAMERS WITH A DEEP AND PROFOUND KNOWLEDGE OF ACTION GAMES AND PLATFORMERS. AT LEAST, I LIKE TO THINK WE ARE.
"PRO-FOUND" KNOW-LEDGE, HUH? OKAAAY... SO WHAT?

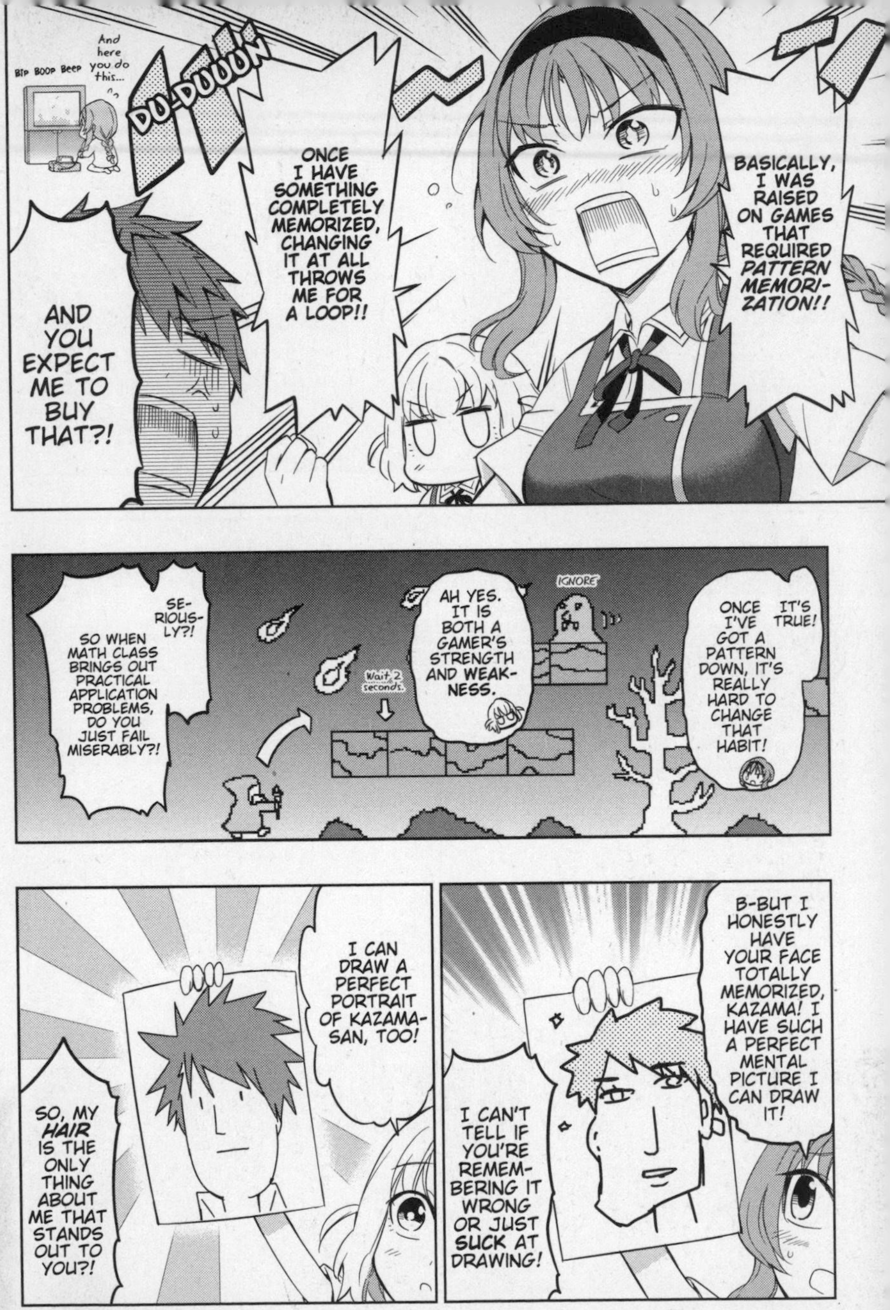
BASICALLY, I WAS RAISED ON GAMES THAT REQUIRED PATTERN MEMORIZATION!!
ONCE I HAVE SOMETHING COMPLETELY MEMORIZED, CHANGING IT AT ALL THROWS ME FOR A LOOP!!
DU-DUUUN
And here you do this...
BIP BOOP BEEP
AND YOU EXPECT ME TO BUY THAT?!
IT'S TRUE!
ONCE I'VE GOT A PATTERN DOWN, IT'S REALLY HARD TO CHANGE THAT HABIT!
IGNORE
AH YES. IT IS BOTH A GAMER'S STRENGTH AND WEAKNESS.
Wait 2 seconds.
SERIOUSLY?!
SO WHEN MATH CLASS BRINGS OUT PRACTICAL APPLICATION PROBLEMS, DO YOU JUST FAIL MISERABLY?!
B-BUT I HONESTLY HAVE YOUR FACE TOTALLY MEMORIZED, KAZAMA! I HAVE SUCH A PERFECT MENTAL PICTURE I CAN DRAW IT!
I CAN'T TELL IF YOU'RE REMEMBERING IT WRONG OR JUST SUCK AT DRAWING!
I CAN DRAW A PERFECT PORTRAIT OF KAZAMA-SAN, TOO!
SO, MY HAIR IS THE ONLY THING ABOUT ME THAT STANDS OUT TO YOU?!

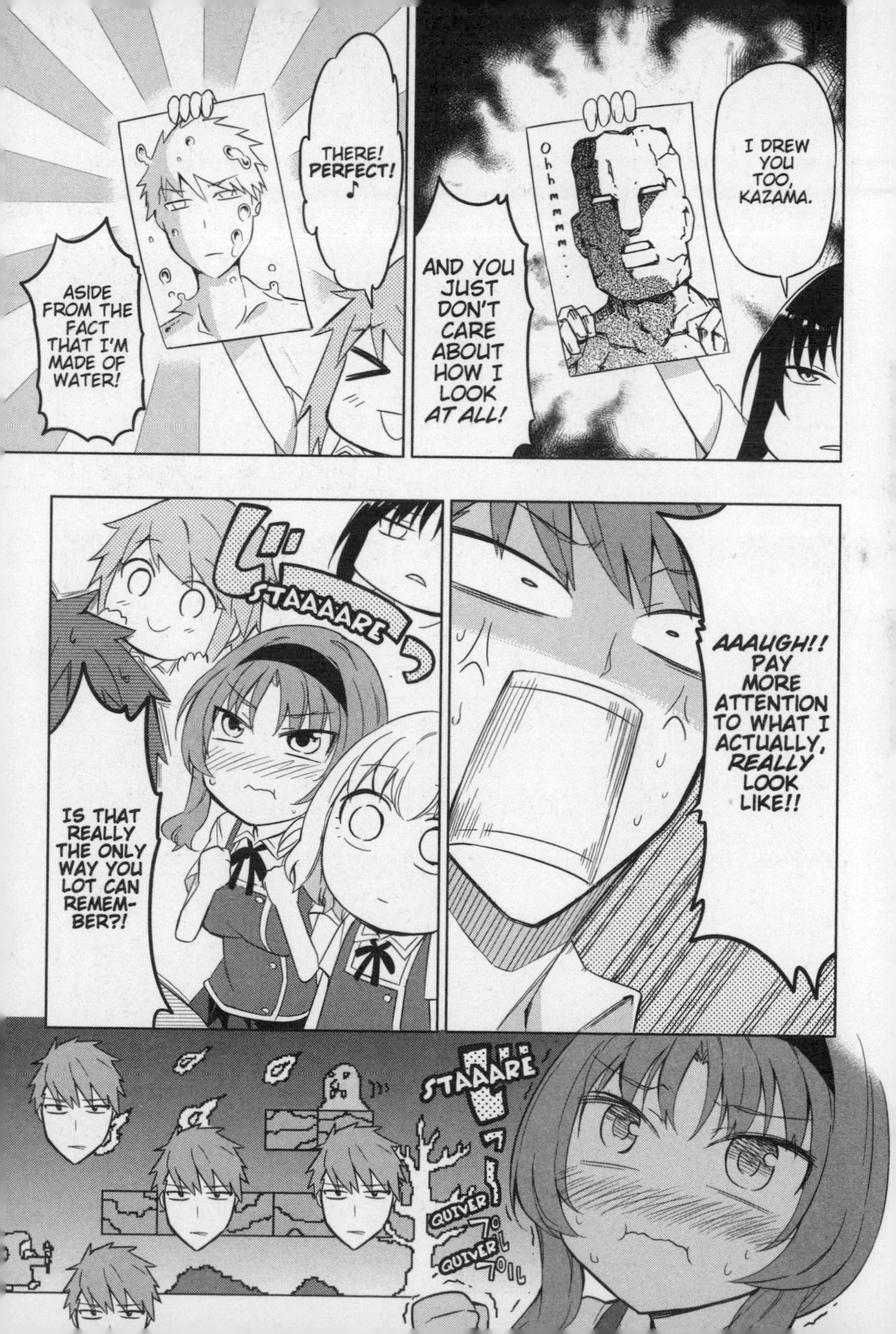
I DREW YOU TOO, KAZAMA.
Ohhmmmm...
AND YOU JUST DON'T CARE ABOUT HOW I LOOK AT ALL!
THERE! PERFECT! ♪
ASIDE FROM THE FACT THAT I'M MADE OF WATER!
AAAUGH!! PAY MORE ATTENTION TO WHAT I ACTUALLY, REALLY LOOK LIKE!!
STAAAAARE
IS THAT REALLY THE ONLY WAY YOU LOT CAN REMEMBER?!
STAAARE
QUIVER
QUIVER

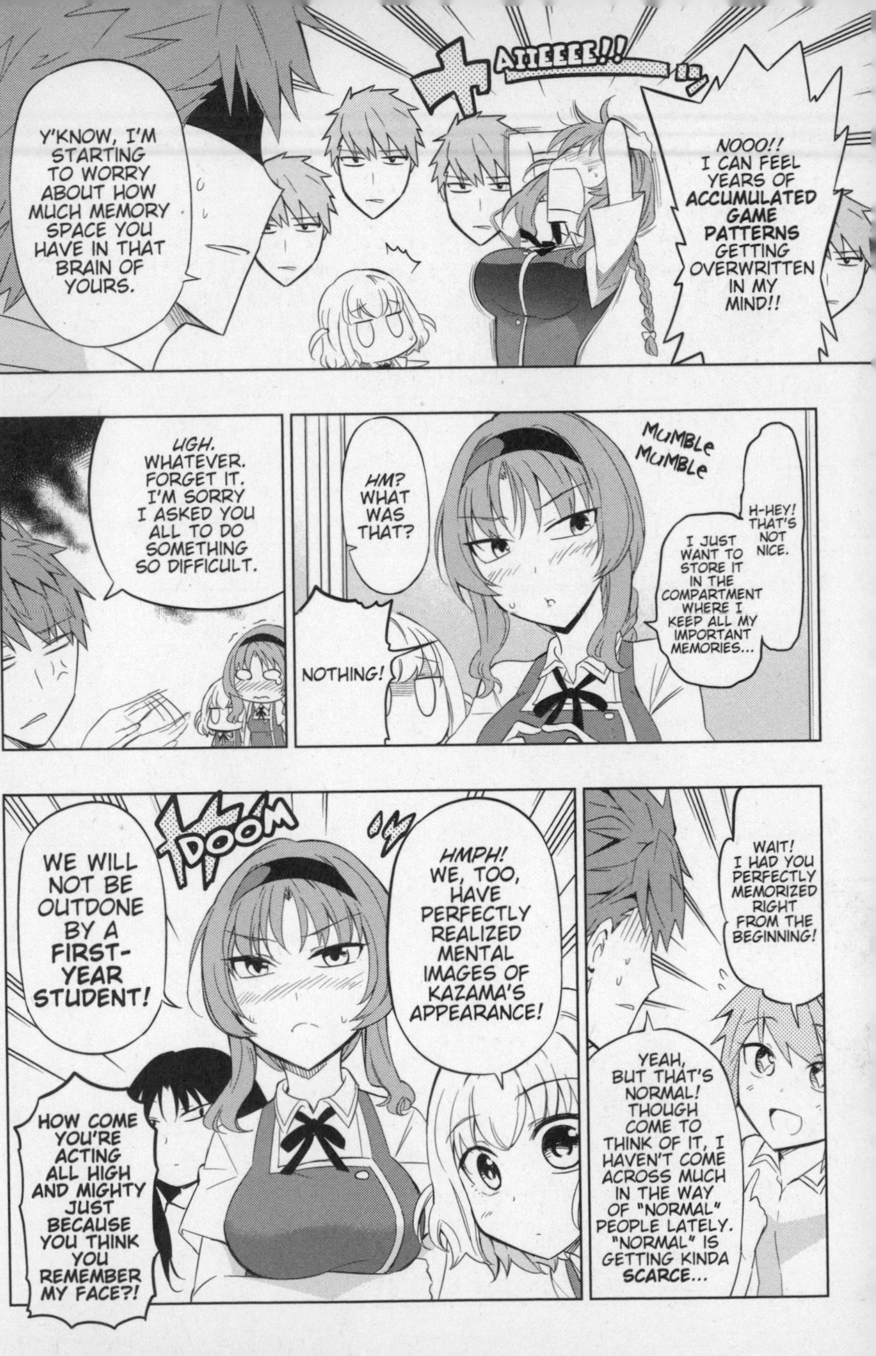
AIIEEEE!!
NOOO!! I CAN FEEL YEARS OF ACCUMULATED GAME PATTERNS GETTING OVERWRITTEN IN MY MIND!!
Y'KNOW, I'M STARTING TO WORRY ABOUT HOW MUCH MEMORY SPACE YOU HAVE IN THAT BRAIN OF YOURS.
MUMBLE MUMBLE
H-HEY! THAT'S NOT NICE.
I JUST WANT TO STORE IT IN THE COMPARTMENT WHERE I KEEP ALL MY IMPORTANT MEMORIES...
HM? WHAT WAS THAT?
NOTHING!
UGH. WHATEVER. FORGET IT. I'M SORRY I ASKED YOU ALL TO DO SOMETHING SO DIFFICULT.
WAIT! I HAD YOU PERFECTLY MEMORIZED RIGHT FROM THE BEGINNING!
YEAH, BUT THAT'S NORMAL! THOUGH COME TO THINK OF IT, I HAVEN'T COME ACROSS MUCH IN THE WAY OF "NORMAL" PEOPLE LATELY. "NORMAL" IS GETTING KINDA SCARCE...
DOOM
HMPH! WE, TOO, HAVE PERFECTLY REALIZED MENTAL IMAGES OF KAZAMA'S APPEARANCE!
WE WILL NOT BE OUTDONE BY A FIRST-YEAR STUDENT!
HOW COME YOU'RE ACTING ALL HIGH AND MIGHTY JUST BECAUSE YOU THINK YOU REMEMBER MY FACE?!

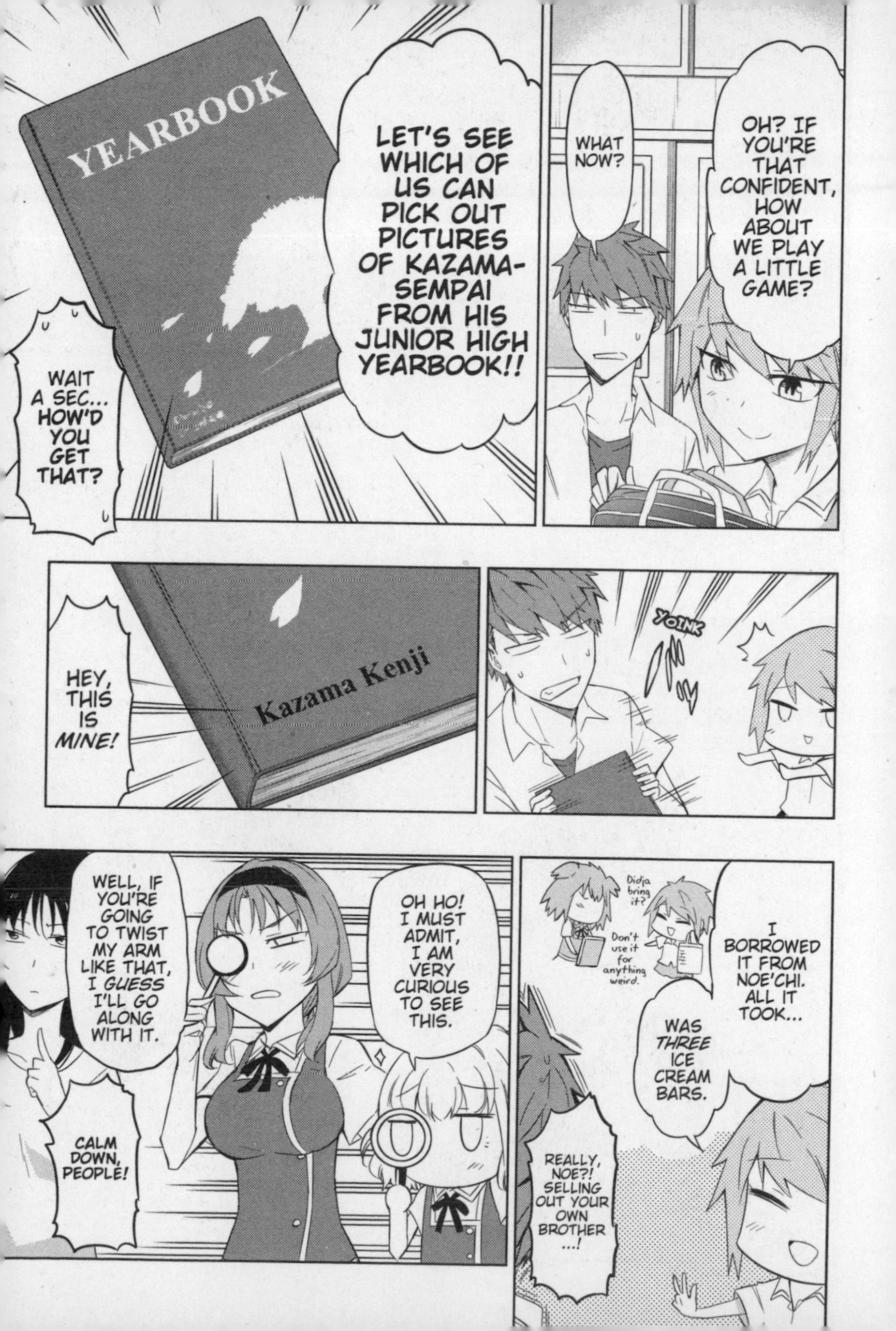
OH? IF YOU'RE THAT CONFIDENT, HOW ABOUT WE PLAY A LITTLE GAME?
WHAT NOW?
LET'S SEE WHICH OF US CAN PICK OUT PICTURES OF KAZAMA-SEMPAI FROM HIS JUNIOR HIGH YEARBOOK!!
YEARBOOK
WAIT A SEC... HOW'D YOU GET THAT?
YOINK
Kazama Kenji
HEY, THIS IS *MINE!*
I BORROWED IT FROM NOE'CHI. ALL IT TOOK...
Didja bring it?
Don't use it for anything weird.
WAS *THREE* ICE CREAM BARS.
REALLY, NOE?! SELLING OUT YOUR OWN BROTHER ...!
OH HO! I MUST ADMIT, I AM VERY CURIOUS TO SEE THIS.
WELL, IF YOU'RE GOING TO TWIST MY ARM LIKE THAT, I *GUESS* I'LL GO ALONG WITH IT.
CALM DOWN, PEOPLE!

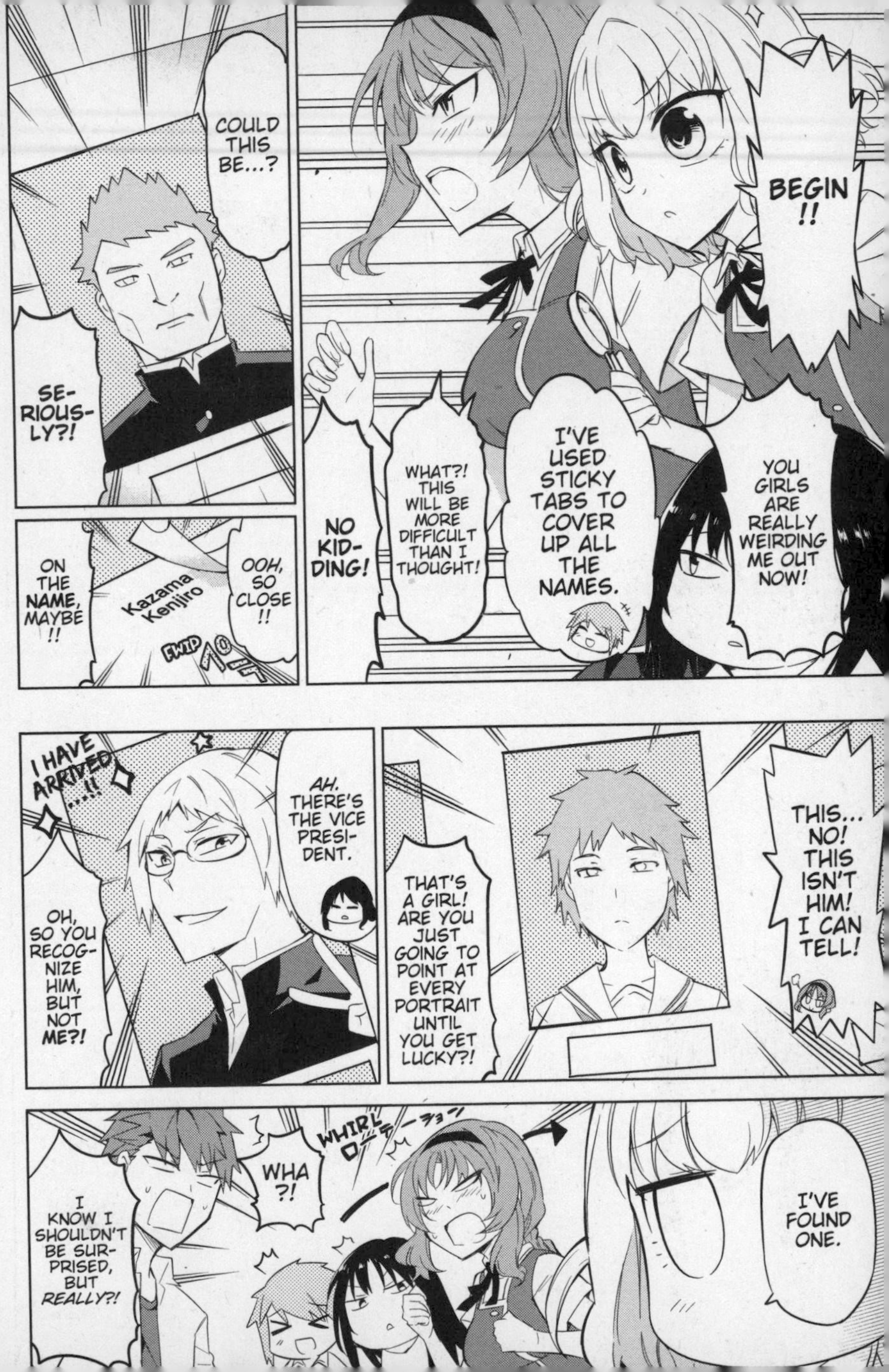
BEGIN!!
I'VE USED STICKY TABS TO COVER UP ALL THE NAMES.
YOU GIRLS ARE REALLY WEIRDING ME OUT NOW!
WHAT?! THIS WILL BE MORE DIFFICULT THAN I THOUGHT!
NO KIDDING!
COULD THIS BE...?
SERIOUSLY?!
OOH, SO CLOSE!!
Kazama Kenjiro
ON THE NAME, MAYBE!!
FWIP
THIS... NO! THIS ISN'T HIM! I CAN TELL!
THAT'S A GIRL! ARE YOU JUST GOING TO POINT AT EVERY PORTRAIT UNTIL YOU GET LUCKY?!
AH. THERE'S THE VICE PRESIDENT.
I HAVE ARRIVED...!!
OH, SO YOU RECOGNIZE HIM, BUT NOT ME?!
I'VE FOUND ONE.
WHIRL
WHA?!
I KNOW I SHOULDN'T BE SURPRISED, BUT REALLY?!

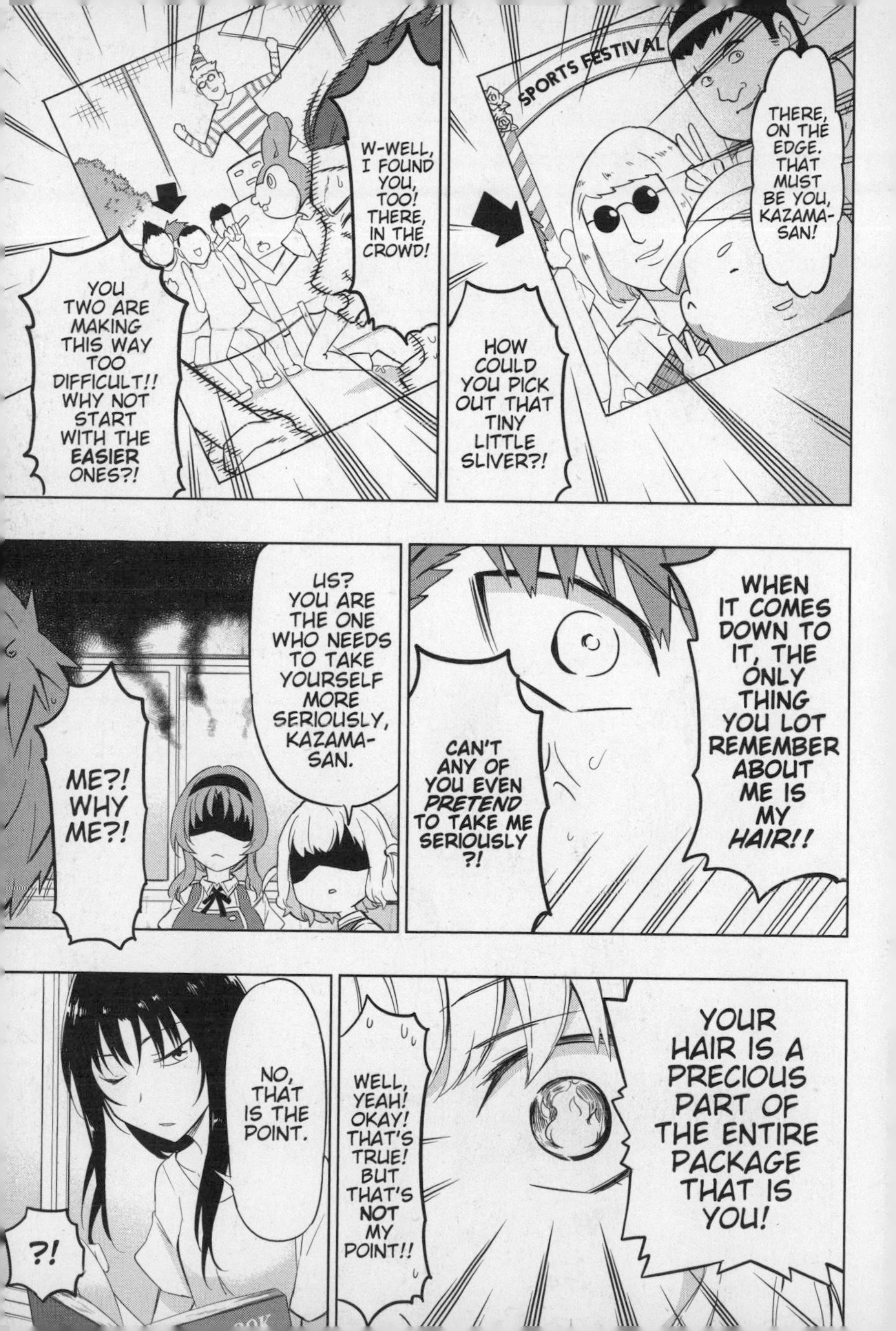
SPORTS FESTIVAL
THERE, ON THE EDGE. THAT MUST BE YOU, KAZAMA-SAN!
HOW COULD YOU PICK OUT THAT TINY LITTLE SLIVER?!
W-WELL, I FOUND YOU, TOO! THERE, IN THE CROWD!
YOU TWO ARE MAKING THIS WAY TOO DIFFICULT!! WHY NOT START WITH THE EASIER ONES?!
WHEN IT COMES DOWN TO IT, THE ONLY THING YOU LOT REMEMBER ABOUT ME IS MY *HAIR!!*
CAN'T ANY OF YOU EVEN *PRETEND* TO TAKE ME SERIOUSLY?!
US? YOU ARE THE ONE WHO NEEDS TO TAKE YOURSELF MORE SERIOUSLY, KAZAMA-SAN.
ME?! WHY ME?!
YOUR HAIR IS A PRECIOUS PART OF THE ENTIRE PACKAGE THAT IS YOU!
WELL, YEAH! OKAY! THAT'S TRUE! BUT THAT'S NOT MY POINT!!
NO, THAT IS THE POINT.
?!

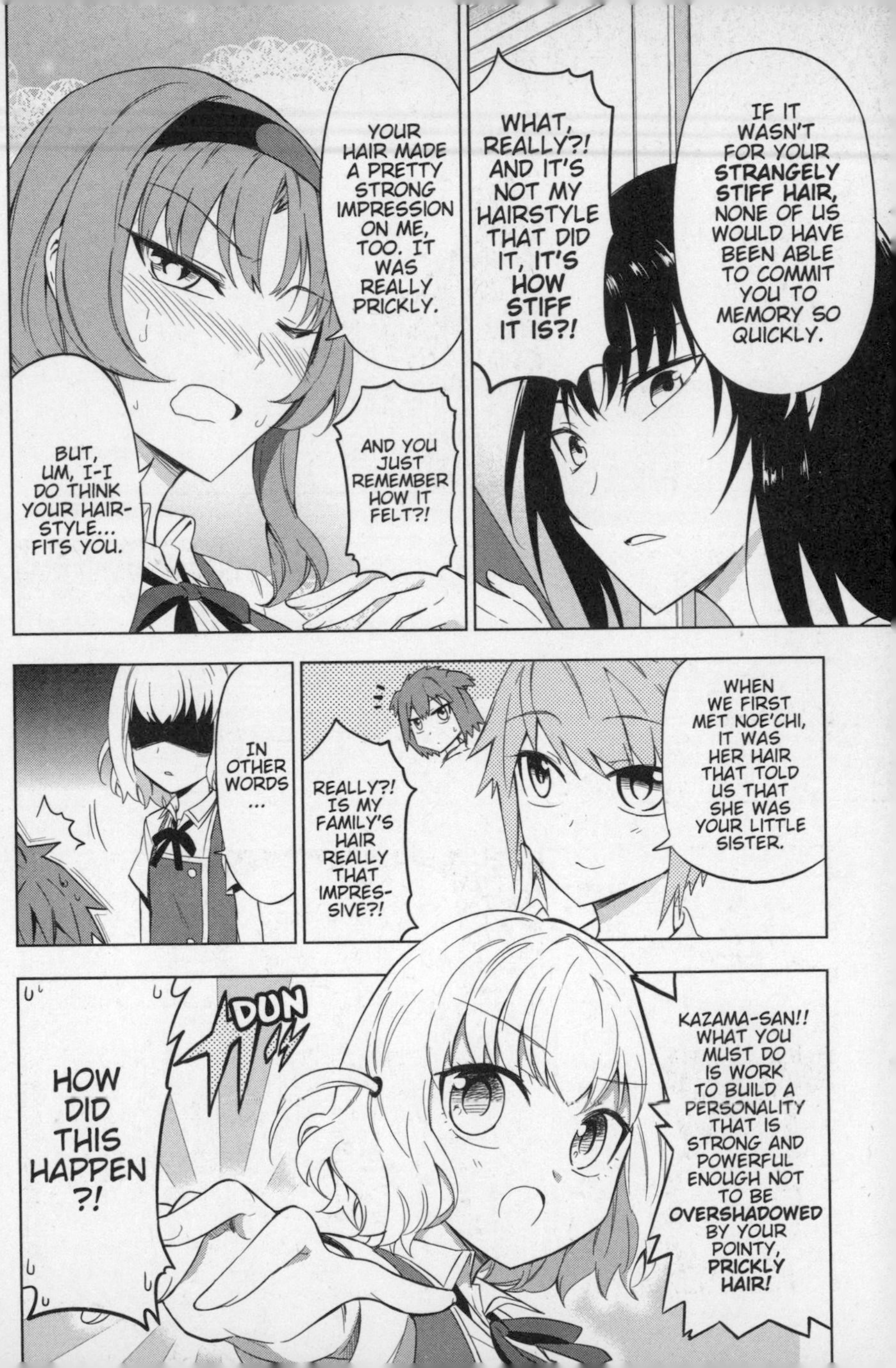
IF IT WASN'T FOR YOUR STRANGELY STIFF HAIR, NONE OF US WOULD HAVE BEEN ABLE TO COMMIT YOU TO MEMORY SO QUICKLY.
WHAT, REALLY?! AND IT'S NOT MY HAIRSTYLE THAT DID IT, IT'S HOW STIFF IT IS?!
YOUR HAIR MADE A PRETTY STRONG IMPRESSION ON ME, TOO. IT WAS REALLY PRICKLY.
AND YOU JUST REMEMBER HOW IT FELT?!
BUT, UM, I-I DO THINK YOUR HAIR-STYLE... FITS YOU.
WHEN WE FIRST MET NOE'CHI, IT WAS HER HAIR THAT TOLD US THAT SHE WAS YOUR LITTLE SISTER.
REALLY?! IS MY FAMILY'S HAIR REALLY THAT IMPRES-SIVE?!
IN OTHER WORDS...
KAZAMA-SAN!! WHAT YOU MUST DO IS WORK TO BUILD A PERSONALITY THAT IS STRONG AND POWERFUL ENOUGH NOT TO BE OVERSHADOWED BY YOUR POINTY, PRICKLY HAIR!
DUN
HOW DID THIS HAPPEN?!

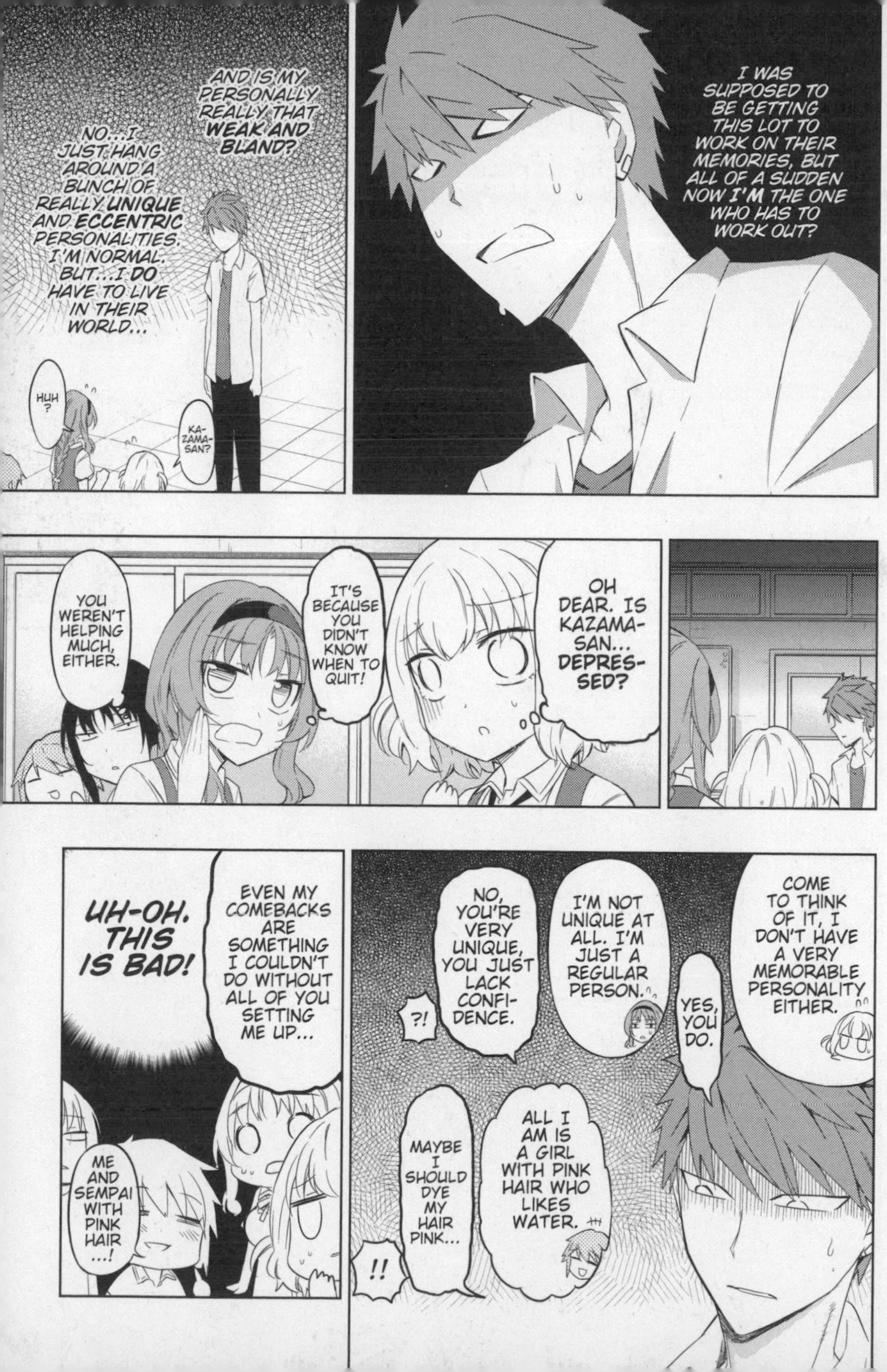
I WAS SUPPOSED TO BE GETTING THIS LOT TO WORK ON THEIR MEMORIES, BUT ALL OF A SUDDEN NOW I'M THE ONE WHO HAS TO WORK OUT?
AND IS MY PERSONALLY REALLY THAT WEAK AND BLAND?
NO...I JUST HANG AROUND A BUNCH OF REALLY UNIQUE AND ECCENTRIC PERSONALITIES. I'M NORMAL. BUT...I DO HAVE TO LIVE IN THEIR WORLD...
KA-ZAMA-SAN?
HUH?
OH DEAR. IS KAZAMA-SAN... DEPRES-SED?
IT'S BECAUSE YOU DIDN'T KNOW WHEN TO QUIT!
YOU WEREN'T HELPING MUCH, EITHER.
COME TO THINK OF IT, I DON'T HAVE A VERY MEMORABLE PERSONALITY EITHER.
YES, YOU DO.
I'M NOT UNIQUE AT ALL. I'M JUST A REGULAR PERSON.
NO, YOU'RE VERY UNIQUE, YOU JUST LACK CONFI-DENCE.
?!
ALL I AM IS A GIRL WITH PINK HAIR WHO LIKES WATER.
MAYBE I SHOULD DYE MY HAIR PINK...
!!
EVEN MY COMEBACKS ARE SOMETHING I COULDN'T DO WITHOUT ALL OF YOU SETTING ME UP...
UH-OH. THIS IS BAD!
ME AND SEMPAI WITH PINK HAIR...!

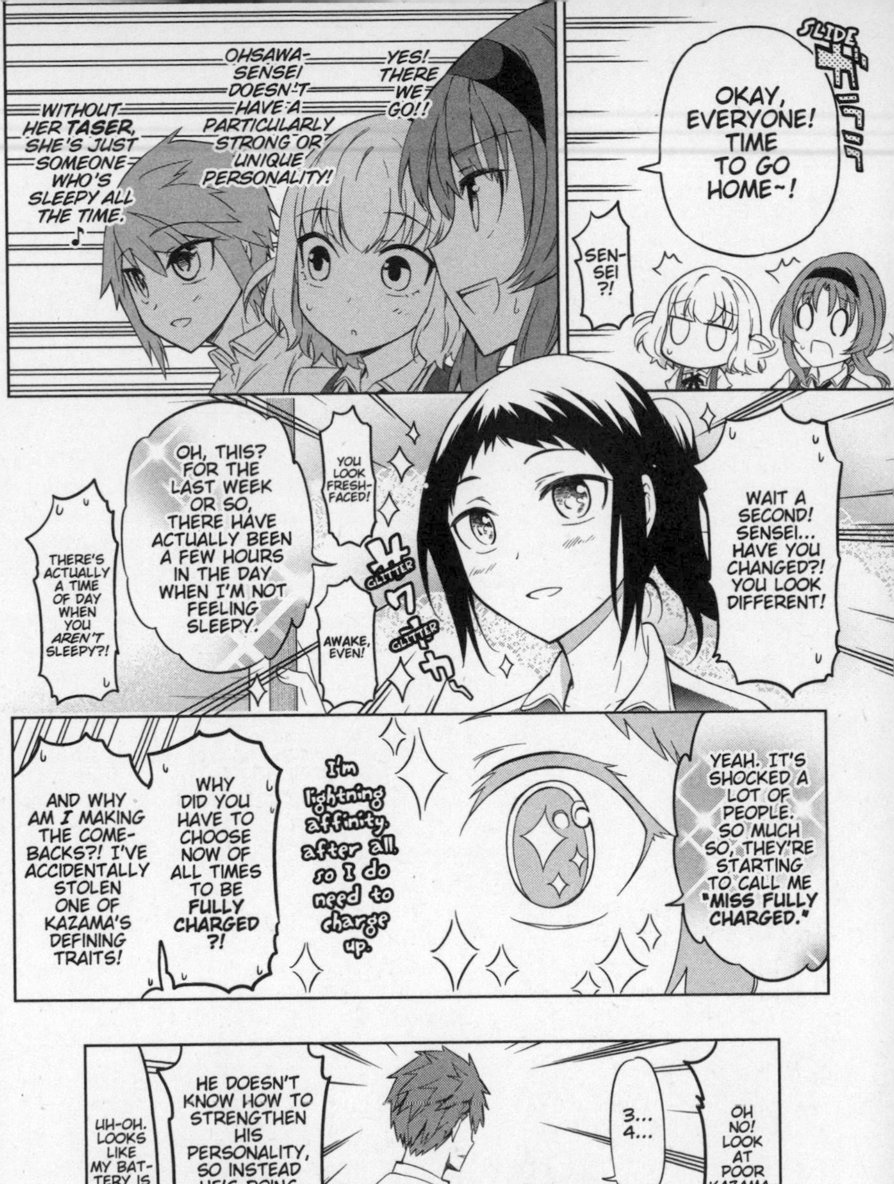
SLIDE
OKAY, EVERYONE! TIME TO GO HOME~!
SEN-SEI?!
YES! THERE WE GO!!
OHSAWA-SENSEI DOESN'T HAVE A PARTICULARLY STRONG OR UNIQUE PERSONALITY!
WITHOUT HER TASER, SHE'S JUST SOMEONE WHO'S SLEEPY ALL THE TIME. ♪
WAIT A SECOND! SENSEI... HAVE YOU CHANGED?! YOU LOOK DIFFERENT!
YOU LOOK FRESH-FACED!
GLITTER
GLITTER
AWAKE, EVEN!
OH, THIS? FOR THE LAST WEEK OR SO, THERE HAVE ACTUALLY BEEN A FEW HOURS IN THE DAY WHEN I'M NOT FEELING SLEEPY.
THERE'S ACTUALLY A TIME OF DAY WHEN YOU AREN'T SLEEPY?!
YEAH. IT'S SHOCKED A LOT OF PEOPLE. SO MUCH SO, THEY'RE STARTING TO CALL ME "MISS FULLY CHARGED."
I'm lightning affinity, after all, so I do need to charge up.
WHY DID YOU HAVE TO CHOOSE NOW OF ALL TIMES TO BE FULLY CHARGED?!
AND WHY AM I MAKING THE COME-BACKS?! I'VE ACCIDENTALLY STOLEN ONE OF KAZAMA'S DEFINING TRAITS!
OH NO! LOOK AT POOR KAZAMA-SAN!
3... 4...
HE DOESN'T KNOW HOW TO STRENGTHEN HIS PERSONALITY, SO INSTEAD HE'S DOING STRENGTH TRAINING?!
UH-OH. LOOKS LIKE MY BAT-TERY IS RUNNING LOW...

NEXT: Vol.09...

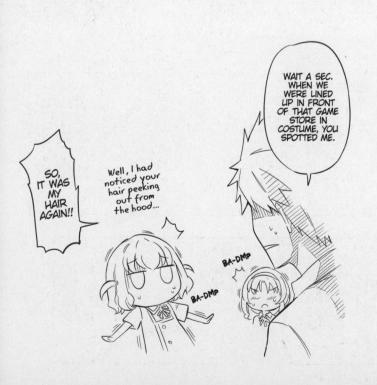

WAIT A SEC. WHEN WE WERE LINED UP IN FRONT OF THAT GAME STORE IN COSTUME, YOU SPOTTED ME.
Well, I had noticed your hair peeking out from the hood...
SO, IT WAS MY HAIR AGAIN!!
BA-DMP
BA-DMP

D-FRAGMENTS ディーフラグメンツ!

Bonus

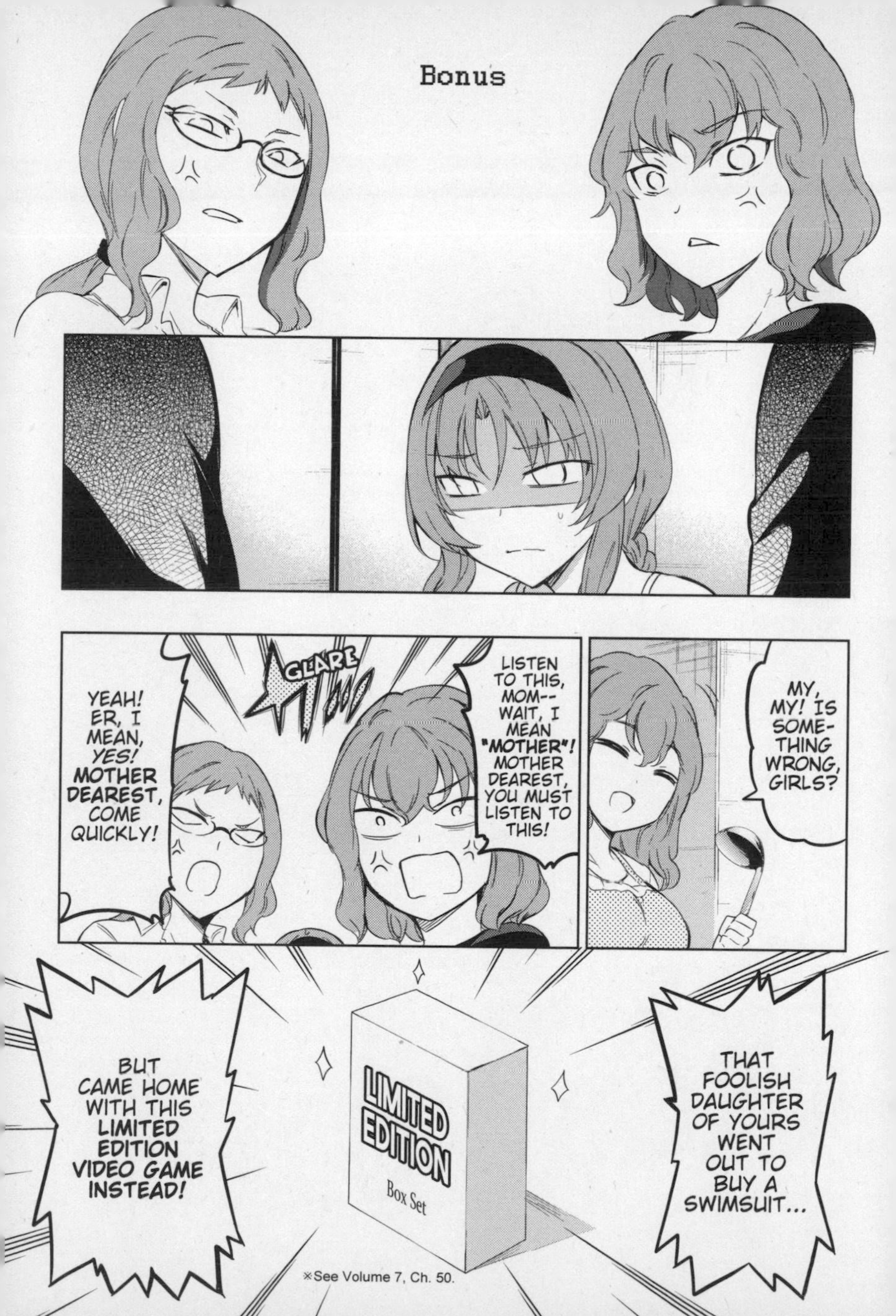
MY, MY! IS SOMETHING WRONG, GIRLS?
LISTEN TO THIS, MOM--WAIT, I MEAN "MOTHER"! MOTHER DEAREST, YOU MUST LISTEN TO THIS!
GLARE
YEAH! ER, I MEAN, YES! MOTHER DEAREST, COME QUICKLY!
THAT FOOLISH DAUGHTER OF YOURS WENT OUT TO BUY A SWIMSUIT...
LIMITED EDITION
Box Set
BUT CAME HOME WITH THIS LIMITED EDITION VIDEO GAME INSTEAD!

※See Volume 7, Ch. 50.

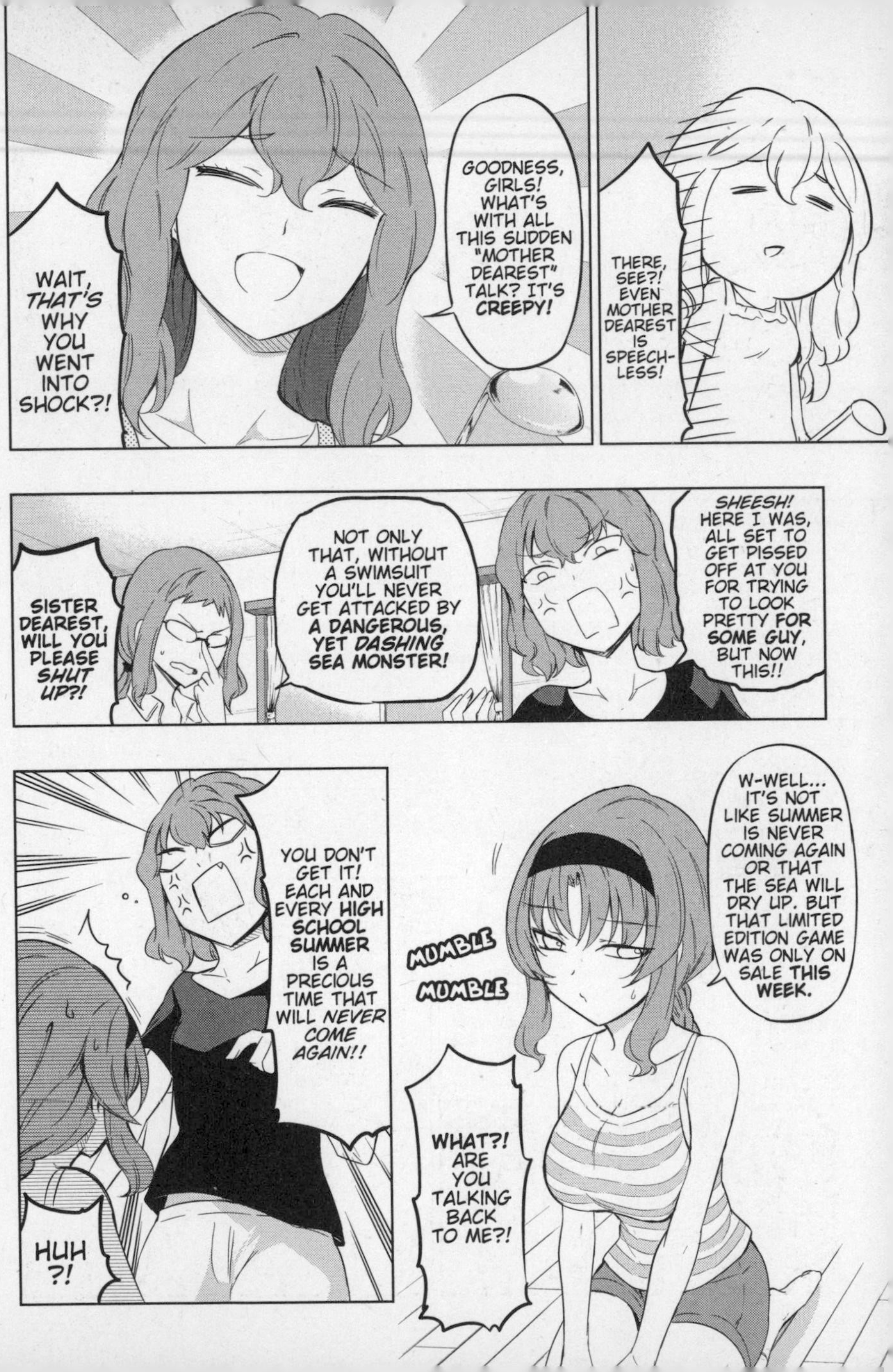
THERE, SEE?! EVEN MOTHER DEAREST IS SPEECHLESS!
GOODNESS, GIRLS! WHAT'S WITH ALL THIS SUDDEN "MOTHER DEAREST" TALK? IT'S CREEPY!
WAIT, THAT'S WHY YOU WENT INTO SHOCK?!
SHEESH! HERE I WAS, ALL SET TO GET PISSED OFF AT YOU FOR TRYING TO LOOK PRETTY FOR SOME GUY, BUT NOW THIS!!
NOT ONLY THAT, WITHOUT A SWIMSUIT YOU'LL NEVER GET ATTACKED BY A DANGEROUS, YET DASHING SEA MONSTER!
SISTER DEAREST, WILL YOU PLEASE SHUT UP?!
W-WELL... IT'S NOT LIKE SUMMER IS NEVER COMING AGAIN OR THAT THE SEA WILL DRY UP. BUT THAT LIMITED EDITION GAME WAS ONLY ON SALE THIS WEEK.
MUMBLE
MUMBLE
WHAT?! ARE YOU TALKING BACK TO ME?!
YOU DON'T GET IT! EACH AND EVERY HIGH SCHOOL SUMMER IS A PRECIOUS TIME THAT WILL NEVER COME AGAIN!!
HUH ?!

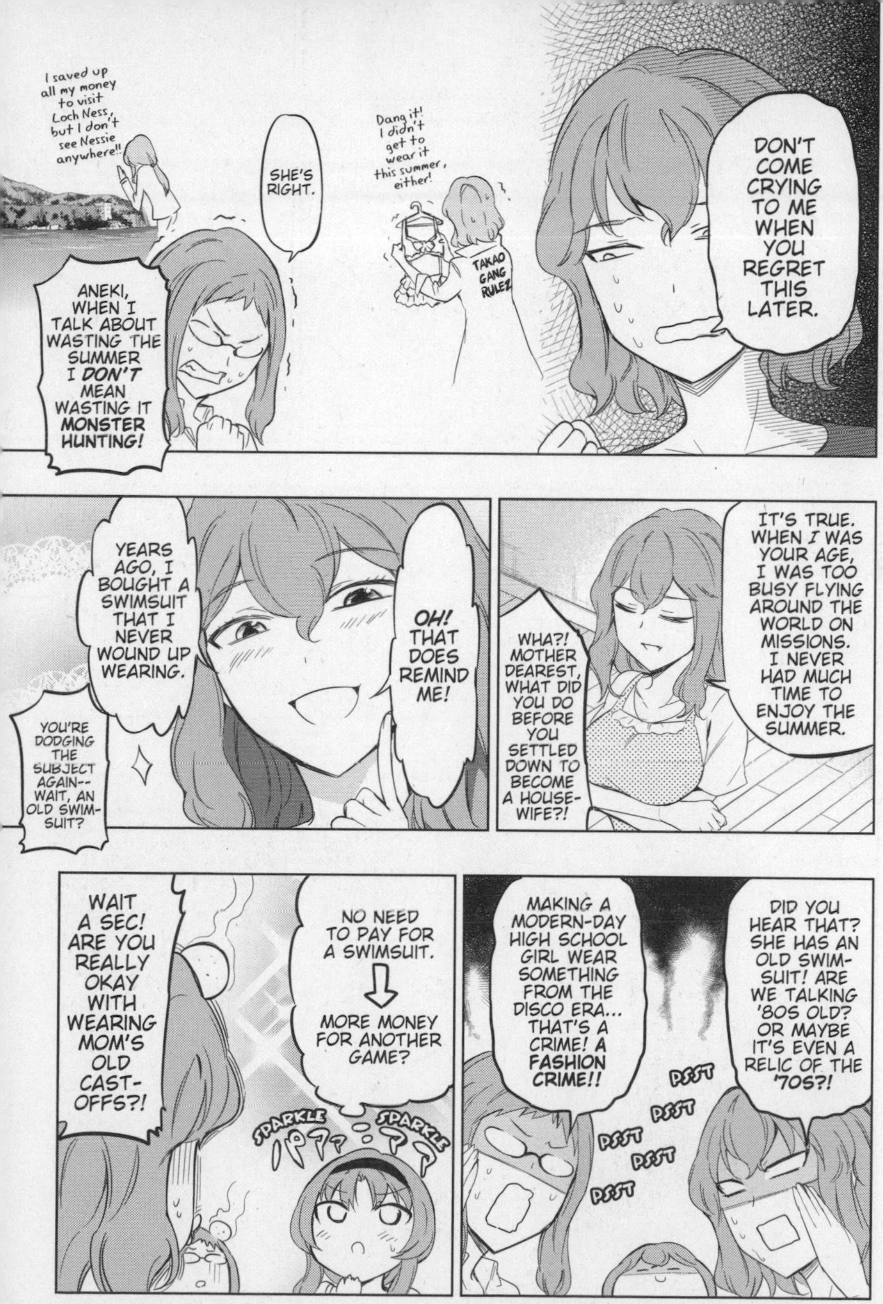
DON'T COME CRYING TO ME WHEN YOU REGRET THIS LATER.
SHE'S RIGHT.
Dang it! I didn't get to wear it this summer, either!
TAKAO GANG RULEZ
I saved up all my money to visit Loch Ness, but I don't see Nessie anywhere!!
ANEKI, WHEN I TALK ABOUT WASTING THE SUMMER I **DON'T** MEAN WASTING IT **MONSTER HUNTING!**
IT'S TRUE. WHEN *I* WAS YOUR AGE, I WAS TOO BUSY FLYING AROUND THE WORLD ON MISSIONS. I NEVER HAD MUCH TIME TO ENJOY THE SUMMER.
WHA?! MOTHER DEAREST, WHAT DID YOU DO BEFORE YOU SETTLED DOWN TO BECOME A HOUSEWIFE?!
OH! THAT DOES REMIND ME!
YEARS AGO, I BOUGHT A SWIMSUIT THAT I NEVER WOUND UP WEARING.
YOU'RE DODGING THE SUBJECT AGAIN-- WAIT, AN OLD SWIMSUIT?
DID YOU HEAR THAT? SHE HAS AN OLD SWIMSUIT! ARE WE TALKING '80S OLD? OR MAYBE IT'S EVEN A RELIC OF THE '70S?!
MAKING A MODERN-DAY HIGH SCHOOL GIRL WEAR SOMETHING FROM THE DISCO ERA... THAT'S A CRIME! A **FASHION CRIME!!**
PSST
PSST
PSST
PSST
PSST
NO NEED TO PAY FOR A SWIMSUIT. MORE MONEY FOR ANOTHER GAME?
WAIT A SEC! ARE YOU REALLY OKAY WITH WEARING MOM'S OLD CAST-OFFS?!
SPARKLE
SPARKLE

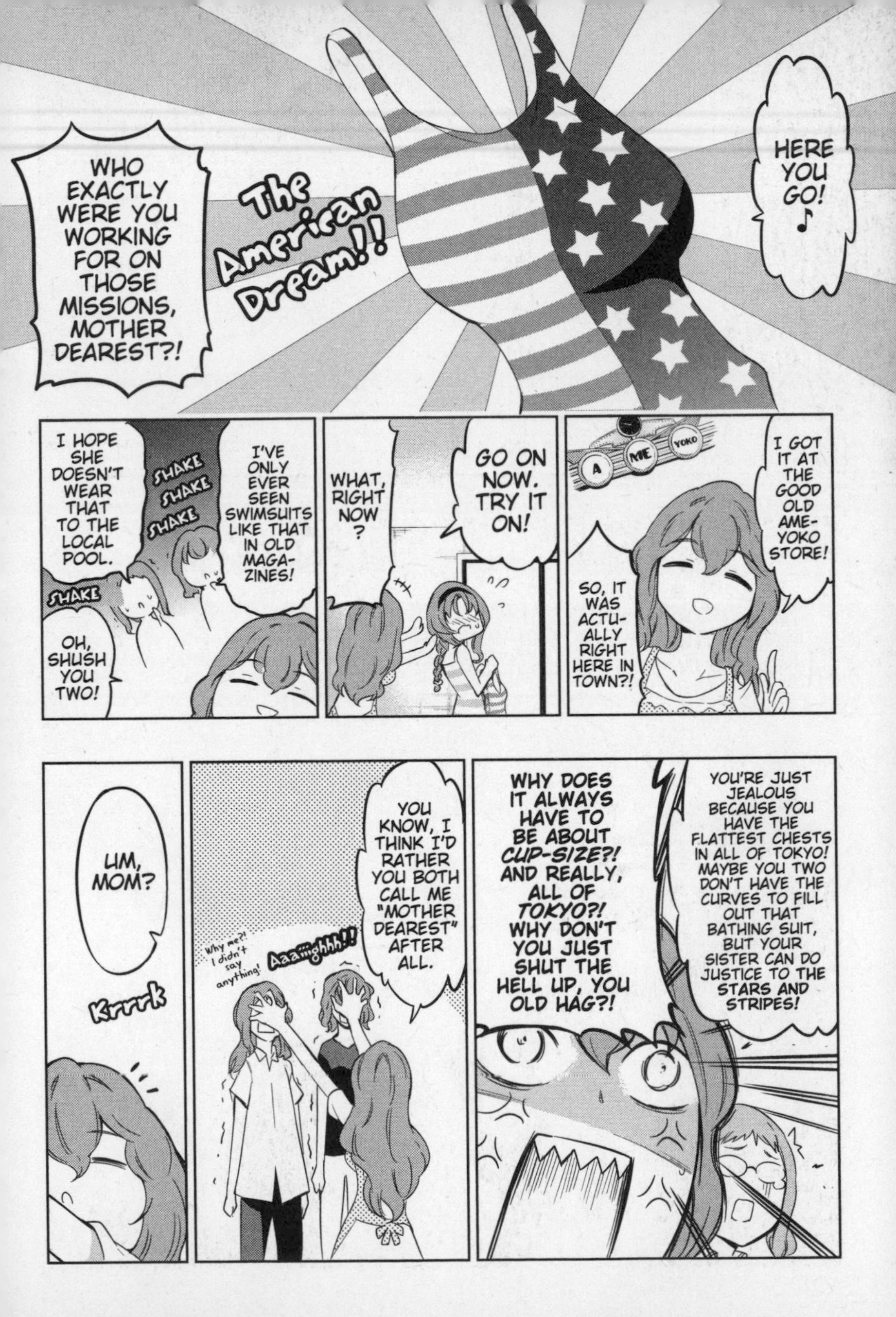
HERE YOU GO! ♪
The American Dream!!
WHO EXACTLY WERE YOU WORKING FOR ON THOSE MISSIONS, MOTHER DEAREST?!
I GOT IT AT THE GOOD OLD AME-YOKO STORE!
A ME YOKO
SO, IT WAS ACTUALLY RIGHT HERE IN TOWN?!
GO ON NOW. TRY IT ON!
WHAT, RIGHT NOW?
I'VE ONLY EVER SEEN SWIMSUITS LIKE THAT IN OLD MAGAZINES!
SHAKE SHAKE SHAKE
I HOPE SHE DOESN'T WEAR THAT TO THE LOCAL POOL.
SHAKE
OH, SHUSH YOU TWO!
YOU'RE JUST JEALOUS BECAUSE YOU HAVE THE FLATTEST CHESTS IN ALL OF TOKYO! MAYBE YOU TWO DON'T HAVE THE CURVES TO FILL OUT THAT BATHING SUIT, BUT YOUR SISTER CAN DO JUSTICE TO THE STARS AND STRIPES!
WHY DOES IT ALWAYS HAVE TO BE ABOUT *CUP-SIZE?!* AND REALLY, ALL OF *TOKYO?!* WHY DON'T YOU JUST SHUT THE HELL UP, YOU OLD HAG?!
YOU KNOW, I THINK I'D RATHER YOU BOTH CALL ME "MOTHER DEAREST" AFTER ALL.
Aaaiiighhh!!
Why me?! I didn't say anything!
UM, MOM?
Krrrk

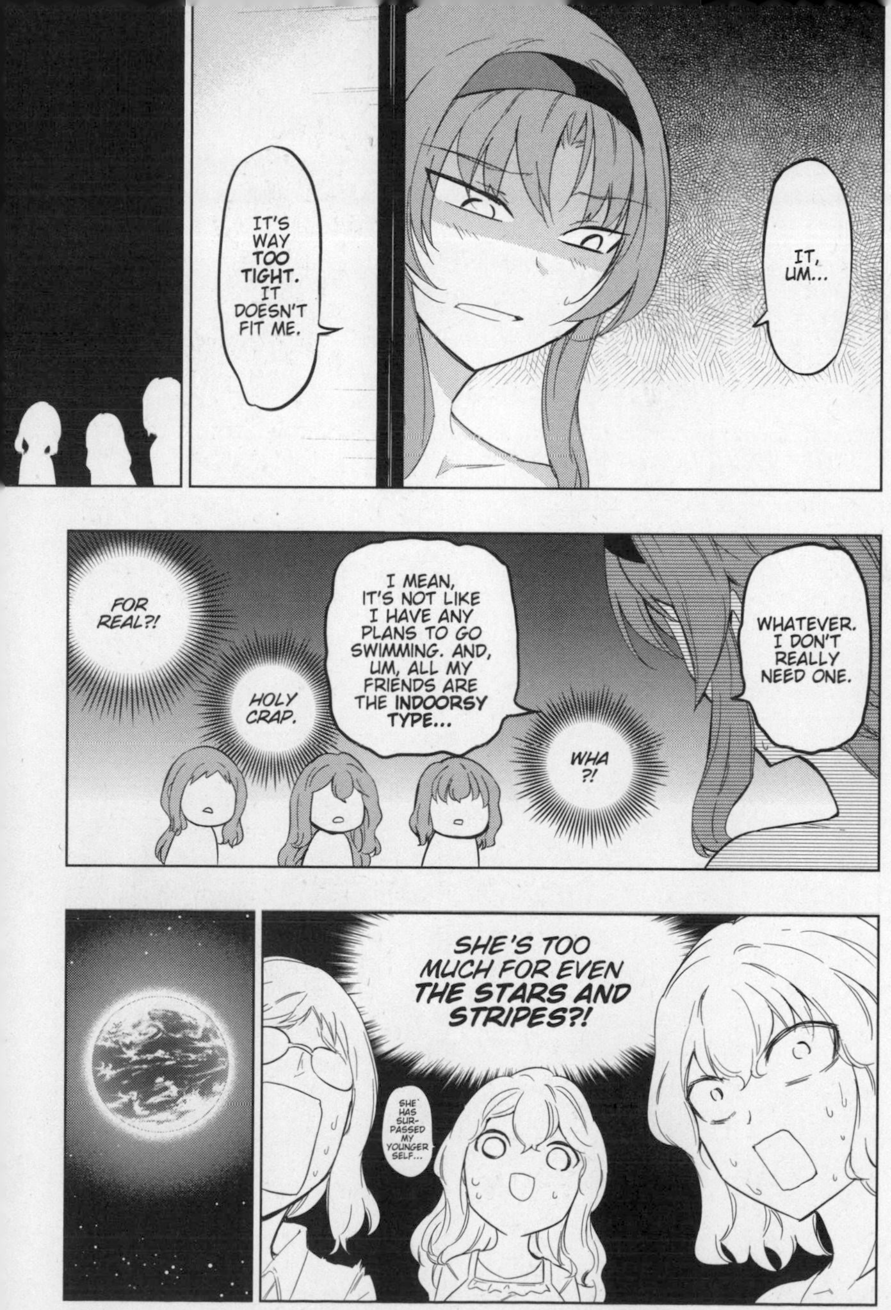
IT, UM...
IT'S WAY TOO TIGHT. IT DOESN'T FIT ME.
WHATEVER. I DON'T REALLY NEED ONE.
I MEAN, IT'S NOT LIKE I HAVE ANY PLANS TO GO SWIMMING. AND, UM, ALL MY FRIENDS ARE THE INDOORSY TYPE...
WHA ?!
FOR REAL?!
HOLY CRAP.
SHE'S TOO MUCH FOR EVEN THE STARS AND STRIPES?!
SHE HAS SUR-PASSED MY YOUNGER SELF...

END

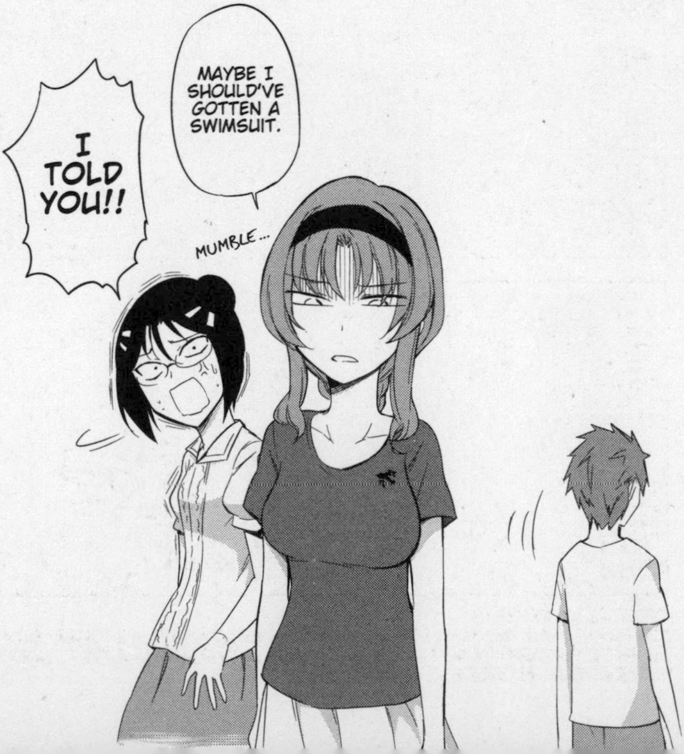
MAYBE I SHOULD'VE GOTTEN A SWIMSUIT.
MUMBLE...
I TOLD YOU!!

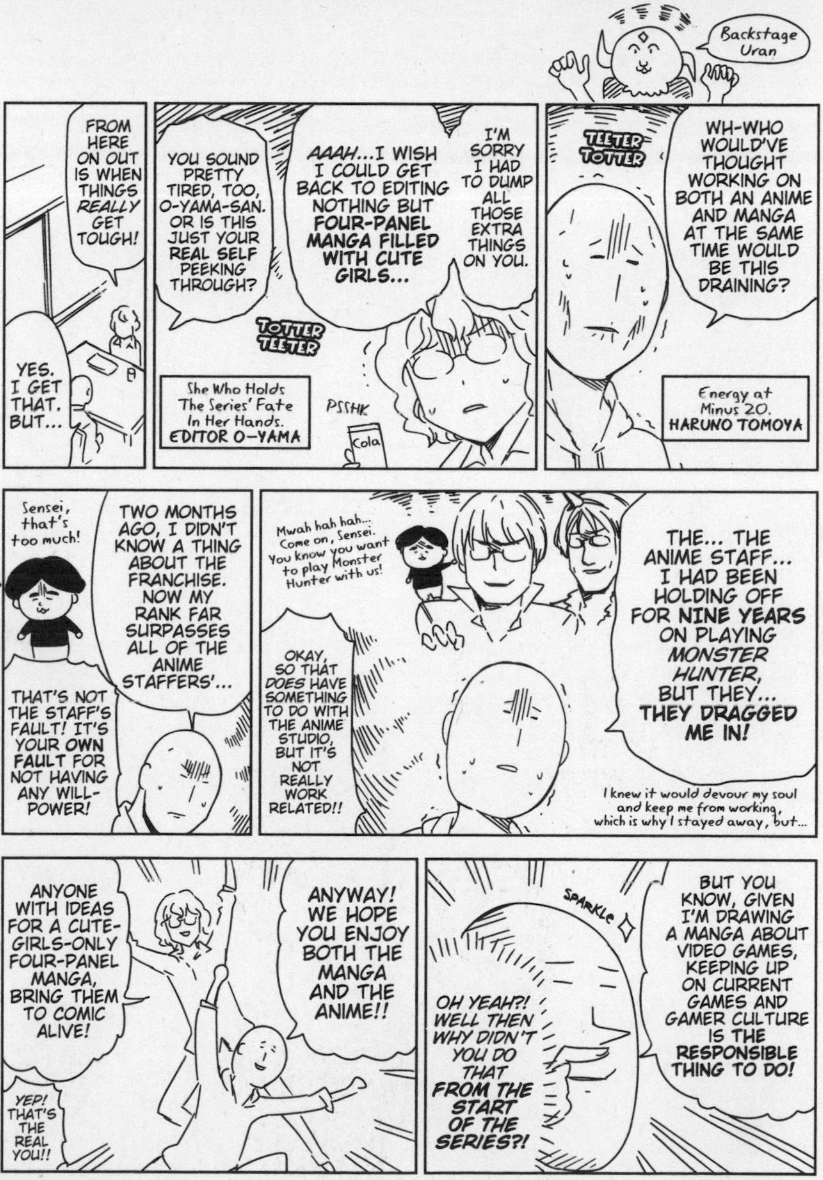
Backstage Uran
WH-WHO WOULD'VE THOUGHT WORKING ON BOTH AN ANIME AND MANGA AT THE SAME TIME WOULD BE THIS DRAINING?
TEETER TOTTER
Energy at Minus 20. HARUNO TOMOYA
I'M SORRY I HAD TO DUMP ALL THOSE EXTRA THINGS ON YOU.
AAAH...I WISH I COULD GET BACK TO EDITING NOTHING BUT FOUR-PANEL MANGA FILLED WITH CUTE GIRLS...
YOU SOUND PRETTY TIRED, TOO, O-YAMA-SAN. OR IS THIS JUST YOUR REAL SELF PEEKING THROUGH?
TOTTER TEETER
PSSHK
Cola
She Who Holds The Series' Fate In Her Hands. EDITOR O-YAMA
FROM HERE ON OUT IS WHEN THINGS REALLY GET TOUGH!
YES. I GET THAT. BUT...
THE... THE ANIME STAFF... I HAD BEEN HOLDING OFF FOR NINE YEARS ON PLAYING MONSTER HUNTER, BUT THEY... THEY DRAGGED ME IN!
Mwah hah hah... Come on, Sensei. You know you want to play Monster Hunter with us!
OKAY, SO THAT DOES HAVE SOMETHING TO DO WITH THE ANIME STUDIO, BUT IT'S NOT REALLY WORK RELATED!!
I knew it would devour my soul and keep me from working, which is why I stayed away, but...
TWO MONTHS AGO, I DIDN'T KNOW A THING ABOUT THE FRANCHISE. NOW MY RANK FAR SURPASSES ALL OF THE ANIME STAFFERS'...
Sensei, that's too much!
Director
THAT'S NOT THE STAFF'S FAULT! IT'S YOUR OWN FAULT FOR NOT HAVING ANY WILL-POWER!
BUT YOU KNOW, GIVEN I'M DRAWING A MANGA ABOUT VIDEO GAMES, KEEPING UP ON CURRENT GAMES AND GAMER CULTURE IS THE RESPONSIBLE THING TO DO!
SPARKLE
OH YEAH?! WELL THEN WHY DIDN'T YOU DO THAT FROM THE START OF THE SERIES?!
ANYWAY! WE HOPE YOU ENJOY BOTH THE MANGA AND THE ANIME!!
ANYONE WITH IDEAS FOR A CUTE-GIRLS-ONLY FOUR-PANEL MANGA, BRING THEM TO COMIC ALIVE!
YEP! THAT'S THE REAL YOU!!

SPECIAL THANKS!!
ODAKURA-SAN, MIKAGE BAKU-SAN, YUKINOJOU-SAN, OHYAMA-SAN (EDITOR), LIGHTNING TOMIYAMA-SAN (FINAL BOSS), THE ANIME STAFF, AND MY WONDERFUL READERS!!

A Tale from the Seitachigawa Academy for Girls

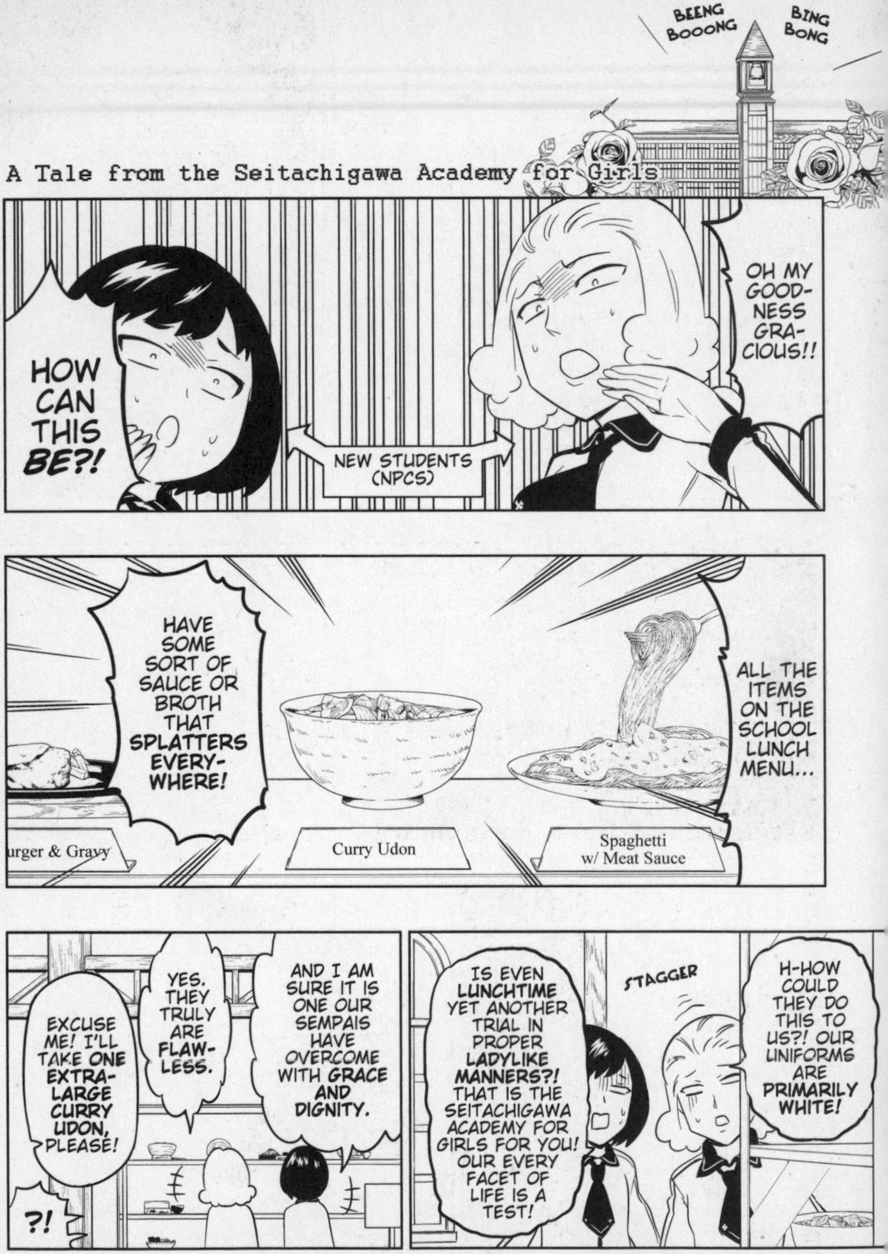
BING BONG
BEENG BOOONG
OH MY GOODNESS GRACIOUS!!
HOW CAN THIS BE?!
NEW STUDENTS (NPCS)
ALL THE ITEMS ON THE SCHOOL LUNCH MENU...
HAVE SOME SORT OF SAUCE OR BROTH THAT SPLATTERS EVERYWHERE!
Spaghetti w/ Meat Sauce
Curry Udon
urger & Gravy
H-HOW COULD THEY DO THIS TO US?! OUR UNIFORMS ARE PRIMARILY WHITE!
STAGGER
IS EVEN LUNCHTIME YET ANOTHER TRIAL IN PROPER LADYLIKE MANNERS?! THAT IS THE SEITACHIGAWA ACADEMY FOR GIRLS FOR YOU! OUR EVERY FACET OF LIFE IS A TEST!
AND I AM SURE IT IS ONE OUR SEMPAIS HAVE OVERCOME WITH GRACE AND DIGNITY.
YES. THEY TRULY ARE FLAWLESS.
EXCUSE ME! I'LL TAKE ONE EXTRA-LARGE CURRY UDON, PLEASE!
?!

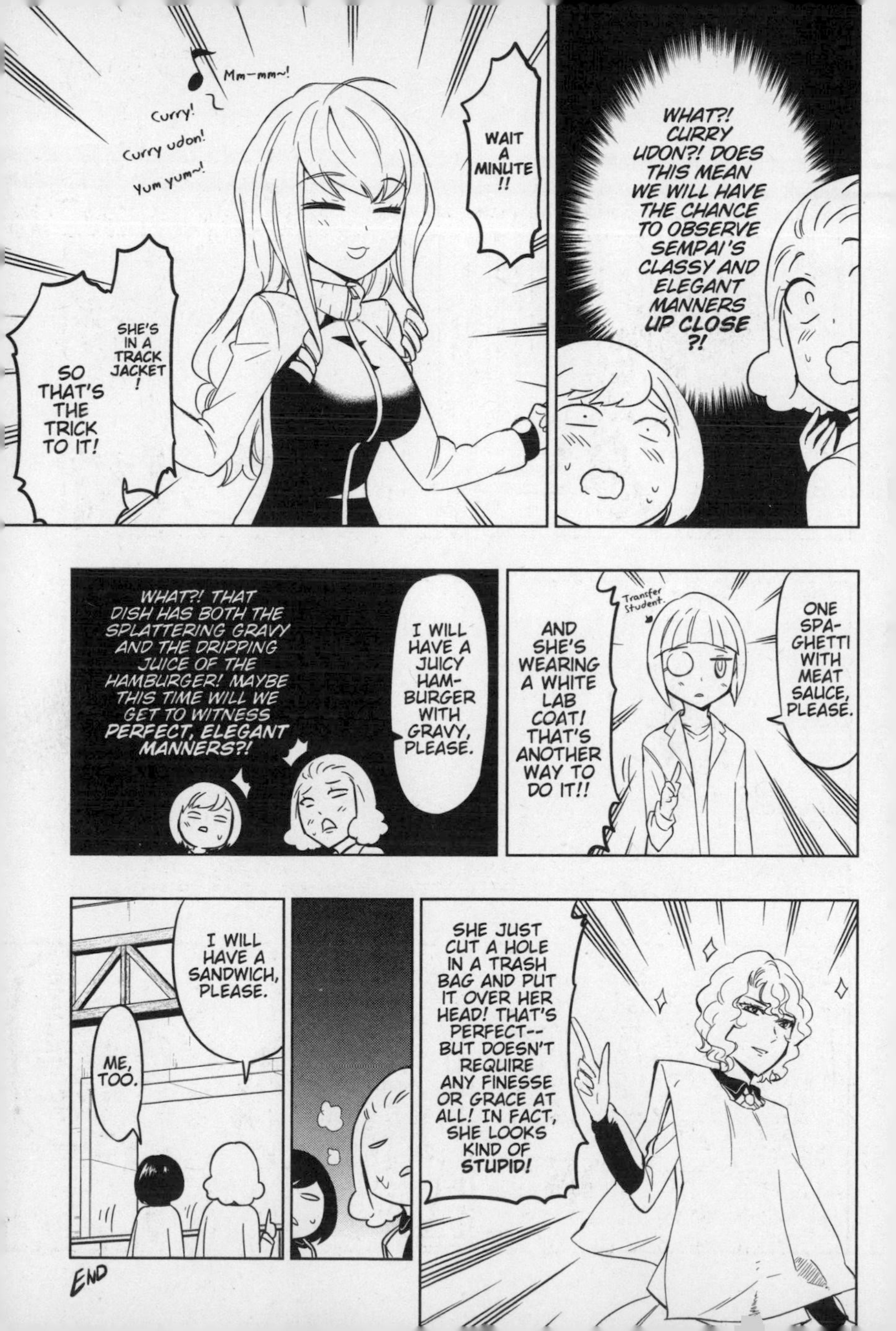
WHAT?! CURRY UDON?! DOES THIS MEAN WE WILL HAVE THE CHANCE TO OBSERVE SEMPAI'S CLASSY AND ELEGANT MANNERS **UP CLOSE** ?!
WAIT A MINUTE !!
Mm-mm~!
Curry!
Curry udon!
Yum yum~!
SHE'S IN A TRACK JACKET !
SO THAT'S THE TRICK TO IT!
ONE SPA-GHETTI WITH MEAT SAUCE, PLEASE.
Transfer Student.
AND SHE'S WEARING A WHITE LAB COAT! THAT'S ANOTHER WAY TO DO IT!!
I WILL HAVE A JUICY HAM-BURGER WITH GRAVY, PLEASE.
WHAT?! THAT DISH HAS BOTH THE SPLATTERING GRAVY AND THE DRIPPING JUICE OF THE HAMBURGER! MAYBE THIS TIME WILL WE GET TO WITNESS **PERFECT, ELEGANT MANNERS?!**
SHE JUST CUT A HOLE IN A TRASH BAG AND PUT IT OVER HER HEAD! THAT'S PERFECT-- BUT DOESN'T REQUIRE ANY FINESSE OR GRACE AT ALL! IN FACT, SHE LOOKS KIND OF **STUPID!**
I WILL HAVE A SANDWICH, PLEASE.
ME, TOO.
END

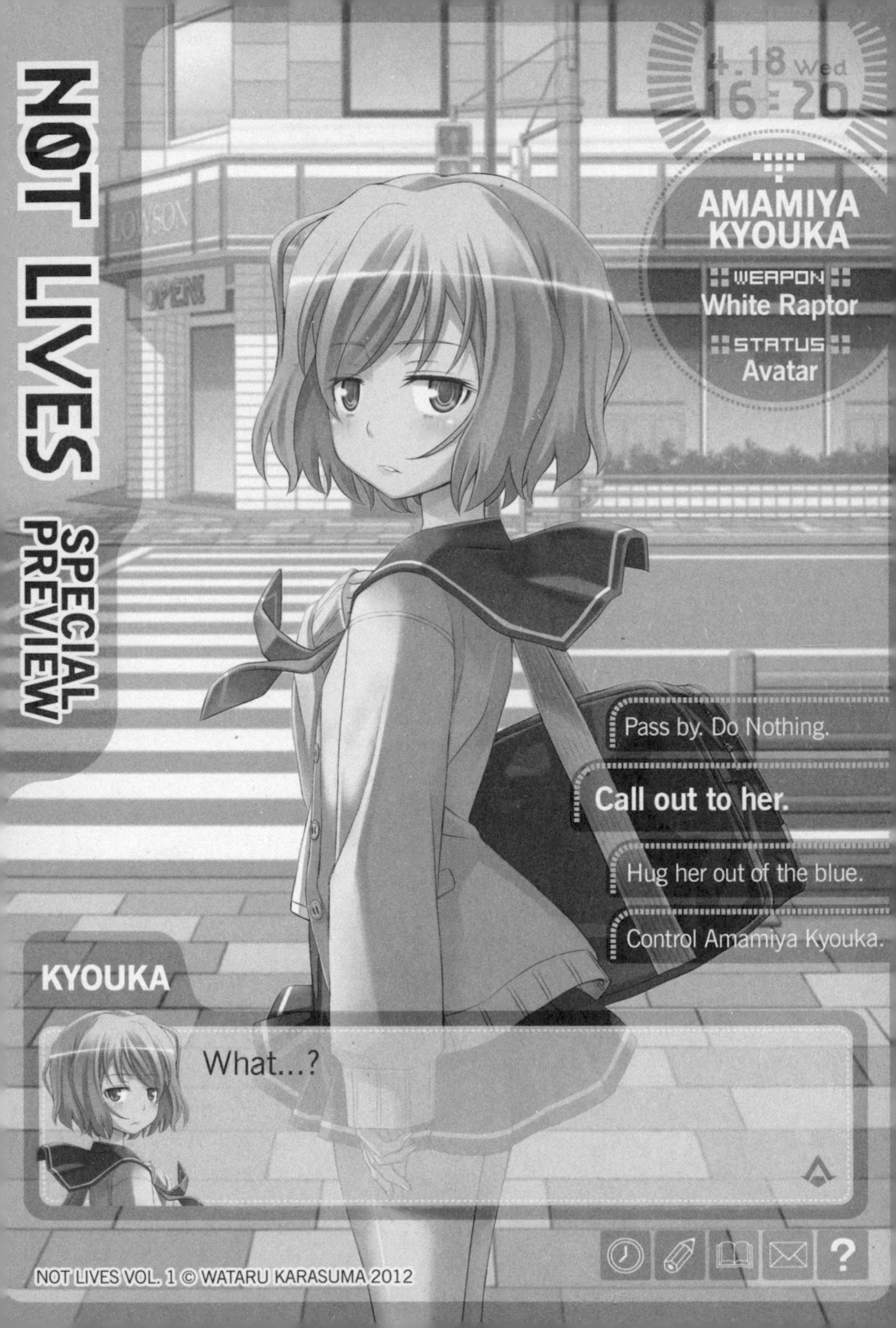
NOT LIVES
SPECIAL PREVIEW
4.18 Wed
16:20
AMAMIYA KYOUKA
WEAPON
White Raptor
STATUS
Avatar
Pass by. Do Nothing.
Call out to her.
Hug her out of the blue.
Control Amamiya Kyouka.
KYOUKA
What...?
?

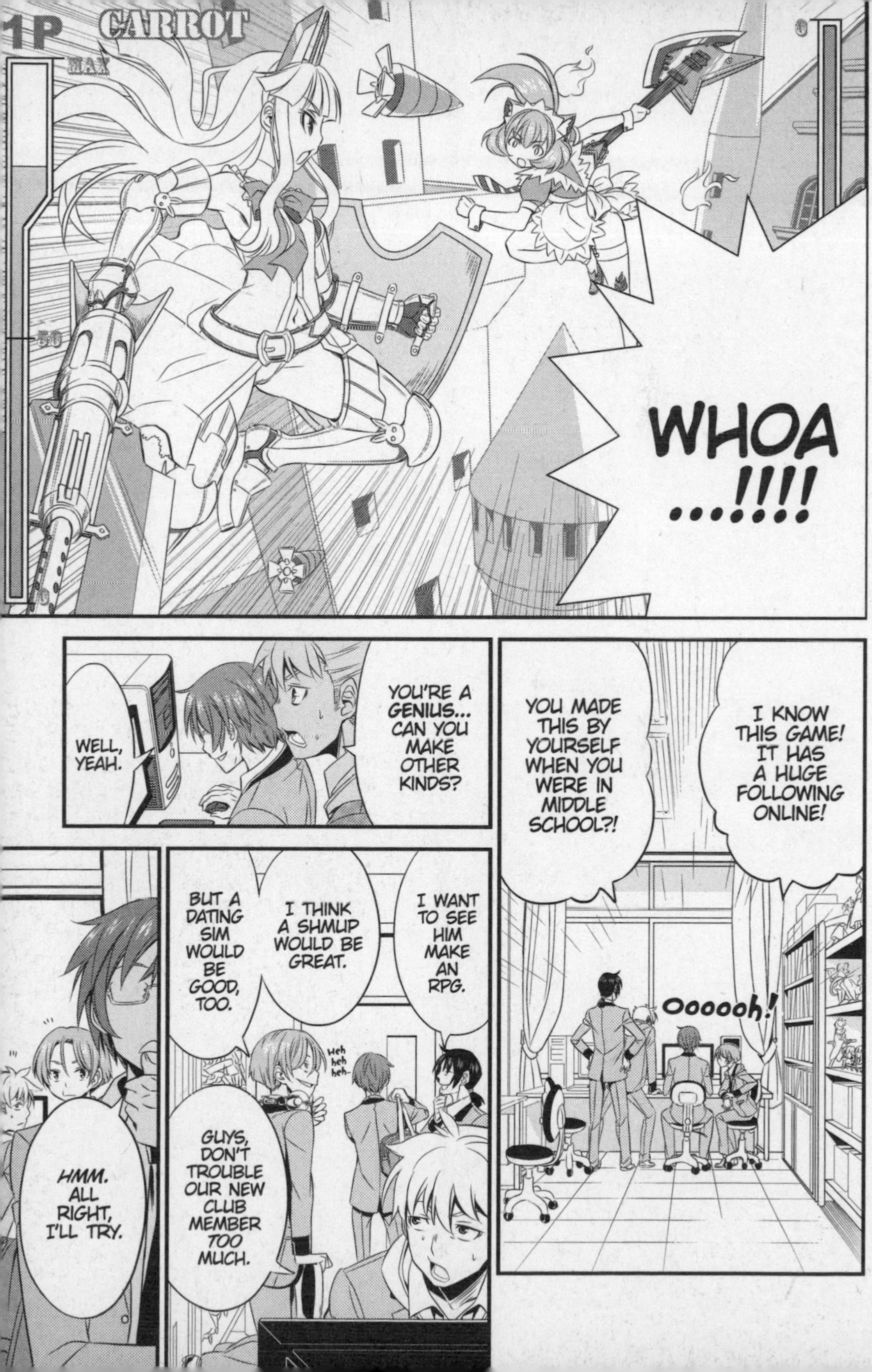

1P
CARROT
MAX
50
WHOA ....!!!!
I KNOW THIS GAME! IT HAS A HUGE FOLLOWING ONLINE!
YOU MADE THIS BY YOURSELF WHEN YOU WERE IN MIDDLE SCHOOL?!
Oooooh!
YOU'RE A GENIUS... CAN YOU MAKE OTHER KINDS?
WELL, YEAH.
I WANT TO SEE HIM MAKE AN RPG.
I THINK A SHMUP WOULD BE GREAT.
BUT A DATING SIM WOULD BE GOOD, TOO.
Heh heh heh
GUYS, DON'T TROUBLE OUR NEW CLUB MEMBER TOO MUCH.
HMM. ALL RIGHT, I'LL TRY.

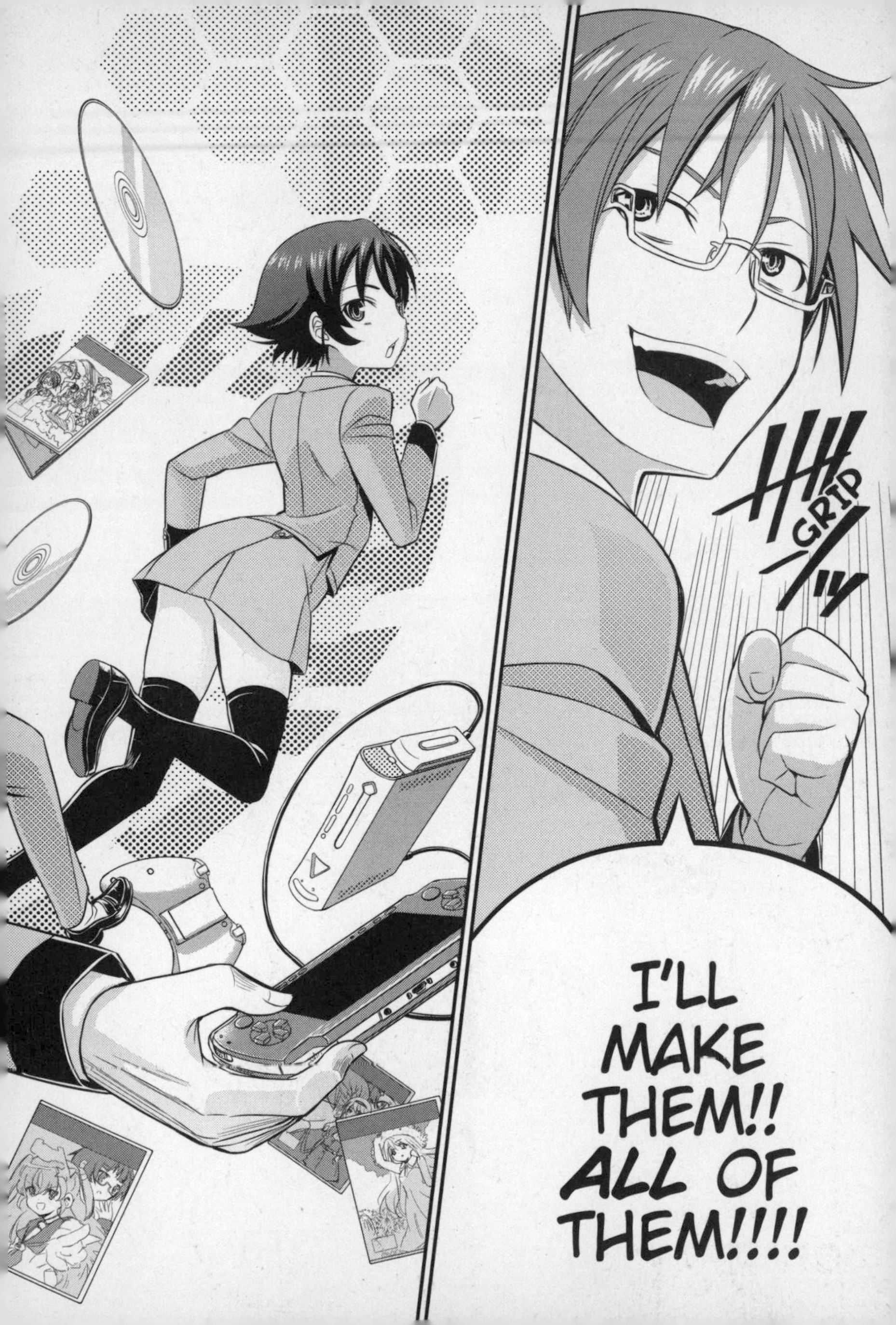
GRIP
I'LL MAKE THEM!! ALL OF THEM!!!!

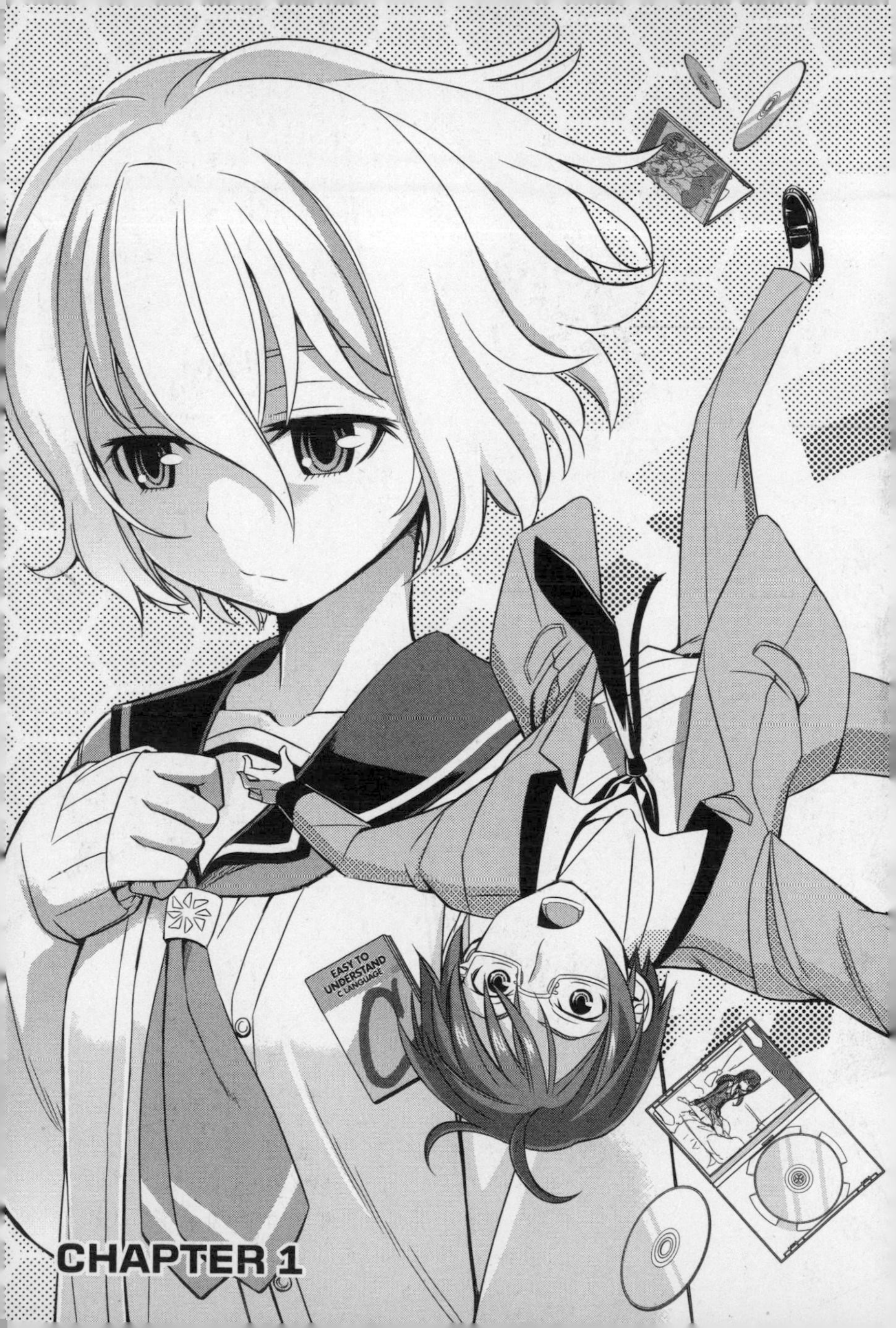
EASY TO UNDERSTAND C LANGUAGE

CHAPTER 1

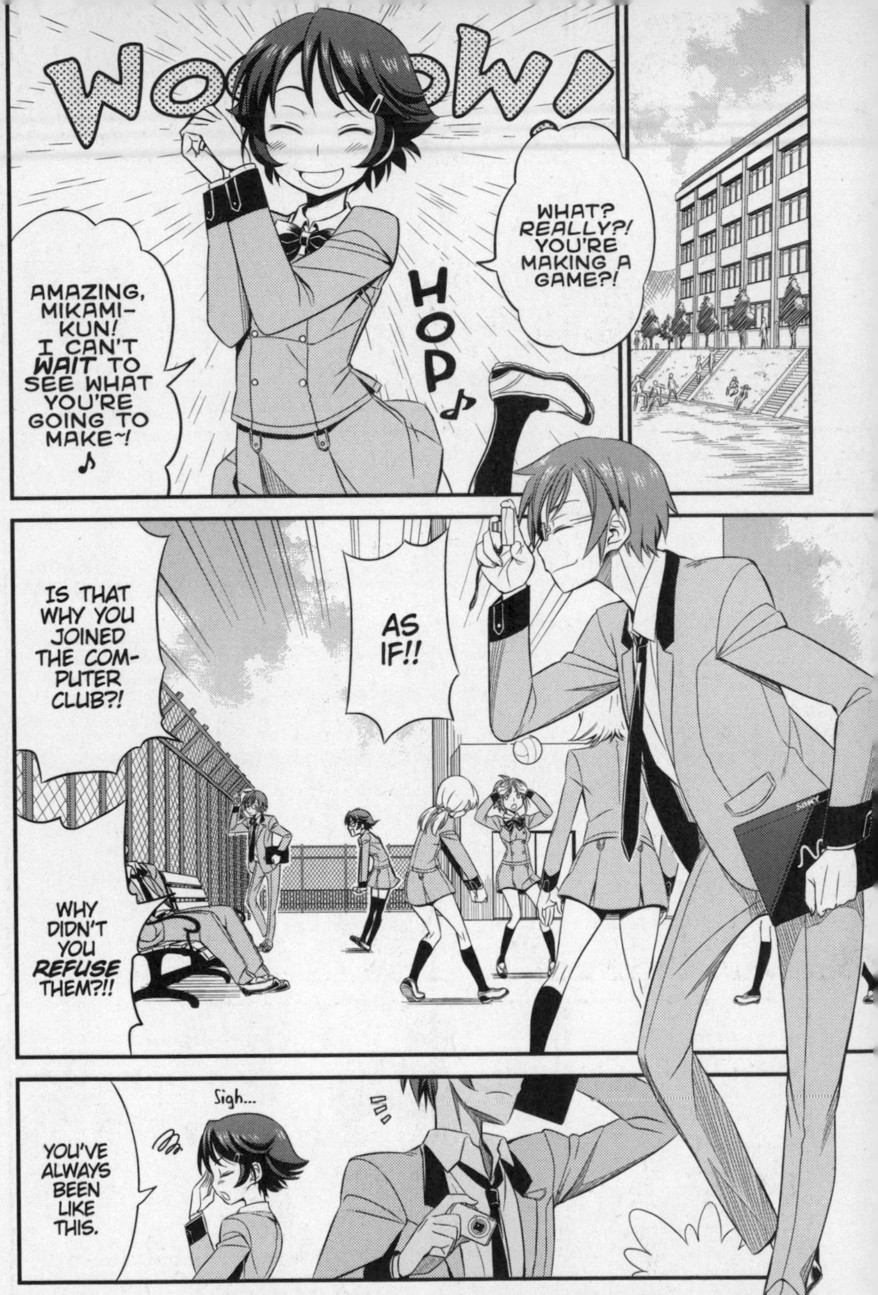
WHAT? REALLY?! YOU'RE MAKING A GAME?!
WOOOW!
HOP♪
AMAZING, MIKAMI-KUN! I CAN'T WAIT TO SEE WHAT YOU'RE GOING TO MAKE~! ♪
AS IF!!
IS THAT WHY YOU JOINED THE COM-PUTER CLUB?!
WHY DIDN'T YOU REFUSE THEM?!!
Sigh...
YOU'VE ALWAYS BEEN LIKE THIS.

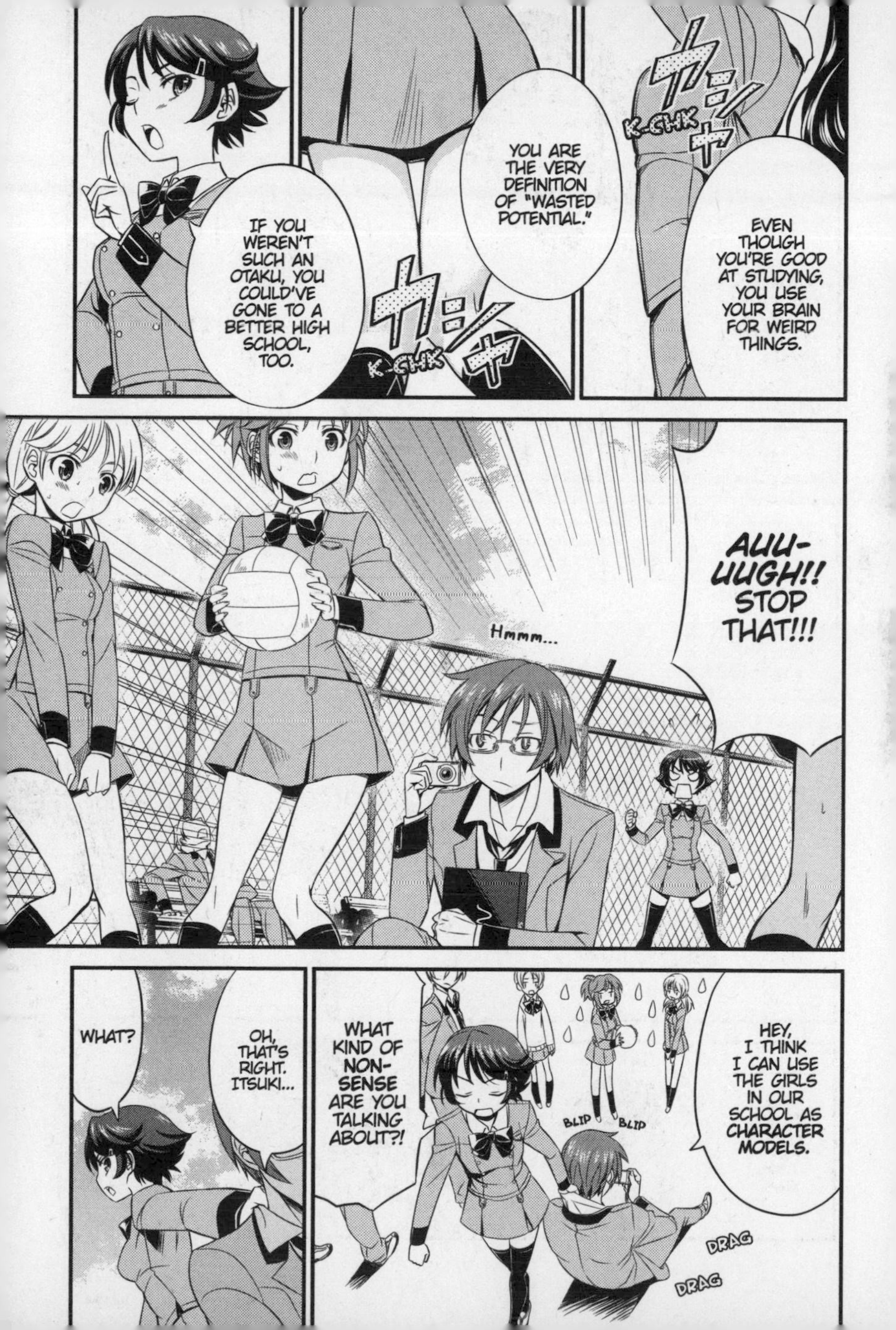
K-CHK
EVEN THOUGH YOU'RE GOOD AT STUDYING, YOU USE YOUR BRAIN FOR WEIRD THINGS.
YOU ARE THE VERY DEFINITION OF "WASTED POTENTIAL."
K-CHK
IF YOU WEREN'T SUCH AN OTAKU, YOU COULD'VE GONE TO A BETTER HIGH SCHOOL, TOO.
AUUU-UUGH!! STOP THAT!!!
Hmmm...
HEY, I THINK I CAN USE THE GIRLS IN OUR SCHOOL AS CHARACTER MODELS.
WHAT KIND OF NON-SENSE ARE YOU TALKING ABOUT?!
BLIP
BLIP
DRAG
DRAG
OH, THAT'S RIGHT. ITSUKI...
WHAT?

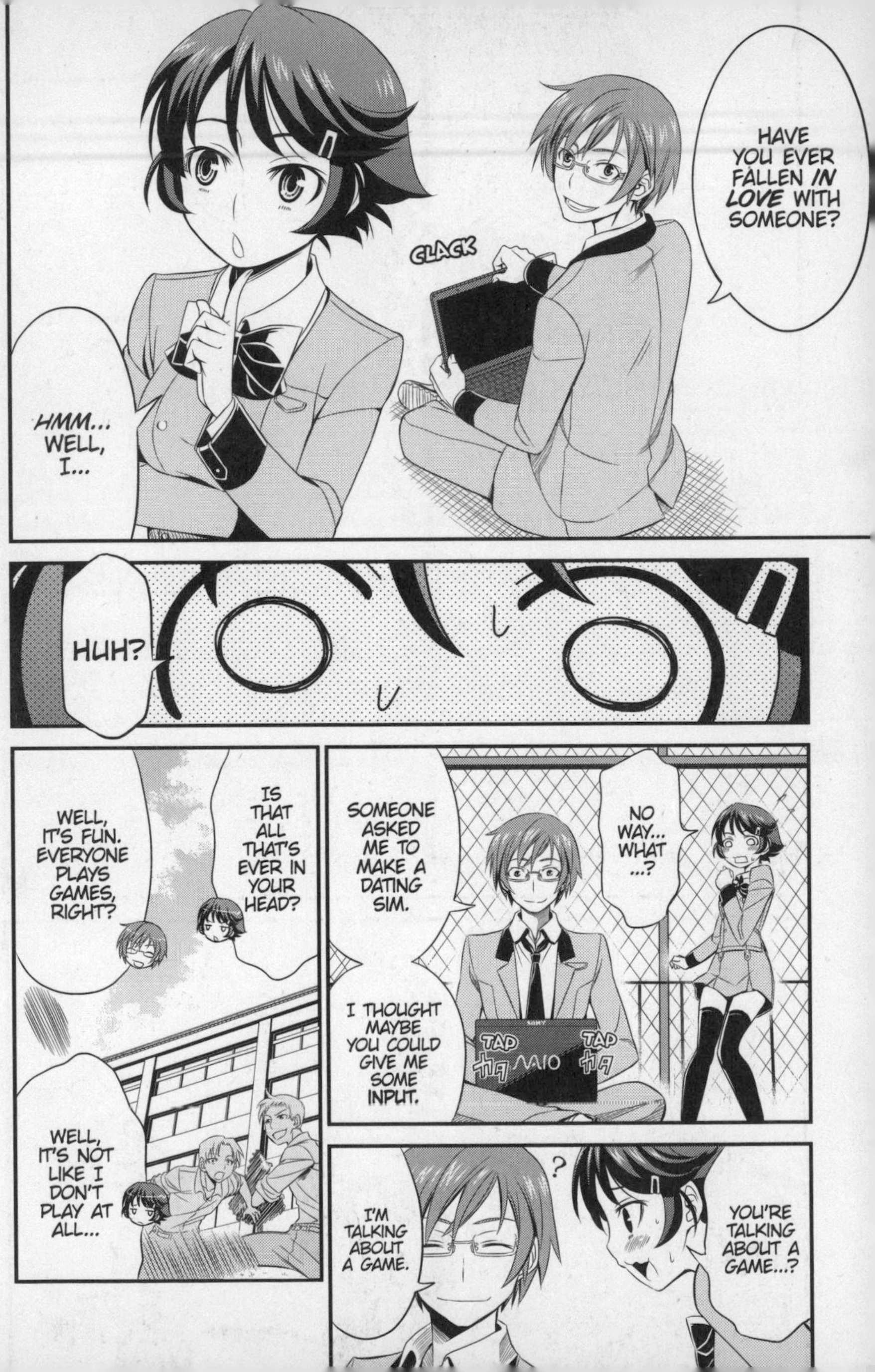
HAVE YOU EVER FALLEN *IN LOVE* WITH SOMEONE?
CLACK
HMM... WELL, I...
HUH?
NO WAY... WHAT ...?
SOMEONE ASKED ME TO MAKE A DATING SIM.
I THOUGHT MAYBE YOU COULD GIVE ME SOME INPUT.
TAP TAP
?
YOU'RE TALKING ABOUT A GAME...?
I'M TALKING ABOUT A GAME.
IS THAT ALL THAT'S EVER IN YOUR HEAD?
WELL, IT'S FUN. EVERYONE PLAYS GAMES, RIGHT?
WELL, IT'S NOT LIKE I DON'T PLAY AT ALL...

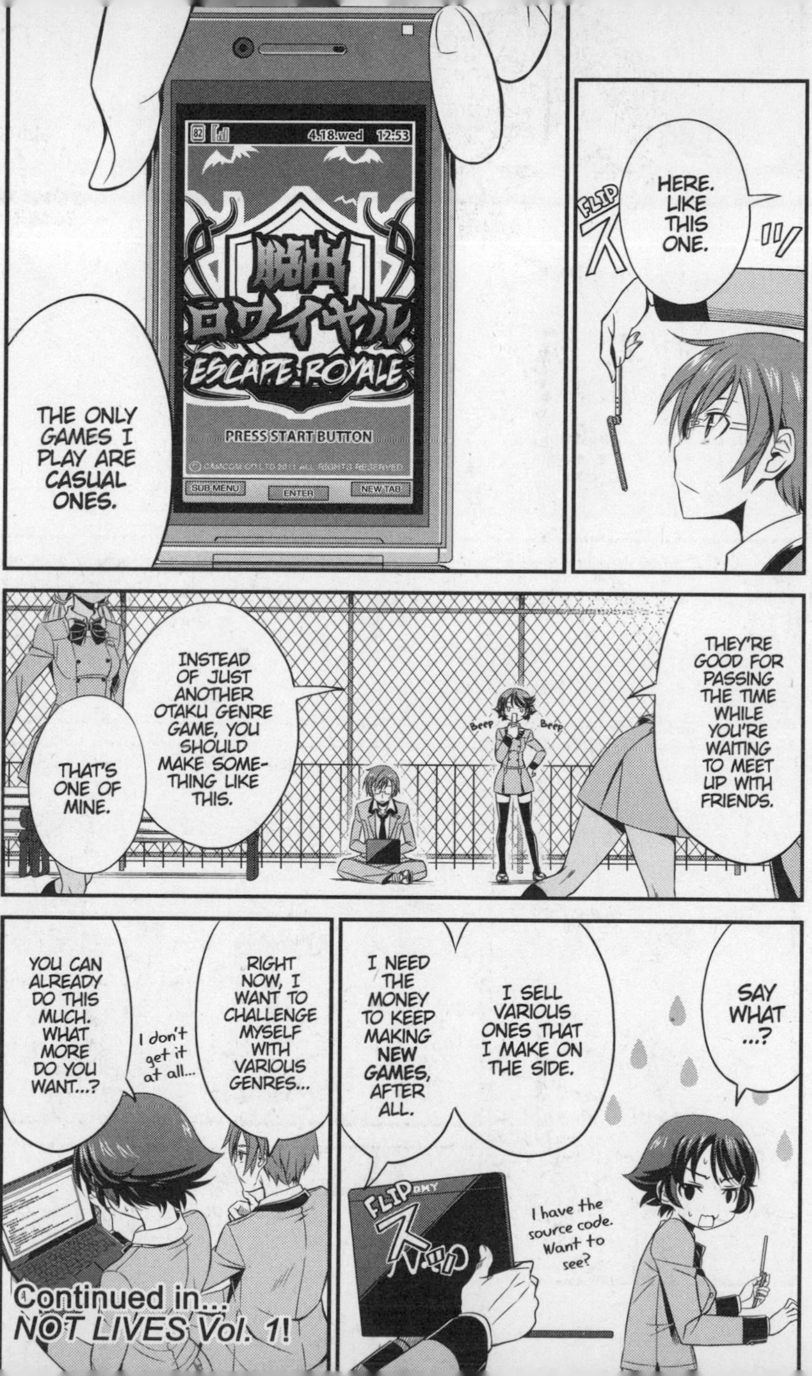
HERE. LIKE THIS ONE.
FLIP
4.18.wed 12:53
脱出ロワイヤル
ESCAPE ROYALE
PRESS START BUTTON
SUB MENU
ENTER
NEW TAB
THE ONLY GAMES I PLAY ARE CASUAL ONES.
THEY'RE GOOD FOR PASSING THE TIME WHILE YOU'RE WAITING TO MEET UP WITH FRIENDS.
Beep
Beep
INSTEAD OF JUST ANOTHER OTAKU GENRE GAME, YOU SHOULD MAKE SOME-THING LIKE THIS.
THAT'S ONE OF MINE.
SAY WHAT ...?
I SELL VARIOUS ONES THAT I MAKE ON THE SIDE.
I NEED THE MONEY TO KEEP MAKING NEW GAMES, AFTER ALL.
FLIP
I have the source code. Want to see?
RIGHT NOW, I WANT TO CHALLENGE MYSELF WITH VARIOUS GENRES...
I don't get it at all...
YOU CAN ALREADY DO THIS MUCH. WHAT MORE DO YOU WANT...?
Continued in... NOT LIVES Vol. 1!

SEVEN SEAS ENTERTAINMENT PRESENTS

D-FRAG!

story and art by TOMOYA HARUNO

VOLUME 8

TRANSLATION
Adrienne Beck

ADAPTATION
Shannon Fay

LETTERING AND LAYOUT
Ma. Victoria Robado

LOGO DESIGN
Courtney Williams

COVER DESIGN
Nicky Lim

PROOFREADER
Lee Otter
Janet Houck

PRODUCTION MANAGER
Lissa Pattillo

EDITOR-IN-CHIEF
Adam Arnold

PUBLISHER
Jason DeAngelis

D-FRAG! VOL. 8

Edited by MEDIA FACTORY.
First published in Japan in 2013 by KADOKAWA CORPORATION, Tokyo.
English translation rights reserved by Seven Seas Entertainment, LLC.
under the license from KADOKAWA CORPORATION, Tokyo.

Seven Seas books may be purchased in bulk for educational, business, or promotional use. For information on bulk purchases, please contact Macmillan Corporate & Premium Sales Department at 1-800-221-7945 (ext 5442) or write specialmarkets@macmillan.com.

ISBN: 978-1-626922-48-8

Printed in Canada

First Printing: April 2016

10 9 8 7 6 5 4 3 2 1

FOLLOW US ONLINE: ***www.gomanga.com***

READING DIRECTIONS

This book reads from ***right to left***, Japanese style. If this is your first time reading manga, you start reading from the top right panel on each page and take it from there. If you get lost, just follow the numbered diagram here. It may seem backwards at first, but you'll get the hang of it! Have fun!!

1
2
3
4
5
6
7
8
9

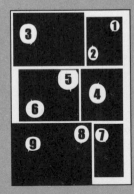